CW01022075

TITO'S SECRET EMPIRE

WILLIAM KLINGER

DENIS KULJIŠ

Tito's Secret Empire

How the Maharaja of the
Balkans Fooled the World

HURST & COMPANY, LONDON

First published in the United Kingdom in 2021 by
C. Hurst & Co. (Publishers) Ltd.,
41 Great Russell Street, London, WC1B 3PL
Printed in Great Britain by Bell and Bain Ltd, Glasgow

A Cataloguing-in-Publication data record for this book
is available from the British Library.

ISBN: 9781787383142

This book is printed using paper from registered sustainable
and managed sources.

www.hurstpublishers.com

To the memory of the authors, Denis Kuljiš and William Klinger

RIP

Il y a deux histoires: l'histoire officielle, menteuse, puis l'histoire secrète, où sont les véritables causes des événements.

Honoré de Balzac

On Stalin's secret orders. The American magazine *Liberty* depicts Tito, who had been an organizer on the side of the communists during the Spanish Civil War. After England and the USA had to drop Peter II at Stalin's request, Tito was glorified by them as a Balkan freedom fighter. From *Signal*, a magazine published by the German Wehrmacht from 1940 to 1945.

CONTENTS

CONTENTS

III. THE SECRET EMPIRE

CONTENTS

LIST OF ILLUSTRATIONS

All images are reproduced with permission from Belgrade Museum and Archives.

LIST OF ILLUSTRATIONS

12. Passing through Nyaung-U on the way to visit the temples of Bagan, Burma, January, 1955.

13. Receiving Gamal Abdel Nasser, president of Egypt, on the yacht *Galeb* during the return voyage from state visits to India and Burma. Suez, February, 1955.

14. Josip Broz Tito receives Nikita Khrushchev during the first official visit of the Soviet delegation to Yugoslavia. The White Palace, Belgrade, May, 1955.

15. The first official visit of the Soviet delegation to Tito's Yugoslavia. The White Palace, Belgrade, May 1955.

16. Formal reception for the Soviet delegation at the White Palace, Belgrade, May, 1955.

17. Josip Broz Tito awarded a medal by Emperor Haile Selassie during the official visit to Ethiopia. Addis Ababa, December, 1955.

18. A motorcade through Moscow streets on the way to the residence, June, 1956.

19. The official meeting between Nasser, Nehru and J. B. Tito. Brijuni Islands, Vanga, July, 1956.

20. J. B. Tito and Khrushchev on the terrace of the White Villa. Brijuni Islands, September, 1956.

21. J. B. Tito and Ho Chi Minh, the president of the People's Republic of Vietnam in Tito's speedboat. Brijuni Islands, August, 1957.

22. The reception for Marshall Zhukov, Soviet minister of defense, at the hunting lodge, Brdo near Kranj, October, 1957.

23. Grand reception on the occasion of J. B. Tito's official visit to India. Delhi, January, 1959.

24. The reception for the Cuban goodwill mission headed by Ernesto Che Guevara. Brijuni Islands, August, 1959.

25. J. B. Tito and Khrushchev meet during the Fifteenth Session of the United Nations General Assembly, New York City, October, 1960.

26. Nikita Khrushchev consulting with J. B. Tito during the Fifteenth Session of the United Nations General Assembly, New York City, October, 1960.

LIST OF ILLUSTRATIONS

I

A COMINTERN AGENT

1

A STAR IS BORN

PANTOVČAK 1928

Ninety years ago, a small group of conspirators gathered in a tavern on the wooded slopes on Zagreb's northern outskirts. The inconspicuous house on Pantovčak 178, surrounded by a secluded garden, is still standing as the only single-storied structure among the urban villas of the *nouveau riche* of newly independent Croatia. It is a protected historic building, with a plaque on its dilapidated front commemorating a meeting that took place almost a century ago. All the participants of the meeting held on 25 February 1928 are now long dead, most of them long forgotten, too. One of them, however, became a global revolutionary star of the modern age—half Stalin, half Che Guevara.

Across the street, a high wire fence surrounds an entire forested hill with huge trees in full leaf. Sheep graze contentedly in this urban forest. Treetops hide the modernist Villa Zagorje, now the official residence of the Croatian president. Its first owner began his miraculous political rise in the nondescript blue-collar tavern across the street. He never developed a liking for the grandiose edifice built for him by his thoughtful aides. As one of the most famous communist internationalists, he found odious anything that reminded him of Bauhaus, "worker's aesthetics," functionalism, international style, and other similar monstrosities of the twentieth century. He preferred imperial estates and royal residencies, with paintings by the Old Masters on the walls.

The conspirators in the tavern belong to a communist cell, and they are attending the Eighth Conference of the Zagreb party organization. Albeit tattered, these well-organized and indoctrinated terrorists scrupulously attach imposing names and numbers to their illegal gatherings, as if they were world's fairs or the Venice Biennale. This time, in addition to local activists from Trešnjevka and other Zagreb districts where leftist unionists and the industrial proletariat mingle in machine shops and other manufacturing operations, "many higher-level representatives" are present. When not discussing the world situation or the status of the Japanese proletariat, the communist conspirators are engaged in factional struggles. Here, we find ourselves in the middle of one such struggle, initiated and controlled by Moscow. Mihajlo Vranješ, a Zagreb communist, gives his account of the first recorded appearance of this story's hero:

> The issues discussed were not unexpected because pretty much everyone was familiar with them. What surprised us was the fact that the problem was presented so openly in front of so many people and that it was done by the organizing secretary himself, in the presence of the main protagonists of the factional struggle who were also responsible for the inactivity of the party's top ranks ...[1]

The organizing secretary of the Zagreb party organization who "presented the problem so openly" is Josip Broz, later to become a famous statesman known as Marshal Tito. But at the moment, he is merely a thirty-six-year-old unemployed steel worker and trade union member, a proletarian known by the alias Georgijević:

> In other words, in the presence of the representatives of the right faction headed by Dr Sima Marković and those of the left faction headed by Đuka Cvijić ... Also attending was a representative of the Communist International, and some fifteen other people, all higher level. The Comintern representative showed unusual interest in the discussion. He was a red-haired Ukrainian, I cannot remember his name any more. It was not his real name anyway ...

Dr Marković, from Belgrade and classified here among the "rightists," is one of the founders of the Communist Party of Yugoslavia (CPY) and its secretary. A university professor of mathematics and Lenin's friend, he was a member of the "management board" of the world revolution—the Executive Committee of the Communist International (ECCI; Ispolkom). When the CPY—the third strongest party in the parliament at the time—had been declared illegal under the Law on the Protection of the State (1921), he spent two years in prison. He then engaged in an ideological dispute with Stalin himself at a Comintern conference in Moscow. Referring to Marković by his pseudonym "Semich," Stalin says: "Semich has not fully understood the main essence of the Bolshevik presentation of the national question."

The whole thing was not about Marković, or Yugoslavia, or the Balkans for that matter; it was about the communist strategy after the October Revolution. The protagonists of the conflict were Stalin and eight other members of the Politburo of the All-Union Communist Party (Bolsheviks)—AUCP(b). Stalin's chief antagonist is Comrade Trotsky, the "prophet of the revolution." Comrade Trotsky thinks that all revolutionaries in all corners of the world should be supported, including the Chinese communists who were inciting the Shanghai proletariat to rise up in arms. Comrade Stalin knows better—the only one to receive support is Chiang Kai-shek, who is crushing the very same Bolshevik uprising but is fighting a national liberation war against the Japanese, thus preventing them from seizing Russian Siberia.

The "left faction" at the meeting in the Pantovčak tavern consists of the alleged followers of Cvijić. Cvijić and the Octobrist romanticists, among them the leading Croatian men of letters, will be pushed to the margins in the same way as the legal leaders of the CPY, dubbed the "right faction" on instructions from the comrades from Moscow, represented at the meeting by a Comintern delegate. The Moscow headquarters no longer trusts them—they have failed to grasp the agenda and are not up to carrying out the new instructions of the revolutionary high command. The command has no need of agitators or writers who would wage a "kulturkampf" in leftist magazines or campaign among union members. A street fight against fascism and the regime's police is about to begin. Political activists acting as missionaries of enlightenment, such as the Belgrade professors at the helm of the CPY, or revolutionary activists and writers, will rarely submit to a command mechanism because they are thinking people, not agents with contacts in the intelligence apparatus.

The Soviet State Political Directorate (GPU) was just beginning the process of transforming itself into a ministry, the People's Commissariat for Internal Affairs (NKVD)—the state political police—which would henceforth run all the "assets" in the field (in Europe and the rest of the world) via its Foreign Department. According to the new Bukharin–Stalin line, the revolution is to come under the state's complete control, together with all resources, including the Comintern. It is no longer an international fraternity of revolutionaries, but a subversive apparatus consisting of people with suitable qualifications. The Comintern's Balkan Secretariat creates a "receivership," sending "Comrade Milković" to inspect the situation.

Of course, he is no "Comrade Milković." His real name is Vladimir Nikolayevich Sakun—he is the "red-haired Ukrainian." He has been in charge of Yugoslavia. When Stalin's "general line" triumphed at the Comintern

Congress in 1928, he became a member of the Comintern's highest body, the Presidium of the Executive Committee. He and Vasil Kolarov, an old Bulgarian communist, have taken over the "Balkan Secretariat," controlling the fluid region between Vienna and the Aegean Sea for which the Kremlin has not yet developed a detailed political strategy. The unsuspecting Vranješ observes: "Then he [Sakun] talked with Broz. We later heard he was very happy with the conference and with the decision—proposed by Georgijević— that an open letter be sent to the Communist International."

So who is this Georgijević-Broz, a confidant of the Moscow-based Comintern headquarters? A year earlier, in July 1927, he was arrested in Kraljevica for communist activities. In October of that year, in Ogulin, he was sentenced to seven months in prison. He was released pending an appeal. Upon returning to Zagreb, he resumed his involvement in the network of unions that served to disguise the subversive apparatus. When he came into the limelight in the Pantovčak tavern at the beginning of this exhilarating story, Broz was an inconspicuous figure—a short, stout man of rather rough features or, to use the terminology from criminal records, "with no special distinguishing marks." First he was apprenticed to a locksmith and then he became a mechanic and test driver for Daimler-Mercedes in Austria. Neither his appearance nor his legal biography contained anything that would stand out in stark relief. The importance of this figure lies in secret spheres.

Naturally, while looking for cadres, Sakun is not working on his own. The most important part of the cadre selection just before the Pantovčak conference was done by a man who was not even attending it. His name is Karlo Štajner, who would achieve worldwide acclaim with his book *7,000 Days in Siberia* (1971). It was published—albeit only in Croatian—before Aleksandr Solzhenitsyn's *The Gulag Archipelago* (1973). The book dealt with the same subject matter but was initially not translated in the West because the Yugoslav authorities hesitated to instigate trouble that would damage their relations with Brezhnev's Soviet Union. Štajner lived to a very old age, without anybody ever really grasping his role in the Soviet apparatus and in Broz's promotion.

As early as 1922, Štajner became a party instructor of the Comintern International Relations Department (OMS) stationed in Zagreb, in charge of the Yugoslav parts of the former Austria–Hungary. As the Law on the Protection of the State banning the Communist Party had just been passed in Yugoslavia, the party went underground. Until 1931, Štajner was in charge of the illegal party apparatus (*tehnika*), funds, and cadres, maintaining contacts with the OMS headquarters in Moscow. The OMS was founded as the Secret Department of the Communist International in October 1920, and in July 1921 it was renamed International Relations Department. Its original name clearly indicates the nature of these relations. In the beginning, the OMS had its main stations in Berlin, Constantinople, Baku, Sevastopol, Odessa, Chita, Riga, Antwerp, and Tallinn. These are mostly port cities—suitable for maintaining secret international connections. But the OMS correspondence goes via the GPU; in other words, the Soviet secret service has penetrated the apparatus of the international communist organization. The GPU is fully familiar with the dislocated OMS centers in the Soviet Union and abroad that maintain international party relations and communication. GPU's foreign department was then headed by Mikhail Abramovich Trilisser, aka "General Moskvin."[2] In the ensuing decade, the service would gain full control over the Comintern apparatus. Walter Germanovich Krivitsky (the *nom de guerre* of Samuel Ginsberg), the coordinator of Soviet secret agents in Western Europe, who defected in 1937,[3] explains:

> We created a permanent network of dislocated agents who operated as liaison officers between Moscow and the nominally autonomous communist parties in Europe, Asia, Latin America and the United States … As Comintern residents, the OMS representatives kept under their control the heads of the communist parties of the countries they were stationed in. The party rank and file, even some of the party brass, were not even aware of these OMS representatives. The latter ones answered only to Moscow, but took no part in local party activities.

Comintern officials like Sakun could of course use their insight into the local situation when choosing new cadres for leading positions. The creation of the new Yugoslav "proletarian" party organs, which were to replace the former leadership, launched at the Eighth Conference two characters who seemed to come out of nowhere: Andrija Hebrang and Josip Broz.

Hebrang, a Croatian Jew from Virovitica, worked in Royal, a Zagreb-based mechanical shop. Before that, he was in Kumanovo, Macedonia, carrying out some highly classified missions. Broz had the same assignment, but he was not so disciplined. He came from Zagreb to Belgrade and, instead of proceeding to Kumanovo, he decided to return to the parts familiar to him. He found a job in a metal workshop in Zagreb and immediately got involved in union activities. He remembered the episode in an interview he gave more than half a century later:

> There we began—how shall I put it?—to make strenuous efforts to bring workers together and strengthen the party organization. We had thirty party cells in

factories. A very strong network—the strongest in Yugoslavia, actually. As I was the secretary of the Metal Workers' Union, I traveled all across the country. And there were strikes to be led in Zagreb. Our people were killing strike-breakers, and police suspected I had my hand in it. So they would come to my office. A detective is sitting opposite me. I'm typing and he's staring at me. And I go, phlegmatically: "Sir, if you feel like sitting here, be my guest." So he keeps sitting and staring at me all day, because they thought it was I who had organized the killings of the strike-breakers.

Clearly, locksmithing did not take him a lot of time. He led strikes in which strike-breakers would be done away with—a mysterious character, this extraordinary, yet seemingly ordinary Mr Josip Broz. But anyway, how did he end up at this fateful meeting in the non-descript Pantovčak house, in a tavern open to select clientele only, like some Carbonari club?

There is no doubt that it was Štajner, the OMS representative informing Sakun about available cadres, who recommended Broz. While there is no archival evidence of it, the whole thing is clear when you follow their future relations. Štajner left Zagreb in 1932. There was a security lapse and the police were after him, so he went to Paris and Berlin, and then, in the same year, he arrived in the Soviet Union. He worked in the Comintern apparatus until November 1936, when he was arrested together with all the leading Yugoslav cadres that he had kept in contact with as an OMS operative back in Zagreb. The wave of arrests in Moscow began when the NKVD (a GPU derivative) had taken over the entire "transmission" institution of the International Relations Department, abolishing the OMS. In October 1937, Comintern heads Georgi Dimitrov and Dmitry Manuilsky sent a letter to the Soviet Party Politburo, warning it that the OMS had become a center of foreign spies and enemies of the people. They hurried to distance themselves from the people they had worked with, as soon as the latter ones fell from grace. The organs of repression then carried out a mass liquidation of the OMS cadres. Only Štajner miraculously survived; he was sentenced to twenty years' hard labor. Very strange; it implies he somehow deserved the grace he was granted—the grace the people of his sort were normally denied.

Tito was also in Moscow during the OMS purge. However, he remained unscathed. He wrote "character references" for all of his Yugoslav comrades who ended up in Siberia, but that was only a secondary form of insurance. More importantly, he was connected and working for the people who, at that moment, were taking control of the international apparatus and purging it, remolding a revolutionary Marxist brotherhood into a Stalinist steel blade of the Soviet secret foreign agent network.

Štajner and Georgijević, the enigmatic characters from the Zagreb party circles of the 1920s, will thus be separated by fate for two decades. Štajner will be serving his 7,000 days in Siberia, and Broz—the Georgijević from the Pantovčak tavern—will be experiencing the avatars of his subversive and statesman careers. He has finally made it to the top of Stalinist Yugoslavia. He will turn apostate from the Kremlin and, when Stalin dies, will return to them, but as an equal partner of Nikita Sergeyevich Khrushchev, the Soviet leader who began the revisionist project of the destalinization of the Soviet Communist state. So Nikita Sergeyevich will rehabilitate the victims of Stalin's purges, including Yugoslav comrades. However, Tito, as his crucial ally in this undertaking, never rehabilitated any one of those whose "character references" he once wrote because he belonged to another team—the one that carried out the purges. But he used his influence with Khrushchev to rescue the only man he cared about—Štajner. Released from his Siberian exile, Štajner returned to Zagreb where he died in 1992, aged ninety.[4]

Appointed by the highest levels in 1928, based on abilities and merits that have yet to be understood, Broz followed his strictly defined course. At the Eighth Conference in the Pantovčak tavern, he and Hebrang were going to bust both "left" and "right" factions, discrediting General Secretary Marković and his deputy Ljuba Radovanović, another Belgrade-based math professor, as people who cannot efficiently run the organization.

Having witnessed the support given to Hebrang (who is allegedly chairing this Zagreb party branch conference) and Broz—something party cadres can easily detect with their in-built radars—the plenum votes in favor of their motion. It was decided that a letter be dispatched to Moscow, requesting the Comintern to arbitrate directly in the internal affairs of the CPY. As if it had not been doing so already! Inspections from Moscow had been permanently coming here since 1922, and special commissars had been operating in Vienna. The "Balkan Secretariat" was founded there, thus disowning the CPY's autonomous leadership.

In all probability, it was Hebrang who wrote the letter to the headquarters: while "Faty" (Hebrang's pseudonym) is a longstanding contributor to the illegal party bulletin *Borba* (Struggle), "Georgijević" is semiliterate—his proclamations are so poorly formulated one can hardly understand them.

Having decided to contact Moscow directly, thus avoiding the Belgrade leadership and even the Viennese Balkan Bureau, the Eighth Conference plenum appointed a ten-member delegation to go to the Comintern in Moscow and brief it about the situation. The delegates included Marković and Hebrang (the latter representing the Zagreb party chapter, part of the Provincial Committee for Croatia). The Zagreb Conference delegate Vranješ was also one of the group that was about to leave for the capital of world communism. On 13 March 1928, they were all arrested in Graz, Austria, and deported to Yugoslavia, where they received long sentences, ranging from five years (Vranješ) to twelve years (Hebrang, as the ringleader). But Broz was nowhere around. His rivals always disappear from the stage, as if fate itself has intervened. When you grasp the *modus operandi* and realize how he treats those standing in his way, you hesitate to even hypothetically take a peek into the utmost depths of his soul ... Now that the ten delegates have been arrested, the stage is bare and the main character of this historical drama can step in— "Bolshevik Georgijević," a new man for the new assignments. But when and where did this Georgijević become a Bolshevik in the first place?

2

THE SIBERIAN ODYSSEY OF
A ZAGORJE CORPORAL

OMSK 1917

It would appear that everything about this story's protagonist is already known. Those who lived during Tito's rule, the best-informed contemporaries, and almost all professional historiographers will agree about the basic biographical data accepted as facts. Born and raised in the Croatian village of Kumrovec, he joined the CPY as a worker in Kraljevica Shipyard in 1925. As for the pseudonym Tito—he could have gotten it who knows where, but it doesn't really matter; as he himself once told his official biographer Vladimir Dedijer, "Tito? Well, it's a nickname ... a nickname like any other!"

And yet, none of the above is correct; the truth is complex, and a legend has been created to veil and mystify both the person and his deeds. In his lifetime, Tito's personal history was a closely guarded secret. While he was in power, the state he ruled took care of that. Great powers were interested in a programmed reception of his activities. When he died, experts and the public more or less lost interest in him, or identified him with the regime that survived for another ten years. They thus glorified or questioned his work, his crimes, his achievements. What they failed to notice was a thrilling story about a cryptic man who, like a phantom, emerged from the Balkan mists and became one of the key protagonists of the modern history of Europe and the world. His fate was not linked with Yugoslavia alone. Both Yugoslavias—the

11

one he inherited and the one he created—were too small for him. His ambitions were oriented to the creation of his clandestine global empire.

Broz was born on 7 May 1892. He spent his earliest years in the village of Podsreda in Slovenia, on the fief of the Austrian princely family Windisch-Graetz, where his grandfather Martin Javoršek worked as a forester. His mother was a Slovene and his mother tongue was Slovene. His father Franjo Broz was from the Croatian village of Kumrovec, on the opposite bank of the Sutla, a small river that then divided two tribes of the same Kajkavian dialect and now divides two European countries and peoples of the South Slavic tribe.

Josip was the seventh child of Marija Javoršek. She gave birth to fifteen of them but eight died before reaching the age of two. Of the surviving siblings, there were two older brothers, a younger brother, and three younger sisters. Thus, six sisters and two brothers died in their infancy; male children clearly received better care and had somewhat better chances to survive—the political economy of rural life in a time of privation. "I was not her favorite," he admitted, showing true pain while recollecting his childhood days eighty years later, when he lived like a nabob in his imperial residence on the Brijuni Islands in the Adriatic. "My two sisters, she loved them ... A mother with many children cannot become equally attached to every one of them; they all need something, and then kids become jealous ..."

Josip lived in Slovenia with his grandfather until he was seven. They went dormouse hunting together. It became his most cherished childhood memory. The experience was also his initiation as a hunter; later on in his life, he killed herds of trophy deer, ibex, bears, and various exotic wildlife in Bosnia, Africa, and Asia. Wherever he went, he always had his hunting carbine and his pistol at hand. At the age of eighty-eight, while on his deathbed in the University Clinical Center Ljubljana, he kept in a small bag in the bedside cabinet a licensed Yugoslav version of the Tulski–Tokarev (TT) pistol after which he had been nicknamed. It was like a metaphorical summary of his entire political biography.

When Joža (as he was called) turned seven, he was sent to his uncle's home in Kumrovec—the house now playing the role of his childhood home. Every year, toothless nostalgists gather there on his (false) birthday on 25 May, playing accordions and waving the banners of his failed state.

Joža was sent to Kumrovec to go to elementary school there. He failed the first grade because he could not speak Croatian. Actually, he never really learned the standard Croatian language; the Slovene language and the Croatian dialect used in his Zagorje region were his original idioms. In the army and during his career as a Comintern agent, he only used the Austrian version of German, which he spoke fluently. He spoke Russian, too, but he never properly learned its orthography and grammar. Not being an intellectual, he would never win the Nobel Prize for Literature even if he did break his vow of silence and publish his memoirs. He was certainly no Churchill in this respect, but he did play with him in the same Premier League.

In Kumrovec, Josip finished four grades of elementary school plus fifth, intended for the schoolchildren to consolidate the knowledge acquired up to then, modest as it was. After six years of education (he had to repeat the first grade), he was sent to his uncle's household as a servant. He did not like it one bit. The last remaining witnesses claim that Josip, as a fourteen-year-old, had an affair with a married woman so he had to be sent elsewhere. This gossip—now almost archeological—can be heard from some ninety-year-olds in Zagreb:

> A sergeant major came to us from Sisak then. To me, he was like a general. My folks asked him if I could go to Sisak with him. He was looking for a young fellow who would be a waiter in the canteen of the 25th Home Guard Regiment, held by some German family. So, my brother came to me and told me, "You're going to Sisak to become an apprentice." So, I packed my things. My uncle was not happy about it. He grumbled: "I took you, and now you're leaving." And I said, "I have to. I need to learn a trade, to live my own life."

His older brother took him to Sisak to wait tables in a canteen. He had just turned fifteen. There was a bowling alley there and, in addition to other busboy's duties, he had to set up the pins. He immediately learned the tricks of the trade. For a tip, using a hidden string, he would pull the pins that were not knocked down by the ball. When he was caught, an officer slapped him in the face. Josip was instantly fed up with the job. He went to the Hašek and Karas workshop across the street and asked if he could be an apprentice there. The owner agreed to take him on, and his father came over to sign the contract of apprenticeship. Josip learned the locksmith's trade there between 1907 and 1910. He left that job for the same reason: while absorbed in a *Sherlock Holmes* novel, he broke a drill on the boring machine and the owner hit him. Then he went to Zagreb, looking for a real job. He found a job as a steel worker in Izidor Haramina's metal workshop on Ilica Street. It was a renowned workshop—they had just gotten a contract for wrought-iron decorations for the Zagreb University Library, a jewel of secessionism. But he wasn't much into this craft. Very soon, he moved on—to the Knaus machine shop—where he trained to be a lathe operator and a mechanic, while preparing for new adventures.

Josip's story clearly highlights one of the fundamental traits of his character—defiance. Instead of fear and self-pity—a resolve to outwit fate. In his political biography, this trait prevails in all circumstances. Boldness, audacity, resistance to authority, and absence of fear manifest in him at all times, followed by cunning, astuteness, self-confidence, and secretiveness. He never confided his ambitions and intentions even to those closest to him.

Quitting his job at Knaus, Josip goes abroad, in keeping with the medieval rule that a journeyman who is about to obtain his trade license must first undergo further training abroad. He walked all the way to Trieste, then to Kamnik, Slovenia, where he worked at Titan, a large metal manufacturer. Then he found a job in Čenkov, Bohemia:

> The pay was very good. Could buy a new suit every month. The living standards in Czech lands were higher than in Austria then. But we were spenders, too. Every Saturday we would go to another place, another village. Every Czech village had its own brass band, so we would go to dances and we would drink and spend money there.

In 1913, having turned twenty-one, Broz received his draft notice. He was in Wiener Neustadt near Vienna. He lived there with his brother, who had also come there looking for a job in industry. Josip got a job in the Daimler factory, where they made limousines. He says he was a mechanic and a test driver. He could remember details of their engines even sixty years later. Having received the draft notice, he found himself in a dilemma for a while: Should he report to the army or borrow some money from a relative in Hamburg and emigrate to America? During his visit to Germany as a statesman in the 1970s, they asked him what he would have become if he had made it to America. He replied without hesitation: a millionaire! However, instead of going to America, he returned to Zagreb and reported to the draft board:

> I applied for the arsenal—the technical arsenal. I was sent to Vienna. They didn't give prison haircuts there, they would leave some hair on your head. But there were only Germans there and I didn't like it. So I requested to be transferred to Zagreb, to the 53rd Regiment. And they sent me to Zagreb, but not to the 53rd—it was full. Instead, I was sent to the 25th Home Guard Regiment. All right, not bad. And so I ended up in Zagreb. None of my family knew I had returned, not even my father and mother, for I had not written to them. My father found out when someone told him, so he came to see me.

Josip wanted to join one of the three battalions of the elite 53rd Hungarian–Croatian Infantry Regiment garrisoned in Zagreb. However, he ended up in the ordinary 25th Agram Honvéd Regiment (in Hungarian) or

Zagreber Landwehr-Infanterie-Regiment (in German). Most of its conscripts (97 percent) were Croats and Serbs. The insubordinate journeyman who has spent the past three years as an itinerant worker in Central Europe and learned some German and Czech in the process is now training in fencing. The story of his participation in an army tournament in Budapest—where he was sent as a gifted fencer—figures prominently in his TV memoirs. He claims he won second place there. He says he came first in rapier and second in thrust fencing, eventually placing second among 600 participants. The silver medal was presented to him by "Archduke Joseph" himself:

> There sits the duke up in the grandstand, presenting awards and diplomas. Having placed second, I won the silver medal. The winner got the gold one. The duke is presenting the awards, shaking the hand of every medalist. I was the only ordinary soldier there—all the others were big shots, officers ... The duke shaking my hand—it's really something. In both disciplines, thrust and rapier, I had to win duels with all these people—Hungarians, gendarmes, cavalry officers ... It's quite a big deal!

All such subsequent accounts are not reliable because in them Broz presents himself as an exceptional man before he actually became one. It is true, however, that in 1913, Archduke Joseph August Victor Clemens Maria von Habsburg-Lotharingen of Austria, in the rank of vice-marshal, was in command of the 31st Budapest Division, where the tournament took place. And the statement of Broz's commander Milutin Stipetić, recorded for TV, also confirms the story to a certain extent.

When the war broke out, Broz and his regiment were stationed in Ruma, between the Sava and the Danube, 40 miles west of Belgrade. Since the chief of the Imperial and Royal General Staff, Field Marshal Count Franz Conrad von Hoetzendorf, could not decide whether to concentrate the troops on the southern or the eastern front—against the Serbs or Russians—a huge army was waiting in Srijem. Broz explains:

> The Austrian army had been crushed in Serbia by then. One of our battalions was deployed on the border, preventing the Serbs from crossing over. We were in Ruma, preparing for Galicia. The Russians had crossed the Carpathians and advanced all the way to Marmor Sziget. We stayed in Ruma for a month, a month and a half—the winter was already coming.

Broz often uses German expressions in his story. Besides, those who would "cross over" into Bosnia are the Serbs—the enemy—and it is "our battalion" taking a stand against them. Broz readily reveals his affiliation: he does not identify himself with the Slavs—Croats, Serbs, or Russians—but with the

Austro-Hungarian army in which he has moved up and got his first bars as an NCO—a corporal. He actually claimed he had become a *feldwebel* (sergeant), but that should be taken with utmost skepticism. At any rate, there is no hint of any revolutionary impulse in his positioning in the cosmos of the big, civilized European country of Austria–Hungary.

The 42nd Home Guard Division (known as the Devil's Division) that the 25th Regiment belonged to participated in the Serbian campaign. It suffered heavy losses during the Serbian counteroffensive at the River Kolubara. Later, during the thrust into Serbia in 1915, its soldiers committed war crimes against civilians. This information has given ground for a widespread hypothesis that Tito was involved in that.[1] But in December 1914 his unit was urgently sent to Marmor Sziget to contain the Russian offensive and participate in the winter counteroffensive toward Lvov.

Broz's division arrived in Galicia by train in December and was immediately sent via high Carpathian passes to attack the Russians. It was forced into a senseless charge across a rugged terrain, in freezing weather. Field Marshal Svetozar Borojević, the commander of the Austrian Third Army, tried to defy the order and was replaced. The army fell apart immediately. This is Corporal Broz's account:

> We were supposed to push the Cossacks back because they had already crossed the Carpathians. And there was deep snow. So we engaged in some fighting there, forced them back and then followed them across these high peaks and very deep snow. When we crossed to the other side, the strong Russian artillery stopped us. We dug our trenches there, in the snow. It was bitter cold at night. Some of the soldiers froze to death. We found them in the morning, wrapped in their tent-halves. It was hard to move on, to chase the Russians. But I was in an advance party—the *Nachrichten patrole*—so for me it was easy: If I felt like fighting, I'd fight; if I didn't, I wouldn't. I was always in reconnaissance and no one could control me. And I never lost a man while we were there.

But it did not last long. The Austro-Hungarian winter offensive failed, and the Slavic soldiers started surrendering on a massive scale. Broz's entire battalion was taken prisoner. As for Broz himself, a Cossack from the Dniester Group on the left flank stabbed him through the chest and a shoulder blade with a lance. Tito's company commander Milutin Stipetić's account of these events can be found in the Belgrade Military Archives.

Like Broz said in his statement at the Zagreb court, he had been wounded near Okno in the Austro-Hungarian province of Bukovina (present-day Vikno in Ukraine). When he remembered those moments, he did not dwell on details:

The Russians kicked the hell out of us near Jaroslav, so we pulled back. Then we were pulled out from Galicia and redeployed in Bukovina. I was taken prisoner there. That's how it ended. When taken prisoner, I was badly wounded. The train transporting the wounded was very slow; it made lengthy stops at stations en route. It was terribly rough. We didn't always have food. First they drove us to Kiev, to the fort up on the hill. We lay there for a few days and then they transported us to Sviyazhsk. There was a monastery there, full of us, wounded. There were typhus cases, too. Doctors were our people—there were eighteen POW doctors. Standing out among them was Dr Kralj. He used to be a head doctor in Graz. After the war he worked in Zagreb, too.

Broz was seriously wounded. In captivity, with no antibiotics, his chances of recovering were not good. He recalls:

What can I tell you ... It was all right while I only had this wound. But several months later, I picked up typhus, too. In combination with the unhealed wound, I took a turn for the worse. When I became delirious, they put me in a separate room, with a red ribbon tied on my bed. That meant I was a goner, my condition was hopeless. Apathetic as I was at that point, I said to myself, "Well, so be it." One doesn't care anymore. But my condition improved and I got out of that room. The crisis was over. There was a fellow in my room—his name was Zrinski. He was from Zagreb. Delirious, he gets up, comes to me and stares at me. He goes, "Hey, you're going to kick the bucket." He told me that, but it was he who died the very next day. While still conscious, he had continually spoken of his two well-behaved children and his beautiful wife. And he died, that Zrinski. These small episodes in life—one doesn't always remember them, but they're interesting.

While such material would suffice for a lengthy anti-war story, to our mundane adventurer it is hardly worth telling even as an anecdote:

I couldn't eat. Fortunately, Dr Kralj, our fellow-countryman, stood up for me, cared for me, and treated me. They were getting edible food for me from the outside, at their own expense. I lay there for thirteen months, but my wound wouldn't heal completely. It did get better, but it still leaked. After these thirteen months, they moved me from the hospital as a convalescent. The Russian mayor of this small town became tired of having a sick Austrian for such a long time— on a special diet, no less—so he wanted to get rid of me as soon as possible. One of his staff came and took me to his place in Ardatov near Nyzhni Novgorod— actually, in the village of Kalasyevo, some 10 miles farther. We came to his home at night and he says to his family, "Here, I've brought an Avstriyets [Austrian] with me." For I was an Avstriyets for them—we all were. "He's a mechanic," he says. "He's going to work in the mill." So I worked in the mill and various things happened to me there.

In Sviyazhsk near Kazan, the present-day fairy-tale-styled capital of the Republic of Tatarstan, resembling Las Vegas, Broz was free to move at will and was, by and large, treated well. He did not end up on a frontline, with the "volunteers" from Slavic countries in whose ranks the flames of the Bolshevik Revolution would soon be fanned. It passed him by because he always tried to stay away from collectivist projects while searching for his own, realistic solutions, as typical of a true individualist. However, after this POW idyll, he was sent and interned in the Urals, in the town of Kungur near Perm, on the Kazan–Novosibirsk section of the Trans-Siberian Railway:

> One day, we were all picked up from these villages. It was a huge transport of POWs, mostly Romanians. They took us to the Urals. First to Yekaterinburg and then to Kungur. In Kungur, we worked on the railway line. I was in charge of some 200 captives, I can't remember exactly. They were supposed to repair the line between Perm and Kungur.[2] Both in winter and in summer. I didn't have to work, I was a foreman. Mine was to make sure they go to work, to keep records of those on the sick list and so on. God, what nasty times they were—being stuck in that terrible vastness, far away from everything, with some 200 Romanians. People were dying like flies. Someone dies and you just bury them. Then winter came, a terrible winter. They always worked in the same overalls; their army uniforms had been torn to pieces. Scantily clad, they ailed constantly. One of them had torn trousers and had to stitch them, so he stayed at home. And then the *provyerka* [inspection] came. "Where is he?" "Here he is," I reply. "He's in rags, can't go to work." And then the gendarme, a Cossack, slapped my face. I was furious. I was so mad I would have killed him if I had a gun. And then they locked me up, on account of deceiving the management.
>
> I had been in jail for a few days when the February Revolution broke out. Suddenly, the door burst open and they tell me: "Come on, get out. There's been a revolution." I saw it coming. There was an engineer at the depot there, a Bolshevik, so I had a contact with them.
>
> After a few months spent there, I got fed up. There had been a revolution, everybody was exuberant. Soldiers were leaving frontlines, they did not want to fight any more. So I decided to escape. The Romanians all chipped in and gave me some money, so I had a civilian coat sewn—I had been wearing an army overcoat until then. The train dispatcher at the local station had a son who worked as an engineer in Leningrad—it was Petrograd then. He gave me the address and helped me obtain my travel papers. So, one night, I escaped through a window and started walking.
>
> I boarded a train near Perm. There was this train, you know, plying between Petrograd and Siberia—they called it "Maxim Gorky." It was half a mile long. It was very slow, stopping at every single station. There was no control, everybody was dodging fare. Soldiers were escaping aboard it. So I arrived in Petrograd and I found that engineer. He was a Bolshevik and had a job in the Putilov Works.[3] I told him I was a metal worker and I would like to work in a factory, too. He

says, "All right, I'll take care of it." And they gave me a job. Demonstrations then took place—Bolsheviks had prepared them well, there were huge crowds in the streets. But the word had leaked out and there were machine-guns and the *okhraniki*, as they were called there, on all the buildings [members of Okhrana, secret police in imperial Russia, used by the Provisional Government against the demonstrations of 16 July 1917]. In front of the Warsaw Station—I remember, I was there—a huge crowd had gathered. Suddenly, machine-gun fire was opened. Many people were mowed down, others fled. I hid under a small bridge and stayed there until it was over. Then I got away. First I went to Devil's Island—a small island, it was still called that back then. I hid there for a while and then I walked to Finland.

I decided to run away from Russia. I thought—the whole thing had failed. It was over. I wanted to go back to Austria, to my home in Croatia, but I was arrested. The Russians were still there—Russian policemen, gendarmes. They were hunting Bolsheviks after the demonstrations. So they grabbed me there. They thought I was some dangerous Bolshevik. They asked no questions, they just put me on a transport to Petrograd, to the Petropavlovsk Fortress. I spent three weeks in the fortress. Nobody asked me a thing there. One day, they finally took me to interrogation. I decided to tell them I was an Austrian POW and that I wanted to escape. "Durak" [You, fool], they said, "Why didn't you say so? Go." But they wouldn't let me go free. Instead, they decided to dump me back to where I had come from, to Kungur, and they assigned a guard to escort me there. But I managed to escape on the way. I got away from the guard somewhere near Vytka, close to Perm. Then I walked again. By God, I must have walked a good couple of days. And when the "Maxim Gorky" train came, I got aboard again.

On the way to Omsk, near Tyumen, they were checking papers. I sit in a compartment with some women. They ask us: "Is there an Austrian with you?" And I say, "Nyet. Nyet u nas" [No, there isn't]. I used a dialect. And off they went. So, at night, the train reached Omsk—the Atamanski Hutor Station. I got off. The town was a mile and a half away from the station. There was nothing there at the time; today, there are boulevards ... I walked to the town, it was a dark night. Suddenly, they stopped me. "Halt! Who goes there?" What could I do? I told them, an Austrian prisoner. "All right, you can pass." When I came closer, I saw red stars on their hats. One of them says, "Have no fear, we took power today." While I was on the train, there was a revolution in Leningrad. Here, too, because they were well organized. All right, now what? "Go to the POW camp and report there. They are recruiting Red Guards. International Red Guard units are being formed." So I happily went there and joined the Red Guards.

Broz needed this early Bolshevik experience as a reference in his subsequent biography, but—in his own words—it seems he "was not the most dangerous of the Bolsheviks, but rather some small fry": "Then I went to countryside again. I had arranged with a Kyrgyz—Issay was his name—to be his machinist. I stayed at Issay's for a long time ..."

Broz stayed at Issay Djaksembayev's place, in a "German Village" 40 kilometers from Omsk, from August to December 1918. There, he started a relationship with Pelagija Denisovna Belousova, who was fourteen at the time (he was twenty-seven). And now comes the pivotal episode of the whole story. Tito says: "In November 1919, I was admitted to the party by Yugoslav comrades, represented then by Dimitrije Georgijević."[4]

Dimitrije Bugarski, whose pseudonyms were "Georgijević," "Starik," and "Stari," was an Austro-Hungarian army officer who fought on the Eastern Front. Upon surrendering to the Russians, he joined the 1st Serbian Volunteer Division. In September 1919, he joined the Bolsheviks in Yekaterinoslav (Dnipro), whence he was sent to Siberia as an agitator. In the Regional Committee (Obkom) of the All-Russian Communist Party (Bolsheviks)—VKP(b)—he becomes president of the Regional Yugoslav Bureau—the man in charge of all the Yugoslavs in Siberia. In November, he admitted Broz to the party, too. In early 1920, the Central Yugoslav Agitation and Propaganda Bureau was established in Moscow. Nine successive political courses were organized there. As part of the second class (generation) of the regular Soviet command course (for Red Commanders), the Yugoslav Section was formed. A total of 165 attendees would complete the course as part of the section. Among the lecturers is Pavle "Speedy" Gregorić, a very important character in this story. In a statement given just before his death in 1959, Georgijević-Bugarski claims: "Broz spent the remaining part of 1919 in various places in Siberia. When these parts were liberated and when party organizations were formed there, he, like most of the Yugoslav communists, was sent to Moscow to attend various courses."[5]

But this does not add up with the dates in Broz's itinerary. Either Dimitrije or the dates are wrong. Broz married Pelagija in September 1919 and they left Russia together. Georgijević-Bugarski, his first party secretary, was then in charge of the repatriation of the Yugoslavs from Soviet Russia. It is logical to assume that it was he who sent Broz and his wife to Broz's native country. Tito, for his part, was more nonchalant when giving his explanation:

> While still in Omsk, I read in the press that there was a revolution in Yugoslavia, too, that peasants were revolting around Zagreb, I don't know, that the army had been engaged ... I felt like going home. So I managed to obtain the papers and I went home. With Pelagija. It took us three weeks aboard "Maxim Gorky" to reach Leningrad. In Leningrad, they placed us in some barracks, where we stayed

for quite a while. Then they transported us to Narva, a fortress on the Baltic Sea, south of Leningrad.

From the port of Narva, prisoners of war were being evacuated to their countries of origin via the German port of Stettin (Szczecin). His claim that the news of peasants revolting around Zagreb made him want to go home sounds like a subsequent explanation or a description of a mission he was given. Be it as it may, the truth remains that *Zugsfuehrer* Broz, the Avstriyets who managed to avoid conscripting into the Serbian Russian Corps, flees from the Russian quagmire with his underage wife Pelagija. Consequently, he did not become "Lenin's comrade-in-arms" in the Soviet Union. In Omsk, however, he did enter the Soviet cadre machinery. And he would meet Dimitrije Georgijević again. The bond forged in those days was unbreakable.

Dimitrije Georgijević *née* Bugarski became a member of the Presidium of the Yugoslav Soviet in Moscow, the highest body of the émigré party hierarchy. He will remain in the Workers' and Peasants' Red Army (RKKA) until 1922. In 1936, he and some other important Yugoslav cadres will receive military training in Ryazan (where the Frunze Military Academy is placed), as part of their preparations for the Spanish Civil War. Some 1,500 Yugoslavs fought in Spain. The main point for dispatching volunteers to Spain is in Zagreb. It is run by Gregorić. In short, the same old bunch from 1917 is running the show.

Bugarski will spend three full years fighting in Spain. He was the artillery commander in the 15th International Brigade that included British and American battalions. Upon returning to Moscow in 1939, he joined the group of authors who were to prepare a report for the Comintern's "household magazine" *Bolshevik*, elaborating on the causes of the defeat in the Spanish Civil War. In the autumn of 1939, in Hotel Lux, among the people occupied with those analyses and lessons for military strategy in the ensuing revolutionary war in Western Europe, Dimitrije Georgijević meets Josip Broz, who has also been using the pseudonym "Georgijević" since 1928. After that, Broz will be referred to by the codenames "Walter," "T. T.," and, eventually, "Stari" (Old Man). They seem to be ranks, not pseudonyms. Tito corroborates: "Later, in Moscow, I met Georgijević again. I had already been the general secretary of the Communist Party of Yugoslavia then. He had returned from Spain in autumn 1939. So we renewed our acquaintance from our days in Omsk."

In the Great Patriotic War, Georgijević-Bugarski performed various duties in the Red Army. In 1944, he participated in the founding of the 1st Autonomous Yugoslav Infantry Brigade in the Soviet Union as its political commissar. In October 1944, the brigade is deployed in Yugoslavia under the command of the 3rd Serbian Division. Tito trusted him. He was transferred to his secret police, OZNA, later UDBA. After Tito's 1948 split with Moscow, Georgijević was invaluable as an "insider" in the fight with Stalin's agents. He made it to the rank of lieutenant general. He retired in 1952 but remained an active member of the Central Committee of the CPY. When he died in 1959, he was interred in the Alley of the Greats at Belgrade's New Cemetery. He had been connected with Broz for more than forty years.

3

THE COMBAT CELL

VELIKO TROJSTVO 1920

I was in charge of a whole transport from Omsk to Leningrad ...

This is how Broz begins the description of his return from Russia in November 1919. He led a group of twenty-five POWs returning to Yugoslavia via Stettin and Vienna. He carried all of their travel papers, and, above all, commanded their confidence. When they arrived in Vienna, Béla Kun, the leader of the failed Hungarian revolution, was also there.

Two months earlier, the Romanian army, supported by the Serbian army, had crushed the Hungarian communist uprising and overthrown the Hungarian Soviet Republic. Kun then moved to Vienna and stayed there until July 1920. At its 1919 founding congress, Comintern had decided to create its branch office in Vienna. They had a well-proven team for it—Mieczysław Broński (Lenin's closest associate and the Comintern's former representative in Germany and Austria) and Béla Szántó (Béla Kun's aide). The Vienna Bureau's tasks were extensive ones. It was supposed to liaise and control the communist parties of Czechoslovakia, Austria, Hungary, Romania, Yugoslavia, Albania, Greece, and Bulgaria. This, of course, required appropriate logistics—the Communist International's money was sent to all these organizations via Vienna, the meeting place of all those fighting on the Balkan secret front.

The very active agents of the Department for State Security of the Kingdom of Serbs, Croats, and Slovenes (SHS), headed by Vasa Lazarević, a prewar chief of Belgrade police, keep these foreign activities under close scrutiny. He provides the Zagreb regional office[1] with very detailed information on the Viennese "mission of Dr Bronski Warszawski." Indeed, he is not just anybody. Broński accompanied Lenin on the "sealed train" from Zurich to St. Petersburg, on his return to Russia across German territory. One secret report says: "Disguised as the Mission for POW Issues, they have their seat in the spacious premises on Belvederegasse 34," a building in Vienna's 4th *bezirk*, in the immediate vicinity of the Belvedere Palace:

> Russian "prisoners" in Vienna are accommodated in the barracks in Ausstellungstrasse in the 2nd *bezirk*. They get their food and quality clothes there and are regularly paid. They come and go, and there are never more than fifteen to twenty-five of them at any one time ... The Mission of the Moscow Republic is headed by the well-known terrorist Dr Broński-Warszawski ... By enabling permanent contacts between Moscow and all communist parties and by carrying out intensive military and political espionage, particularly in the successor states [of Austria–Hungary], as well as in Hungary and our Kingdom, Bronski's Mission serves as the main and only link between Moscow and the communist movement here, as its sole spiritual guide and source of funds. All the decisions of the Central Committees of the Yugoslav, Hungarian, Bulgarian, and Romanian parties must be approved by the Viennese Mission as the highest authority. No relevant decision made by the committees of these parties can be carried out without consent of this Mission, operating on instructions directly from Moscow. Because the entire organization is so centralized, the communist parties from all countries are merely sub-committees of the Soviet Executive Committee in Moscow.

So it was via Vienna—where these well-proven communists were creating their Balkan network—that Broz, accompanied by his wife, returned to his native country. He immediately found a job in a company in Zagreb's main street, Ilica. According to some sources, he organized demonstrations against the "Obznana" (Proclamation), a decree promulgated in December 1920 "in order to protect the state," putting the Communist Party outside the law. What was his next task? Broz himself explains:

> I found a job in Veliko Trojstvo. Here I stayed quite a while—a couple of years. Then Šabić came to me one day, Stevo Šabić. He had been an Austro-Hungarian officer, an *obleutnant* [first lieutenant]. He, too, had been taken prisoner in Russia. He was in the headquarters of Muravyov, who was a traitor. That Šabić was his chief of staff. When Muravyov was exposed and shot, he went home via Vladivostok. Then the two of us met. His parents were rich, so he had a lot of money. I had money, too ... We went around, agitating for the Communist Party. And he says—we were rather naïve in those days—we should collect arms,

rifles, to have something when the time comes. I was assembling a saw-mill at the time. We were laying the foundations there, pouring a thick layer of concrete. I made special hollows and we kept those rifles in them.

In the Civil War, Colonel M. A. Muravyov headed the armed detachments of Left SRs (the Left Social Revolutionaries, who were then allied with the Bolsheviks). He defeated the White troops of General Nikolai Yudenich, who was loyal to the parliamentary Provisional Government of Alexander Kerensky, the legal Russian government formed in the Duma in the wake of the February Revolution of 1917. Muravyov was then sent to the Eastern Front. But when the SRs revolted against Lenin's government in the summer of 1918, he also defected from the Bolsheviks. He was captured and killed because he allegedly resisted the arrest. Broz simplifies the whole story with an informed comment that Muravyov was liquidated. Clearly, First Lieutenant Šabić ranked very highly in the headquarters of that Soviet strategic formation. Upon returning to his homeland via Vladivostok, he came to Bjelovar, established contact with some mechanic from Zagorje, and, together with him, became an agitator and started obtaining and stashing rifles. When viewed in a larger perspective, the whole thing no longer seems that naïve.

The subversive career of Šabić, a lieutenant in the Austro-Hungarian army in Sisak and a revolutionary commander in Russia, reveals something very important—he was one of the numerous returnees sent on new missions as soon as the success of Lenin's revolution was ensured.

The revolutionary army that fought in the vast Russian spaces between Poland and Vladivostok was now being redeployed to a new front—Europe. Its mission: exporting the revolution. This is also the reason why Šabić, a Red Army staff officer, is hanging around in a village near Bjelovar, awaiting the developments that are to come. Bjelovar is not far from the border with Hungary, where Kun started a Bolshevik revolution and established a Soviet republic that lasted 133 days (from March to August 1919). After its collapse, Kun moved to Vienna in September (Broz passed through Vienna in October). Two months later, in January 1920, the demobilized Corporal Broz joined Staff Captain Šabić in Bjelovar. They realized by then that the Hungarian revolution had been put off; however, as early as April, street riots began in Vienna. This is a new round. Therefore, arms are to be collected. An autonomous military line of command was established among the communists. Their political activities in Western Europe had hitherto been overt, taking place on the public scene, and they were active as agitators, politically committed writers, or union leaders. This new Soviet agent network, however, is of a completely different nature. The well-intentioned Belgrade Socialists who held their Second Congress in Vukovar in April 1920, formally dropping the "Socialist Workers" label and becoming the Communist Party of Yugoslavia, are not even aware of it.

As communist organizations were to be prepared and trained for an armed revolution, combat cells were organized. In the Vienna headquarters for illegal activities (in Belvederegasse), in charge of the Balkans and Italy, a plan for a revolution in Bulgaria was drawn up in 1923. Other communist groups, the fighting nuclei of the "combat cells," were now studying it.

What was really going on in Bjelovar is best reflected in a discussion held a few years later, at the Third Congress of the CPY. It was only then, in 1926, that the delegates, including General Secretary Marković himself, first heard of a secret "combat cell" in the party, with "two sections with twenty members and twenty-seven candidates." "The discussion about the combat cell came as a great surprise for some delegates, including Sima Marković, for they had no idea it existed." Marković said that "such an organization is of dubious nature and is not part of the party."[2] At his proposal, a political commission was formed to investigate the whole thing. However, no records of an investigation have been preserved. At any rate, at its Fourth Congress in 1928—the last one before the Second World War—the CPY would be suspended and all the naïfs at the Eighth Conference in Zagreb, who wanted to learn more about the secret apparatus in their own ranks, would be politically liquidated.

For the Comintern in the late 1920s, the activities of bodies like the OMS (Secret Department of the Communist International), GPU (the political police), and GRU (the military intelligence agency) were of much more importance than the ideological work among union members. To fulfill a revolutionary protocol, one does not need research but well-organized armed masses. This, in turn, requires special cadres working as networked secret agents. So, beside the illegal but visible party (visible to its members), there is a parallel group, small and secret. In this sphere, top positions are not occupied by the professors masterfully debating with the leaders of the international workers' movement, but by "proletarian" revolutionary cadres with the required military qualifications. By the late 1920s, the process that had started by establishing "combat cells" completely changed the very nature of the communist parties of the Third International.

At the election for the Constituent Assembly in November 1920, the CPY won sixty-nine out of 419 seats. Just before that, in June 1920, it held its Second Congress and was transformed from a "Socialist Workers' Party"

THE COMBAT CELL, VELIKO TROJSTVO 1920

(established in 1919) into a "Communist Party" by adopting Lenin's "Twenty-One Points"—the programmatic principles dictated by the Comintern. The Party had 65,000 members and there were also 210,000 members of the unions influenced by it. A remarkable force. But, regardless of the revolutionary ideals, it is basically a democratic mass organization with very elaborate internal "checks and balances," as can be seen in the party statute that Lazarević's Department for Public Security promptly managed to obtain. However, with the instinct of an autocrat who cannot tolerate any opposition, Regent Alexander Karađorđević abolished all communist activities. The "Obznana" enacted in 1920 meant a restriction of civil rights of the regent's subjects in the Kingdom of SHS. His state, created in Versailles, was quite unstable.

After the "Obznana," there was a division in the Communist Party. A "soft" formation was created—the Independent Workers' Party of Yugoslavia, intended to continue the activities legally, on the political scene. However, it only won about 3.7 percent of the votes in the 1923 election, failing to cross the required threshold for entering the parliament. Other communists went underground. One of them, Alija Alijagić, assassinated Milorad Drašković, the royal minister of police. Drašković, a lawyer, banker, and former minister of war, was Regent Alexander's mentor and the author of the "Obznana." In response to the assassination, the state imposed the Law on the Protection of the State in 1921, stipulating long-term sentences for mere membership of subversive political organizations "promoting, justifying, or glorifying dictatorship, revolution, or any kind of violence." At the same time, the European revolution is at its last gasp. Crushed in Germany and Austria, defeated on battlefields in Poland, where Polish forces led by the Lithuanian aristocrat Marshal Piłsudski routed the Red Army led by the Russian aristocrat Marshal Tukhachevsky. How does all this affect Croatia, where Broz and Šabić operate?

This is how a memo sent from the General Staff of the 4th Army Military District of the Kingdom of SHS to the royal provincial governor for Croatia and Slavonia on 9 September 1922 analyzes the situation:

The following report has been received from a reliable source:

Russian Bolsheviks have been forced to give up their plan to roll over Poland and Romania, the vanguards of Western Europe, by force of arms.

The reasons are as follows:

I. Chaos in the Red Army, caused by starvation and the lack of foodstuffs and various supplies.

27

II. The failure of their propaganda among the Western proletariat, something that revealed itself recently. All the nations are so exhausted from the lengthy world war that the only thing they want is peace. There is but one thing that could start a fire again—the resentment of the defeated nations who feel humiliated as a result of the lost war and lost territories.

This weakness of the defeated nations is the only thing Bolsheviks and their ally, the German General Staff, are counting on today.

The situation in our Kingdom is as follows:

After the clampdown, communist activities in towns have decreased significantly, even ceased completely in some places. The only exception are the railway committees, which are still operating in high gear. They are linked with [centers] abroad. For example, from Russian "Vneshtorg" in Vienna (Belvederegasse 32) they receive all instructions, literature, money etc.

In December 1922, the Presidium of the Ispolkom—Executive Committee—of the Communist International (the Comintern's highest body) appointed its plenipotentiaries for the communist parties of France, Italy, Norway, Czechoslovakia, England, and Ireland. These are not some endemic communists any more, this is Moscow's all-star cast. Clara Zetkin (a German) was responsible for France, Mátyás Rákosi (a Vojvodina Magyar) and then Dmitry Manuilsky (a Romanian/Moldavian) for Italy, and Kolarov (the universal Bulgarian) for Great Britain. In this context, an intriguing conclusion/instruction was noted down in Moscow: "In Yugoslavia—keep N. Milyutin in mind. Before the dispute is settled—Kolarov must talk to secretary Radovanović ..."[3]

Since Moscow is not happy with the ideas of Marković and the very existence of Yugoslavia—an "unnatural" creation of Versailles with its dictatorial regime engaged against Comintern operations in the Balkans—Marković is not present at the Comintern's Fourth Congress. His deputy secretary Ljuba Radovanović goes to meet Kolarov, who becomes the general secretary of Ispolkom. After the meeting, Kolarov appoints Commissar Vladimir Pavlovich Milyutin as the person in charge of all the Balkans. A Ukrainian with a law degree from the University of Petrograd, he was the people's commissar (minister) for agriculture in Lenin's first government. And the dispute mentioned in the conclusions of the Comintern's Ispolkom—what is it about? What has caused such displeasure at the headquarters? The answer can be found in the "Brochure on the Communist International's Views on the CPY Dispute"—an excerpt from Stalin's report at the Fourth Congress of the International. Here, Joseph Vissarionovich—the "people's commissar for nationalities" in Lenin's cabinet—says that "Semich has not fully understood the main essence of the Bolshevik presentation of the national question." And he goes on, specifying: "This lack of understanding and this underestimation constitute a grave danger, for, in practice, they imply an underestimation of the potential might latent, for instance, in the movement of the Croats for national emancipation. This underestimation is fraught with serious complications for the entire Yugoslav Communist Party."[4]

This is why, since way back in 1924, Moscow has been working on establishing contacts with Stjepan Radić's Croatian Republican Peasant Party (HRSS), a national peasant movement with anticlerical and separatist agendas. True, it is characterized by populism and antisemitism, but one cannot really expect Fabians or liberals in Croatia. Still, they, too, are good popular front material—this is what Stalin tried to explain to Marković in his congress discussion.

So the CPY had been under the receivership of the Comintern's branch in Vienna since January 1923. The party tried to re-establish and unite itself at its Third Congress in 1926, but Moscow had basically written them off. In the meantime, the OMS had been creating a new network of agents in the field. In Veliko Trojstvo, Broz established closer contacts with the Bjelovar–Križevci party organization and achieved recognition in the communist ranks for the first time. According to records, in 1925 he and Šabić were elected to the CPY District Committee for Bjelovar.

Just after Broz had found a job in Polak's mill in Bjelovar, Pelagija fell pregnant and gave birth to a baby girl, Zlatica. They went to Broz's younger brother Stjepan, in Kupinec near Zdenčina, 30 kilometers south of Zagreb. The second child, Hinko, died as an infant in November 1922. Zlatica would die six months later, aged two. Žarko was born in 1924 and survived. However, these personal matters are always of little importance in the story of our hero—he himself does not pay particular attention to them. The mill in Veliko Trojstvo was completed in 1925, and Broz's revolutionary activity in villages had become pointless now that armed insurrection was removed from Moscow's agenda. So he switched from subversive to intelligence activities.

4

PROLETARIAN GEORGIJEVIĆ

KRALJEVICA 1925

The Soviet apparatus started transforming itself from a secret network, paving the way for the revolutionary onslaught of the Red Army to a classic agent network integrated in the communist parties, members of Comintern. A memo sent by Lazarević's Department for State Security to the Zagreb County authorities on 25 September 1925 contains precious information on their Balkan activities.[1] For instance, that the delegation of the Comintern's Ispolkom, in charge of the Balkans, was established in Vienna (its abbreviation is DIKI). It took charge of the bureaus in Trieste and Gorizia—in other words, of the Italian Communist Party (PCI), crushed by fascists everywhere except in the ethnically mixed regions adjacent to the Yugoslav border. Established in Livorno (Leghorn) as late as 1921, PCI lasted merely four years.

Two different levels of activities can already be seen. In addition to the political one, the Balkan Federation headed by Dimitrov, there is also a separate intelligence structure. It was immediately clear which group Broz belonged to. When the work on the mill where the guns are stashed was completed, he moved to Zagreb with his family. It was Antun Mavrak, the organizational secretary (orgsec), who put them up at his place. This Bosnian Croat from Travnik (a high school in his hometown would later be named after him) had the pseudonym "Cerberus" and a matching face. As the

31

organizational secretary of the party's Regional Committee for Croatia and Slavonia, Mavrak was undoubtedly in touch with the OMS and Štajner. Štajner remained close to Mavrak when both of them moved to Moscow. While there, in 1932, "Cerberus" was expelled from the party. Štajner tried to help him before his own fall.

Having arrived in Zagreb from Veliko Trojstvo with his wife, Broz finds a new job—one never mentioned in his numerous biographies and hagiographies, despite readily available evidence: a document confirming it can be found on top of the pile in the Croatian State Archives in Zagreb. It is not a locksmith's job this time, nor a mechanic's job, or any such "proletarian" job. Broz becomes no less than a "sub-representative" (an agent) of Jugoslavenska Express Agencija A. D., with its seat in the very center of Zagreb—on Ban Jelačić Square. Jugoslavenska Express Agencija represents International Mercantile Marine Co., a New Jersey-based shipping company owned by J. P. Morgan, the largest in the world (Morgan also controlled White Star Line, which had *Titanic* in its fleet). The Yugoslav government gave the company a concession on the transport of immigrants to the United States and Canada. And the company's branch office in Belgrade was opened by—Josip Broz.[2]

That Broz lived at Mavrak's place and worked as a travel agent clearly shows that his entire metal worker's career was but a cover-up story. When one looks at his employment record in Zagreb, it turns out he spent no more than two to three months on every job—the minimum period required for obtaining the employment certificate (usually from some Jewish sympathizers) that he could submit to the police in order to become a union representative. And the "Red Unions" and Red Aid (MOPR) were merely a front for the intelligence and subversive apparatus.

Mavrak sends Broz to Kraljevica. Why there? The neighboring port city of Rijeka (then Fiume) is the most important revolutionary center in the Adriatic. Throughout 1920, the Italian poet and proto-fascist ideologist Gabriele D'Annunzio led in Fiume his Regency of Carnaro, a rogue utopian state that even declared war on the Italian government. After the collapse of the Hungarian Revolution, a large number of Kun's supporters came to this former Austro-Hungarian autonomous crown territory, a Croatian–Hungarian condominium administered by the parliament in Budapest. The Italian government ousted D'Annunzio and annexed the city in December 1920. In 1921, the Comintern sends a group of its operatives to the border town of Kraljevica, 17 kilometers away from Fiume, supplying them with substantial funds.[3] It was the Comintern's biggest Yugoslav project that year.

However, in 1925, when Tito came to the shipyard, where he would find a job, he did not find many communists among the local workers. Moscow's agents in that region were then focused on Italy via Fiume, engaged in a completely different mission.

And who is Broz's contact in Kraljevica? Gregorić, who taught at the Moscow school for the Red Commissars in 1919. He worked in Kraljevica as a physician. As the secretary of the local party committee, Gregorić admits "Georgijević" Broz to the CPY—this is Broz's third admission to the communist movement. This time, however, he adds a relevant political position to the one he already holds in the illegal *nomenklatura*: he is elected to the Kraljevica District Committee. Immediately, he organizes a strike in the shipyard and gets fired after only four months of his proletarian activism. Anyway, there was not much for him to do there—the area was run by the brothers Vujović, who were based in Rijeka. The oldest among them, Radomir (born in 1895), was sent to Vienna, to the Balkan Secretariat. He organized youth detachments, which, in accordance with the Comintern tactics of the moment, were to be used for street fights. Later, in Moscow, he became the organizing secretary of the CPY. Vojislav (born in 1897) became the first secretary of the Communist Youth International (KIM), founded in Berlin in 1919. Eventually, he became a member of the Comintern's Ispolkom (IKKI). The youngest brother, Grgur (born in 1901), after having been appointed into the IKKI, became the organizing secretary of the CPY. Clearly, all three of them were part of the OMS network. In the late 1930s, they were arrested and executed in the purges.

While in Kraljevica, Broz is still not a high-ranking operative, although he is older than all of the Vujović brothers. But they are intellectuals, educated abroad. They speak foreign languages and write and teach at communist cadre schools. Broz is merely a field worker, suitable for some specific actions of the combat cells, yet he is but an *unteroffizier* of Moscow's agent network. But this is the sort of man required for field work at this time.

In late 1926, Bolshevik "Georgijević" returns to Zagreb once again. From there, he is sent to Belgrade. Unfortunately, the shipping agency has been wound up in the meantime, so he finds temporary employment at the railway depot in Smederevo, where "the railway committee is operating in high gear." He was supposed to go to Kumanovo (Macedonia), where Hebrang, his opposite number in Zagreb, already resided. Kumanovo is a base for venturing into the untamed frontier, Komitadji territory. There, among local Slavo-Macedonians, the Bulgarian pro-communist Internal Macedonian Revolutionary Organization (VMRO) is conducting field training for revolutionary cadres. With the perfect instinct of a man who always avoids taking unnecessary risks, Broz gives up this plan after a short period of hesitation. He returns to Zagreb in late March 1927 and proceeds as usual:

> I found a job at Hamel in Medulićeva Street. I didn't like it, it was a metal workshop. I only stayed there for a while. Then I had a fight with the foreman again. So I left. Went straight to the metal workers' union and was appointed secretary there. First for Zagreb and then for the whole of Croatia. After that, I led a strike of the union members and then I was elected organizing secretary of the Zagreb party organization.

The following year, 1928, was a pivotal year in Tito's career, one that saw this disgruntled locksmith quickly rise to a prominent political position. His rise is easy to explain. It was in that year that the mysterious Vladimir Nikolayevich Sakun was inspecting the party organizations in the country as a Comintern emissary.[4] Unlike the Belgrade bunch, the characters he found among the Zagreb metal workers and in the railway depot left a favorable impression on him.

The workers Sakun encountered in the railway depot included cadres fitting the needs of the new, anti-fascist strategy of the communist movement. This is how "proletarian" detachments are formed, which, if required, undertake subversive activities and initiate street fights, thus creating an urban guerrilla front. Agitation among the general public is thus abandoned, including the activities of committed leftist artists (*kulturkampf*)—hitherto a favorite field of intellectuals, who have now become undesirable. What they lack is toughness. Besides, they are already known to the police.

Whenever the party apparatus is reorganized or the political course changed, the adaptable and intelligent Broz easily advances to a higher level. He is a locksmith who describes himself as a precision mechanic, because he worked as a test driver in the Daimler factory in Wiener Neustadt. Whoever had an opportunity to read his speeches and written comments would clearly realize his limitations and lack of book-learning, regardless of his social and political intelligence. A scrupulous analysis of his life and career indicates he was a secret agent by vocation. When Sakun began to organize a new, Stalinist CPY, Broz finally got a chance. Overstating his role as per usual, he eliminates Hebrang from history just like he had him eliminated from the face of the earth. He says:

> So I organized the Eighth Conference. From Belgrade came Sima Marković and Ljuba Radovanović, to hear what workers have to say, what they are thinking. A man from Herzegovina, Dušan Grković, was the secretary of the local party

committee. The two of us delivered reports. He glossed the whole thing over. I said the proletariat was revolutionary, but the [party's] job was not being done well. The tables turned at the conference. Grković was an intellectual, he never mingled with workers, while I regularly visited all the cells. So I was elected secretary then. It was also agreed that we send a letter to the Comintern.

Only the context can help us understand the political purpose of the Eighth Conference that took place in the Pantovčak tavern on 25 February 1928. This was the time of the conflict between Stalin and Trotsky over power and the fundamental issue of revolutionary strategy. Trotsky argues for revolution at home and abroad, while Stalin wants to build the state and introduce a foreign policy that would help the Soviet Union find a way to escape its isolation. And he does not need an international revolutionary brotherhood, but a normal secret service. That same year, Trotsky will be exiled into Alma Ata, and at the crucial Sixth Congress of the Communist International (17 July–1 September), Stalin's line—socialism in a single country—will triumph. Later, at the Fourth Congress of the CPY in Dresden (6–12 November 1928), the Yugoslav party will be practically abolished and turned into an agency.

Two months after Broz was elected to the leadership of the Zagreb party, there was an attempt on the life of the Croat national leader Radić in the National Assembly in Belgrade. Radić died at the beginning of August, causing riots to break out in Zagreb. The communists had some rifles. "Georgijević" saw an opportunity to gain prominence as a revolutionary star. First he won recognition at the Eighth Conference, then he excelled in the street fights, and, eventually, received publicity in a sensational court drama. He will thus brand his name in public, with the help of the tabloid press.

5

THE BOMBING PLOT TRIAL

ZAGREB 1928

Tito's descriptions often resemble the telegraph dispatches of the Associated Press, but he is less than scrupulous when relaying certain facts:

> Following Radić's death, we organized demonstrations that turned into a conflict, an armed conflict. We tipped the trams over and what not. For instance, in that street near Jelačić Square, our men dug in and opened fire. As for the gendarmes and police, they fired from the opposite side of the square. After midnight, I went there with one Martinović, who had just returned from the Comintern and was pretending to be very brave. But when the gendarmes fired at the two of us, he took to headlong flight. He had long legs, so he ran faster than me ...

Jovan Mališić Martinović from Danilovgrad in Montenegro is in fact the general secretary of the Central Committee of the CPY. Since 1924, he has lived in Moscow, where he teaches philosophy. However, his character reference written by Tito in 1937 for the NKVD reads: "I have known him since summer 1928, when he worked back in our native country. He was very daring, but I had an impression he was an adventurer. The way things are there, sending him home would not be useful."

Instead of sending him home, the Comintern sent him to Spain. After that, in 1939, he perished in the purges. He would be rehabilitated in 1958, but only in the Soviet Union. For Tito, he is just "one Martinović," even when he talks about him for his TV memoirs in the mid-1970s. Generally, he perceives Marković and Radovanović as "professors," sissies, people without real revolutionary enthusiasm; their brave conduct during police investigations means nothing to him. CPY General Secretary Martinović is merely "Martinović with long legs." He will describe the interim secretary of the CPY as a semiliterate worker with fat fingers who cannot even type, to say nothing of having an appeal to workers, whereas Tito, who has just become head of the Zagreb City Committee, formulates the proclamation brilliantly in no time, although he is in fact semiliterate.

The leaflet has been preserved—the text is full of distinctive empty phrases, revealing an uneducated author who is now overstating the quality of this worthless agitprop *oeuvre* while looking back at it through the prism of his subsequently achieved status. Besides, it was the embittered citizens and members of Radić's party who started the demonstrations. Communists merely seized the opportunity to use some of the rifles they had started collecting in Polak's mill seven years earlier.

Broz fell in the police ambush; the pistol he was carrying was confiscated and they brought him in. In the station, the chief detective hit him with a chair. Tito is philosophical when recollecting this episode:

> They already knew who was in their hands. They did. And I told them: One day we will discuss this. And when our army entered Zagreb in 1945, the chief detective killed himself. He knew what he was in for. But I wouldn't touch him! Perhaps he would even get a pension.

Or he would be shot together with 15,000 other people who were executed in Zagreb at that time. The police were obviously aware of the illegal organization's structure and the roles of its members. Allegedly, they had a highly positioned informer. Who was tipping them off? The suspicion fell on Matija Brezović, the secretary of the Central Committee of the League of the Communist Youth of Yugoslavia (SKOJ). Was he really a police spy? This *Tinker, Tailor, Soldier, Spy*-style enigma is practically impossible to solve, but the basic topography of relations can be seen: all of Broz's rivals and redundant fellow-travelers disappear in Russia or fall into the hands of the police. Only he gets away, untouchable and unscathed, as if he is coated with Teflon. But now his turn came too. Broz was brought to court in Zagreb and the sensational "Bombing Plot Trial" ensued. At the trial, which took place in Zagreb in November 1928, the state prosecutor was Dr Ivo Marokini, and he—naturally—remembered the whole thing very well fifty years later. Not a hair of his head was harmed:

The trial was named "Bombing Plot Trial" because of the two hand-grenades that had been included in the evidence. It was generally believed that the hand-grenades had been planted by the police.

It was during the judicial hearing that Broz said his famous words: "I do not recognize this bourgeois court; I consider myself responsible to my organization only." He admitted belonging to the organization, which, under the Law on the Protection of the State, was a criminal offense as such. Dr Ivo Politeo was his defense counsel. He said that the Criminal Procedure Act stipulated that, when the offense had been proven (because the accused had pleaded guilty), there was the benefit of a direct indictment. It was the state prosecutor's job to raise such an indictment at the trial. So that is what I did, keeping in mind that the proceedings would thus be shortened and that there would be no preliminary inquiry nor would he have to be remanded in custody. Which certainly suited Broz and he accepted it. For the remand prison, particularly in Zagreb, was not very pleasant. It was very unhygienic. In Lepoglava or Mitrovica, the hygienic conditions were better. Josip Broz gave an impression of a stable and courageous man, capable of saying such words in the court of law. His behavior and his bearing indicated good upbringing and it was a very good and useful thing to allow him the benefit of a direct indictment.

The former state prosecutor who had pressed charges against him at the Bombing Plot Trial guessed that Tito had used the trial and the sensational press coverage for his own promotion. To use modern terminology, he "used the media to create his own brand." Without five years of hard labor, he would be nobody among the party brass. When one looks at a list of top communists, his five years (plus the earlier eight-month sentence received for initiating a strike in Kraljevica—a suspended sentence that was now activated) would only make him a second-rater. To play in the first league, like Hebrang or Ivan Milutinović (a member of the wartime Politburo of the CPY), one had to serve ten to fifteen years. The true champions would be forwarded straight to the communist Valhalla—the police would liquidate them during a (staged) escape attempt or they would jump through a fourth-floor window. At the very first opportunity he got, Tito showed a phenomenal talent for managing his public image—one of the key characteristics of a skilled leader. He adds: "I thought I was in for at least ten years. And it turned out to be five. I was honestly surprised. Five years!"

6

CRIME AND PUNISHMENT

LEPOGLAVA 1931

In the penitentiary in Maribor where he was sent to serve his jail term, Broz met Moša Pijade, a Jewish painter and journalist from a middle-class Sephardic family in Belgrade. Together with Rodoljub Čolaković, Pijade translated Marx's *Das Kapital* while serving time in prison. Plain-looking, hunch-backed, hard-line, and fanatical, Pijade would become Broz's most reliable man and his most capable administrator. Until his imprisonment, Broz was merely an executive cadre of the Comintern's apparatus. The formation of this special relationship with the only two years older but incomparably better educated Pijade marked the beginning of the famous Tito-style cadre selection. He creates his own apparatus within the apparatus, a secret group of henchmen within the global communist empire. Never making a mistake in selecting his aides, even when they came from a completely different milieu, he began creating a group composed of his closest confidants. There would always be very few of them, and their duties would never correspond with the hierarchy of the party *nomenklatura*. Consequently, selecting people for "official" duties is one thing, whereas forming a group of "clandestine mandarins" he can always rely on is something completely different.

Pijade remained a *consigliere*, a person of utmost trust, until his death in 1957. He carried out the most delicate missions: politically liquidating rivals like Hebrang, commanding troops and entire provinces in wartime, and singlehandedly performing peacetime tasks for Tito that—in a different social order—would be assigned to entire institutions. Pijade wrote the Yugoslav Constitution, led the highest-ranking diplomatic delegations, and was the deputy chairman of the Presidium of the Federal Assembly (hierarchically, the deputy head of state). Pijade's loyalty to Broz was endless. But he viewed Broz through the eyes of a painter—he had studied painting in Munich and Paris—and the prison portrait that has been preserved shows the cruel, distrustful, frenetic look of a still unaccomplished street-level operative of the international communist conspiracy. Tito did not like the portrait one bit. In his residency, he kept it next to the door in his office, where visitors would not notice it. When the National Museum in Belgrade requested the loan of the painting for an exhibition after Pijade's death, he sent a note to his chief of protocol: "Not to be given on loan, because it [the portrait] is of very low quality and unfinished. T." But he was more than willing to give on loan a much worse, sycophantic monumental portrait depicting him in his marshal's coat, a work by Đorđe Andrejević-Kun. A reliable party painter, Andrejević-Kun had fought in the Spanish Civil War and had joined the Partisans at the beginning of the uprising. In 1949, he made that representative poster of Tito in his marshal's uniform. Members of the State Security Administration, the secret political police UDBA, presented it to Tito at some appropriate occasion.

Pijade had a nickname, "Uncle Janko", but he was not a good-natured man. He was a short-tempered, irascible, and harsh individual. Undoubtedly intelligent, perhaps the most capable of all those who helped Tito rise to power, this Balkan and Parisian expressionist of tiny stature clearly admired "Georgijević," the overtly aggressive, immensely resolute, physically strong, and unusually intelligent "proletarian of action." They established a feudal relationship—the only type of relationship the future communist power-wielder will ever have with the people in his immediate environment.

When the two men met in the prison in the small town of Lepoglava in Zagorje, Pijade was only at the beginning of his endless Calvary. Sentenced to a twelve-year prison term in 1925, he will serve fourteen years altogether. So he will translate not only *Das Kapital* but also two other works by Marx, *The Poverty of Philosophy* and *A Contribution to the Critique of Political Economy*.

Čolaković, a member of the assassination squad who killed the minister of interior, describes his meeting with Broz in Maribor, newly arrived from Lepoglava penitentiary, an old-fashioned Austro-Hungarian prison built on the foundations of a Paulist monastery way back in 1854. He says:

> In the spring of 1931, a group of convicts was brought to Maribor from the Lepoglava prison. Among those convicts was Josip Broz, a metal worker sen-

tenced to five years of hard labor. It was in the days when we, old Maribor convicts, were preparing for a hunger strike. Our main demand was that all the communist prisoners should share the same room. While inspecting the new arrivals from Lepoglava, the warden came to Tito, too. And Tito told him straight away that he would not serve his time the way the warden and the management had planned. He insisted on the same room. So we ended up in the same room. We organized ourselves immediately. We created our party organization and Josip Broz became its secretary.

However, it was not firm conduct against the class enemy that helped the small communist cell gain its special status in Lepoglava. Even in the mid-1970s, when these reminiscences of his were recorded on film, Čolaković did not know the whole truth. Tito explains it in his own TV memoirs:

The warden in Lepoglava was Bohaček, my wartime comrade. He had been a cadet, a one-year volunteer. He, too, had been in Sviyazhsk, in captivity. So we were good friends, we knew each other really well.

When he saw me, he was glad, and, by God, I was glad, too. Then he says: "You know what, let's agree on our future relations. I will help you as much as I can. You don't have to eat the regular food, it's not good. I'll arrange that you eat the hospital food." And he would let me leave the prison compound, to install electrical wiring around the village. ... There was a tavern there and I held meetings in it. Pajo [Pavle] Gregorić would come.

When explaining his relationship with Broz, Čolaković resorts to a retrospective analysis:

Slowly, while serving a prison sentence together with him, learning and working in the prison committee, I got to know a true proletarian and party official. I had been sentenced to a long term of imprisonment as a young man and my earlier contacts had mostly been limited to high-school students. There was an occasional worker in Sarajevo, but in Bijeljina, a small undeveloped place I lived in, there were 100 or so apprentices, mostly sandal makers, shoemakers, tailors, a few mill apprentices. They were unsophisticated, undereducated, illiterate, rather rough-hewn people, with undeveloped class consciousness. Suddenly, I meet a proletarian of a different sort, who has been around. An industrial worker who worked in Austria, Germany, Russia, and then in Zagreb—one of the strongest party centers then.

The union officials and agitators like Hebrang and Broz now have the edge, because, for them, socialism is not some fashionable teaching but a mission that required building a new, organized, and disciplined underground movement. Stalinism made everything comprehensible and clear for uneducated proletarians. In the account of one of the most literate revolutionaries in

Broz's immediate environment, Broz figures as a metal worker tempered in steel in the street, in unions, and committee struggles. Suddenly, his patchwork biography begins to look like the résumé of some future leader or power-wielder. In the turbulent twentieth century, riding the wave of populist movements, such people of exceptional abilities but with no regular civic background would either turn into dictators or end up on the gallows—or sometimes both. How does one become a historical leader? By experiencing a world of poverty, combat, and revolution. A convict with an ascetic face and a flaming gaze, as Čolaković describes him, is ready for the final ascent. But the days of success are still far ahead. First he must find his Queen of Hearts and see the light of the Lux.

7

QUEEN OF HEARTS

VIENNA 1934

In the spring of 1934, when Broz was finally released from the prison in the ancient Frankopan Tower in the Croatian town of Ogulin after 2,046 days, he was still a bit-part actor in the global revolution on the European continent. While he was serving time, Pelagija left him. He had brought her from Russia and put her at his brother's place in the countryside. She lost a baby boy in childbirth and soon afterward, in 1923, the two-year-old girl too. The third child—a boy—was born in the following year while Broz was operating around Bjelovar. When Georgijević was arrested and sentenced in 1928, Pelagija returned to the Soviet Union with her only remaining child, the four-year-old Žarko. They gave her a job in the Comintern.

Having served an additional seven months in Ogulin for organizing the strike in Kraljevica, Broz finally leaves the prison. In the meantime, he had lost contact with the organization. His existence and his future depended on whether he could re-establish contact with the communist network. But the network's fabric did not last very long. The people who introduced him to the underground structures have disappeared. Fleeing from police, the OMS head Štajner left the country three years earlier. The just-released prisoner is of course aware of the importance of his former position as the organizing secretary of the Zagreb party cell in touch with the Comintern section that had been gradually absorbed into the Foreign Department of the GPU, later renamed NKVD. But the organization does not have a contact to approach;

it is perfectly fluid and secretive, and since he lost his contacts, he has to re-establish them and reaffirm his role.

When the prison gate closed behind Broz, the Great Depression was just beginning. In 1934, when he was released, the Depression was in full swing. Fascism had triumphed in Europe. In Italy, Mussolini had been in power for twelve years. A year before, Hitler won control of Germany. France had seen riots organized by the extreme right/fascist movement called Cross of Fire. Maurice Thorez, general secretary of the French Communist Party, pro-claimed a new policy, in line with the Moscow headquarters: forming an anti-fascist national front. All the forces of the left were being urged to rally together and abandon the Trotskyist doctrine that perceived social democrats as enemies because they were not ready to start a revolution, right there and then, regardless of the odds of success.

The Second Republic has been established in Spain and José Antonio Primo de Rivera has founded the Falange, a wide right-wing coalition of nationalist trade unions. The civil war looms large. In Austria, Chancellor Engelbert Dollfuss, who has ruled with dictatorial powers for a year, has sus-pended the Parliament and founded the Austro-fascist "Ständestaat," which will last four years. It is spring, and new battles are taking place in the streets of Vienna between the Schutzbund (socialist "protection units") and Heimwehr (home guards loyal to the conservative government, supported in this fight by the regular army). Things are still quiet in Yugoslavia, due to the hardline policy of the regime that will remain unshaken for only another six months or so.

To the untrained eye, the spy who has just come in from the cold and returned to the revolutionary scene looks like an ordinary rebellious worker and union member of the 1920s. But he was the one who, on the orders of the Comintern and the representative of its Executive Committee, organized and led the Zagreb demonstrations supposed to destabilize King Alexander Karađorđević's regime. Moscow wants Yugoslavia to collapse or disintegrate, because it would make possible the creation of a national front-style coalition of left-wing, bourgeois, and anti-fascist movements within the nations consti-tuting the composite kingdom. In 1929, when Broz started serving his prison term, the king abolished both the constitution and the Parliament and assumed power himself, while appointing his favorite Petar Živković prime minister. An ideology of integral Yugoslavianism was proclaimed. The Special Court for the Protection of the State was established, thus giving impetus to the persecution of communists, Croat right-wing Ustashe, and populist democratic HSS, Macedonian VMRO terrorists, and any Albanian activist that would open their mouth. Even Serbian patriots of any democratic profile were being imprisoned on a regular basis. Broz thus returns to the scene after civil order has been abolished. There are no union centrals where agitators could gather and receive funds and instructions from OMS representatives. While he was on trial in 1928, the Fourth Congress of the CPY took place in Dresden, Germany. The party was practically suspended at the congress; instead of a general secretary with real authority, an organizing secretary was elected, a kind of *chargé d'affaires*. It was his colleague from the Zagreb union movement, Đaković. But Đaković was soon arrested by the royal police, together with the head of MOPR. Gendarmes took them both to the state border and shot them during a staged "attempted escape."

Straight from prison, Broz goes to Zagreb. He is actually on probation, interned in Kumrovec, where he has to report to police regularly. The municipal gendarmerie station in the nearby municipal center of Klanjec had received instructions to keep him under strict surveillance. He went to Samobor to his sister Terezija's place. From there, he can easily go to Zagreb, where he will find a contact sooner or later:

> When I was released from prison, the situation was very difficult. So, in Zagreb, I gathered a few members I could find—there was one Breyer, a Jew in charge of Red Aid, also a few other comrades. Students liked me. We would meet in the Samobor hills, up there in the woods. They found places for me to stay in Zagreb. There were very nice people among them. There were some girls, too: a physician, Beba Krajačić, Vanda Novosel. I wrote a long report on fascism, based on the writings of that Italian writer, what's his name ... I made comparisons with the situation in Yugoslavia, anticipating a military-fascist dictatorship. Fascism in Germany, fascism in Italy—it had to have some effect on the most reactionary classes in Yugoslavia. I gave it to them to read. It was distributed at the university; a brochure was also made later. However, I had to flee the country soon.

One should not take too seriously these alleged studies on fascism of his, written on the basis of "that Italian writer, what's his name." He is probably referring to Antonio Gramsci, a brilliant intellectual and founder of the Italian party newspaper *L'unità*. Bosiljka Beba Ević will become the wife of Ivan Stevo Krajačić, Tito's most reliable policeman, and Vanda Novosel will become Broz's "courier." She and some other young girls will remain infatuated with him even as pensioners. When he begins to operate in European capitals as a Soviet secret agent, they will become his "Bond girls." Right now, in Zagreb, they are of no use to him as a link with the organization. However,

Mirko Breyer from Red Aid is a real contact. Through him, he would find his Queen of Hearts and the cards would start opening as in solitaire.

Breyer, an antiquarian and publisher, put him in contact with Alfred Bergman, a Zagreb-based physician and an active communist with the operational pseudonym "Nenadov." His wife Braina Voss-Rudin, a Latvian Jew from Riga, was also a physician and active communist. Born in 1902, she was thirty-two at the time. She had obtained her medical degree in Berlin and started working in a hospital. When Hitler took power, she had to leave the country. Accompanied by her husband, she moved to Zagreb, found a job, and was placed in charge of maintaining party links with Vienna. Braina's husband, Bergman, was head of the OMS for the whole of Yugoslavia, connected with Breyer of the MOPR.

In July 1934, when all this was taking place, the Soviet security apparatus was incorporated into the NKVD as an autonomous department named Main Directorate for State Security (GUGB). At the same time, the NKVD's Foreign Department became a separate section—the First Main Department. Trilisser—"General Moskvin"—has been assigned a triple function. First, he runs this (civilian) foreign intelligence service. In his second avatar, he is an OMS inspector—meaning that the intelligence apparatus and the Comintern's communication infrastructure have become amalgamated. Third, Trilisser is responsible for the Baltic Secretariat, the Comintern's political bureau covering Poland, Finland, and the Baltic nations—a formation similar to the Balkan Bureau. This is why there are so many Latvian Jews in the OMS and MOPR as transmission organizations. Trilisser himself is from Riga, and there is no doubt Voss-Rudin was directly linked with him.

Voss-Rudin will send Broz to Vienna and become his "higher contact," as can be reconstructed from his subsequent activities: when he traveled from Vienna to Moscow in 1935, she accompanied him—otherwise he could not have access to certain places in a country where every foreigner is suspicious. Did Voss-Rudin and Broz remain close after their joint visit to the Soviet Union? It is possible, because they had similar paths in the years that followed; they were on the same missions, too. As of 1937, Voss-Rudin would be based in Paris and so would Broz—who, in the meantime, had dropped the pseudonym Georgijević and become Walter. Both of them will work for the Yugoslav Party's General Secretary Milan Gorkić. Gorkić will send her to Belgrade, entrusting her with the important task of organizing volunteers for Spain. It is Broz's primary mission, too, but on the other, intelligence end of the apparatus.

Broz's Viennese adventure in 1934 is not just an episode in an exceptional biography—it is a procedural example of the *modus operandi* of the Soviet intelligence network. The Zagreb party's organizing secretary arrived in Vienna on 27 July 1934. For a comparison, Harold Adrian Russell "Kim" Philby also arrived there some months earlier. The city had become a mecca for all progressive anti-fascist leftists—like Madrid and Barcelona a few years later. Philby was staying at the Kolmans, a Jewish family in the 9th *bezirk* who were communist sympathizers. Their daughter Litzi, an Austrian Communist Party activist, worked for the Soviet secret service. Being twenty-four, she was two years older than Kim, but she had already divorced her first husband, also an Austrian communist. When she met Philby, she was still having an affair with Gábor Péter, a Hungarian professional revolutionary who in 1945 would become head of Államvédelmi Hatóság, the notorious secret police of Rákosi's Stalinist regime. Litzi soon enthralled the somewhat stiff English leftist with an occasional stutter.[1] When the street fights began in Vienna in February 1934, thousands were interned in Austrian prison camps and nine leaders were executed on the grounds of martial law. Litzi would certainly have fallen victim to these measures, too, if Philby did not marry her in April 1934, two months before Broz's arrival in the Austrian capital. Litzi thus went to England with Philby.[2] There she put him in touch with Arnold Deutsch, who went by the name Otto, obviously corresponding with the function of an illegal (secret) resident—Tito also had such a name for a while when he temporarily took charge of the CPY bureau in Paris.

Broz arrived in Vienna, the regional headquarters and imperial capital, where—in the famous Café Central—many of the revolutionary ideas of the twentieth century had been born. There he would be coopted into the CPY Politburo. For the first time, he would be cast in a leading role—he would become organizing secretary of the CPY.

8

OBERKRAINER COMMUNISM

LJUBLJANA 1934

Gorkić took charge of what had remained of the CPY in 1932, while the Comintern was run by Nikolai Bukharin. The highest-ranking among those responsible for Yugoslavia was Sakun, a member of the Presidium—the Comintern's highest body. But the hierarchy in communist organizations is not that simple: instead of being distributed vertically, power is distributed laterally. Formally, since 1928 and the Sixth Congress, Comintern was run by its Executive Committee (Ispolkom of the Communist International; IKKI). Soviet bigwigs and a few representative party leaders from the West were sitting in its steering Political Secretariat. Gorkić was in the Control Commission—the highest level below the Secretariat. The next level—the third from the top—was occupied by representatives of individual parties, including the Yugoslav party's Organizing Secretary Đaković. However, operations are carried out laterally, via eight regional secretariats. The Balkan Secretariat or Bureau covers Bulgaria, Yugoslavia, Romania, Greece, Albania, and Cyprus, as well as Italy. The Balkan Bureau was at that moment headed by Bohumír Šmeral, one of the founders of the Communist Party of Czechoslovakia. His deputy was Mikhaylov, a Bulgarian better known as Georgi Dimitrov (real name: Georgi Dimitrov Mikhaylov). In addition to Kolarov and Kun, among the members of the Balkan Secretariat was also Angelo Tasca, representing the PCI as a leader of one of its factions. Tasca will later lose his position to the most dedicated Stalinist, also an important sociologist and writer Palmiro Togliatti, known as Ercole Ercoli.

51

This political structure is intertwined with the intelligence structure, which provides communication while controlling everything on behalf of the real authority. And the real authority is the Politburo of the Central Committee of the AUCP(b). In that pivotal year—1928—it had nine members. Lenin had died in 1924; two years later, Stalin ousted Trotsky, Zinoviev, and Kamenev, who had been elected, together with him, to the First Politburo at the Congress of the then Russian Communist Party (Bolsheviks) in 1919. Of the Old Bolsheviks, only Bukharin and Alexei Rykov have remained, but not for long. Gorkić is Bukharin's man. When Đaković was killed in 1929, Bukharin installed Gorkić as general secretary, with full authority.

Bukharin was forty years old at that time. From 1926 to 1929, he headed the Secretariat of the Comintern's Ispolkom. He wielded great authority as political commissar of the world's shadow government—the headquarters of the global revolution. Having allied himself with Stalin, he thoughtlessly helped him eliminate all three main rivals in the party leadership: Trotsky, Zinoviev, and Kamenev—all of them Jews. They were declared the "left opposition" because they had demanded an uncompromising revolutionary course. Bukharin then rose to defend Lenin's New Economic Policy (NEP)—a pragmatic answer to the postwar adversities and practical problems of the communist economy.

British science-fiction writer H. G. Wells, a socialist and communist sympathizer, visited Moscow in the early 1920s as a guest of Lenin himself. He realized with astonishment that even the highest-ranking officials' clothes were falling apart. Trams were out of commission, city people lived in family communes, there was a shortage of staple food, chaos and terror reigned, congresses of various mass organizations were taking place one after another. Lenin tried to loosen up the revolutionary course by introducing the NEP, which was supposed to stimulate small farms on private plots to produce basic market supply. It was incompatible with the revolutionary "general line"—the immediate worldwide export of the revolution in its purest form—the fundamental Trotskyite concept based on a belief in the spontaneity and inevitability of the dialectical wringer of Marxist social fission theory. However, the "armed export of revolution" failed after the defeat on the banks of the Vistula and after the uprisings in Budapest, Vienna, and Berlin had been crushed. Being a cautious realist, Bukharin then chose a "middle way." Stalin, on the other hand, believed that only uncompromising collectivization and development of heavy industry by means of ambitious five-year plans headed by the all-powerful apparatus of the state could ensure the survival of the Soviet

Union. He won that factional struggle because it was possible to mobilize the lower-ranking party officials for the project of the reconstruction of the authoritarian, repressive, and centralist state run from the Kremlin, instead of firing enthusiasm for a postponed revolution, with endless congresses of the party, the Red International of Labor Unions (Profintern), Comintern, Red Peasant International (Krestintern), Young Communist League, and so on.

Milan Gorkić, whose real name is Josip Čižinski (Josef Čižinský in Czech), nicknamed himself after the writer Maxim Gorky. He came from a Czech family who had moved to Sarajevo while it was part of Austria–Hungary. Having emigrated to Moscow back in 1923, Gorkić became the CPY's representative in the Comintern and, in 1927, a member of the Comintern's Presidium. As an instructor for Western countries, he often traveled to Austria, Germany, and Czechoslovakia. He was the Comintern's field instructor in the Communist Party of Great Britain, where he married Berta Glen. Then he was appointed head of the CPY's Moscow headquarters, with Blagoje Parović and Vladimir Ćopić as his assistants.

Broz met Gorkić for the first time in Vienna, in the Balkan Bureau. Looking back, he claimed to have been skeptical about Gorkić's qualities right from the start. In the last days of the Great Purge, Walter wrote the following character reference of Gorkić: "He has but one flaw: he wants to keep everything under his control. I mentioned that at one meeting of the Central Committee. It is hard to say why he does that. Perhaps he has little confidence in the political capabilities of his comrades ..." It is as if Broz is writing about himself.

Broz came to Vienna in late July 1934. In August, he attended a meeting of the CPY Central Committee for the first time. The party had gone underground because the situation in Vienna had changed substantially: when Hitler came to power in Germany the year before, Austrian Chancellor Dollfuss dissolved the Parliament and installed a right-wing clerical dictatorship. He declared war on the Viennese workers' detachments barricaded in the Karl-Marx-Hof complex on the city's outskirts. As a result, the CPY headquarters—in reality, a regional OMS station—would be moved to Prague.

At around the same time, Stalin liquidated Bukharin, head of the Comintern. The advance of fascism is pushing more and more parties underground, leading them to become utterly dependent on organizational and material assistance from abroad.

A totally new, pragmatic national front strategy was formulated in Moscow after the pathetic failure of the "proletarian" terror tactics in the urban environment. Not later than 1930, the concept of a revolutionary takeover after street fighting was abandoned—it had yielded poor results everywhere in Europe. The class enemy mobilized nationalists and right-wingers, and the proletarian actionists remained in a minority. In *Class Struggle*, a theoretical journal published in Moscow, Stjepan "Štefek" Cvijić, the organizing secretary of the Young Communist International (KIM), wrote the article "Against Terrorist Tendencies in Our Movement." A graduate of the Sverdlov Communist University, which was founded in 1918 as the first cadre school, Štefek would always move around with a gun in his pocket. In 1929, when he was taken to the police station in Dubrovnik, he pulled the gun and shot two gendarmes. So, if a person of Štefek's profile declared that the days of terrorist actions were over, it meant that the directive came from the very top, just like the directive that the whole left should come together and that an "anti-fascist movement" should be formed. This is when the syntagma "anti-fascism" was born as a Stalinist political construct and one of the most successful communist slogans of all time.

Broz soon returns to Yugoslavia on an important mission he was entrusted with as the only efficient operative who always survives in the field. The newly appointed organizing secretary of the CPY must create party networks in Slovenia and Croatia that will grow into separate national front compatible parties. In other words, the instruction is to break the CPY and initiate the national front policy. It was implemented for the first time in France in 1935. In Yugoslavia, it will only take hold in Slovenia: Osvobodilna Fronta (Liberation Front) existed there from 1941 to 1953, carrying out activities in the way specified by Moscow. Conceived by Stalin, it was bureaucratically implemented by Dimitrov.

Deep underground, Broz spent the whole of the autumn of 1934 in Ljubljana carrying out that mission. Sergej Kraigher, then a twenty-year-old member of SKOJ in charge of party communications and logistics, gave his account of those days:

> In 1934, the Regional Committee led by Comrades Kardelj and Kidrič revitalized the party organization in almost every major industrial center in Slovenia, but it was also active in villages, among peasants. Involving them meant a commitment to the solution of the problem of the Slovene national question. Slovenia was then fragmented and divided by three countries—Austria, Italy, and Hungary—with its largest part in Yugoslavia.
>
> I became aware of all the above from the letters that I decoded as a party technician. They were sent from Vienna, mostly by Comrade Tito, signed "Rudi." This

is also how I found out preparations were being made for his arrival in Ljubljana. Indeed, he arrived in June.

Sent to Yugoslavia, Broz went to Ljubljana, where he managed to make contact with a group of young Slovenian activists inspired by nationalist ideas. The support Moscow gave to them in their attempts to become independent from Belgrade and—in the Littoral (Friuli) and Venezia-Giulia—to shake off Italian domination had made the party popular not only among the circles of young intellectuals but also the broader public. It was during this period that romantic ideas about national emancipation started to develop in Slovenia's peasant society for the first time. This will eventually lead to a brew of specific, Slovenian "oberkrainer" communism, a universal revolutionary doctrine with undertones of shepherd's music from the idyllic hills of Oberkrain (Upper Carniola).

The Slovene party has one card up its sleeve here: its "Trieste section" is completely autonomous, despite being formally part of the PCI, which, in turn, answers to the Balkan Secretariat. This makes it possible for Slovenian communists in Trieste to have direct contact with Moscow. For them, the CPY does not exist, except as represented in the persons of Gorkić, who is based in Vienna but will have to move to Paris, and "Comrade Rudi," who comes for inspection visits. But, as Rudi, like them, speaks the Kajkavian dialect used in the Slovenian–Croatian border region and has to promote the same national front agenda, they will easily find a common language. Kraigher explains the conclusions of the conference they held:

> By then it was perfectly clear that the old line that the Central Committee was still supporting—fighting frontal battles and undertaking activities against social democrats, who were to be perceived as social-fascists—could not be maintained any more. I think it was then—in Comrade Kardelj's report—that we in Slovenia finally addressed the class aspect of the national questions the way it should have been addressed. This enabled the Regional Conference to give full support to the initiative for founding national parties—the Slovenian Communist Party, Croatian Communist Party, and, later, the Macedonian Communist Party.[1]

In December 1934, just before Christmas Eve, another conference took place in Ljubljana, the Fourth State Conference of the CPY—an interim party congress. Broz was elected to the CPY Central Committee, which now had eleven members. At the Central Committee's first session, which took place only a day later, on 26 December, he was elected to the committee's Politburo, among the party's top officials. The Politburo appointees included Čižinski/

Gorkić (absent); Broz; Blagoje Parović (also from the "Zagreb proletarian cell"); Kamilo Horvatin, a "left-faction" intellectual who was kept as a member because he was a deputy of a legal political party in the Zagreb city assembly; and Adolf Muk,[2] Gorkić's man in the field who will soon fall into the hands of the royal police.

In Ljubljana, Broz recruited his crucial associates: Edvard Kardelj, Boris Kraigher (Sergej's older brother), and Boris Kidrič. Kardelj was twenty-four and the other two were only twenty. As a forty-two-year-old participant of the October Revolution, with a relevant position in the organization and with contacts in Moscow, Broz will impress these young people, who will become attached to him for life. The insecure Kardelj will become Tito's "second banana," the regime's nominal number two for the following forty-five years. And when Marshal Tito eventually dies, Sergej Kraigher will take his place as the "rotational" head of Yugoslavia.

While in prison, Tito established relationships with his two key men: Pijade, who would remain loyal forever, and Čolaković, who would play an important role in Tito's promotion. Here, in Ljubljana, Tito started creating his own "base," with his own people in the field. He will use them to colonize the local Soviet revolutionary network. While he never questions the format, ideology, strategy, and tactics of the Moscow headquarters, he only relies on the people he personally trusts when it comes to implementation. All the others—those stuck to some Marxist or Moscow canons and guidelines—will soon fall off, disappear, end up in prison or in front of a firing squad in Siberia, or be forgotten. Pijade was the first man in his confidence and Slovenia was his first base. Like everything else, no one gave it to him—he won it; he snatched it away from the bear's claws, but in his special, cunning way, without direct confrontation—all under the pretense of the triumph of the revolution and world communism.

9

THE LIGHT OF THE LUX

MOSCOW 1935

Having successfully carried out the missions in Vienna and Ljubljana, Broz leaves for Moscow in early 1935. Ostensibly, he visits his wife Pelagija, who returned to the communist capital after he had left her in the Prigorje backwater. There was a promotion in store for this secret agent. In Dimitrov's diary, Walter is first mentioned on 27 November 1934.[1] The Comintern's secretary sent him a letter in Vienna. Clearly, Walter has direct contact with the Communist International's top official—which, judging by the diary of its boss, is not the case with other Yugoslav party cadres.

Broz arrived in the Soviet Union in February 1935, after having been coopted in the CPY Central Committee and elected to the Politburo, because he had already been the organizing secretary of the CPY and a confidant of the Viennese leadership for the Balkans—a capable operative and a rising star. And now he is working on bypassing the Vienna authority and establishing direct contact with Moscow.

Broz arrived in the communist capital together with Dr Voss-Rudin. Somewhat earlier, in mid-January 1935, Dimitrov had made an entry in his diary, as if he had known Broz well. It revealed his excitement about Walter's (his new assumed name) departure for the Soviet capital scheduled for 27 January. Obviously, they are counting on Broz, who arrives accompanied by an OMS case officer and lodges at the Hotel Lux. The once luxurious pre-revolutionary hotel "Fantsiya" on Tverskaya Street is now used as the head-

57

quarters of the global revolutionary project. Broz checks in as Walter Friedrich. His metamorphosis from "Georgijević," "Otto," and "Rudi" to "Walter" has thus been confirmed: "I came to the Soviet Union to become an officer for Yugoslav affairs at the Comintern ..."

In fact, his mission was of a completely different nature and his function of a "CPY representative in the Comintern" was but a cover, a legend. He moves "under the Comintern iceberg," as this clandestine sphere was defined in a book by Vladimir Pyatnitsky, the son of the first head of the OMS. The book is a collection of precious "second-hand" accounts. The conclusions about Tito's real function have been made by the young Russian historian Nikita Bondarev, who dedicated an entire study to this analysis. The study was a result of his access to the holdings of the Moscow archives, which is not available to everyone.[2]

Everything indicates that Walter worked for a special "cadre department" of the Communist International (KI), belonging not to the party—either AUCP(b) or CPY—but to the Soviet intelligence apparatus. After a careful analysis, Bondarev linked Tito's activities with Ivan Karaivanov, Yakubovich, and Gevork Alikhanian (Alikhanov), heads of the KI Cadre Department. The "official version" that he worked in the Yugoslav party office at the Comintern cannot be accepted. Among other things, his Russian writing skills were less than basic. He is a military-trained cadre, a specialist in secret agent activities, organizing secretary, and underground activist—not some pencil-pusher collating the classics of Marxism–Leninism. Broz says: "I stayed in Moscow for around ten days. Then I was sent to the Caucasus on vacation. I stayed there for a month."

This was the period, shows Bondarev using a pattern of indications and his profound knowledge of the Soviet apparatus structure, that Broz spent attending special training at the Comintern's Partisan Academy. Karol Wacław Świerczewski, another revolutionary that went by the name of Walter, taught that class in Balashikha on Moscow's outskirts, and not in the Caucasus: "When I came back, I took the job in the Comintern. My superior was Pieck,[3] one of the Comintern's secretaries. A very decent man, an older man. He liked me. I grew accustomed to them there."

Who were those he "grew accustomed to"? When country secretariats had been abolished in 1935, the German Wilhelm Florin was put in charge of all the Scandinavians, and another German, Wilhelm Pieck, of all the Balkan nationals. Finland and the Baltic nations were directly under Trilisser-Moskvin, head of the NKVD's Foreign Department. This is the structure of the apparatus, and communist parties of the Comintern are the visible political manifestation. KI Secretary Dimitrov himself belongs to "Pieck's Secretariat," which means that the famous leader of the world communist organization is subordinated to Pieck, a skilled carpenter working for the NKVD. Pieck was such a reliable Russian man that, after the Second World War, he was installed as president of the German Democratic Republic—a function abolished after his death.

Broz will become a star of that crew with a "pistol" cover name "Walter." The name is quite appropriate—it is a small-caliber (7.65mm) handgun suitable for concealed carrying. Its classic version, Walther PPK, is also associated with that other secret agent, James Bond.

From Vienna, where war was raging in the streets in 1934, and from Yugoslavia, where police had successfully eliminated communist cells, Broz came to Moscow during the Great Purge, Stalinist *coup d'état*, and general terror. Three months earlier, on 1 December 1934, Sergei Mironovich Kirov, the secretary of the Leningrad party organization and Stalin's most prominent rival in the party, had been killed in his office. Stalin used it as an excuse for a purge that would reach unimaginable proportions. After an investigation that took several days, GPU "found evidence" of a widespread counterrevolutionary conspiracy. As a result, not just the man pinpointed as the assassin was executed; more than 100 alleged helpers were shot, too. But that was only the beginning. Stalin used the affair to deal with all his opponents and independent political bases. He begins to transform the *nomenklatura*, changing it from a revolutionary organization to a state hierarchy with the command system of the state security apparatus as its backbone.

In January 1935, Grigori Zinoviev, Comintern's first secretary, and Lev Kamenev, Lenin's deputy in the first government, were indicted with the anti-party and counterrevolutionary ideological deviations that had led to Kirov's assassination. They were executed in August 1936, after the first of many spectacular show trials. Thousands of party appointees would be executed or sent to Siberian prison camps. The old Bolsheviks were the first ones to bear the brunt of the purge.

Broz, however, saw rapid promotion in those days—the broom of the Stalinist purges did not sweep him away. On the contrary, on 25 March 1935 he is appointed by the CPY Central Committee as the representative of the CPY section in the Comintern. In the summer of 1935, Broz is in the Yugoslav communists' delegation at the Seventh Congress of the Communist International. Taking place in the ballroom of the former Assembly of the

Nobility, the congress has as its main theme the "forming of a popular front against fascism." Walter supervises the Yugoslav delegates attending the congress "on behalf of the secret service."

Comintern officially adopts the national front policy as its "general line." The reasons are obvious: Hitler's triumph has deprived Moscow of its most important ally in the West—the German Communist Party. It was in Germany that the congresses of most of the European parties forced to go underground were taking place (e.g. the 1927 congress of the Italian party in Cologne; the 1928 congress of the CPY in Dresden, in the Central Party School of the German CP). Once the base of European communism, Germany is now a fascist stronghold. In other countries, communists are a substantial minority and, as such, must adapt their activities to that fact. However, while the pragmatic reasons for this twist in the political general line are clear, it is hard to explain it to the old idealists and revolutionaries— the alliance with bourgeois parties and countries formed after the Versailles Treaty in Europe should be recognized. That goes for Yugoslavia, too. And the unofficial recognition of this "creation of Versailles" has—finally—opened an opportunity for the recognition of the integral CPY.

At the congress, it was decided to dissolve the regional secretariats (including the Balkan Secretariat). As a result, the KI became a monolithic, centralized organization with direct control over communist groups and organizations in various countries. Pieck's branch of the service, for instance, will be working on the creation of new, underground communist organizations in Bulgaria, Greece, and Albania, still non-existent at the time. The task and authority over the groups in the field in the Balkans, Europe's southern periphery, would be given to Walter.

How does Tito describe his two-year stay in Moscow and the beginning of the purge in which almost all high-ranking CPY officials except him and a few other similar characters were liquidated?

> I simply minded my own business in the Comintern and spent my time learning. I had a good library and I spent most of the time at home. And that's what saved me. I would walk to Comintern and back. I would buy some sausages and a chicken in Univermag[4] and, as I have a kitchenette in the hotel, I prepared my own meals. That's what saved me. I was not under suspicion. I took Žarko with me—he was still very young, I can't remember his exact age right now ...[5] He behaved like a stray child then, like a true young hooligan. So he would come to my room and he would say various things. And I would give him a lesson then: "Are you aware that you eat the bread produced by the Russian workers?" And I would add, "the same ones who shed their blood so that your generation would have a better life?" Things like that. And I know they are listening ... "What a

rascal you are!" And I said: "You'll get spanked if you keep behaving like this." But there was no use. He was very stubborn then.

Tito's relationship with his son was not an easy one. They were not close either. The wild boy had been growing up in children's homes, his mother having gone with another man. At the same time, his father had an affair with Johanna Anna Köenig, an Austrian political emigrant who also lived at the Lux and went by a suitable pseudonym there—Lucia, Lucia Bauer.

According to his own account, Tito occasionally went to the Communist University of the National Minorities of the West (KUNMZ), a recruitment center for young European party members.[6] There he again met Kardelj, the frail Slovenian teacher whom he had recognized in Ljubljana as the leader of the Slovenian communists. Kardelj, a reliable Moscow cadre and both a student and teacher at the college for professional revolutionaries, has given his account. However, his assessment of Stalin's political motives is unreliable. The old stager learned to change his opinion as the situation requires:

> The Comintern was built as a center of a revolution—at least European, if not global. It turned out, however, that the revolution would not spread after the Second World War. Its sparks had been put out immediately. Even Lenin himself began to have doubts in the Comintern's efficiency. In such a situation, naturally, communist parties would have to change their tactics. However, the Comintern continued with its "class against class" course, with a slogan that "democracy and fascism are twins." This resulted in putting communist parties in an isolated position, separating them from the masses. Let me mention here the example of a truly fatal mistake of the German Communist Party, immediately before Hitler's rise to power, when they, together with the Nazis and reactionary parties, voted in the parliament against the Social Democrat government! The German party did that in order to follow Comintern's line. Objectively, it was against the working class and it helped Hitler to assume power. Unfortunately, as always, Stalin realized this too late; this is why Comintern changed its sectarian course much too late. If it changed it earlier, the catastrophic mistake made in Germany probably would not be made.

The "class against class" tactics was a late compromise, after the intransigent Trotskyite and Zinoviev–Kun revolutionary line had failed. The idea was to form the Left Front. It was launched by Bukharin in September 1928, and abandoned in 1934 when Stalin brought Dimitrov to the helm of the KI in order to implement even wider alliances. But, it was too late. Nobody believed the tame communists and their new constructive approach.

In that very period, between 1934 and 1938, purges were carried out at every level of the Soviet apparatus in order to eliminate the revolutionary radicalism that had proven detrimental and threatening to the very existence of the Soviet Union. Stalin entrusted the task to the dwarfish executor Nikolai Yezhov.

The Stalinist purges in the Soviet Union ensued after ideological and political struggles had been tearing the Soviet state apart for ten years. The party elite polarized between universal revolutionaries (Trotskyists) on one side and statists (Stalinists) on the other. The latter won. Stalin relied on a state built on repression, while Trotsky only cared about the ideological discourse. The purpose of the purges was not merely to liquidate those who had committed any sin, but to recompose society. In his seminal work, Soviet historian of the KGB Roy Medvedev reveals that in all Soviet institutions—the party, administration, universities, the army—80 to 90 percent of all personnel were purged by execution or exile in Siberia. Altogether, around 14 million people passed through the Gulag system. This means that the entire superstructure of the revolutionary Bolshevik state was eliminated and fully replaced with the people connected with the new backbone of the state authority—the security apparatus.[7] This is how the Russian Revolution evolved into the Soviet state. Kardelj describes the purges in the USSR and Tito's role in them:

> Of my Moscow encounters and conversations with Tito, I particularly remember two of us sorting out the files of our party cadres scattered all over the Soviet Union. It was the time of Stalinist show trials and purges, an atmosphere of strong pressure, when people did not know what was awaiting them the next day.
>
> Tito tried his best to get as many of our people as possible out of the Soviet Union. It was decided then that those who had a chance of legalizing their status at home should do so, even if that meant spending some time behind bars. Or they should go to Spain. Some were sent to work in America and other countries, as emigrants. Of course, Tito's success in it was only partial because others had also been making lists of a different kind. Soon after he left Moscow for Paris in order to work in the CPY Central Committee there, Tito requested from the CPY office at the Comintern to send me home to resume my underground party activities—particularly in connection with the preparations for the founding congress of the Communist Party of Slovenia.

Kardelj claims that Tito tried to save as many comrades as possible from Stalin's repression by sending them back home or to the Spanish battlefields. But at the same time, we also know that he wrote, by order of Yakubovich, informer reports about his comrades. He sent them to Karaivanov, a member of the Executive Committee. Tito proved himself by writing those secret character references, and all these comrades were shot, including his Moscow partner Lucia. He admitted that, as far as she was concerned, "he was not vigilant enough." It was not his character references that sealed the fates of his colleagues, but they did help him to stay alive. The only thing he could do in Moscow in those days was to distance himself from all his associates and family members, and wait to see how the NKVD and dear God—that is, Stalin—would judge him.

While Stalinist terror reigned in Moscow, the Yugoslav police began the large-scale repression and persecution of communists and Croatian Ustashe after the assassination of King Alexander on 9 October 1934. Alexander was shot by the VMRO terrorist Ivan "Vancho" Mihailov Gavrilov, with the participation and help of the Ustashe. The Yugoslav royal police correctly perceived the Ustashe as Italian agents and the communists as Soviet spies. The mass arrests of party members and political repression made any popular front-style arrangements impossible. And then, Franjo Kralj, secretary of the Regional Committee of the Communist Party for Croatia and Slavonia, and Đorđe Mitrović, chief of ZEMBILJ (the "united revolutionary command" in charge of activities in the country), were both arrested in November 1935. Mitrović had on him numerous party materials with coded names of activists. Police tortured him savagely until he gave them away. Some 1,000 communists throughout Yugoslavia were arrested. Even the police were surprised by the party's widespread network, so the government launched a strong campaign to suppress the CPY.

On 10 February 1936, Comrade Walter reads his report on the situation in Yugoslavia at the party conference of the Yugoslav sector at KUNMZ and admits that the arrests have shaken the organization. In Walter's opinion, the solution is to give up sectarianism and start forming front-style organizations—primarily in the unions, in order to weaken the socialists' position. These are all typical committee-style delusions, but the failure of political directives to function in practice does not mean one is permitted to question them in the party forum.

After this public appearance, Tito disappears again. Officially, in late February and early March 1936, he is receiving medical treatment, although he has not reported any health problems and it has been less than four months since he returned from his vacations in the south. Historian Bondarev believes that Broz's lengthy absences have to do with the military courses he attends. The European fight between the reds and the blacks is about to escalate into an armed conflict. The Comintern is on the warpath.

10

WALTER IN THE COMMUNIST UNDERGROUND

PRAGUE 1936

The notes of Pyatnitsky, the son of the executed head of OMS, based on both his own experience as a member of the apparatus and his father's accounts, reveal that the special schools for military training of revolutionaries were opened in the last stages of the Russian Revolution. Successful students would be prepped up in the Intelligence Department (RU RKKA) of the Red Army General Staff. After their training, they would return to their native countries. As they were no longer needed in Russia, their return to their countries of domicile would be organized so that they could become future subversive agents there. Does this not correspond perfectly with Broz's path? Having established contacts with the Bolsheviks, he leaves Russia for his homeland as a leader of a group of former POWs. He travels home via Vienna, the regional intelligence logistics center. Soon afterward, he is found in Bjelovar, stashing rifles together with another similar character.

Between 1927 and 1931, the Comintern's military schools were administered by Tuure Lehén, the son-in-law of the Finnish communist Otto Kuusinen. Between 1931 and 1936, they were run by Świerczewski—"Walter." During his stay in the Soviet Union, Broz first disappeared from Moscow in November 1935, only to reemerge in early September 1936.[1] Some functionaries dubbed the school he attended the "Partisan Academy." Pyatnitsky notes that many of its students later won glory in Spain, Yugoslavia, Poland, China, and Vietnam.

The military and intelligence training in the Comintern intensifies or slows down, depending on the current international situation and the requirements of the apparatus. As a direct participant, Pyatnitsky registered the most intense activity between 1936 and 1939, during the Spanish Civil War. This coincides with Tito's Moscow years and his rise in the party hierarchy. Obviously, this rise has more to do with the events on the Iberian Peninsula than with those on the Balkan Peninsula. The service he belonged to was not divided by countries or nations; instead, it was divided into "fronts," in much the same way as the Soviet strategic military formations. There is a main Western direction, or front, focused on Spain. Yugoslavia is on a sidetrack, totally irrelevant at the moment. It can only be used as a base, where combatants for both real and secret wars are recruited.

Bondarev concludes that Walter completed his military training in nine months, between the autumn of 1935 and the summer of 1936, because no records of his Comintern activities in this period can be found. Another meticulous researcher discovered that the Comintern personnel files contain no documents on Broz's training in Soviet schools and training centers. Alexei Y. Timofeev, Russian military historian and professor of history at the University of Belgrade, explains that this can mean only one thing—Broz was sent to the training centers of the NKVD or the Red Army Intelligence Department. As a rule, they did not notify the Comintern about their decisions and dispositions. It is hard to imagine any other explanation for such an information gap in the dossier of a member of the apparatus.

Everything is rationed, everything is controlled, and every trip or visit to an official building is registered. In addition, there is a recommendation by Karaivanov, "Head of Cadre Affairs of the Balkan Secretariat," dated 21 May 1935. He confirms that "Comrade Friedrich Walter can be entrusted with teaching activities." True, the Balkan Secretariat would be abolished at the Seventh Congress two months later, but the Cadre Department would remain—together with the cadres—because they are the basis of the apparatus.

In volume 3 of Dedijer's book *New Contributions to the Biography of Josip Broz Tito* (1981), Marshal Tito discloses the sources of his military skills: "Clausewitz, classics and Frunze." This could be interpreted as if he read the works of Mikhail Frunze—which is hard to believe because he preferred adventure novels—but also as if he attended the Military Academy named after Frunze, where promising commissioned officers were trained for commanding positions. The academy also organized numerous specialist courses for "part-time students." Besides, in his report at the 1940 Fifth Land

Conference in Zagreb, Broz quotes Stalin's "Address to the Graduates of the Red Army Military Academy" (4 May 1935).[2] Does this mean Tito himself attended it? He says: "Comrade Stalin told us ..." He did not use the formulation "as Comrade Stalin writes ..." Stalin's speech was published in the anthology *Concerning Questions of Leninism* (the first Zagreb edition was published as early as 1939). Tito claims it was he who translated it in Moscow, first with the help of Ćopić, who then—as Tito puts it in his televised memoirs—"let him down" by being arrested and taken for execution, so Broz had to finish the job on his own.

Trainees in all special schools are preparing for the Spanish campaign. The armed conflict in Spain has begun like a proxy war between two global revolutionary blocs. The Comintern is mobilizing. The well-informed Karlo Mrazović, in charge of Yugoslav cadres in the Comintern's Ispolkom, estimated that they were the most numerous members of the International Brigades, second only to the French contingent. According to his field evidence, there were 1,200 to 1,300 of them, mostly Slovenes and Croats.[3] Half of them survived and would become the backbone of Tito's Partisan army and his Mediterranean operative command—the underground apparatus he used to control southern Europe during and after the Second World War.

On the battlefields, the expeditionary corps must conceal the Soviet military presence. Božidar Maslarić, an experienced Comintern operative sent to the headquarters of the 5th Regiment near Madrid, describes a meeting he attended.[4] Bent over the map table, military advisor "General Kleber" (allegedly an Austrian; in fact, his real name was Moshe Stern, a Ukrainian Jew) explains the situation. He is a Soviet military intelligence agent, a graduate of the Frunze Military Academy. Also attending the meeting are General Enrique Lister, commander of the 5th Corps who has just returned from the Frunze Academy; political commissar Carlos—actually, Vittorio Vidali from Muggia near Trieste—a former NKVD agent in Mexico; and General Wilhelm "Gomez" Zaisser, commander of the 13th International Brigade, who was a Soviet military instructor in China. After the Second World War, he will become the minister of state security in the German Democratic Republic.

The language of the meeting is English. This takes time, as everything must be translated into Spanish. Maslarić writes: "I almost shouted—why not use Russian? You've all been in the Soviet Union until recently?!" But as Zaisser explained to him later, it was a directive from Moscow; intervening in the internal affairs of another country must be disguised.

Although Broz, too, attended military courses, he was not sent to the Spanish front; a function of a higher order awaited him instead.

Vlajko Begović, who worked together with Walter, gave his account about the hierarchy of the Comintern cadres.[5] Begović says he was taken to the Lubyanka prison, thrown into a cell and kept there for a couple of months. Then they tried to recruit him, with a Bulgarian from the NKVD offering him the chance to work for the organization and have a "special status." Begović tried to dodge the offer, explaining that he would like to continue his studies and then resume party work back in his own country. To which the Bulgarian replied:

> Party work—what does it mean for you? It means returning to Yugoslavia, going underground, and then, inevitably, falling into the hands of police, and if you survive, a trial and Mitrovica prison. Working for the NKVD, on the other hand, means working with elite cadres only. There is no great danger, one is always paid well, and in this sector one can do more for the revolution and for the Soviet Union than by working in the party. After the revolution, back in Yugoslavia, those who had been party members would receive honors and adequate positions. But those who had collaborated with the NKVD—now, they would be in for high-ranking positions!

In April 1936, while Walter was still training in Moscow, Gorkić convened the April Plenum of the CPY Central Committee in Vienna. He proposed the following members for the Politburo: organizing secretaries Lovro Kuhar ("Glanzner"), Josip Broz ("Otto"), Karel Hudomalj ("Oskar"), and Vladimir Ćopić ("Senjko"), and candidates Stjepan Cvijić ("Štefek"), a member of the Secretariat of the Young Communist International, and Ivan Marić ("Ironmonger"), a representative of the Split Regional Committee for Dalmatia. Lovro Kuhar (with his literary pseudonym Prežihov Voranc) is a trustworthy Moscow cadre, their man for Carinthia. Hudomalj is Kuhar's assistant, also a Slovene from Carinthia, and a "Comintern instructor," in fact a Prague-based executor working for the secret service. Ćopić is the former Moscow head of CPY and Cvijić the top leader of SKOJ. Only Marić, an ironmonger, seems the odd man out here. However, he represents the strong Dalmatian party organization, which is autonomous in the CPY.

The April Plenum took place without the Comintern's consent, which is a grave breach of discipline—selection of cadres is delegated to no one, because it is the domain of the Personal Directorate, meaning the NKVD. An extraordinary session of CPY leaders is immediately held at Ispolkom in Moscow in August 1936. Walter attends. The Vienna Plenum is criticized and, after several days of discussion, new guidelines for the leadership are adopted. The guidelines urge for mobilization "against the advancing fascist reactionaries and for uniting all democratic forces in Yugoslavia into a combat front."

After the security lapse the year before—when Yugoslav police crushed the organization, arresting almost 1,000 out of 3,000 party members (many of whom had joined the party when it was still legal but had distanced themselves from it in the meantime)—the party was practically destroyed and the vast majority of its leaders sentenced to long prison terms. This is why it was decided in Moscow that all CPY Central Committee members should "return to the country," except Secretary Gorkić, who would stay in order to maintain contact with the Moscow headquarters. The Comintern's Executive Committee gave special powers to Organizing Secretary Josip "Walter" Broz, who would start building a completely new organization upon his return to Yugoslavia. The party had ceased to exist in the country, and the "foreign bureau" consisted of Gorkić's unreliable cadres, old communists interconnected via the OMS and run by a crypto-Bukharinite. How long could such a leadership survive?

The Vienna-based Politburo of the CPY Central Committee meets again on 8 December 1936. Like a good soldier, Gorkić reports that the Comintern's Ispolkom has declared the April Plenum decisions null and void and has named new party leaders. He, Gorkić, is again "general secretary with a veto right." Broz, now with the party name "Otto," has been confirmed as the organizing secretary for country activities. Other members of the top leadership now include Walter's prison buddy Čolaković, Slovenian Franc "Luka" Leskošek, and Sreten "Black" Žujović, a law student from the Sorbonne and former soldier of the Légion étrangère who is a member of the French Communist Party.

When Gorkić took over as the party's general secretary in 1932, he knew almost nothing about the country, having lived entirely abroad for the past twelve years. He is deeply rooted in the Comintern's corporate structure. For the headquarters, this is the most important characteristic of a political functionary. However, as the Comintern itself has changed its profile, and theoreticians are now unwelcome (Bukharin is a Marxist theoretician on Lenin's level), the new cadres are of a different sort. Leskošek is a metal worker from Celje, just like Walter, who had a similar job in the nearby Kamnik. Luka was also lodged in the Hotel Lux together with Birk (Kardelj) and Walter.

Walter is sent to Yugoslavia via Prague, to where intelligence logistics have been moved—the Communist Party is still legal in Czechoslovakia because President Tomáš Masaryk is trying to maintain the country's neutrality, counting on the Soviet Union's support. Broz outlines his movements: "First I came to Prague via Poland. In Prague, I had to deal with the old party leadership. I sent some comrades to Spain while the others were simply replaced."[6]

What does this "dealing with" and "replacing" he had to carry out in Prague really mean? Stjepan Cvijić, former secretary of the Young Communist International, is sent by Walter to Paris, an émigré center and the capital of European anti-fascism, from where volunteers are transferred to Spain. Ćopić, the Comintern's delegate at the Czechoslovak Communist Party in Prague, will also be among those "sent to Spain" by Comrade Walter. Ćopić will become a heroic commander of the XV International Brigade that also included the American battalion Abraham Lincoln. He returned to the Soviet Union in November 1938 and was executed in April 1939. Stjepan Cvijić had the same fate. Obviously, Comrade Walter must be wielding great authority if he can dispatch former top cadres of the CPY and Comintern like that.

According to the Moscow decision made to annul the Vienna decisions, the party has two priorities. First, autonomous national parties should be organized in Slovenia and Croatia, because the national front policy cannot be implemented via the unitary CPY. Second, the CPY apparatus must urgently be moved to Paris because the conditions in Austria have become unbearable. Besides, the Paris Bureau will be more suitable for the new task—the transfer of volunteers from the whole of Southeastern Europe to the Spanish theater of operations. The group of NKVD executors and military intelligence agents like Mustafa Golubić, Begović, Josip Kopinič, Hudomalj, and Ivan Kralj will stay in Prague in order to be sent on specific missions. Walter has a crucial role here—he is, in his own words, the one "sending them to Spain" or "replacing them." Only one man stays on his way to the final ascent, the old-school bureaucrat and Bukharinite Gorkić, who, following the next scandal, will inevitably end up before a firing squad in Moscow.

11

COMRADE ORGSEC

ANINDOL 1937

Gorkić fell from favor as a result of the ill fate of the passengers of *La Corse*, the Corsican ship that cast anchor off the Dalmatian island of Brač on the night of 28 February 1937. According to the plan, Spanish volunteers were supposed to embark the ship between 9 p.m. and midnight. The gendarmerie, however, knew the moves of this dubious crowd in advance; a motor boat of the financial border police intercepted them at sea, and the Yugoslav cadres— the striking power of the CPY—ended up in dungeons, except for a few of the bravest ones, who managed to swim their way out of trouble. Gorkić's final attempt to show that his operation still deserved the backing of international investors failed miserably.

Walter pretends he first heard about the failed operation from Gorkić himself, when they met in Prague in December 1936. Gorkić confided to him that a boat had been prepared for transporting the Dalmatian and Montenegrin volunteers to Spain and that Muk, a shoemaker from Kotor, "who knows the sea," had been chosen to lead the operation. To meet Gorkić, Walter came to Prague from Split, where he had stayed in mid-December. Vicko Krstulović, secretary of the Regional Committee of the Communist Party of Dalmatia, claims that Broz came to him in Split with the money for the rental of *La Corse*.[1] But Muk was arrested by police and betrayed his comrades while in jail. If Krstulović's claim is correct—and there are no reasons to doubt it—Walter was all too well informed about this operation and was actually involved in it, because it was the task he had been given at the meeting with the leading party members in Moscow in September 1936, after the ill-fated Viennese April Plenum. But, using his distinctive skills, Walter managed to avoid being identified with this failure. Eventually, the blame was put on Gorkić, who had informed Broz in Prague about the operation Broz had just carried out. Previously, Gorkić had sent Dr Voss-Rudin to Belgrade, instructing her to agitate among potential volunteers for the international brigades in the Spanish Civil War. Maybe she got in touch with the wrong people there, thus enabling the ever alert and organized royal police to prevent this communist expedition. At any rate, the affair took place only a year after the last wave of arrests, when the police got hold of the list of party members. This time, after the failed attempt of sending the volunteers to Spain by boat, another wave of arrests of communists and their sympathizers ensued. All this will be fatal for Gorkić. And for Walter? It will give him an opportunity to finally come to the very top of the whole secret organization. But that will not go so smoothly.

In January 1937, Walter leaves Prague for Ljubljana and Zagreb to start working on another task he was entrusted with in Moscow—the one that will add a political dimension to his hitherto agent-related activities. With the Slovenian and Croatian regional committees, he organizes two founding congresses of autonomous parties (instead of the usual all-Yugoslav "land conferences").[2] According to the usual Comintern procedure, communist parties are founded in the visible, public sphere, while their secret apparatuses are established in the background to keep everything under control. But now, for the first time, it is the other way around—an apparatus has been instructed to establish a party. Such were the conditions of working deep underground, under the relentless repression of the new Yugoslav regency government of Alexander's brother, Prince Paul.

The CPY is maintained as an anomaly: from what is left of it, two national parties have been created in the western part of the country, and the "rest"—meaning the Serbian part of the CPY—remains a non-autonomous section of the Viennese Balkan Bureau and, later, at Manuilsky's and Dimitrov's desk in Moscow. This is how it looks from Stalin's perspective. But Tito has completely different ideas, as it will soon turn out.

After having summoned union leaders to his aunt's wooden house in the village of Trebče near Kumrovec to inform them about the founding of the new, national front-based parties, Walter goes to Paris to submit his report. There was still a commotion about the *La Corse* affair there, so Gorkić and Walter took it upon themselves to investigate the causes of the disaster. But there is nothing much to analyze, really: as the general secretary, Gorkić/ Čižinski is responsible. As for the organizing secretary, nominally his subordinate, he belongs to a different chain of command. In summer, Čižinski will be summoned to Moscow, arrested, and executed. Maybe the trigger was his recommendation of an agent provocateur who soon publicly denounced communism for the post of a Red Army intelligence operative in Yugoslavia. Čižinski simply is not up to the new tasks Moscow has been assigning. And he is, after all, definitely one of Bukharin's crew. After Gorkić's disappearance, the Paris-based Politburo operates by inertia. Anyway, in the beginning they have no idea about Gorkić's falling from grace—as far as they are concerned, the man simply went to the Moscow headquarters, probably for new instructions. In the words of Čolaković:

> There were no cues indicating it was not a regular trip. Then, some fifteen days after his departure for Moscow, I spoke with Bohumír Šmeral, Czechoslovak communist and the Comintern's representative for Western Europe, who was also based in Paris. It was the conversation with him that made me think about Gorkić's trip to Moscow in a different way.

> I retold my conversation with him to Žujović. Then we decided to contact Tito and suggest that he comes to Paris, him being the highest-ranking party official second to Gorkić. And indeed, Tito came in August [of 1937]. We told him about the conversation with Šmeral. He took charge over the party.

> I remember Tito then wrote a lengthy report to the Comintern, about his activities in the country. However, there were no reactions from Moscow, neither to the report nor to our letters.

After Gorkić's disappearance, Živojin Pavlović, editor-in-chief of *Proleter*, the Paris bulletin of the CPY Central Committee and a friend of the arrested General Secretary Gorkić, moves to Belgrade and gets a job there in the government's press office. In 1940, he will publish *The Balance Sheet of the Soviet Thermidor*, an informed account of the purges in the Soviet Union.[3] This is the second most important anti-Stalinist book of the thirties. A year before Pavlović's book, *Au pays du grand mensonge* (The Russian enigma) by Ante Ciliga was published in French. This Yugoslav party in emigration is indeed a nest of "Trotskyists and revisionists." As early as 1937, the NKVD in its Lubyanka headquarters can be certain that, by dissolving the CPY, they are dismissing a totally bankrupt company, a "traitor's lair." Moscow has severed every contact with the CPY Central Committee's "foreign bureau" in Paris.

Broz has found himself at a crossroads. When Gorkić was arrested, he was the organizing secretary, the most prominent cadre of the bureau, with special connections in Moscow. But those connections are now severed, too. Invited by Žujović and Čolaković, he came to Paris and took charge of the party, but the party has lost its contacts and legality in the headquarters, previously the source of its money. Small amounts of money from sympathizers in both Americas have continued to come via the Paris bookstore "Horizons" that serves as a front for this communist lair. As for the "party technics," they rely on improvisation. A group of young women is used as couriers. These Yugoslav students have all been enthralled by secret agent Walter, a handsome forty-five-year-old with inexhaustible self-confidence. As the World Fair is taking place in Paris, numerous tourists are coming to the city, making it easier for the conspirators—now a group of desperados and outcasts—to move around.

Two weeks before Gorkić's disappearance, Walter founded the Communist Party of Croatia in Samobor, thus completing the reorganization of the party in Yugoslavia. The Communist Party of Slovenia had been in operation since March. The Belgrade CPY as the third party is run by his confidants: Milovan Đilas, Ivo Lola Ribar, and Aleksandar Ranković. The first two are in charge of the numerous communist sympathizers among the Belgrade student population. Ranković, on the other hand, is a former Mitrovica prison convict who still maintains contacts with those in prison—it is the main party cadre base in the country. Walter's confidant Pijade is there, too. Ever since Ranković joined him, Walter has put his trust in him. Aside from Đilas, Ranković is the only one in the party leadership without any Moscow training—Aleksandar "Leka" was a member of SKOJ, a former cloth workshop assistant and union activist.

Dissolved in Dresden and patched up as a provisional solution under Gorkić, the party is now run by Walter as his personal network. Formally, it consists of three separate national party organizations of equal status. Comintern does not recognize "party super-organizations" or "federal" parties above national ones. There is only one organization superior to all others—the Comintern itself, the "one ring to rule them all."

Of the three Yugoslav parties created by a far-from-immaculate parthenogenesis, only one has a general secretary, Kardelj in the Slovene party, who enjoys Tito's full confidence. They became close in Moscow. There is also a close-knit coterie of Kardelj's Slovenian associates. The Slovenes were the first to adopt the Stalinist doctrine and the national front format. The Moscow headquarters' support for the Slovene communists in their efforts to become independent from Belgrade and free themselves of Italian domination in the border areas made the party attractive to the general public. The goal of annexing Friuli–Venezia Giulia (including Trieste) and Carinthia will become the Slovene communists' fundamental aspiration in the Second World War and the postwar years. As early as 1934, they managed to secure a tripartite declaration on the status of the Slovenian people, by which the communist parties of Austria, Italy, and Yugoslavia committed to support Slovene "national unity" within extended borders. Behind that move was Slovene communist Dragotin Gustinčič, who had been in Moscow for a long time and, together with Dimitrov, was one of the leading men in the Balkan Secretariat of the mid-1920s. Meanwhile, Kuhar ("Prežihov Voranc"), born in Carinthia, was in Moscow, representing the Austrian Communist Party. Ivan Regent, a Slovene from Trieste, was also in Moscow representing the PCI.[4] It was of course not particularly difficult for three Slovenes to reach an agreement on the Slovenian territorial claims. However, eventually, the "Greater Slovenia" was not meant to be.

The political commissar Comrade "Rudi"—or Comrade "Walter" for the intelligence community—accepts these Slovenes and their program, which corresponds with the Comintern's intentions. He has adopted them, and they have become his political base, his primary political cell. They came to an understanding easily, speaking the Kajkavian dialect used both in Slovene Lower Carniola and in Croatian Zagorje. They had all been roommates in the Hotel Lux, where they had stayed while acquiring their doctrine in the same political academies and special military schools.

Unlike the Slovenian party, the Croatian party is a tentative solution, created under Moscow's strict instructions and in accordance with the national front formula. In Croatia, Radić's formerly republican HRSS—now the Croatian Peasant Party (HSS)—would play first fiddle in the creation of a composite national-liberation "anti-fascist" political formation. However, the problem with the middle-class Croats is that they tend to incline toward some consociational combinations. Radić's successor, Vladko Maček, sincerely accepted the option of Yugoslav cohabitation by reaching an agreement with the Serbian premier Dragiša Cvetković, kept in power by Prince Paul. Although the Croatian question in Yugoslavia was thus more or less solved by 1939, the agreement-based state could not survive the war. But an order is an order, and the Stalinist Comintern tolerates no alternative formats—whether in China or Croatia. Therefore, in Anindol in 1937, Comrade Tito formally founds the Croatian Communist Party—only two years before the Serbo-Croatian Cvetković–Maček Agreement makes this effort of his totally superfluous.

Not one person of Tito's trust can be found in the Croatian Central Committee, except Vlado Popović, who is Montenegrin. Rade Končar, a Croatian Serb, is a field operative, not a historical leader. Very conveniently, Hebrang is in jail. So the party secretary will become Đuro Špoljarić, a completely irrelevant character. Immediately after the war, he will end up on Goli Otok island—Tito's Gulag for his followers and potential rivals.[5]

The group of sixteen delegates that Tito has gathered in a pavilion in the forested hills above Samobor for the founding congress of the Croatian Communist Party includes battle-hardened communists like Gregorić, his "red commander" from Russia who admitted him to the Communist Party in Kraljevica thirteen years ago. However, he is allied to Moscow, of course. There are also prominent intellectuals like Božidar Adžija, and brave and loyal field operatives. Most of them will perish in prisons or be killed in war. However, the Central Committee made up of these people will never play an important or independent role. Under Tito's leadership, the Croatian Communist Party, founded in accordance with the Comintern's national front format, will never get off the ground. Things will change only when Hebrang, a communist-internationalist who takes instructions from headquarters seriously, assumes the leadership after his release from prison. But, while Tito is founding the Croatian party in Anindol, Hebrang is serving his ninth year in the royal prison, with four more years to go.

In addition to the founding plenum in Anindol, Walter also gathered his own operatives in Zagreb—members of the SKOJ. The most relevant among them are Leo Mates, a twenty-seven-year-old intellectual from a Jewish family from Osijek, and his twenty-six-year-old friend Vladimir Bakarić. The Bakarićs were once Kupferbergs, but Vladimir's father adopted Christianity and became a judge in Austro-Hungary. In the Kingdom of Yugoslavia, he advanced to the Chamber of Seven, a court of cassation. As a Delnice judge, it was he who sentenced Broz to eight months in prison for organizing the strike in Kraljevica. But it did not bother Walter one bit when he appointed his son to the leadership—on the contrary. It was these people from the bourgeois milieu, idealists, whom Tito trusted the most. He relied on the solid, educated Jewish intelligentsia that had constituted the backbone of Croatian society way back in Austria–Hungary: lawyers, engineers, the military elite. His most trustworthy diplomat will become Vladimir Velebit, a Serb and a descendant of a line of Austrian generals. This is only natural, given the social stratification of the revolutionary avant-garde, not just in Yugoslavia but also in the home of the communist revolution—Russia. Young middle-class intellectuals and Jews predominated. Tito's preference for young men from the upper middle class shows not so much his social pretensions—he considered himself better than everyone else anyway—as his pragmatism in creating his "personal network." In doing so, he was never subdued to Marxist ideas about the historical predestination of the working class. First, he was not a trained Marxist, and, second, he was not stupid enough to mix propaganda with the management of his revolutionary project. At that moment, he needed capable men. But for the "executive" line of the "proletarian" organization, the most suitable choice will, of course, be shoemakers, locksmiths, carpenters.

In Belgrade, in the CPY station, Tito's man is the fiery Montenegrin Đilas; among the elite of the cosmopolitan Yugoslav capital, it is Ribar, secretary of the SKOJ, a son of a respected Croatian bourgeois politician Ivan Ribar, an honest Yugoslav unitarianist. According to Krstulović, Ribar was the only one on equal footing with Tito and could have pretended to succeed him had he survived the war. Somewhere in the background in this Belgrade party station is "the most reliable man," Ranković. When you count Tito's closest aids, it is obvious that they are mostly very young, twentysomethings. There are Montenegrins—the supermen of the Balkans—and a few proven older guys, like Popović or Velebit to add to the mix. Except for the Slovenians, they are not the usual Moscow-trained crew. Walter obviously has his own plan and goals, and two principal ambitions: to eliminate anyone in the CPY who could challenge his supremacy and to win recognition from Moscow. One thing leads to another—if the CPY's "foreign" Politburo is dissolved, the transmission mechanism will be destroyed and he will become Moscow's only reliable man in the rugged Balkans. The headquarters will then have no other choice but to confirm him as the communist viceroy of Balkania.

12

THE REVOLUTIONARIES FROM BOULEVARD SAINT-GERMAIN

PARIS 1937

"The process of purging various elements from the party mostly took place in Paris," says Walter at the beginning of his reminiscences on his anti-faction campaign that ensued when he came to the CPY secretariat after Gorkić's disappearance:

> One of the biggest problems I had to deal with back then was the factionalism among the communists in the Mitrovica prison. One of them was Petko Miletić. He was widely known, foreign press and communist press wrote about him a lot. In fact, we all tried our best to promote him. Even a battery in Spain was named after him. Signatures and money were collected in America and progressive press wrote about him as a communist hero. I found the whole thing suspicious because he had been trying to destroy our best and most deserving men in the prison. For instance, Moša Pijade, who was an old revolutionary. Miletić tried to discredit our old cadres in the eyes of our imprisoned comrades. Many of them were young people and they became his followers because they couldn't see through him.

> Our men were released from prison as true "Petkovites." Even those who went to Spain. I spoke with some of them. They wouldn't hear of anyone else in our party but Petko Miletić. Struck by it, I spent a lot of time getting the facts straight and unmasking the whole thing. I analyzed the materials from the prison—huge quantities came from Petko Miletić and his group and some came from the opposite side, from Moša Pijade.

In reality, "purging various elements from the party" will be Walter's attack on the strongest party organization in the country: most of the 200 communists, the core of the party, served long-term prison terms in Sremska Mitrovica. The arrests of 1935 and 1936 thus had a twofold impact—they destroyed the party's field operatives and created an alternative organization behind bars. In Mitrovica, Hebrang came under the attack of Petko's "Wahhabists," and he had to request that he and fifteen of his followers be locked in solitary cells. The only one Walter could rely on at that moment was Pijade, transferred from Maribor to Mitrovica. He also had his own party network that he had established in Slovenia and Croatia. But the factionalism from the Mitrovica prison continued to spread.

Marić, a member of the Regional Committee for Dalmatia, decided to play on Petko, bitter at having been admitted to the Politburo at the annulled 1936 April Plenum in Vienna only to be left out from the top leadership by the same decision by which Walter was imposed on them as an unquestionable authority. Čolaković explains this personal conflict:

> Marić established contact with Petko Miletić in the Sremska Mitrovica prison through Gorkić. And all of a sudden, *Rundschau*—a Comintern weekly in German, French, and English—runs an article on Petar "Petko" Miletić as one of the prominent leaders of the Yugoslav Communist Party who, while in prison, is educating CPY cadres there as true Bolsheviks. In late December, Ivo Lola Ribar came from Yugoslavia with very important messages from Milovan Đilas, who was then the secretary of the temporary Regional Committee for Serbia. He said Petko Miletić's escape from the Mitrovica prison was being prepared. Miletić was the secretary of the party organization in the prison. That organization outnumbered all other party organizations in the country.

The idea was that Petko, once he was free, would establish a new, authentic leadership in the country. Finally, with his distinctive feeling for timing, Walter made his move. He says:

> One day I had to make a sharp decision. I wrote a letter to Moša Pijade and, on behalf of the Central Committee, I gave him a mandate to lead the party organization in Mitrovica. This saved the day because Moša energetically took matters into his own hands. Also, there were lots of other old comrades who joined him.

But Marić, with a stubbornness typical of someone from Split, does not give in. Čolaković explains:

> When Tito convened a meeting of the Central Committee, the decision was made to send the letter to the communist inmates in Sremska Mitrovica. The Prison Committee headed by Petko was replaced and Moša Pijade was appointed plenipotentiary of the Central Committee, with the task of solving

the problems in the party organization. Then, after the meeting, Ivo Marić wrote a letter to Tito, saying that he only trusts him and that he will not attend any meeting where Čolaković, Žujović, and others from Paris leadership are present. Tito realized Marić wanted to divide the leadership. He informed the Comintern about it, but the Comintern did not reply. At the same time, the Comintern delegate, who was on his way to Spain, was passing through Paris. Instead of contacting Tito, he met Marić. Tito felt he had to act. Instead of just waiting for whatever message comes from the Comintern, he, invoking a detail from one of the dispatches, dissolved the Paris leadership, returned to Yugoslavia, and formed a temporary CPY leadership there.

In January 1938, Moscow sent a dispatch confirming it had "received the message of 17 December" about the replacement of Miletić as the leader of the Mitrovica Prison Committee. The dispatch also said that "the leadership should take care about the House until its dissolution, with Comrade Otto bearing the heaviest responsibility." In other words, the Paris leadership will soon be dispersed and more Moscow-style cadre combinations will follow. Walter viewed this as unacceptable—he decided to capitalize on his invest- ment in the network he had singlehandedly formed in the country in accord- ance with Comintern's general instructions. Čolaković explains:

It took political courage—it was an unusual move in a relationship between the Comintern and a communist party. Until then, it was the Comintern that had appointed leaders and selected people in general. So he forms a new, temporary leadership made up of people in the field, in Yugoslavia. In his view, the several hundred emigrants working in the USSR or somewhere in Europe—they were not the party. The people in our country, factory workers, employees in institu- tions, party members, union members, those fighting for the general CPY and Comintern line—they were the party.

Čolaković describes the events as a conflict of principles, while in fact it was a competition of two party power centers seeking support of the headquarters, one in emigration, led by Otto, or Walter, which has only started establishing its network at home, and the other in prison, where most of the leading party cadres are, albeit unable to take action. On 23 March 1938, Walter sends a letter to Dimitrov from Paris in which he announces:

After eight months without any moral or material assistance, I have decided to liquidate the headquarters here and leave only a commissioner ... I am coming back to my country where I will try to establish a headquarters made up of responsible people, members of the Central Committee. I am aware of what this decision means and of the responsibility I have taken, but I think it is necessary for the salvation of the party.

Having arrived in Zagreb, Tito first hides in the vineyard of his courier Novosel at the city's outskirts. Then he goes to Kočevje by bus and returns to Samobor to his sister's family. Later, he leaves for Slovenia again and organizes a "conference" of the Slovenian party's Central Committee. In early May 1938, he goes to a climbers' lodging on Lisca Hill[1] above the town of Sevnica.

Here, in the mountains between Krško and Trbovlje, Tito will organize a meeting of his people and elect the "temporary leadership" consisting of himself, three Slovenes (Kardelj, Leskošek, and Miha Marinko) and two Belgrade commissars (Đilas and Ranković). From Croatia, came Josip Kraš, Drago Petrović, and Andrija Žaja. Tito internally proclaimed this group the "CPY Politburo," which means that he established his own Balkan Comintern out of the Slovenian, Croatian, and Yugoslav Communist Parties. Three parties have formed an umbrella organization without Moscow's consent. From the perspective of the Third International, this is totally unacceptable, as it clashes with the "principles of Leninism" that every party must adopt at its congress when joining the International. Even more importantly, it clashes with the "principles of Stalinism," which envisage strict control of every party formation by means of the vertical chain of command of the secret apparatus. But Tito now has his own apparatus, consisting of people he trusts, though it is true that he does not trust them enough to tell them that he is doing all this on his own initiative. He disguised the creation of his own apparatus and its fictitious party superstructure with the form of "temporary leadership." However, it managed to survive for more than half a century, all the way to the collapse of the regime in 1990.

Walter then leaves Slovenia for Belgrade, where he meets Ribar, whom he appointed head of SKOJ, and convenes the CPY's Regional Committee for Serbia. The Belgrade organization functions as the "parent body" for the entire southern territory that the man from Lisca Hill wants to control. He will establish contacts with Montenegrin and Macedonian activists via Belgrade. Nobody has realized it yet, but he has already started building his own Balkan empire.

As soon as Tito returned to Zagreb, the nature of the relationships that were to exist in this seemingly complex organization became clear. He dispersed the entire Anindol team—he could not care less about these national front-style combinations. Not one of those intellectuals and respected communists has remained, not even Gregorić, who had trained him in Russia twenty years ago and admitted him to the party in Kraljevica a decade earlier. Walter only kept Kraš, Petrović, and Žaja, three common workers. As they were all killed at the beginning of the uprising in 1941 and 1942, they took themselves off the agenda. Other communist champions from the Anindol national front phase of the Croatian Communist Party will last merely nine months, and then they will be arrested by Ivan Šubašić, the ban of the Banovina of Croatia (Banate) under the Serbo-Croatian compromise government formed under regent Prince Paul. His police had at their disposition a detailed list of those men, excluding Gregorić, given to them by a well-informed source. They will later be shot by the Ustashe. Party President Špoljarić will be arrested by Marshal Tito after the war and will end up in Goli Otok prison camp—the Alcatraz of the Adriatic. So much for the autonomous Croatian Communist Party.

Čolaković, a terrorist and a convict, played on Walter in 1938. He miraculously survived the war and everything that followed, including his treason, when he opted for Stalin in 1948. But he had a deep vault in the favor bank. And in the 1970s, still alive and well, a regular apologist of the personality cult and an informed insider, he gave an account of Tito's unsurpassed combinatorial mind, working under pressure in times of crisis:

> Tito spent around two months in Paris waiting for a visa. Only after personal intervention from Dimitrov, the visa came in August 1938. He went to the Comintern to explain the situation in the CPY. As he had recently returned from Yugoslavia, he was able to give a much more detailed report than he would if he had spent his time in Paris. He could explain the real situation with the CPY, its activities, its organizations, its successes, its achievements since December 1936.

> Also, Tito urged the concept that the leadership should be where the fight is—in the country, not in emigration. Indeed, Dimitrov shared this opinion.

> The third favorable circumstance was the fact that they knew Tito well. A respected Zagreb cadre, secretary of the local committee, and then a member of the Central Committee, organizing secretary, and political secretary who has established contact with younger generation ...

> So, like I said, when Tito came to Dimitrov with his report and his proposals, Dimitrov sensed it was a man who could—if anyone could—get the party out of the situation it was in. The thing is, the Comintern had been seriously considering dissolving the CPY as a party full of spies, waverers, and Trotskyists. If anyone can at least try to do something, it is this man. And so, Tito was given a chance.

Dimitrov met him in early November 1938. Politically, Comintern was almost bankrupt by that time and Walter is a godsend—he claims he has a well-organized communist organization distributed across the Balkans. This is the only organized communist group anywhere abroad to have survived the onslaught of fascism, except the one in China. Tito submitted a report and made up stories about the party's successful implementation of various national front initiatives in Slovenia, Serbia, and Vojvodina—the usual fiction communists feed each other at meetings and conferences. Dimitrov heard what he wanted to hear and the operative apparatus backed their member and, as early as 5 January 1939, Walter was given a mandate by the Comintern's Ispolkom, albeit a temporary one, as Dimitrov's diary reveals, to sort things out as the general secretary. They gave him a chance to do what he could—within three months.

13

THE STALINISTS

BOHINJ 1939

With a forged passport in the name of John Alexander Karlsson, an engineer from Stockholm, Walter left Leningrad for Copenhagen and arrived in Paris on 27 January 1939. He will stay in France for two months, then he will proceed to Fiume via Italy, cross the Yugoslav border there, and take a train to Bohinj in Slovenia. In the beautiful alpine village of Bohinjska Bistrica, where Jean-Paul Sartre would be coming after the Second World War, a four-day constituent meeting of the entire leadership would be held—this time with Dimitrov's temporary patent.

All of Walter's activities in Slovenia and Croatia are based on his good contacts with the well-connected people of the Kajkavian microcosm. Here, in Upper Carniola, logistics are provided by Tomaž Godec, a skiing champion and a member of the Yugoslav national team, otherwise a carpenter from Bistrica. It is in his carpenter's workshop that this crucial plenum of Walter's group will be taking place, now that they wield the legitimate mandate received from the head of the Comintern. The narrow circle of Walter's confidants has gathered here: the failed Montenegrin student Đilas, half-schooled teacher Kardelj, and Leskošek, a worker, union leader, and alumni of the "Leninist School" in Moscow. Also present are Kraš, a correspondent for the illegal party newspaper *Borba*, and—as the most promising adept—Ribar, secretary of SKOJ. Ranković and Marinko are absent with consent. From this meeting of 19 March 1939, a report on disciplinary measures is sent to

Moscow. This is done by publishing it in the illegal Paris-based party bulletin *Proleter*, which is then dispatched to the Comintern by well-established channels. Item 1 on the agenda: "Due to the devastating anti-party activities, attempts to resume factionalism in CPY, sowing confusion in the party ranks, propagating rumors from abroad, liaising with Trotskyists and other suspicious elements etc., I. Marić and M. Marić, Labud Kusovac and his wife have been expelled from the CPY."

This is how the "Petkovites"—Marić and his brother, Kusovac (a Belgrade lawyer and a contact with the Mitrovica prison), and his wife—were politically liquidated. Condemned, Marić will return from Paris to Split and live deeply underground, hiding from both police and communists. Under Italian occupation, he was interned in a prison camp. After the war, he was arrested as a Gestapo spy and sentenced to ten years' hard labor. However, in 1948, they attached him to the Stalinist contingent on Goli Otok, where he was confined in a special military prison on the nearby island of Sveti Grgur. Labud Kusovac and his wife joined him there. Although physically very weak, Kusovac was regularly beaten. He stayed there longer than anyone else, with the exception of Radovanović, the prewar CPY secretary. Marić managed to survive. Released in 1954, he lived a quiet life until his death in 1967.

Besides the "Petkovite factionalists," others were also expelled from the party by the Bohinj decision "due to factionalism and anti-party activities, maintaining close contacts with Trotskyists and informing them about party secrets": the entire "Dalmatian faction" of the incorrigible "Petkovites" including Vicko Jelaska, were arrested in Graz after the Eighth Conference in 1928. After the war, he too will end up in Goli Otok prison camp. Although more than sixty years old, he will be forced to carry rocks from the quarry barefoot. They regularly "beat the living daylight out of him," remembers his Montenegrin inmate Vlado Dapčević.

These factionalists were Walter's main problem, despite his attempts to present them as a side issue by focusing, in the rest of his report, on the people who are far from his reach but are important to Moscow:

> As elements who inflicted extensive damage to our party and the working class over the years by their factionalism and contacts with the class enemy, by cheating the Communist International, by hindering the party's development with their destructive activities and thus creating confusion in the Yugoslav workers' movement and assisting the class enemy, the following CPY members are hereby expelled from the party ranks ...

This is followed by a list of party pseudonyms and an occasional family name, starting with—Gorkić. The list also includes Dr Marković, brothers

Cvijić and brothers Vujović, Jovan Martinović Mališić with those long legs of his, and many others. The names published in *Proleter* are mostly pseudonyms, mainly for conspiratorial reasons, but also because the expulsion of all well-known leaders would demoralize party members. His letter of denunciation to the Comintern with these conclusions will be officially dispatched to Moscow by Kuhar, who also works for the 5th Directorate of the NKVD.

Walter also ousted Ćopić, who had helped him translate Stalin's *History of the All-Union Communist Party (Bolsheviks): Short Course* from Russian (which Broz had never learned particularly well) into Serbo-Croatian (the standard form of which he would never acquire). And even Rade Vujović, with whom he shared room 275 at the Comintern's Hotel Lux during his first stay in Moscow in 1935.

Of the nine leaders of the CPY before Broz, six of them—listed in the Bohinj letter (Horvatin, Đuro and Stjepan Cvijić, Gorkić, Ivan Gržetić, and Mavrak)—are long dead by that point. They were shot the year before, in the first wave of the purges. This Yugoslav party decision is merely a "confirmation," "legalizing" the decision Broz must have heard of in Moscow beforehand. Reportedly, that happened at a "narrow-circle meeting" he attended five months before Bohinj, while staying at the Hotel Lux in September 1938 and waiting to be received by Dimitrov. He was summoned and briefed by a competent commission consisting of the leaders of his operative branch, the true bosses of the Comintern—Manuilsky, Trilisser, and Kuusinen.[1]

Filip Filipović is not mentioned in the Bohinjska Bistrica decision, although he, too, was arrested in 1938 and shot with these demoted cadres. But it would simply be too big a scandal to announce that even the very founder of the CPY had been ousted.

As soon as Tito's list was published in *Proleter* in March 1939, the NKVD rushed to apprehend all those omitted in the previous wave of the purge. In April, the learned Dr Marković—who once debated with Stalin—was arrested in Moscow, and so were Ćopić, a Spanish Civil War hero, and Akip Šerment, a former organizing secretary of the CPY. Šerment had been interned as a Trotskyite in the early 1930s, when one could still survive expulsion from the party. Exiled to Kazakhstan, he was eventually released and allowed to return to Moscow. They obviously forgot about him until the Bohinjska Bistrica decision was made. He was arrested immediately after that, and so were Martinović, who led the Zagreb demonstrations of 1928, and Radomir Rade Vujović, a cofounder of the PCI. Death caught them all on the same day, in October 1938, when they were shot and cremated in the Donskoy Cemetery Crematorium in Moscow. Their ashes were thrown in a large, unmarked grave.

At the end of the Bohinj anathema, after the petty factionalists from Paris and Dalmatia and after the major sinners who either were shot in Moscow or will be shot as soon as *Proleter* reaches its subscribers in the Comintern apparatus, Walter inserts the thing that troubles him the most:

> On account of factionalist behavior in the party, lack of discipline, and failure to submit himself to party decisions, bringing confusion into the party's ranks, insincerity to the Central Committee, and treasonous conduct before the class enemy—all of which resulting in misleading the Communist Party and the entire working class, Petko Miletić is hereby expelled from the ranks of the CPY. Due to their factionalism and anti-party activities, Vojnilovič and Korski are also hereby expelled.

Petko is head of the Prison Committee in Mitrovica and Boris Vojnilovič and Ivan Korski are his aides. By denouncing these leaders of the prison party organization, serving long-term sentences, Walter eliminated the greatest threat to his authority. While it was easy to denigrate the former Moscow-based leaders, the authentic engagement and revolutionary commitment of these prisoners could not be denied, because they had been sitting in the Mitrovica prison, and not up in Moscow. And for Moscow headquarters, it was easier to interfere in Walter's domain through these prisoners than through the spent Moscow-based cadres or anybody else in these émigré communist circles. His authority as the temporary leader is actually protected by the efficient royal political police, which prevents Moscow agents from accessing the field. For Walter, it is of paramount importance to monopolize all communication channels between the headquarters and the field base. In carrying out this maneuver, he has learned the most important trick of all future strategies: your enemy is the best protection from your dangerous friends. He will later apply this principle even in his military strategies.

Thus, Tito dissolved the Paris Bureau, sent the Moscow cell members to their deaths, and declared the prison cadres "factionalists." But the job was not done yet. He went to Moscow. How does Tito himself describe his fight to survive and prevail in the conspiratorial communist organization?

> When I got there, I found no one except Ćopić, and some teacher from Serbia, who was also a police informer. I was given the task of translating the history of the Russian Communist Party.[2] There were three of us working on it—Ćopić, myself, and another man. No sooner had we finished the first chapter, they were arrested, so only I remained. I had to work day and night for three months. I even had to be in the printing-office for the layout. Upon finishing the job, in 1939, I went to Yugoslavia via Turkey. But while I was still there, a group of Bulgarians headed by Damjanov, head of the Balkan Section of the Control

Commission, were allowed to bring Petko Miletić from Yugoslavia on their own initiative and without my knowledge.

Some of my friends from the Russian party informed me later. They told me he was writing a report against me, claiming I was a Trotskyist. One day, I met Petko Miletić on the bus. He was on his way to the Comintern. So I asked Damjanov Belov—what is this Petko Miletić doing here? Who has brought him here? He says, "I don't know." I say, "Not true—you've brought him here! You have interfered in our internal party affairs again. You will hinder our consolidation! Don't you know that he is a factionalist, that he has destroyed our organization?" He said he knew nothing about it. All right, I said, we'll see. And, after a while, Petko Miletić was arrested. I didn't know why, but the NKVD arrested him. And they arrested him because they had spies in contact with the Belgrade police who had informed them that Petko Miletić had spilled the beans during the interrogation. Later, when we came to Belgrade and when Ranković took over all the archives as the minister of interior, it was established that Petko Miletić had actually worked for the police. The police created his heroic image to make it easier for him to work for them. It turned out I had a good instinct when I thought there was something wrong about him.

Le Carré would praise the setting and all this double-crossing in bleak Moscow during the purges; the hero of the story has to work daily with the other spy, while the indictment he has written against him hangs over the fellow's head. After that, he is in a tram clattering down Tverskaya (then Maxim Gorky Street), together with the other guy he has denounced, while the other one is desperately trying to prevail by denouncing him in return.

And the happy end, the victory of truth and justice, always follows the same pattern that will be used again after the war for compromising Hebrang. The political secret service finds a dossier in the archives, conveniently substantiating the alleged collaboration. As the NKVD supposedly has its agents everywhere, it was only logical that they would use the knowledge of the traitor's guilt to blackmail him and turn him into a double agent.

II

COMMANDER OF A SECRET ARMY

14

T. T.

ISTANBUL 1940

After the auto-da-fé in Bohinj, before leaving for Moscow—to go back in chronology for the moment—Walter goes to Belgrade, where his clique is still not widely accepted. He meets Pijade, just released from jail. They confer about the successful coup in Mitrovica prison, where "differentiation" was carried out and the "Petkovites" had been temporarily subdued. Tito then leaves for Moscow. Due to the itinerary he has chosen, it will take him three months to get there. First, he goes to his native soil, to Zagreb and Maribor. Then he pays a visit to his village Podsreda—more precisely, to the Slovenian hamlet of Trebče, some 6 kilometers from Croatian Kumrovec. His aunt Ana Kolar has a cabin there, and the preliminary meeting of the new national—Yugoslav—party leadership will take place there.

Thanks to the funds made available to the (temporary) general secretary, the field work has now become much more comfortable. Having thoroughly inspected the Slovenian franchise, he goes on vacation on the islands of Susak and Krk. In late summer, he goes to Fiume/Rijeka and then, by car and using the name Karl Seiner, he proceeds to Paris via the Côte d'Azur. He is neither nervous nor in a hurry. War is in the air, but he will stay in Paris for almost a month. Nerves of steel, always concentrated on his missions and priorities, not on world affairs. In the port of Le Havre, he embarks the Soviet ship *Sibir*.

The outbreak of the Second World War finds Tito on the Baltic Sea, on his way to the Soviet Union—on the same latitudes where the end of the war found him on his way *from* Russia. He reaches Leningrad on 1 September 1939—the day Germany invaded Poland. The next day, he will take an express train to Moscow, where he will spend two months. He is back in the headquarters again, in room 128 in the Hotel Lux, where he checked in as Walter Friedrich. He will get a new assignment—establishing a strictly subversive organization intended to prepare the party for armed engagements behind enemy lines. The differences between the political and intelligence network on the one hand and the subversive military network on the other have now been erased—the two networks are being integrated on the same operational axis.

On the same day that Broz left Le Havre aboard *Sibir*, the Molotov–Ribbentrop Pact was signed in Moscow. While its political motives may have been insincere, strategically it was highly logical and of great importance for both partners—neither of them wanted to fight on two fronts. This is why, on 24 August, only a day after the signing of the pact in Moscow, Commander of the First Army Group Georgy Zhukov ordered a meticulously prepared attack on the Japanese army in Manchuria, and, a week later, Hitler will approve the invasion of Poland. Stalin only has a small window of opportunity to stabilize his eastern borders before the Red Army is deployed on the defensive positions on the Western Front, because it will take only two weeks for the German blitzkrieg to crush the Polish defense. But it was enough for Zhukov to defeat the Kwantung Army in the massive Battle of Khalkhyn Gol (Nomonhan).

Soon after the battle, on 15 September 1939, the Soviet Union and Japan signed a truce. Two days later, the Soviet Union invaded Poland. The next day, the Red Army entered Estonia and Latvia, as well as Lithuania, which, under a clause in the Molotov–Ribbentrop Pact, was supposed to maintain neutrality. Then, in November, the RKKA attacked Finland after proclaiming the "Finnish Democratic Republic" headed by Kuusinen, Walter's superior from the intelligence structures. But the Winter War will drag on, with very little success for the Soviet forces. Only in the spring of 1941, after having lost 130,000 troops, Finland will yield one-tenth of its territory (with one-third of its industry)—the Karelian Isthmus. In that border region, adjacent to the Greater Leningrad area, Kuusinen's Finnish Soviet Socialist Republic was then proclaimed. Instead of using the national front approach, Finlandization was implemented by establishing a small Soviet province.

The finale of the strategic game in which Stalin, having reached an agreement with Hitler, will liquidate its Comintern network in the West began when Walter arrived in Moscow on 2 September 1939. In geostrategic terms, it turned out that, militarily and politically, the whole pack run by Dimitrov was not worth a dime. The Spanish war ended in defeat, France took a right turn, and the Daladier government started hindering the communists and interning the fleeing international republican combatants in the camps scattered between the Pyrenees and Toulouse. There is no chance of fighting fascism in Europe by forming some fictitious national front formations any more. Austria was annexed in March 1938 and Czechoslovakia was occupied in March 1939. Hungary used the opportunity to wrench off a part of Slovakia in the Little War in which a total of thirty troops were killed. In the officially neutral Romania, the fascist Iron Guard rules the streets. Nevertheless, the secret protocol of the Molotov–Ribbentrop Pact allows the Red Army to enter Moldavia. The communist–Nazi agreement envisages strict demarcation of the spheres of interest in Europe, giving up any subversive activities in the divided regions and mutual liquidation of subversive networks in the new partner's territory.

On 26 August, while Walter is still on his way to Leningrad, the Cvetković–Maček Agreement was signed as a result of the same forces dominant in European politics. Yugoslavia was also divided into German and Soviet spheres of interest. It was a "Yalta before Yalta," an agreement in which Stalin always claimed half a portfolio.

Yugoslav regent, Prince Paul Karađorđević, has been ruling on behalf of the minor King Peter II. In order to reach a deal with the Croats, in February he replaces the legally elected Prime Minister Milan Stojadinović, who is opposed to the Serbo-Croatian agreement. The agreement has divided the country into two spheres. The Banovina (Banate) of Croatia, headed by Šubašić, has been established in its western part. It is clear that German influence will dominate in Zagreb, and Soviet influence in Belgrade. The Kingdom of Yugoslavia and the Union of Soviet Socialist Republics have started negotiating mutual recognition and exchange of diplomatic personnel.

After less than two months spent in the Soviet Union during the Polish campaign, and many other dramatic events in Europe, the secret agent—now called "T. T."—takes a boat from Odessa to Istanbul, with the passport and identity of a Canadian mechanic, Spiridon Mekas. In Constantinople, he must contact the head of the Soviet agent network in the Balkans and Eastern Mediterranean, Mikhail Matveyevich Baturin. Baturin was the resident in Ankara, deputy resident in Istanbul, and then, from May 1942, chief NKVD resident in Turkey. Between May 1940 and March 1944, he managed to recruit nine key agents that enabled the Soviet intelligence to operate in Turkey even after his departure.

Istanbul was Europe's most important spy center at the time, more important even than those in neutral Switzerland or Portugal. From the exotic Turkish capital, it is possible to oversee the Balkans and the whole of the Mediterranean. Three rival networks operate there—the British and German ones and the Soviet one headed by Baturin. According to the Moscow routine, a resident is accompanied by a young female code clerk. This one obtained her degrees in telecommunications and French in Moscow. Baturin will marry her upon their return to Moscow and they will have a son, Yuri Mikhailovich Baturin, a future academic, Yeltsin's aide, cosmonaut, and a very important witness for the Broz story—he clearly remembers hearing his father saying that this top agent of the Comintern network had always been given "pistol nicknames."[1]

It was the Istanbul headquarters of the British intelligence that organized the 1941 anti-Axis coup in Belgrade ("Better War than Pact!"). Baturin was engaged on the other side, because the "general line" was to maintain the Molotov–Ribbentrop Pact. As a result, Yugoslav communists would remain passive in these events that had shaken Stalin's basic strategy.

Based on Yugoslav soil, Tito will be the head of Baturin's agent network in the Balkans and Mediterranean theater of operations. He came to Istanbul for instructions in late 1939 and stayed there until March 1940, more than three months, before returning to Zagreb. His task was to take charge of the CPY now that it had merged with the intelligence apparatus for the Western Balkans and Western Europe. Why did agent T. T.—Tito—spend almost four months in Istanbul? According to the instructions received from Moscow, he was to take over a huge portfolio, a wide range of duties. Upon arriving in Zagreb in October 1940, he would organize the Fifth Land Conference of the CPY. Instead of the "Fifth Congress of the CPY," it was named the Fifth Land Conference because, despite the long-term tasks with which he had been entrusted, Tito had not really been given any substantial political legitimacy. This is why the conference is actually a subversive cadres' briefing on how to operate behind enemy lines. But Tito compensated this lack of quality with quantity. In addition to the Yugoslav network—meaning three Yugoslav parties established in 1937—he has been given charge of the activities in Slavic Macedonia (and, indirectly, in Greece), in Albania (where there is no party organization at all), and also in Italy (because no other communist groups except his Slovene group exist there either). He has also been given a free hand in Austria, where the communists were mostly apprehended by the Gestapo during the Ribbentrop–Molotov idyll. Now annexed into the German Reich, it still has some Slovenes in Carinthia. There are also Germans and Austrians, former Spanish combatants in French prison camps, and they are also part of the portfolio. With the exception of Tito's clandestine network, Moscow has no other credible organization in the West.

Tito spent his time in Istanbul frequenting the Pera Palace Grand Hotel and staying at Park and Continental, luxurious hotels in Beyoğlu that have now vanished. Here, he is to receive a delegation from Zagreb: Herta Haas, a twenty-five-year-old courier whom he romanced in Paris (and who would give birth to his child in 1941), and the reliable Velebit, a lawyer and a descendant of a line of Austrian and Yugoslav generals, an intriguing character recruited as part of Tito's personal network in Zagreb. The two brought his new passport to Istanbul. Velebit says:

> There were two other comrades in the hotel, who had come from the Soviet Union together with Tito. They were Comrade Kopinič and his wife. They had come to Istanbul with a special mission to slip across into Yugoslavia and establish radio-contact with the Comintern. I had no idea at the time that it would fall to me to be their assistant in that project. When I showed the passport to Tito—a "masterpiece" of our party forgers—he laughed and said, "I can't use it for walking around here in Istanbul, to say nothing of crossing the Yugoslav border with it!" Eventually, he managed to cross the border in a different way—he used a Canadian passport, the one he had brought with him from Moscow.

And so, in Istanbul, Spiridon Mekas disappeared and John Alexander Karlsson reemerged. He traveled to Yugoslavia by train, via Greece. Tito arrived in Zagreb on 15 March 1940. On practically the same day, the Croatian ban's government in Zagreb arrests all prominent communists, intellectuals, and leading cadres of the episodic "Croatian Communist Party" established by Tito in Anindol. But no one touches Tito and his operative contacts. The arrested communists were interned in Bileća together with other opponents of the regent's politics. As for the communists, after a short while they were released. However, the moment they reappeared in Zagreb, Ban Šubašić sent them to Lepoglava prison. He was then—or later became—a Russian agent, with the pseudonym Seres.[2] Communist internees will spend ten months in prison, and in May 1941 they will be taken to the special prison camp in Kerestinec Castle in the vicinity of Zagreb. Almost 100 men, the leftist intelligentsia and leaders of the ill-fated Croatian Communist Party will be forgotten and abandoned by Tito. They will be killed as soon as the Ustashe take power in Zagreb upon arriving in the wake of the German occupation army.

As soon as he came to Zagreb, Tito rented, and later (with the help of Velebit) bought, a two-story house on Zagreb's western outskirts. This became a safe house. Kopinič will be the radio-operator there and his wife Stela the code clerk. Incidentally, Kopinič is yet another Slovenian from the area adjacent to the Croatian border. All they now needed was a two-way radio. The resourceful Velebit will solve the problem. He managed to find a man who would build a radio station and soon they would establish contact with the Comintern in Moscow.

In June 1940, in the new climate of the "gentlemen's agreement" between Hitler and Stalin, the regent's Cvetković–Maček government established diplomatic relations with the Soviet Union. The Soviet ambassador, military mission, and intelligence arrive in Belgrade. The Soviet military mission headed by General Alexander Georgiyevich Samokhin ("Sophocles") arrived in Belgrade. The Red Army intelligence service (GRU) establishes its center (sector Yugoslavia East) on Dedinje hills in Belgrade, in the villa of Vladislav Ribnikar, the publisher of the daily newspaper *Politika*. He is the illegal resident of the Soviet intelligence service that he joined in 1927.

Meanwhile, in Zagreb, Tito has been preparing a large-scale party conference and a session of his Balkan Command. A conference of the Slovenian Communist Party is held in advance near Ljubljana, the District Conference for Dalmatia is held in Split and Makarska, and, finally, the Regional Conference for Montenegro, Boka Kotorska, Sanjak, and Kosovo takes place in the mountain resort of Žabljak, Montenegro. To attend the latter, he traveled aboard a passenger plane from Belgrade to Podgorica. Under the protection of the Molotov–Ribbentrop Pact, he is moving freely around the country as a communist operative. In the meantime, war is creeping to the borders of his secret empire in the making.

15

MICKEY MOUSE IN WAR SCHOOL

DUBRAVA 1940

"It was Kardelj and I who prepared the conference," says Tito about the Fifth Land Conference, which, after the Eighth Zagreb Conference, was the next pivotal moment in his political career. It was held in 1940, instead of a party congress: "I bought a new Ford, a small car—we called it Mickey Mouse. So we drove around, looking for a suitable place. We needed a room large enough for more than 100 people."

The political preparations were much more important than the logistics. As Nikola Petrović, a member of Tito's personal network and his liaison officer for Moscow, explains:

I went to Moscow and stayed there from mid-September to early October ... In the Comintern building, I met the secretary of the Comintern's Balkan Section, Wilhelm Pieck. I handed to him the false-bottom suitcase that Comrade Tito had given to me to bring to Moscow. I told him I had the latest information about the most important political and organizational issues related to our party activities.

Pieck immediately convened the Comintern's Balkan Secretariat: Pieck, Vasil Kolarev, and Ercoli [Palmiro Togliatti, whose pseudonym was Ercole Ercoli]. Detailed discussions about our party affairs were taking place in the secretariat for six full days. After it was over, I was instructed to write a report for the Comintern's Executive Committee (IKKI), which was to meet specially for this purpose.

The meeting was attended by the famous communist leaders: Dolores Ibarruri, Andre Marti, Dmitri Zaharovich Manuilsky, Vasil Kolarov, Togliatti, and a number of well-known communists who were in Moscow, either just as emigres or working in the Comintern. Georgi Dimitrov was absent as he was on vacation. When I read my report, a discussion ensued.

After a few other speakers, Vasil Kolarov, a member of the Balkan Secretariat, took the floor and started making some critical remarks, which, I have to admit, I did not really understand. At that moment, I noticed Manuilsky, the representative of the Soviet Union in the Comintern and, thus, practically the second most important man in the organization, nervously walking up and down the conference room. He suddenly stopped, interrupted Kolarev, and said: "Vasili, I don't understand you at all. I don't know what are you trying to say. Say it clearer." Kolarov got confused and there was an awkward silence that lasted for several seconds.

Excited, I was waiting to see what was going to happen. Manuilsky then pulled himself upright and briefly said: "Yugoslav communists are brave [*molodci*]. They have done a lot."

Such a resolute and favorable judgment, given by a man of such authority as Manuilsky, made a strong impression on all the Comintern leaders present at the meeting.

Naturally, Comrade Tito was very pleased to hear that the achievements of our party were being judged so favorably.

However, the answer to the most important of the four questions Petrović had been instructed to ask in Moscow was negative. The crucial question was if the CPY could finally hold a congress, like any other exotic communist party in the far corners of the world. But the Comintern could not transfer to him the one thing of which it was in charge: formal authority over various communist parties (the Communist Party of Slovenia, the Communist Party of Croatia, the CPY). Tito, on the other hand, wanted to merge them because of his own political motives and in accordance with his unlimited ambitions.

As usual, T. T. informed no one about Petrović's Moscow trip. This was typical of him: he maintained his crucial contacts by using the people he placed full confidence in—the people who acted outside the party hierarchy. He recalls:

Convening the Fifth Conference was a huge responsibility for me.

The conference lasted three days. Only Kardelj and I would regularly come and go. The others were in there all the time. The conference was prepared well. It was a big success—no one was arrested. It was a big thing at the time—it meant that the police had lost their ability to penetrate the party by using their spies.

When the conference was over and the couriers had escorted all the delegates without any one of them having been arrested, we decided to organize the party school there. We held classes in the same room for twenty days. I taught there, too. Almost every day I would come by car from Sevnica, where I lived then.

Slovenes call this conference the First Land Conference of the Slovenian Communist Party. Josip "Vokšin" Kopinič, a GRU agent, attended it as an observer from headquarters. So Walter, Vokšin, and Birk (Kardelj) all have a direct line to Moscow. Between themselves, they communicate in the dialect spoken in the Slovenian province of Lower Carniola. Kardelj is the only one born in a city, in Ljubljana.

For the Fifth Land Conference—held between 19 and 23 October 1940— and the military course after it, the Comintern is sending its cadres to Yugoslavia. But unlike before, when the top brass would come from Moscow with instructions, it is now young, promising operatives from Italy, Austria, and Slovakia, coming here to learn something about conspiracy and how to build a combat-ready party under the protection of Tito's agent network. One such man is Franz Honner, a strongman of the Austrian Communist Party.[1] He was in Spain in 1938, and in 1940 he founded the underground Austrian Communist Party after meeting Tito in Split. (The earlier, "official" Austrian Communist Party had been crushed by Stalin after the Molotov–Ribbentrop Pact.) Moscow notifies Tito that Rigoletto Martini has arrived in Yugoslavia in order to renew the national party organization in Italy. This is the first really important task Tito has been entrusted with that is outside his immediate Yugoslav domain.[2] Tito will retain a substantial influence on the Italian party and politics for the rest of his life.

The year 1940 is the *annus mirabilis* for the secret agent Walter who has become Tito. The Comintern added a large chunk of territory to his provinces. After the fall of France—the capitulation was signed near Compiègne on 22 June, three months earlier—communists lost the opportunity to operate legally in Western Europe. Instead of political experiments with national fronts, Moscow is now creating a paramilitary organization. Its agents, including the "Spaniards" (Spanish Civil War veterans, now underground), will be operating in France and Italy, controlled from the detached field command in the Balkans.

Regardless of the permissive climate resulting from the communist–fascist détente, 1940 saw preparations for an all-out warfare again. Consequently, instead of the civilized and cultural avant-garde of the Croatian Communist Party that immediately ended up interned in Bileća prison and then in Lepoglava and Kerestinec, a new, much tougher team is being formed in Zagreb. It includes Ivan "Antonov" Srebrnjak, a Soviet military intelligence resident, former GRU agent, and demolition expert from the battlefields in Spain, and Kopinič, head of the Comintern's intelligence center, who has come to Zagreb together with Tito, accompanied by his sister Angela (who is also in the Comintern's special service) and his wife Stella Bamiadzidos, a Moscow-trained radio operator. Of course, Comrade T. T. is here too, teaching at the underground school for subversion. Twenty-day courses held after the Fifth Conference include a comprehensive introduction to military doctrine, encryption, and the use of radio-equipment. Attending these extended seminars are Spanish combatants that will become generals of Tito's future army.

Martini and Umberto Massola have been entrusted with establishing a new PCI. Bamiadzidos is in charge of contacts between Greece and Moscow, and she will stay in Croatia even after Kopinič's departure to Slovenia in 1942. Metodij Šatorov has been appointed secretary of the Regional Committee of Vardar Macedonia. He is attending the Fifth Conference in Zagreb, too. However, Dimitrov will entrust Greek operations to his Bulgarians, and in 1941 they will establish a new Greek Communist Party (KKE). Šatorov will then join the Bulgarian party, and transfer to them the Regional Committee of the Vardar Macedonians in Skopje.

Tito also took it upon himself to establish a party organization in Albania. The war had already arrived there—the country had been invaded by Italy in 1939. The Italian forces are now about to attack Greece from eastern Albania. The operations will begin five days after the Fifth Conference. Tito will send to Albania his two delegates—Dušan Mugoša, a military organizer later decorated with the Order of the National Hero, and Miladin Popović, a political cadre and future governor of Albania. When Tito opened the war school in Zagreb, the conflict on his southern front had already begun but no action could be taken as long as the Molotov–Ribbentrop Pact remained operative (and that meant one whole year).

Tito holds a lecture on the strategy and tactics of an armed uprising. Written in shorthand, the lecture is handed out to those attending the military and party course. The lecture is based on the scenario the Moscow instructors insist upon: the focus is on diversions that small groups will be carrying out in cities.[3] These classic (Leninist) general-strike and street-combat tactics are inapplicable in a war where large armies carry out large-scale military operations. All the attempts at starting a revolution in the German,

Austrian, and Hungarian capitals failed in the collisions with organized military forces. So, riots can serve as a detonator for a conflict, but action should immediately be moved from cities to villages.

For Tito, the crucial premise for a successful uprising is that it is led directly by the party, consolidating the political and military activities and thus ensuring centralized management of war efforts and efficient commanding. As an example to follow, he used the Bolshevik Red Guard from 1905 and the Cantonese organizations of the same name, consisting of basic units or detachments of ten men, merging into larger formations. According to Tito, refusing to establish such units on account of not having any arms is not acceptable, because acquiring arms is actually the primary purpose of these units. This means that combat detachments are to be created on the entire territory—in both urban and rural areas—regardless of the circumstances (which are not going to be favorable in the beginning anyway).

The military courses in the party school, intended to prepare the party for guerrilla warfare, lasted three weeks. Experiences from the Spanish Civil War were analyzed. And yet, despite all the theoretical preparations, the reality of war will find them all ill-prepared—politically and militarily.

16

NEITHER WAR NOR PACT

ZAGREB 1941

When the anti-government demonstrations began in Belgrade on 27 March 1941, after the signing of the Tripartite Pact, Russophile army pilots flew Tito from Zagreb to Belgrade, where he had a meeting with the Belgrade-based members of his leadership. The meeting took place in an apartment in a building near the old Kalemegdan Fortress.

The Belgrade demonstrations were a public reaction to Prince Paul's attempt to avoid involvement in the forthcoming world war by joining the Tripartite Pact. But the loss of a neutral position was perceived as capitulation, although there was no chance that Yugoslavia could avoid either the war or the pact. Traumatized by the Calvary of the earlier wars—two Balkan wars and the Great War—the Serbian people did not want to take part in another wholescale massacre, be it on the Axis or anti-Axis side. This is why they rose against the pact. In any case, the party did not take part in these events. Inciting the masses in the street was the task of the British subversive service SOE, as part of its efforts to stage a coup that would bring down Prince Paul's compromise-prone government.[1]

On 28 March, Stalin sends a wire to the Central Committee of the CPY, instructing them to take a cautious position. He will substantiate this with another telegram, sent the next day, 29 March.[2] These instructions from Moscow are reflected in the proclamation of the CPY. Stalin instructed Yugoslavia to stay neutral and divided into two spheres of interest. If not, then the status similar to the one of Bulgaria would be acceptable. As a signatory of the Tripartite Pact, Bulgaria ensured a special clause stipulating it would not have to declare war on the Soviet Union.

While the Italian army is taking a bad beating during its invasion of Greece, British troops have landed in Attica and the whole "South European flank" is undergoing tectonic shifts. The Soviet intelligence services are trying to parry the British ones: in Prague, a meeting was organized between attaché Zubov (actually, the NKVD resident) and the representatives of the Yugoslav army chief of staff who wanted money for their services. Believing that—as he put it in his report—they cannot provide any relevant services, Zubov refused them. On the margin of the report of his hasty envoy, who is saving his money while Europe is burning and everything is falling apart, Stalin himself wrote, "To be arrested immediately!"[3]

Neither the secret services nor the underground party network operating as their extension will change the course of events. The war in Europe cannot be avoided, and the same goes for the German attack on Yugoslavia on 6 April 1941. Stalin does not seriously countenance acting on the provisions of the Soviet–Yugoslav friendship agreement signed in Moscow at 1:30 a.m. on the day of the attack, but antedated to 5 April. It was initialed—in Stalin's presence—by Yugoslav plenipotentiary minister Milan Gavrilović and Soviet Foreign Minister Vyacheslav Mikhailovich Molotov. Stalin took them to dinner, where he showed off with his usual witticism and black humor. He asked General Staff Colonel Savić, who was in Moscow with the delegation, how long the Yugoslav army would be able to fend off the Germans if war broke out, to which Savić replied three months. Stalin then turned to the Yugoslav military attaché in Moscow, Major Žarko Popović, and asked him the same question. Popović replied that they could last a month. Stalin shook his head in disbelief and said, with regret—not more than two weeks. In fact, everything was over within a few days.[4]

Of course, the German air raid on Yugoslavia that began as *Unternehmen Strafgericht* an hour or two after this insincere toast did not trigger any Soviet reaction except the claim that "a nation has the right to fight for peace." As early as 7 April, on the second day of war, the Central Committee of the Slovenian Communist Party sends on a special mission two of its highest-ranking officials—Kidrič, a militant SKOJ member, and Dr Aleš Bebler, a member of the "Operating Commission of the Liberation Front" (a body of the party's Military Committee—the Supreme Command in the case of war). Bebler is also a Moscow student, Spanish combatant, and demolition expert—

which reflects his GRU background. The two of them go to a local commander of the royal army offering him their communist forces. Not trusting them, he declines their offer. This shows that the Slovenian party leadership acted independently of Tito's CPY, according to the general national front guidelines. For Tito and the CPY, who are strictly adhering to the instructions from Moscow, the German attack and invasion of Yugoslavia are not a good enough reason to rise up in arms and fight the invader.

Based on the account of Krsto Popivoda, Tito's closest associate in Zagreb, a Montenegrin who managed and directed the training of party cadres and who was also in charge of maintaining the party network throughout the country, the general secretary's predictions about the war developments were much more similar to those of the representative of the Yugoslav army chief of staff in Moscow than to those of the more realistic Stalin. Popivoda testifies:

> We met in Zagreb on 27 March. In a lengthy conversation, he described the general situation our country and our party were in, and gave me the tasks I was supposed to carry out. Having assessed the situation, Comrade Tito said we should do everything in our power to resist the enslavement of our country, that the masses are willing to fight, and that the tradition of our peoples—particularly the Serbs—will manifest itself in the liberation struggle.

> Comrade Tito was confident that the resistance would be much fiercer than some maybe thought ... Particularly in Serbia, with its rich combat traditions from the First World War. The conglomeration of the terrain was such, said Comrade Tito, that our forces would probably withdraw to the mountains and organize resistance there.

This was also the plan of the Yugoslav army's General Staff, but it never came to be. After four days of uncoordinated resistance, the army would fall apart. Only General Dragoljub "Draža" Mihailović, chief of operations of the General Staff of the II (Sarajevo) Army, refused to carry out the Supreme Command's order to lay down arms and, accompanied by a small group of officers and members of Chetnik (reserve) units, marched across the Ozren Mountain to the Ravna Gora Mountain between Užice and Valjevo, where he would establish his base.

After the 14th German Panzer Division entered Zagreb on 10 April, the retired Colonel Slavko Kvaternik, who had maintained secret contacts with the Ustashe émigrés, proclaimed the puppet state called the Independent State of Croatia (NDH). According to some earlier combinations, Maček's Croatian Peasants' Party was supposed to give it political legitimacy—Hitler's Balkan specialists from Ribbentrop's Reichsministerium of Foreign Affairs had the same idea as the Comintern's practitioners. Leaving the political problems behind, the Wehrmacht advanced: on 15 April, the 14th Panzer Division entered Sarajevo, a city in the central part of Yugoslavia.

Meanwhile, on Derenčinova Street 33 in Zagreb, Tito began to gather his team, holding instructive meetings and reaching conclusions that were to be dispatched to Moscow either via Kopinič's radio station or by being printed in *Proleter*. The paper's editorial board had moved from Paris to Belgrade in the meantime. In a new building in Belgrade's Senjak District, two printing machines had already been installed. This was only possible with Soviet logistics and in the permissive climate of the Molotov–Ribbentrop Pact, when police surveillance in the capital was somewhat less strict. Only a few of the highest-ranking party leaders and the party's academic forger Đorđe Andrejević Kun, a sculptor, knew about the secret printing office that would operate here without interruption until 1943.

In subsequent party hagiographies, the meetings in Zagreb, held in April, will become known as the "May Conferences," when Tito, even before the German attack on the Soviet Union on 22 June, allegedly made a call to arms, exceeding the "legitimate fight for peace" allowed by Stalin. However, looking back, it is clearly not possible that some autonomous political strategy was pursued months before Operation Barbarossa—the attack on the Soviet Union—that began on 22 June. The absurdity of such a claim can be seen in the fact that Tito and the network he had been preparing for the war since the Fifth Land Conference of 1940 did not even think of violating the gentlemen's agreement between Hitler and Stalin by, for instance, liberating the 100 "most precious party cadres" imprisoned in Kerestinec. Nothing was done about it even when Yugoslavia was invaded by the Axis powers and when the Ustashe regime was installed in Croatia by the German occupying administration because they could not find any civilian collaborationists. The conservative and pro-British Maček preferred being interned in the Jasenovac concentration camp to handing over his party to the Ustashe—although he had appealed to the members to be loyal to the new state. This is why the German occupying administration was forced to ask Rome to send them the members of the marginal fascist movement, "Ustashe in exile"—in fact, the subversive agents of the Italian secret service who, until then, had been isolated on the islands of the Tyrrhenian Sea. Trucks with some 230 members of the Ustashe "assault unit" came from Pistoia, Italy, to Zagreb not earlier than 15 April. It was clear that, as soon as they took over the Kerestinec prison, the inmates there would certainly be killed.

An article published in *Proleter* in April—not a call to arms but merely describing the situation—explains Tito's political platform for the imminent war. Tito first points out that only his organization—unlike Yugoslavia and all other parties and institutions, now fragmented—has remained intact and under a single—his own—command. This is the original, operational, not doctrinal, meaning of the "brotherhood and unity" policy. It is not a slogan for the national coexistence of Yugoslav socialism after the war, but an offensive war doctrine that Tito has recognized as a fundamental political prerequisite for success in the armed struggle that is about to begin. The occupiers have divided the country into several zones, thus fragmenting their forces. He will fight them where he can count on success; it will be territorial, guerrilla warfare, but with a united force. This is just a military perspective that will be refined over time. Crucial, however, is the political conclusion that the fight against the invaders can only be carried out by a united political movement that will not allow fragmentation of war efforts and creation of several autonomous factions, each with its own national program—for that would inevitably lead to civil war, as had happened in Greece. Those who have made arrangements with the Axis powers are not a problem. One way or another, the Axis powers will lose the war against the Soviet Union (as Comrade Tito believes and knows) and the local clients of the occupiers—the "quislings"—will go to the dogs with them. But those who could snatch from him his monopoly of the national liberation struggle—they are a problem. Like the Allies' stock, their strength will be rising, unlike the strength of the "national traitors." This is why he sees the Croatian Peasants' Party as the most dangerous rival. They opted for neutrality, which is but a nuance of collaboration during occupation, but will nevertheless remain a constant political threat—not because they are real collaborators, but because they are not.

The programmatic text in *Proleter* underlines that the CPY does not recognize the country's partition. Also, the party's Central Committee proclaims that the communists must lead the struggle for liberation in all parts of the country, *including the ones that remained under foreign sovereignty after the First World War*. Tito has thus defined his maximalist national war plan—he has promised Istria, Trieste, and Friuli–Venezia Giulia to the Croats and Slovenes—also a sign that the post-First World War territorial gains in Vojvodina and in the south will be preserved and that other territorial issues will possibly be raised from a likely position of strength. This was a far-reaching political platform—no one else had a project for the impending special war in the Balkans that would be even remotely as potent as this one. But, as this is totally different from the national front format, Dimitrov—the old Comintern parrot—reacts on the dispatch from Zagreb by sending a warning that "this is no time for a revolution, but for a national liberation war." Luckily for Tito, Stalin was too busy to exchange opinions with the rigid Comintern bureaucrat (to whom he will deny personal access and telephone calls in the bad times of the first year of war). For the moment, however, while the Molotov–Ribbentrop Pact is still on, all this is merely a theory. The party is as neutral as Switzerland. Until things change, communist agents wage war on paper, printing illegal subversion studies and militant bulletins. Still, some incidents will not be avoided.

17

A SPY NEST IN DEDINJE

BELGRADE 1941

Although the Molotov–Ribbentrop Pact is still valid, the situation in occupied Zagreb has become uncomfortable for the chief of the communist network. The capital of the quisling Independent State of Croatia is to become a mousetrap for communists. With his perfect sense of timing, Tito—who has until now lived in a small house built for him by his nephew in the western part of the city—leaves Zagreb for Belgrade on 15 May. In the house, located in the vicinity of the NKVD radio station, remains Tito's wife Herta, who will give birth to their son Aleksandar (Mišo) within days of his departure.[1] Tito travels to Belgrade by train, via Zemun. The German–Soviet pact is still on and no one touches communist agents yet. Prepared as a strategic surprise, "Barbarossa" will be launched five weeks later. Tito goes to a safer, Soviet sphere of interest, leaving behind his wife, newborn son, some 100 communists in Kerestinec, and the GRU team Srebrnjak–Kopinič, who are maintaining contact with Moscow.[2] Nominally in charge of the communist cell is the "troika" consisting of Hebrang, just released from prison, the steadfast Montenegrin Vlado Popović, loyal only to Tito, and Rade Končar, a worker and old hand of the network.

In Belgrade, Tito is met by Davorjanka "Zdenka" Paunović, a new courier, with whom he will begin a relationship that will last until the end of the war. This is his James Bond-style *modus operandi*—Comrade T. T. is fifty-three, Herta is already twenty-seven, and Zdenka—a student—is barely twenty. He saw her at the railway station. An eyewitness describes the scene:

The Zagreb train has arrived at the Zemun station. People are hastily getting off it, carrying suitcases full of various destinies. Other people are welcoming them on the platform, with open arms or with their heads bowed. The most impatient ones among them are Slobodan Penezić "Krcun" and two lovely young ladies, Davorjanka Paunović and Veselinka Malinska. They are awaiting the most important guest. They came closer to the railway cars to give him a warm welcome. And then, passing through the steam of the locomotive, in his elegant suit and hat, a suitcase in his hand—there he was—Josip Broz Tito.[3]

Jaša Rajter, a Belgrade communist and an ethnic German, now joins in:

In the early days of the occupation in 1941, I was one of very few Belgrade citizens whose automobile had not been taken away by the occupiers. Because of my ethnic background, they let me keep my little Steyr, so I could drive around the town. In May, I was given the task of giving a ride to a comrade, because it could be dangerous for him to walk the streets of Belgrade.

Since my Steyr had a convertible roof which was down, the comrade asked if I could close it up, adding that otherwise it would be risky. He then explained that he also had such a car back in Zagreb. I watched him while I was driving, but I could not guess his identity. I drove him to Kalenića Market and there, in a back alley, he got out and disappeared. I knew nothing about this man. This is how our first encounter ended.

As soon as he arrived in Belgrade and found lodgings in a house between two villas in the posh Vračar District, close to Kalenića Market, Tito went to the Soviet secret service headquarters in the Ribnikar family's villa in Botićeva Street in Dedinje District. A radio station codenamed "Pavlodar" was concealed there. In the immediate vicinity of this Soviet base in Botićeva Street, just across the street, in the villa of an eminent lawyer, the General Staff of the LXV Corps was quartered. It was the headquarters of the German occupying forces in Serbia, subordinate to the commander-in-chief of the southeast, Field Marshal Wilhelm List in Thessalonica.

A few days later, in March 1941, the head of GRU sends a dispatch to Dimitrov complaining that "Walter has been obstructing the activities of Mustafa Golubić," the GRU's resident in Belgrade.[4] This intervention of the Soviet military intelligence on behalf of Golubić certainly did not help him: the moment the Germans took Belgrade—with Tito arriving at practically the same time—the Gestapo received a tip about Golubić. Mustafa was soon arrested, tortured, and shot. Although his name was mentioned in the context of some acts of sabotage on the Danube (a depot with confiscated ammunition), they were certainly not organized by the Soviet secret service—probably by the British one. Stalin had strictly insisted on a policy of caution and neutrality, still hoping at that moment that he would manage to avoid or delay the war with the Germans that would ensue three months later.

On 22 June 1941, the day the Soviet Union was attacked, all radio stations in Hitler's "Fortress Europe" aired *The Internationale* as a sign to start arresting communists.

Having been given the right of free passage under the law of war, Soviet diplomats left Belgrade. From the Ribnikar villa, right across from the German headquarters, the GRU operatives of the Soviet military attaché Colonel Maslov followed suit. Colonel Maslov handed over his precious radio station to radio-operator Miloš "Giant" Brašić, instructing him not to give it to the party organization but to keep it as a separate relay station.

On 4 July, a meeting of the Politburo of the CPY Central Committee is held in an abandoned house. Tito proclaims the armed uprising here. Seven days have passed since the German attack on the Soviet Union. The German army is just entering Athens. It has surrounded 300,000 Soviet troops near Minsk. Svetozar "Tempo" Vukmanović, then a twenty-nine-year-old lawyer, a party organizer from Montenegro in charge of the CPY Central Committee's printing machines in Senjak who will later become Tito's most important commander during the campaign in the south, gives his account of the Dedinje meeting:

> It was on 4 July 1941. We were supposed to decide whether to start an armed uprising or not. Seemingly, it would be an adventure: Hitler's armies were pushing on into the Soviet Union; people in Belgrade were saying there were no front lines there and that the Germans were cutting through the country like a hot knife through butter.

> By then, Hitler's troops had been in Yugoslavia for two months. We met in Botićeva Street in Vladimir Ribnikar's house. Besides Tito, there were six of us—Ranković, Đilas, Milutinović, Lola Ribar, Žujović, and I. When I entered the room that morning, he told me, "No more printing machines for you. The time has come to get a gun and organize an uprising!"

> The situation on all fronts, not just in the Soviet Union but elsewhere in Europe, was far from favorable: the Allies had been holding their ground only on the British Isles. Europe was quiet. The Comintern kept broadcasting appeals for uprisings, for acts of sabotage ... Appealing to the European proletariat to rise in arms. But no one fought back.

> I was aware of the Comintern's directive that only a liberation struggle against the invaders should be waged, without launching a socialist revolution. And yet, Tito was resolute that the liberation struggle could only be won if it was turned into a socialist revolution.

While I listened to him, I was thinking, what will the revolutionaries in other European countries and other communist parties do? Will they submit to the Comintern or grab the opportunity to win the revolution?

On the same day, in Zagreb, a combat communist group captured the former Yugoslav royal gendarme Ljudevit Tiljak. He was an assistant of Đorđe Kosmajac, head of the Glavnjača, a fortified prison in Belgrade where communists were regularly beaten during investigation. There was no such specialist in Croatia, because the anti-communist repression had been directed from the Belgrade headquarters. When the Gestapo took over Kosmajac's institution, they transferred Tiljak to Zagreb, installing him in the police headquarters in Đorđićeva Street. His duty was to put his experience at the service of the Ustashe Surveillance Service (UNS)—the political police of Croatia's quisling regime—and help them in the repression of politically unsuitable elements. Unlike the eager amateurs who had been transported into the country on trucks from Italy, Tiljak posed a real danger to the underground communist movement in Zagreb. Pavle Pap, "Comrade Goofy," who had been beaten by Tiljak in the Glavnjača, followed him for days. They managed to lure him into the apartment of a woman near Vlaška Street. They questioned him there, killed him, and chopped him into pieces. They used buckets to carry the remains to a ditch near Radnička Road and threw them there. Four days later, on 8 July, when the remains were found, ten Kerestinec prisoners were put to death, including Dr Bergman, Braina Voss's husband.

After the first wave of executions, the communist organization started preparing to escape from Kerestinec. The operational leadership of the Croatian Communist Party—Hebrang, Vlado Popović, and Končar—had nothing to do with the operation. It was led by Kopinič, who—now that Tito had gone to Belgrade—saw an opportunity to assume a more important role. In his regular communication with Moscow, he must have received instructions to begin guerrilla actions. He decided to act independently, relying on his authority among the members of the Zagreb party organization.[5] Three weeks after the German attack on the Soviet Union, he initiated a rescue operation. It began five days after the execution of the first group of inmates, on the night of 13–14 July. We know it was an independent operation of Kopinič and not of Tito's party network from the letter Kardelj wrote two weeks later (on 2 August) and sent to Tito in Belgrade.[6] In it, Kardelj describes the situation in Slovenia and Croatia:

The party failed to organize itself on time. As a result, the Frankists [Croatian nationalists, Ustashe] have totally destroyed the party or forced its members into the woods, thus isolating it. And—no reason to deny it—our people in the field panicked in most cases, as much as I could see. Both of these moments—which are interconnected—have contributed to the fact that the liberation movement in Croatia (among Croats) is still very weak. So the fact is, the hardest situation we are now facing is the one in Croatia.

This should be kept in mind, including in the context of the [N. N.] affair. He obviously panicked and showed fear when he pulled it off. Not understanding the real conditions here, he simply wanted to skip the hardest part of the preparations, which cannot be skipped. Also—and I am totally convinced of it—he may have had a subconscious intention to strike you and the entire leadership. I say subconscious, but I cannot say there had not been some clear intentions here, too. He lied to Grandpapa [the Comintern] in the hardest times and he sabotaged the firm [the CPY]. Objectively, what he did was a provocation. Besides, he was politically helpless. He could give no advice. He only kept saying what they themselves kept saying: we should take action. But he didn't know how to do it. No wonder his two operations were more than unsuccessful.

The accused is, of course, Kopinič, Comrade Vokšin (radio call-sign Vozdukh). The editors of the collection in which the facsimile of the letter is included—a group of experts working under General Fabijan Trgo, head of the JNA Institute of Military History—left a remark here: "This refers to the ill-prepared escape of prisoners from the Kerestinec concentration camp (the preparations for the escape were inadequate)." Kardelj adds:

> It was an unforgivable and irresponsible act. I haven't spoken with him yet because I wanted to receive your instructions first. However, I changed my mind today (because of the report) and I will talk to him tomorrow morning. I will not discuss the whole affair with him before I get your opinion.

What happened in Kerestinec? Some 111 inmates attacked and overpowered the guards. Then they scattered in groups. However, as no one awaited them outside—because only a part of the communist organization had participated in it—almost all the inmates were captured and executed. Only a couple of them survived the war. Even those who had come to their rescue lost their lives. But Kopinič definitely positioned himself as a menace, a man who had challenged Tito's authority. And that was fatal for anyone.

The combat group that killed Tiljak consists of the members of the Zagreb Local Committee. Their higher command is the troika of the "operational leadership" of the CPY for Croatia (codenamed Papa), installed by Comrade Tito. Also operating in Zagreb are the GRU network run by Srebrnjak and an autonomous agency connected to the Comintern (codenamed Grandpapa), embodied in Kopinič himself. However, Tito does not believe in parallel lines of operation; quite the opposite, he considers them a lethal threat to be dealt with immediately and by any means.

18

THE SURREALIST REVOLUTIONARIES

FRUŠKA GORA 1941

As general secretary of the CPY, Tito proclaimed himself the commander-in-chief of the National Liberation Partisan Detachments of Yugoslavia (NOPOJ). Unlike the Spanish Civil War and subsequent popular front guerrillas in occupied Europe, where the military and political functions are separated, he applies his own doctrine: he keeps all power in his hands. In the first issue of the NOPOJ headquarters bulletin, Tito's article "The Task of the National-Liberation Partisan Detachments" was printed, in which he defines the formations and tactics to be used. So, the army has been organized, together with its hierarchy, doctrine, internal structure, and political goals. This is what makes communists successful when fighting on secret fronts or waging guerrilla warfare—they have detailed plans. They do not believe in inspiring leadership, they believe in organization. On the other hand—as Comrade Stalin put it—it is all about cadres. But here we have hardened old communists—underground activists who took severe beatings in the jails of a semi-oriental brutal dictatorship and, most importantly, Spanish war participants who commanded battalions, brigades, and divisions in battles. True, the largest pool of cadres is still in prison. The Kerestinec internees all perished, but they were obviously not counted on anyway. There is also another prison group—the one in Sremska Mitrovica. As it is now on the territory of the NDH, the Ustashe have taken it over. However, the communist prisoners there are mostly "Petkovites," so Tito's team does not really care about them.

117

They were freed practically by accident. Vladimir "Vlada" Dapčević, an old revolutionary who later turned Stalinist and did not like Tito, explains:

> Do you think it was a coincidence that the local party committee in the occupied Sremska Mitrovica banned any attempt to free the Mitrovica prisoners? The escape was organized at the initiative of Slavka Veselinov, a SKOJ secretary, because she was in love with Jovan Veselinov, who was in that prison together with other communists. There were around sixty of them and most of them were Petkovites. They were facing an imminent threat of getting butchered by the Ustashe. It was probably in someone's interest not to help the people of such skills, knowledge, and influence escape from prison.[1]

In any case, thirty-two inmates managed to escape the Mitrovica prison; only two were killed in the process and the rest got away because helpers awaited them outside. Escorted by their comrades, they went to Fruška Gora, a mountain that, together with the rest of Syrmia, had become part of the NDH. Eight of them would later receive the Order of the National Hero—an apostolic status in Tito's revolutionary sect.[2] Ivan "Matija" Maček, the brother of Kardelj's wife Pepca, escaped from the prison too, together with Jovan Veselinov, who would become Tito's satrap for the autonomous Vojvodina until his death in 1982.

However, the single most important cadre among the tough people from the communist underground, essential for the ensuing war, is a short, tiny philosopher and writer from a wealthy Belgrade middle-class family, Konstantin "Koča" Popović—Tito's military commander and perhaps the greatest general of the Second World War. He went to war from Belgrade.

Koča spent his childhood in Switzerland and his first language was French. Then he studied philosophy at the Sorbonne, where he joined the surrealists and made friends with André Breton. He wrote film reviews for the *Paris soir* and essays for Surrealist magazines, as well as the programmatic study *Outline for a Phenomenology of the Irrational* (1931). However, he abandoned these ideas after the 1934 Kharkov congress of Soviet writers, where demands had been made that art should be in service of the revolution. He became an orthodox Marxist and went to Spain to join the International Brigades, spending two years fighting as a commander of an artillery battalion.

Koča joined the Partisans in mid-July 1941. He went to the Kosmaj detachment of ten fighters. Čolaković, a member of the Politburo of the Central Committee of the CPY and a revolutionary from Boulevard Saint-Germain, joined them and appointed Koča commander of the detachment. This is where Popović's military career begins. In Tito's army, he will advance from squad commander to chief of staff of the Yugoslav army, which, at the end of the war, was 700,000 strong, with twelve rifle divisions. Save for the three major Allied forces, it was the strongest military force in the European theater of operations at the time. Koča rose to this position by winning battles as a brigade, division, and corps commander, in a war without rear echelons.

While Koča is fighting his battles around Belgrade, Serbia is in flames. Although easily conquered, it was not pacified. German troops came and went farther, to Greece, landed on Crete and proceeded to the Eastern Front. Only a negligible number of them were left in Serbia. This is why the collaboration government of General Milan Nedić was formed. The gendarmerie was armed immediately (in May 1941) and the first Serbian Armed Detachments (Državna straža) were formed in early September (eight companies with light infantry weapons). Militarily, they turned out to be worthless. Volunteers from the prewar Yugoslav National Movement (Zbor), a philo-fascist organization led by member of parliament and reserve Colonel Dimitrije Ljotić, will show more enthusiasm. But they were all good enough only for maintaining order, provided that order had been established and that the mass rebellion spreading in the towns and villages had been crushed. An uprising also began in neighboring Montenegro: an entire garrison of Italian occupying forces there was disarmed in a few days.

However, an Italian counteroffensive—30,000 troops from six divisions—started as early as July. By the end of August, the Italians would retake the towns and territories they had lost, crushing all major insurgent units in the process.

Serbia is strategically important to Germany because the Morava Valley is part of the communication route to Greece. In addition, the copper smelting plant in Bor, eastern Serbia, is vital for the German war industry, and so is the Serbian labor force—some 100,000 Serbian workers volunteered to work in the Reich. The number of Serb deportees and POWs in Germany proper is equally high.[3] However, in order to let local quislings and Bulgarian occupying forces maintain order, the country first has to be pacified.

During the preparations for the German offensive, Tito finally leaves Belgrade. He leaves on 12 September, having received a crucial message from the field the day before: "We had a meeting with the Chetnik military organization led by Draža Mihailović ..."[4] This means that everything is ready for the bilateral cooking of a national front-style broth, ultimately demanded by the Comintern. But the second piece of information is much more important and will prompt Tito to take immediate action.

In the meantime, Comrade "Marko," Aleksandar Ranković, has sent Comrade "Goofy" to Zagreb as a courier. He was supposed to contact Končar, a member of the operational leadership's "troika." "Goofy" is Pavle Pap, the reliable underground fighter who organized the abduction and execution of the Ustashe gendarme Tiljak. What is Goofy's new task? He is bringing a message that Kopinič is supposed to forward to Moscow by radio. However, Končar and Hebrang are to be bypassed. Generally, the dispatches that Kopinič receives from the Moscow headquarters are distributed to the operational leadership in Zagreb (in other words, to Hebrang) representing the Croatian party; to Tito for the CPY; and to Kardelj for the Slovenian party leadership. These three parties are equal, but such a scheme is totally unacceptable for Tito's pretensions of maintaining the monopoly in the apparatus. This is why the other piece of news that he received from Marko is crucial: Ranković has established contact with Ratko Mitrović, political commissar of the Čačak Partisan Detachment. Mišo "Giant" Brašić came to Mitrović, and brought with him the Soviet radio station "Pavlodar." Colonel Maslov ordered him not to hand it over, under any circumstances, to the Central Committee of the CPY because GRU wanted to maintain the autonomy of its communications. However, Brašić had to hide somewhere, and he went to the Čačak detachment. As soon as Ranković notified Tito of the whereabouts of the radio station, the general secretary immediately went to the Partisan-controlled territory. His organizing secretary Comrade Marko was now in control of the radio station. Without it, Tito would be just another outlaw in the woods. "Pavlodar" and Brašić were hidden in Ljubostinja Monastery, halfway between Kraljevo and Kruševac. Taking possession of the radio station will be easy, and then Tito will not need Kopinič's transmissions. So he leaves for the "liberated territory," counting on establishing direct communication with Moscow, instead of through Vozdukh.

In early September, Tito leaves Belgrade with a forged ID, using the name "Petrović." He also has a document identifying him as a company commander in the Chetnik detachment of Vojvoda (local military commander) Javorac. Smartly dressed, he leaves Belgrade by train, accompanied by Dragoljub Milutinović, the Orthodox priest who helped him obtain the false papers. Milutinović is in fact "Vojvoda Javorac"—it is his *nom de guerre*. Three other persons accompanying Tito are two young couriers—Davorjanka "Zdenka" Paunović (twenty), his personal secretary and mistress; Comrade Veselinka Malinska (twenty-four), a Macedonian student of law; and Joachim "Jaša" Rajter, an ethnic German, member of German national organization

Kulturbund, in fact a reliable prewar communist who has joined them now to use the membership as camouflage. He and Tito converse in German during the trip. Gendarmes keep saluting them. Rajter remembers:

> In August 1941 I was given another task—to escort one comrade to the liberated territory near Valjevo ... I took a look at the passengers standing on the railway platform and I recognized the comrade I had driven around Belgrade in May. Comrade "Zdenka"—Davorjanka was with him. An Orthodox priest hanged around them, too. Comrade Veselinka Malinska, my contact and a member of the same party organization I was in, disappeared somewhere. She probably went to the other end of the train.

> We spoke German. Who would think that those who spoke German were leaving for the Partisan territory? When the train suddenly twitched, the suitcase flew forward and Comrade Zdenka said: "Watch it, Tito!" At that moment, I realized it was the general secretary. I had been reading *Proleter* as a young communist, which contained many articles written by Tito.

> After getting off the train, we arrived in a hotel in Valjevo. Next morning, we got up, put our clothes on, and went down to the coffee-shop to make a plan for the rest of our trip. I was instructed to hire a coachman. In the village of Bačevci, we entered an inn. When we came in, we realized it was full of Chetniks. A couple of them jumped up, rifles in their hands, and approached me. I stood next to the wall. One pointed his rifle at me. I did not know what to do. I looked at Comrade Tito, but he gave me a sign to stay calm. He stood up and asked loudly: "Who's in charge here?" One of them approached him. They went aside. I didn't hear what they were talking about. When they returned, the Chetnik commander, or whatever he was, said: "It's all right, it's all right, let him be."

> After the war, I asked Comrade Tito how did the whole thing end up? He told me he had had a document identifying him as a Chetnik commander on his way to negotiations with the Partisans. It was a pass that Milutinović, the priest, had given him. He was a Chetnik *vojvoda* at the time—"Vojvoda Javorski."

Tito came to the headquarters of the Valjevo Partisan Detachment in the village of Robaje near Mionica on 18 September. He met Draža the very next day, on the road to the River Drina. "He seemed to me like a nice, cultural man, a typical commissioned officer," said Tito to Churchill's envoy Brigadier Fitzroy Maclean two years later, describing his first impression of his would-be partner.[5] Bearded, with thick graying hair and steel-frame spectacles on the nose, Draža observed Tito with curiosity and seemingly in a good-natured manner. However, despite his friendly attitude, the General Staff colonel clearly did not take Tito seriously. He thought Tito was some disguised Russian who could not speak proper Serbian, some plotter and agitator chased before the war by the royal police. All the worse for him—five years later, his would-be ally, who will have turned into a merciless enemy in the meantime, will have this royal army colonel, now general and minister of war, executed and buried in an unmarked grave somewhere on the banks of the River Sava near Belgrade.

The meeting gave no results. In expectation of a more suitable moment for the resistance to take root, the defensively minded Mihailović limited the confrontation with the Germans to the smallest possible extent. More importantly, he wanted to maintain the old regime and its claims on Yugoslav territory as an integral state, other national aspirations notwithstanding. The Partisans, for their part, flew a red flag with the hammer and sickle on the house in Užice where Tito took residence on 23 September. They introduced the salute "Death to Fascism," created by Tito. The reply was, "Freedom to the people", suggested by Ranković. The town of Užice supplied them with arms—there was a factory there that could produce large quantities of ammunition within a short period of time. On top of that, the Partisans became self-confident after seizing some territory.

19

THE DEFEAT

UŽICE 1941

The military conference in Stolice, a mountain hamlet of a dozen houses surrounded by orchards, 112 kilometers from Užice, is much more important for the Partisan guerrillas than the chat with General Mihailović. A dozen or so participants that attended the conference formed the wartime political leadership that was to command armies and the revolution in the Balkans. A very unusual group, but these are all exceptional people, stainless-steel communists, Stalin's "seven samurais." First, there is the commander himself, Josip Broz "T. T." (forty-nine). Then there is his organizing secretary, tailor's assistant "Marko" Ranković (thirty-two). There are three Belgrade Law School graduates—head of SKOJ (Yugoslav Komsomol) Ribar (twenty-five), and two Montenegrins, Ivan "Milutin" Milutinović (forty) and Vukmanović (twenty-nine). These four close aides of Tito have *never* received training in Moscow. Somewhat in the background, there are also two loyal and reliable Moscow cadres—the Sorbonne-educated doctor of law Sreten "Black" Žujović (forty-two) and "Roćko" Čolaković (forty-one), former convict, assassin, and collaborator on the translation of *Das Kapital*. With the exception of Ribar—who has only a short prison record—they had all served time with hard labor (thirty-three years between the six of them).

From Slovenia and Croatia, through the occupied country, also came the members of the Military Committee of the CPY. From Zagreb came Rade "Moustache" Končar (thirty) and Vlado "Spaniard" Popović (twenty-seven), captain of the Spanish Republican Army. Slovenian comrades Leskošek (forty-four) and "Poldi" Marinko (forty-one) also made it to Stolice. Hebrang is not here—he was either not invited or did not come. Kardelj got lost along the way—allegedly, he could not find his "contact." The radar of the general secretary must have detected their absence, because, for these two nominal leaders of the Slovenian and Croatian Communist Parties, he represents political authority only if they choose to accept him.

The German command has just launched the First Enemy Offensive—mopping up the rebels. The insurgents have grouped themselves on the territory around the town of Užice, between the River Drina and Zlatibor Mountain—the so-called Užice Republic. Overestimating the strength of their resistance—just like Tito himself did before the war—the German command has deployed two divisions and one infantry regiment. Some Ustashe forces and parts of the German 718th Jäger Division have also been deployed on the Drina's western bank, preventing the Partisans from crossing into Bosnia. Albeit passively, Nedić's State Guard and Ljotić's newly formed Volunteer Corps are also taking part in the operation.

The mop-up operation started in the northern Serbian province of Mačva, where 2,000 people were shot and more than 20,000 were deported to the Reich. Mass executions took place in the centrally located Kragujevac, in which many civilians perished, including students and professors of a high school. At the same time, armed conflict between Partisans and Chetniks flared up in Užice, turning their cohabitation into an open clash. General Mihailović reports to the Yugoslav government-in-exile in London: "I am doing my best to unite all progressive forces in a decisive fight against the Germans."[1] In the meantime, Tito informs Moscow he has evidence that Mihailović has been overtly collaborating with the Germans. In fact, General Mihailović is not hoping for a merciless war with the occupational forces nor is Tito willing to merge his forces with the Chetniks and thus legitimize his adversary. Draža is preparing for going into winter quarters and Tito is preparing for the revolution. An agreement was reached, but Mihailović backed down from it on 5 November. Tito is resolute to defend the town. The best unit, the Workers' Battalion from Užice—like the one he saw in Omsk—was sent to fight the Germans at the Kadinjača Pass on 29 November 1941. Not being an elite proletarian unit but merely four companies of manufacture workers, bakers, and tailors, the battalion was crushed. If all 260 workers were not tragically killed to a man, it would be a farce, because advancing against them was the regular 342nd Infantry Division of the Wehrmacht, with 15,000 regular and 8,000 support troops.

The Partisan state in Užice was crushed after two months of existence. The XVIII Corps under command of the "plenipotentiary commanding general in Serbia," Franz Böhme, annihilated the Partisan forces. Tito and his Supreme Command escaped to the south, toward the impenetrable woods of Zlatibor Mountain. They were lucky that the Germans chased them only to the Uvac River—the demarcation line between the German and Italian occupational zones—the area where Miletić came from and where Tito was not particularly popular. The Partisans slipped into Sanjak, a predominantly Muslim territory on the border of Serbia and Bosnia. However, in the spring of 1942, Operation Trio was launched there against them. Although Yugoslav sources perceive it as two operations—the Second and Third Enemy Offensives—it was a single, large-scale synchronized operation carried out by the joint occupational forces and some quisling units.

At the Politburo session held in the village of Drenova on 7 December 1941, Tito allegedly offered his resignation. It is not quite clear whether he was referring to the position of supreme Partisan commander or general secretary of the party.[2] All in all, it was a debacle *par excellence*. While trying to follow the diktat from Moscow to join forces with the Chetniks as partners in the national liberation war, he chose the wrong tactics and the wrong strategy, using the same military doctrine that had been used in the Spanish Civil War. At the same time, an uprising in Dalmatia pressed ahead, although the situation there was not ripe yet: the Italian occupation administration tried to win the population over with massive supplies of foodstuffs; also, the numerous troops deployed in the region were permanently stationed there, unlike the German troops who only intervened in their occupation zones by sending sporadic punitive expeditions.

In the winter of 1941, the unstoppable German forces were advancing toward Moscow. In December, they came within sight of the city, 20 kilometers away. Simultaneously, they laid sieges to Leningrad and Sevastopol. Soviet intelligence services that had taken over the Comintern's channels were now demanding urgent attacks and acts of sabotage, while Dimitrov was asking for the creation of a general national anti-fascist front. The uprising in Montenegro was launched and failed on this premise, the same as the one in Užice, the Serbian Alesia with its two irreconcilable Vercingetorixes. The proletarian actions in Dalmatia also ended disastrously. Rade "Moustache" Končar, member of the Politburo of the Central Committee of the CPY, was captured in November and shot. The First Detachment from Split went to the hinterland as early as August. The entire detachment was ambushed and executed by the Ustashe.

Tito's superior acumen now had to process all three major failures in the first year of the Partisan uprising. He then came up with a very complex, original solution that he would impose on Croatia, Slovenia, and then everywhere else. This unique combination resulted in a successful revolution in Yugoslavia. The uprising in Greece, on the other hand, eventually failed; although it took place under the same circumstances, it lacked Tito's command and his management and credibility.

Having rested in Sanjak, Tito arrives in the village of Rudo, in the rugged mountainous area on the border of Serbia, Montenegro, and Bosnia, and establishes the 1st Proletarian Brigade. It is 21 December 1941—Stalin's birthday. Tito abandons the concept of national liberation war. The new unit boasts communist insignia—red star with hammer and sickle. The communist revolution has begun.

One of Tito's best generals, second only to Koča Popović, will be Petar "Peko" Dapčević. This Montenegrin from Cetinje, the son of an Orthodox priest, studied law in Belgrade and then, having turned twenty-four, joined the volunteers in Spain. He became a lieutenant, political commissar, and company commander in the Dimitrov Battalion of the 15th International Brigade "Abraham Lincoln." When the uprising erupted in Montenegro, he was appointed commander of the Lovćen Partisan Detachment. He immediately destroyed a motorized battalion of the Italian Messina Division. But the uprising failed, Tito escaped from Užice, and the Wehrmacht was just taking Tolstoy's estate Yasnaya Polyana on the outskirts of Moscow. In this toughest moment, Peko had to report to Tito. He managed to reach him only on 18 December, in a village 100 kilometers southwest of Užice.

> When I came there, they ushered me to the backyard of a large house and they showed me a well-built man in uniform, with a binocular and a holstered revolver. I paused for a moment—this was the first time I saw Tito. I approached him and told him who I was. He shook my hand, but he was focused on something else—he was watching a horse being unloaded. I found it strange, but soon I was told it was the radio station that the Supreme Command had been using for communication with the units of the National Liberation Army across Yugoslavia.

Although giving his account thirty years after the war, Peko was wrong here. The Supreme Command of the National Liberation Army had no radio communication with its units—messages were sent by couriers. And this was the "Pavlodar" radio station, used only for communication with Moscow. It had been taken away from Brašić:

I was told that the 1st Proletarian Brigade was to be formed. We made it to Rudo as early as 20 December, together with some other members of the Supreme Command. Among them was Comrade Kardelj. Tito then told us his decision. I myself had supported the idea of organizing a regular army as soon as possible, because of my Spanish experience. Tito, actually, gave us the fundamental elements of his idea, tactics, and strategy of our future war efforts. When I interrupted him and asked him if we should form such brigades, too, he quickly and resolutely answered: "No, not without our approval. Because of the 1st Proletarian Brigade, we will have difficulties as it is."

So it was about establishing a party army, as Tito admitted to the confused Montenegrin commander who was not particularly versed in things political. Set up on 21 December 1941,[3] the 1st Proletarian Brigade—formed in Rudo—had around 1,200 combatants. Of these, 700 were Serbs. The first and second shock battalions (Lovćen and Zeta Battalions) were made up of Montenegrins. There will be one Bosnian battalion, too, with fighters of mixed ethnicity. This brigade would remain Tito's "officer factory" for the rest of the war. Some 22,000 combatants will pass through its ranks, 7,500 of whom will be killed in action.

When he arrived in Rudo with the shattered remnants of his Partisan group from Užice, Tito was at the lowest point of his military career, but also at the outset of his triumphant war exploits. The Comintern had practically stopped communicating with him. What is the use of a loser who cannot start a national liberation uprising in Yugoslavia based on the prescribed national front formula? In his dispatches, Tito is trying to convince them he has loyally done his best to cooperate with the Chetniks but was obstructed by some English agents who had disembarked from a submarine in Montenegro and were now fighting with the Germans against the Partisans. No one in Moscow was willing to listen to these fabrications. He was practically written off. Besides, the Chetniks are the army of the royal government-in-exile, recognized by the Soviet Union in 1940. Stalin certainly had no intentions of antagonizing its British patrons because of a revolution in the mountains of the Balkans, where Tito's elite bakers and shoemakers had suffered a crushing defeat at the very beginning.

The first convoy with war materiel reached Murmansk on 1 September 1941, while Tito was still in Belgrade. When he was conferring in Stolice in September, US diplomat Averell Harriman and Churchill's envoy Lord Beaverbrook arrived in Moscow, promising abundant assistance for the war against Germany. Stalin, who had extradited communists to Hitler not to jeopardize the Molotov–Ribbentrop Pact, certainly would not think of entering a dispute with Churchill over some Walter. Soviet relations with the Yugoslav government in London and with General Mihailović, its minister of war in the woods, had been suspended for two months but were renewed and maintained unhindered for three years, until October 1944, when the whole thing was eliminated from the agenda.

Later, Tito admitted to Dedijer that, had he obeyed the instructions from Moscow, he would certainly have gone to the dogs. In a country that was just splitting into separate nations, where would he find allies for the national liberation struggle? He would have to side with each of them, thus automatically siding against everyone else; he would also have to fight against his own forces, which would side with one such partner or another. After all, these theoretical national allies were not willing to go to war at all: the Croats had been given their state—even if run by the Ustashe—and the Serbs, having been defeated after the large-scale German pacification of Mačva and Šumadija that ended up with the Partisans' debacle in Užice, would try to avoid yet another war after the one that had decimated their population. The Serbs from Serbia were willing to fight about as much as the French. Only the Serbs in the NDH, terrorized by the quisling regime, would rise up in arms on a massive scale. Besides, being in the Italian zone of occupation, they would have against them a weaker adversary.

Tito left Rudo for Foča on the River Drina. Foča is only 100 kilometers from Sarajevo, but there are rugged Bosnian mountains between the two cities. The communist strategist has realized that he must create an insurgent authority capable of surviving the winter. In the autumn of 1941, party members were convinced that the Soviet forces would reach the Yugoslav border no later than 1942. Instead, in the winter of 1942, the Soviets had just managed to stop the German thrust toward Moscow (Operation Saturn).

But even after the crossing of the Drina, Tito's army was still in a very dangerous situation, despite the forming of the 1st Proletarian Brigade and, six months later, of the Supreme Command's operational group consisting of six brigades. Or—precisely because of this. Major military formations attract enemy forces; if it is Germans, it always ends badly. Operation Trio was launched along the entire Drina Valley in order to eliminate the remnants of the Partisan army crushed in Serbia. But Tito found a recipe for Partisan warfare: marching on and spreading the revolution on the move instead of defending a territory. Here is the account of Peko Dapčević:

> Tito kept mentioning that the fact that we have formed the 1st Proletarian
> Brigade and the main Operational Group as a core of our operational army must

in no way affect the wide scale of our struggle. We stick to the Partisan detachments. The character of our struggle must become even more comprehensive. Tito also made a suggestion—which was realized in a few days—that we should go to central Bosnia as soon as possible, because it is the center of Yugoslavia. He said that things were going very well in Dalmatia and that the entire region was about to rise up in arms, adding that fierce fighting was going on in Bosnia and that our units, despite heavy losses, managed to maintain the initiative.

Soon afterward, the proletarian brigades started their march. By successfully engaging the enemy while in motion, we soon advanced to central Bosnia. Livno, Duvno, Petrovac, Drvar ... We got there at the right moment. We linked up with the brigades from Bosnian Krajina and the entire Dalmatia had joined the national liberation struggle in the meantime.

Like Mao Zedong before him on the other side of the world, Tito came to the solution by combining a Leninist–Trotskyist approach (revolutionary war) with Stalinist pragmatism (relying on peasant masses). In other words: dynamics, maneuvering, marching on, constant military and political offensives outside cities, and a simultaneous revolution. The bourgeoisie must be liquidated and their land divided; mandarins should be terrorized, "war speculators" and "economic collaborationists" should be shot. As political and military dominance can only be achieved by a revolution—and no frontlines can be established around such an insurgent republic for defending it—one must find some place out of the way and establish a temporary communist Shangri La, a sanctuary where the new political system will be introduced immediately. This is why Mao undertook his "Long March"—he wanted to create his Yan'an Republic. Tito went to the wilderness of central Bosnia, where he would create his first Partisan communist state in the Bihać area.

20

THE LONG MARCH

BIHAĆ 1942

Driven from Serbia, Tito and his army are undertaking their "Long March" across Bosnia. However, although he is really in the gutter, it does not mean he has neglected other territories under his authority. Mugoša and Miladin Popović were sent to Albania in 1941. Now, in early 1942, he is sending Dobrivoje "Orce" Radosavljević to Macedonia as an instructor, together with his former courier Malinska who accompanied him to Užice. Vukmanović, a great Partisan commander—a Montenegrin—will soon join them in the south. But these lands where there is not yet a communist organization are not a problem. The biggest problem is the two regions where the movement is developing in an unwanted direction, based on the prescribed national front-based organizations created by the autonomous communist parties of Croatia and Slovenia.

As a special agent with the task of rectifying the wrong course, Tito sends to Zagreb his most efficient man, Ribar, a member of the Supreme Command and Politburo, and head of SKOJ. This twenty-five-year-old lawyer arrives in Zagreb on 8 January 1942. Kardelj soon joins him there. Tito appointed both of them as members of the "CPY Central Committee's Organizing Secretariat for Non-liberated Regions." On 16 February 1942, he ordered them to "purge the techni-cal apparatus of the Central Committee of the Communist Party of Croatia."[1]

What are the "non-liberated regions"? Primarily Slovenia and Croatia, and all the other parts of the country not covered by his marching army. Formally,

Ribar and Kardelj are also in charge of Serbia and Macedonia, but there is very little they can do from occupied Zagreb.

Tito's operational group is being chased—notwithstanding the underground network at his disposal, his substantial authority extends only to the territories where his armed proletarians have set foot. At the same time, there are some vast "liberated territories," or uncontested territories created by guerrillas in the two western provinces of Yugoslavia occupied by the inefficient Italian army. The problem, however, is that the "non-liberated regions," even when they are liberated, have their own political authorities functioning as national front parastates. This is why Tito sends Kardelj to subdue Slovenia, and Ribar to pacify Croatia and, above all, to "purge the technical apparatus." The "technical apparatus" refers to the Soviet intelligence network embodied in Srebrnjak and Kopinič "Vokšin." They have been trying to ruin the "firm" and establish their own agent network, of which Kardelj notified Tito way back in August 1941.

So the main problem is that, besides Tito's unreliable Pavlodar radio station, which often loses signal as they are always on the move and the power grid is not available at all times, there is also the main communication channel—the one controlled by Kopinič, who has a reliable radio station. Also, another Soviet residency—the military "rezidentura" run by Srebrnjak—is based in Zagreb. Srebrnjak, a military intelligence agent, and his wife, a code clerk, have their special center in Vrapče (Zagreb's western district), where they share a house with Hebrang, the nominal secretary of the Croatian Communist Party. Tito sees things like this: while he is busy fighting behind enemy lines, Srebrnjak and Kopinič are operating as a fifth column behind *his* lines. When one works for Stalin's agent network, paranoia is always understandable. All the more so since Comrade Hebrang maintains regular communication with the Comintern through Kopinič. Besides being a member of the Croatian "operational leadership" in Tito's hierarchy, Hebrang is also the secretary of the autonomous Croatian party in Stalin's hierarchy, as Kardelj is of the Slovenian party. While this is not so relevant at the moment, current formations and directives are to be followed in the Soviet network until new ones are introduced at a congress or after purges.

This proliferation of authority does not suit the CPY general secretary one bit. But Comrade Tito trusts Comrade Kardelj because he himself selected and installed him. He knows him well and always keeps him under control. As for Comrade Hebrang, Comrade Tito does not trust him. While the Croatian Communist Party was headed by the inert Bakarić, there was no fear of such a thing. But as soon as Hebrang was released from prison, he immediately reassumed his secretarial position (to which he had been appointed by Moscow way back in 1928). This is why a pressing issue needs to be dealt with—the rival Soviet network in the field must be eliminated. Ribar reports to Tito from Zagreb on 21 February 1942:

> Dear T. T.,
>
> We are writing to you primarily because we have noticed you have established contact with Grandpapa. I am attaching here the related message of Valdes [Kopinič's pseudonym from the Spanish Civil War]. We are very happy about your success. It is important now—and Valdes suggests the same—that you agree with Grandpapa about new operating conditions, so that both of you could keep operating without obstruction ... As regards the code, you must have noticed that some of the messages were incomprehensible in the beginning— they were encrypted using the new code ordered from the above. Valdes will be using that code and you will be using the old one ... Otherwise, arrests keep taking place here. Since our last letter, we have been forced to take even more radical measures: we are moving from Z[agreb] all the endangered cadres and are reorganizing the apparatus. Vlado and Fati [Bakarić and Hebrang] are being sent to the liberated areas these days because their position here has been compromised. Instead of them we will leave a single commissioner of the Croatian Papa [Central Committee of the Croatian Communist Party]. Fisher.

However, only three days later, the problem solved itself. The police stormed the GRU safe house in Vrapče. Srebrnjak, a GRU officer, fell courageously, as a true soldier. Hebrang was seriously wounded and captured. While in prison, and later in Stara Gradiška concentration camp, he was tortured. Vlado Popović, Tito's closest confidant who is running the party network in Croatia on his behalf, reports to Tito about Hebrang's conduct under torture:

> His conduct has been appropriate. He was offered a deal. He refused, saying he was a communist. He is blind in the right eye. We got a short letter from him saying: "I expect torture. But I am not concerned about my personal fate, which is sealed. My only concern is to keep carrying the flag of our party untainted until the end."

On 25 February, the very day when the police captured the badly wounded Hebrang, Ribar went to Velebit and told him that the two of them have to take a Sarajevo train the same evening. Using their contacts, they traveled to Foča (Herzegovina) via Bosnia and joined the Supreme Command there. Until his dying day, Velebit did not understand (or did not want to understand) the reason for such a hurry. He describes it in his memoirs:

Immediately after lunch, I met Lola and conveyed to him the news from Sarajevo, where I had just returned from. To my astonishment, Lola decided, without hesitation, that the two of us should go back to Sarajevo the same day, on a night train. I tried to remind him that he had planned some other meetings and that we should better postpone our departure for a few days. Lola wouldn't hear of it and he stuck to his decision. It would turn out later that he was almost a clairvoyant ...[2]

The underground organization planned to abduct Hebrang from the hospital, but the rescue attempt was canceled as he was transferred to the Stara Gradiška concentration camp while the action was being prepared. Six months later, in September 1942, he and thirty-odd other prisoners will be exchanged at a Partisan's initiative. Among the released prisoners was Olga Kohn, a friend of Srebrnjak's wife. Being Jewish and a member of the underground, Olga had been arrested in December 1941. She ended up in a concentration camp together with her husband Marko Kohn and their nine-year-old son Zlatko. Marko starved to death, and then their child died there, too.

The exchange of prisoners and high-ranking Ustashe officials took place near Okučani in Posavina. Hebrang left for Otočac and joined the Partisan headquarters, reassuming the position of party secretary. He will soon start living with Olga, who will become his wife.

A new inspection by the "Organizing Secretariat for Non-liberated Regions" was carried out immediately: Bevc and Fisher (Kardelj and Ribar) would once again carry out a limited purge and reshuffle some cadres from the Croatian leadership.

After the last wave of arrests, Kopinič and his wife Stela fled to Slovenia. Kopinič went to the Slovenian Liberation Front headquarters "Baza 20" in the Kočevski Rog region.[3] Thus, in February 1942, the "parallel line" in Zagreb was eliminated, just like Golubić's line earlier in Belgrade. Srebrnjak was killed, and Kopinič found shelter among his fellow Slovenes, who are still ambivalent toward Tito, torn between loyalty to him and to Moscow. The divine hand has intervened from the background once again, moving pieces on the chessboard in such a way that it meets the needs of our story's hero.[4]

By now, Tito has realized that his political legitimacy is a major problem. He cannot gain it territorially, by taking an area permanently, because he would have to organize a frontline around it. Instead, he will build his authority by means of the military and security apparatuses (for which he is well trained). But he needs something else, some umbrella organization, without which he and his combatants are merely a bunch of communist bandits (a "pack of vagabonds," as Goebbels once described Tito's Partisans). The Allied countries still recognize only Mihailović, who is sitting quietly on the Ravna Gora mountain, awaiting the Allied victory so that he could realize his political legitimacy. This is why Tito creates AVNOJ (the Anti-fascist Council for the National Liberation of Yugoslavia). Dimitrov had encouraged him to do so. True, in the beginning Dimitrov made some obstructions as regards the new body's "registration." An excerpt from his diary: "21 March 1942—I informed Walter that we have no intention to publish the appeal of his Supreme Partisan Command before we clearly define our relations with the Yugoslav government in London."

At the same time, the Comintern was entering its last days. Dimitrov and his associates were moved to Ufa, 1,400 kilometers away from Moscow, where radio propaganda would be their only job. Finally, on 1 June 1942, he sent a series of telegrams to Walter in which the earlier defined policy was revised. The alliance with the Chetniks is still on the agenda, but some differentiation is now allowed: some should be won over, others neutralized, and yet others—the wild ones—destroyed mercilessly. How does one carry out this politically sensitive triage? And why? As Đilas will later wittily explain to the English Labour Party members who will try to persuade him to adopt the national front-based course after the war, as if they themselves came from Ufa and not from Westminster, not all the Chetniks are equally guilty—so some of them, proposed Đilas, should be hung 100 times and some only twenty times.

Deep behind the lines in the Soviet Union, Dimitrov has finally done something useful—he instructs Tito to include people from prewar public life, such as artists and other distinguished figures, in Partisan propaganda. A national committee of support should be formed, consisting of acclaimed representatives of Yugoslav peoples who would promote the Partisan struggle in Yugoslavia and abroad. In other words, a recipe for the AVNOJ.[5]

According to the instruction, the AVNOJ would be a mere propaganda tool. However, over time, Tito will turn it into his convent and, at its second session in Jajce, it will proclaim his investiture and sovereignty. Nominally, the first session of AVNOJ was convened in Bihać on 27 November 1942 with the task of establishing "the closest and strongest links between the frontline and the rear, thus ensuring more successful war efforts." By its form and composition, AVNOJ is a government, but its members are the representatives of what we would today call civil society. They enjoy a positive reputation and possess moral authority and no political legitimation. Therefore, they will only make decisions that they are told to make.[6]

The Slovenian communists did not show up at the first AVNOJ session, having reservations about this new formation. Kardelj has not fully accepted this project of a joint government, as if he is having second thoughts about it and wants to see how it will all turn out. The Slovenes already have their national assembly—the Liberation Front (OF)—consisting of the Slovenian Communist Party and fourteen other organizations and associations such as the Engineers' Association, the Association of Slovenian Youth, United Unions, and so on. The liberal association Old Justice was expelled from the OF because its leader Dr Črtomir Nagode had opposed the assassinations of collaborationists and functionaries of the occupational administration carried out by the Security and Intelligence Service (VOS) based on the lists made by Comrade Zdenka Armič. After the war, Nagode was tried as a traitor and sentenced to death. As late as 2000, the Slovenian authorities, which always contained some incorrigible communists, refused to reveal the place where he had been buried.

Tito's Slovenian partners are flying their own flag, have their own separate army in which commands are given in the Slovene language, and—most importantly—they have their own separate apparatus. Comrade Armič's VOS is controlled by a three-member board of the Central Committee of the Slovenian party. But the "unitarization" of the Slovenian army will begin soon, in the autumn of 1942, when Tito appoints Arso Jovanović commander of the General Staff of the National Liberation Army and Partisan Detachments of Slovenia and sends him there with a group of General Staff officers, mostly Montenegrins.[7]

Tito left Foča on 25 May. He crossed Bosnia, came to Cincar Mountain in June, took Jajce in September, and entered Drvar in October. In Drvar, he presented the colors to the newly established 2nd Proletarian Brigade. In November, he will take Bihać and, in late December, organize the First Congress of the AVNOJ there. By that time, he will have covered thousands of kilometers, although it is merely 350 kilometers by road. The Operational Group of the Supreme Command is formed, with Koča Popović—who else?—as its commander. But this is too much for the Oberkommando der Wehrmacht. On 16 December, while the AVNOJ delegates are having sessions in Bihać, Hitler summons Colonel-General Alexander Löhr, commander-in-chief of the southeast, and orders him to destroy Yugoslav resistance.

21

THE BRIDGE OF BLOOD

THE NERETVA RIVER 1943

Tito was almost destroyed by his own success. Now that he has gathered a proletarian army and created a whole guerrilla state in the Bosnian mountains, the Oberkommando der Wehrmacht decided they had had enough of that mess in the middle of "Fortress Europe" and ordered two Austrians, Luftwaffe Colonel-General Löhr, commander-in-chief of the southeast who had taken the Dodecanese, and army general of Croatian origin Lothar von Rendulic commander of the 2nd Panzer Army, to destroy the communist Partisan army led by some bluffer named Tito.[1]

The first part of the operation, "Fall Weiss" (Case white), included the strategic encirclement of the main operational force of the National Liberation Army in Bosnia. That force consisted of Tito's Supreme Command, the 1st and 2nd Proletarian Divisions (commanded by Koča Popović and Peko Dapčević, respectively), 9th Dalmatian Division (commanded by Krstulović), and two Krajina corps—some 40,000 fighters in all. It was planned that the high-quality German units—the 7th SS Mountain Division Prinz Eugen[2] and 369th Division of Wehrmacht—would enter the encircled area, cutting the "liberated territories" in half. Following them would be the 717th and 718th Infantry Divisions advancing from the Sarajevo area in order to carry out the pincer maneuver. There was a large number of Italians—six divisions of poor-quality troops ordered to block the Partisan retreat to Dalmatia. There were also four Croatian Home Guard army units with heavy weapons, one Ustashe

137

semi-brigade, and some 10,000 Chetniks. All in all, around 100,000 troops, tanks, numerous vehicles, and the entire NDH air force. A balance of forces indicating rather bleak prospects for the Partisans, who, on top of it all, had their hospital with 4,000 wounded with them.

The operation had three phases (Weiss 1, 2, and 3) and began by exerting pressure on broad parts of Lika and Krajina, mostly inhabited by Serbs, and continued by taking the towns in the "Bihać Republic"—Drvar, Livno, Jajce. Crushing the main force—pushed into the canyons of the Montenegrin mountains in the meantime—was supposed to be the third phase. As soon as the operation began with a breakthrough—forcing the Partisans to withdraw to central Bosnia—the strategic encirclement was complete. Soon afterward, the Partisans were cramped on the bank of the cold and deep Neretva River. Tito ordered all the bridges to be destroyed, including the large railway bridge. He thus protected his rear and cut off his own line of retreat—burnt all bridges behind him—and counterattacked with his entire force. Ten Partisan brigades swooped down on the German 717th Division. But even with only two infantry regiments and one artillery regiment, this Jäger division is an impressive war machine. The Partisans—there are about as many of them as Germans (because Partisan brigades are actually battalions)—fight it all day on Makljen mountain pass, but the battle ultimately ends in a stalemate. When they realized that there was no way through, Krstulović's 9th Dalmatian Division was ordered to climb the remnants of the destroyed bridge by night and destroy the Chetnik bunker on the opposite bank. Logs will then be used to improvise a crossing for the whole main force. General Vladimir Smirnov, the man who blew up the Neretva bridge, gives his account:

> It took me a while to come up with the concept of a cantilever bridge tied up to the metal skeleton of the destroyed bridge. It was the only possible solution, given the fact that the weathered telegraph posts were our main material. It took my young sappers around nineteen hours to build such a bridge under harsh conditions. The work was very dangerous and exhausting. Working in the dark, often hanging upside down above the Neretva's icy rapids, these brave and loyal men really performed their duty in the most honorable way. Tomorrow at night, I escorted Comrade Tito across the bridge, in between the units of the 1st Proletarian Brigade.[3]

There are two interpretations of the event. According to the official account, the destruction of the bridge was a brilliant diversion devised by Tito that enabled the Partisan forces to break out (although they had to leave behind 200 trucks and dozens of tanks and cannons captured from the Italians). According to the second interpretation, it was a mistake partly corrected by the desperate efforts of the people sentenced to death if they surrendered.

This glorified strategic diversion was analyzed regularly in the guerrilla tactics' manuals studied at Yugoslav and foreign military academies. The famous film *The Battle of Neretva* (1969), directed by Veljko Bulajić, also mythologizes the "Battle for the Wounded," taking the limelight off the cruel reality of the episode. The Battle of Neretva was only an introduction to the developments that will lead to Tito's great political victory as well as the tragic loss of human lives.

An account based on first-hand experience can be found in Krstulović's war memoirs, which could not be published until 2012—twenty-four years after his death.

While the proletarian and Krajina units were engaged in the failed breakthrough at Makljen, the 9th Dalmatian and 7th Banija Brigades stayed with the wounded, preparing to take on the infinitely stronger Italian troops and Chetniks who were advancing from the lower reaches of the Neretva and the 7th SS Division approaching them from the Livno–Duvno direction.

At this point, things are as clear to Tito as they possibly can be: the columns with stretcher cases are moving at a speed of about 2 kilometers per hour and, if the entire main force and wounded stay together, no one will ever break out from the encirclement. He calls for Krstulović and orders him to leave the main force together with the hospital. The main force will break through the Neretva using Smirnov's makeshift bridge.

It is clear from Krstulović's memoirs that he did not realize what was at the bottom of that decision—he simply thought Tito was making a mistake. Krstulović refuses to carry out the order and—in a terrible moment—he even threatens Tito. He says he would be ready to kill him if it wasn't for his family (Krstulović has his family with him).[4] After that, Krstulović was of course crossed forever. But at the moment, Tito has changed the order, so the hospital and the 9th Brigade also crossed the river and, having joined the main force, headed for the mountains, thus temporarily relieving the pressure they had been under. However, he immediately disbanded the 9th Division and attached its brigades to other units. Krstulović's Dalmatian army is thus finished for good and, from this time on, Krstulović himself will only be playing a secondary role.

The German casualties at the Neretva included 335 dead and 101 missing in action, as well as 1,200 temporarily placed out of action. According to their estimates, 8,500 Partisans were killed and 2,010 captured. The whole of western Bosnia was mopped up, and all men over fifteen years were deported to Germany to work there. The operation, which took one month, ended on 18 February 1943. This massive battle had elements of a civil war in itself. Croats accounted for a large part of the Partisan side, but also of the Axis side—in addition to the Ustashe and Home Guard units, one *German* division also included them. Even some SS members were Yugoslav citizens, mostly from Croatian parts of the Pannonian Valley.

Defeated and exhausted, the remnants of the Partisan forces were now withdrawing into the mountains of Montenegro, toward the Sutjeska River. At the moment of desperation, Tito decided to send negotiators to Zagreb. They were accepted as parliamentarians in Sarajevo and flown by plane to Zagreb.

When they arrived in the city, they were accommodated in the Feldkommandature building. Đilas and Velebit met officers of the German military intelligence—Abwehr. Tito had given them a rather extensive mandate for the negotiations, in the presence of Ranković, Koča Popović, and General Velimir Terzić from his Supreme Headquarters. Nominally, they were to discuss a prisoner exchange, and then claim that their main enemy were the Chetniks, not the Germans, and to express readiness to cease actions against the Wehrmacht.

The first stage of the negotiations in Zagreb must have been successful, because the negotiators have returned to the Partisan Supreme Command to submit their report. After that, Velebit goes to the 6th East Bosnian Brigade (which had lost contact with Tito's Supreme Command), carrying letters with the orders for the suspension of attacks on the enemy units and rail communications. He goes to Zagreb for the second time, and with the assistance of the German army, he goes to the headquarters of the Slavonian Third Operational Zone in Pakrac. Then he returns to Zagreb once again and there, in the former Jockey Club in the city center, discusses a truce and the political dimensions of such neutrality with the German commanding general in Croatia, Edmund Glaise von Horstenau. Asked if the Partisans would react in the case of an Allied invasion of Dalmatia, Velebit told him that the Partisans, recognizing only the sovereignty of AVNOJ, would put up armed resistance to any landing that would not be authorized by that body. He also added that the arrival of Allied troops would undoubtedly benefit the Partisans' bitter enemy—Chetniks, facilitating their attempts to restore the monarchy and enable the return of the government-in-exile from London. Clearly, it was a serious offer, but with a slight restriction: "We never really discussed the possibility of carrying out joint operations of any kind with the Germans."

The subject of the so-called March negotiations in Zagreb remains unknown. No other accounts have been found or preserved.[5] According to the invaluable memoirs of the main political commissar for the Balkans, German high representative Hermann Neubacher, Hitler refused any form of negotiations or collaboration with Tito. When the Führer asked "Is Tito a true communist"? Neubacher had to reply that he was. Hitler then logically concluded that Tito's loyalty was only to Moscow. Consequently, there could be no negotiations. Churchill would not be so narrow-minded later on.[6]

At that moment, the Partisans are indeed in a disastrous situation and have nothing with which to trade. Naturally, Tito never notified Moscow he had sent his most reliable men—Đilas, practically his deputy, and Velebit, head of Partisan diplomacy and keeper of all secrets—to negotiate with the enemy. When he mentioned it to Moscow later on, he tried to diminish the whole thing, explaining he had merely been probing the ground for the exchange of prisoners. Upon hearing this, the Moscow leadership was highly disgruntled and reacted angrily. Since the German army does not recognize the Partisans as a belligerent, the only thing that could have been negotiated was some kind of armistice, détente, inactivation of the Partisans (like with the Chetniks—not active collaboration, but still). In Moscow, they understood it perfectly well. Any negotiations actually meant acceptance of collaboration with the enemy.

When all this is stripped bare, it is clear that the real subject was the fate of 4,000 wounded Partisans in the central hospital who had crossed to the eastern bank of the Neretva with Krstulović. Either a truce will be negotiated and they will be saved, or they will all be left to their fate, like the Partisan General Kosta Nađ did when he received the order to leave the camp-followers during his march to the Neretva. Nađ later outranked even Koča Popović because he had manifested reliability that had exceeded that of those legendary generals and heroes of the revolution. People like Koča and Vicko never became members of the Supreme Command. Their careers ended with their marginalization under the surveillance of the secret police.

Later on, Tito will even accuse Đilas and Velebit of having fooled him as regards the subjects of the negotiations. However, as there was no agreement—there could not have been one—act 2 of the heroic tragedy began. In May 1943, Löhr's operation will continue on the Sutjeska River, when the Fall Schwartz (Case black) plan will be carried out. This operation was even more ambitious than the previous one. The idea was to disarm the Montenegrin Chetniks as an unreliable element in the Balkan theater of operations and, at the same time, destroy the main Partisan force crowded on the rugged terrain between the canyons of the Tara and Piva Rivers and the formidable Durmitor masiff with its dozens of peaks exceeding 2,000 meters.

Four German divisions were provided for the operation. The elite 1st Mountain Division was brought from the Caucasus, where it had captured Mt Elbrus (5,642m). It was a particularly strong unit with 18,000 troops. Two "light" divisions, the 118th Jäger Division (transformed 718th Division) and 194th Jäger Division (both consisting of two instead of three infantry regiments) were also involved. Also the 369th (Croatian) Legionnaire ("Devil's") Division, 7th SS Division Prinz Eugen, and 4th Regiment of the Brandenburg commandos (German rangers). Then there was a panzer battalion, three inferior Italian divisions, two Bulgarian combined infantry regiments, and a Croatian Home Guard Jäger Brigade with artillery. All in all, troops of a much better quality than the ones used in the Battle of Neretva.

The Partisan units are made up of the very same combatants who had been through the winter hell of the Neretva in the Fourth Enemy Offensive. They include Koča Popović's 1st Proletarian Division, Dapčević's 2nd Proletarian Division, Colonel Pavle Jakšić's 7th Banija Division, and Colonel Sava Kovačević's 3rd Shock Division strengthened by the 1st Dalmatian Brigade of the dissolved 9th Dalmatian Division.

The first phase of the German operation was carried out with ease—the Chetniks were disarmed and captured, together with the Chetnik Commander Vojvoda Pavle Đurišić, without losses on either side. But the Germans had to release them after the demand of the governor of Montenegro, Italian General Pirzio Biroli, who called their capture a violation of sovereign rights in the Italian zone of occupation. They were deported, with only 800 of them left, and turned into mountain porters—the Sherpas of Durmitor.

Near Foča on the River Drina, the Partisans crushed the Chetniks and the Italian Alpine Division Taurinense (some of whom will later join Tito's army as the Garibaldi Division). The second-class Axis troops are no match for the fanatical fighters in rags. But the German army is about to step on the scene.

The 1st Proletarian Brigade was sent to capture Vučevo Peak to enable the Supreme Command's operational group to cross the Sutjeska there and then head north, toward Sarajevo. The proletarians took Vučevo after hand-to-hand fighting, but the German forces took the whole Sutjeska Valley in the meantime, and, as a result, the Partisan main force ended up in a tight encirclement, together with 3,000 wounded and 1,000 typhoid patients in the central hospital.

1. Formal reception on the occasion of the fifth anniversary of the State Security Administration, Belgrade, May, 1944 (left to right, Aleksandar Ranković, Ivan 'Stevo' Krajačić, Slobodan Penezić 'Krcun', Cvetko Uzunovski, Maks Baće, Nikola Vujanović, Jovo Kapičić, Boris Krajger, Veljko Mićunović, Andrija Pejović, Uglješa Danilović, Svetislav Stefanović 'Ćeća').

2. J. B. Tito's vacation on the Brijuni Islands, July, 1949,

3. The reception for John Phillips, photographer for *Life* magazine. Brijuni islands, July, 1949.

4. First snow on 15 Romania Street (later Užička), J. B. Tito's residence, Belgrade, December 29, 1949.

5. A game of pool at 15 Užička Street, March, 1950 (Edvard Kardelj, an unknown guard, Tito).

6. Visit to Pula airport and the inspection of the first shipment of US airplanes, February, 1952 (foreground, Edvard Kardelj, J. B. Tito, Vladimir Bakarić; background, Koča Popović, Jovanka Budisavljević and Ivo Popović 'Đani', Tito's physician).

7. The reception in honor of Louis Mountbatten, 1st Earl Mountbatten of Burma. Brijuni Islands, June, 1952 (from left to right, J. B. Tito, Louis Mountbatten, Srećko Manola, Sir Ivo Mallet, British ambassador to Yugoslavia).

8. The reception for the members of the British Conservative Party in the Yugoslav Embassy in London during Tito's visit to the United Kingdom. London, March, 1953 (foreground, Sir Winston Churchill, J. B. Tito; background, Sir Ivo Mallet with spectacles).

9. Visit to the Acropolis during the official visit to Greece. Athens, June, 1964.

10. Grand reception at the Delhi Municipal Committee when J. B. Tito was bestowed an honorary citizenship of Delhi, December, 1954 (Josip Broz Tito and Jawaharlal Nehru).

11. Formal dinner party with the Maharaja of Gwalior. Gwalior, December, 1954 (from left to right, Radivoje Berović, Tito's private physician, Ivan 'Stevo' Krajačić, an unknown lady, Josip Broz Tito, an unknown lady, Aleksandar Ranković).

12 Passing through Nyaung-U on the way to visit the temples of Bagan, Burma, January, 1955 (Josip Broz Tito and General Milan Žeželj, chief of the military cabinet).

13. Receiving Gamal Abdel Nasser, president of Egypt, on the yacht *Galeb* during the return voyage from state visits to India and Burma. Suez, February, 1955 (left, Gamal Abdel Nasser, Abdel Hakim Amer; right, J. B. Tito, Aleksandar Ranković and Marko Nikezić, the Yugoslav ambassador in Cairo).

14. Josip Broz Tito receives Nikita Khrushchev during the first official visit of the Soviet delegation to Yugoslavia. The White Palace, Belgrade, May, 1955.

15. The first official visit of the Soviet delegation to Tito's Yugoslavia. The White Palace, Belgrade, May 1955 (from left to right, Anastas Mikoyan, Nikita Khrushchev, Jovanka Broz, Josip Broz Tito, Nikolai Bulganin, Andrei Gromyko).

16. Formal reception for the Soviet delegation at the White Palace, Belgrade, May, 1955. The crowd greets Mikoyan, Bulganin, Tito, Khrushchev and Jovanka Broz; also present, General Bogdan Oreščanin in his uniform with the medal of the Order of the People's Hero, Miloš Minić with a bow tie, Spasenija 'Cana' Babović with black gloves, General Ivan Rukavina, and the chief of protocol of the president's cabinet Dr Sloven Smodlaka with a bow tie, in the right corner.

17. Josip Broz Tito awarded a medal by Emperor Haile Selassie during the official visit to Ethiopia. Addis Ababa, December, 1955 (in the background, Dr Sloven Smodlaka, Milan Žeželj and Prince Amha Selassie, the emperor's son).

18. A motorcade through Moscow streets on the way to the residence, June, 1956.

19. The official meeting between Nasser, Nehru and J. B. Tito. Brijuni Islands, Vanga, July, 1956 (Dr Smodlaka in the background).

20. J. B. Tito and Khrushchev on the terrace of the White Villa. Brijuni Islands, September, 1956.

21. J. B. Tito and Ho Chi Minh, the president of the People's Republic of Vietnam in Tito's speedboat. Brijuni Islands, August, 1957.

22. The reception for Marshall Zhukov, Soviet minister of defense, at the hunting lodge, Brdo near Kranj, October, 1957 (in the background Ivan Gošnjak).

23. Grand reception on the occasion of J. B. Tito's official visit to India. Delhi, January, 1959 (Rajendra Prasad, J. B. Tito).

24. The reception for the Cuban goodwill mission headed by Ernesto Che Guevara. Brijuni Islands, August, 1959.

Tito makes a decision he has been postponing since last winter: the army will split into two operational groups. The proletarian and Krajina units will form the first group and will try to break through by crossing the Sutjeska to the north. The second group will consist of the Montenegrins and Dalmatians, who will join the central hospital and try to cross the River Tara toward Montenegro. This is allegedly being done in order to "stretch the enemy forces." In fact, the main force is leaving the wounded and is attempting to breakthrough in order to save at least part of the troops. In that critical moment, an unusual bunch falls from the sky—William Deakin,[7] Captain Bill Stewart, and four other members of the British Military Mission. Deakin is a British historian, Oxford University professor, and the literary secretary of the British wartime premier Sir Winston Churchill. Stewart works for the military intelligence service; he was a prewar consul and head of the intelligence center in Zagreb and speaks Croatian. Nominally, they are the British Imperial General Staff's military mission at the Partisan Supreme Command. In fact, Deakin's duty is to conduct political reconnaissance directly for Churchill.

Although the reports of the British intelligence service described the Partisans as "extremists and bandits" as late as 1942, the vigilant MI-1B (the analytical section of the wiretapping service in Bletchley Park) initiated a change of this perception of the situation in field. Based on German dispatches decrypted as part of Operation Ultra (decoding the German signals sent using the Enigma cipher machine), one can tell that the Chetniks are not fighting the Axis powers at all, whereas the Partisans have distinguished themselves (an MI-1B message from September 1943 reads: "The heroes of the hour are undoubtedly the Partisans").

In April 1943, while the Battle of Neretva was raging in central Bosnia, the RAF parachuted three members of a reconnaissance unit near Brinje in Lika. Two were Canadians and one was British, and all of them were of Yugoslav descent and could speak the local language. When they were taken to the headquarters of the National Liberation Army and Partisan Detachments of Croatia, Commander Ivan Rukavina[8] recognized the Canadians because they had fought together in the International Brigades during the Spanish Civil War.

After the reconnaissance team had established radio contact with the Special Operations Executive (SOE) headquarters in Cairo, Deakin's mission was parachuted to Tito's Supreme Command. Ending up in the thick of combat, Deakin will have an opportunity to witness everything for himself and understand who is on whose side, who is fighting and who is not, and what kind of a fight it is.

Encircled at the Sutjeska, the Partisan forces are desperately trying to break out. Fierce fighting has been going on for three weeks. The 1st Proletarian Brigade has lost 1,500 fighters, almost a third of its initial force. The somewhat stronger 2nd Proletarian (2,600 fighters) also lost one-third of its force. In the fight with the 118th Jäger Division, the 2nd Dalmatian Brigade (part of the 2nd Proletarian Division) had 600 casualties in a single day and was reduced to a platoon. Proportionally, the 7th Krajina Division suffered even worse losses: 1,400 killed out of an initial 2,500 fighters. At Milinklade on the Ozren Mountain, in the encirclement around the Supreme Command, Tito was lightly wounded by aircraft bomb shrapnel on 9 June. British intelligence officer Captain Stewart, Tito's bodyguard, and a few Partisans were killed; Deakin was wounded, too.

On Zelengora Mountain, the 369th Legionnaire Division (Devil's Division) is tightening its circle around Koča Popović. The Devil's Division includes 8,000 mobilized Croats under the command of 3,500 German officers and non-commissioned officers. Koča decides to break out of the encirclement in the northern direction. Although Tito does not give his approval, Koča orders a charge. Antonije Isaković, Serbian writer, member of the Academy of Arts and Sciences, remembers:

> I think it was the only time when the whole 1st Proletarian charged, to a man. Across that clearing. We were all in the same line. All of us, all the battalion and brigade commanders, all the couriers, all the cooks, all the medics—they were all charging. We were all there and we started running. And we all knew: there was no going back!

On that day, 10 June, on Tjentište Plateau, the 1st Proletarian Division crushed the Kampfgruppe Höhne after having crossed the rain-swollen icy Sutjeska. The next day, the 1st Proletarian also repulsed the Kampfgruppe Wertmüller, which was advancing from the west. The operational staff of the 369th Division headquarters reported to the Wehrmacht headquarters in Zagreb that the 2nd battalion of the 724th Regiment of the 369th Division "withdrew in total disorder." It reads: "Commanders report that their battalion has been crushed and that the Partisans have broken out." Löhr forwards the report to Berlin, calling it "a local breakthrough."

Using the "instinct of a natural born warrior," as Krstulović comments in his memoirs, Peko Dapčević ignores Tito's orders and instantly leads his division through the opening created in the enemy lines. Supreme Command follows. They all break out and head for Bosnia, toward Sarajevo. For a moment, Tito was desperate. He considered replacing Koča for disobeying the orders. Unlike the General Staff officers in the Supreme Command, who deploy troops on the maps, Koča charges in the front ranks, fueled by his warrior enthusiasm. It was the stellar moment of his military career.

The seriously wounded were left in the River Piva valley. Aided by dogs, SS men were systematically searching the area; they were tracking them down and killing them. The lightly wounded followed Kovačević, commander of the 3rd Shock Division, in which the Dalmatians from the 9th Division are incorporated. On the same day, 13 June 1943, Kovačević will try to break out from the bridgehead on the right bank of the Sutjeska. He was killed while leading a charge and firing his machinegun. All the wounded were slaughtered. It was here that the Chetniks killed Ivan Goran Kovačić, a Croatian poet and film critic for *Novosti*, the paper that once wrote about Comrade Tito so sympathetically.

Having escaped death and with a shrapnel wound to his shoulder, Tito is heading for Bosnia, to a new adventure. He is escorted by the Supreme Command, his mistress "Zdenka" Paunović, and Deakin (who is also lightly wounded). Once again, Comrade Tito has gained maximum political capital from a near military defeat.

The reports sent by Deakin and Stewart (the latter was killed at the Sutjeska) were substantiated by the emissaries to the headquarters of General Mihailović, as well as by the messages electronically intercepted and analyzed in Bletchley Park.

The bottom line of all this intelligence is this: Tito's Partisans are fighting, and Chetniks are standing aside, not engaging the Axis forces. In a memo to the War Cabinet of 10 January 1944, Foreign Secretary Anthony Eden (who publicly recognized Tito's Partisans as an allied force in his speech of 14 December 1943) gives an accurate description of the situation. In Yugoslavia, he says, there are two resistance movements. One in Serbia proper, led by Mihailović, and the other—the Partisans—spreading everywhere. Mihailović's army is about 15,000 strong but is not much use for the war effort, because Mihailović is now busy preparing to deal with the "communist threat," as he (correctly) perceives the Partisans. In contrast to him, the Partisans have a huge, organized army of perhaps 200,000 fighters, whose primary goal is, undoubtedly, fighting against the Germans. For the British, the situation is complex—the king and his Chetniks represent the best political option, but they have no military relevance in Yugoslavia. On the contrary, they have become one of the factors in a widening split.

This is where Sir Fitzroy Hew Royle Maclean of Dunconnel dramatically appears on the stage.[9] The thirty-two-year-old Conservative MP and

Churchill's confidant was parachuted into the Balkan mountains in order to find a reliable answer to the question of who was killing the most Germans in Yugoslavia.

"Tito is definitely a man one should count on," Maclean will explain. "Tito is a communist, but ..." This "but" would always keep hanging in the air because Comrade Tito was a great communicator: he would always open a door, never close it; he would listen before talking; and he would say exactly what others wanted him to say while keeping his opinion to himself. His opinion was perfectly adaptable anyway—it depended on the priorities of a fail-proof survivor who had survived every disaster by coming out of it even stronger. Maclean recalls:

> Looking back, I think my mission to Yugoslavia was the most important event in my life. Of course, I did not know it then. Mr Churchill told me he wanted me to go there, make my opinion about the situation and then report to him. While we were having this conversation, someone entered the room with the news of Mussolini's capitulation. I remember Churchill turning to me and saying: "This makes your mission all the more important. You must go there as soon as possible."
>
> I was dropped into Bosnia. I landed near a small town called Mrkonjić Grad. The Partisans were waiting for me. I remember my encounter with the first Yugoslav I ever met—now my old friend, Vlatko Velebit. In the evening of the next day we went to Jajce, where Tito's headquarters was.
>
> And there, under a tree, Tito was sitting—or Commander, as they all called him. He was studying a map. For the outside world, Tito was still a vague figure. He was a stout man, about fifty years of age. His clear, light blue eyes were looking directly at me. His face was tanned, with traces of exhaustion. One could see he had been through a lot. He seemed very resolute, a person on whom nothing is lost. We shook hands. A guard brought us a bottle of schnapps ...

The two met on 18 September. It would be a turning point in their careers and biographies. From a commando, Maclean becomes a political operative of the highest order, preeminent Cold Warrior in the future, with Tito as his lifetime project. For Tito, the encounter is a meeting with destiny. He is now leaving the underground world, revealing the undreamed-of aspects of his ambition—to become a statesman and a historical leader.

22

MARSHAL

JAJCE 1943

The Comintern has been pushed into the background. Moved first to Kuybyshev and then to Ufa, it is now even physically away from the Moscow vortex. Out of sight, out of mind. Located some 1,400 kilometers away from the Kremlin, Ufa is the capital of the Bashkir Republic. It was founded by Ivan the Terrible, which indicates the level of local communal standards. This is the place where the Comintern's all-star team—proven Stalinists and future leaders of the Eastern Bloc—are now bivouacking. The Germans are represented by the always reliable Pieck and the totally loyal Walter Ulbricht. The ideologically correct Czech Klement Gottwald is with them—but not for long because he is a syphilitic and an alcoholic. Also here are Mátyás Rákosi ("Stalin's best student," as he calls himself) and Ernő Gerő (real name Ernst Singer), who will personally lead Russian tanks during the 1956 Soviet intervention in Hungary. Brutal Ana Pauker has landed the lead female role—she will be introducing communism to Romania (however, she will ultimately be replaced due to lack of enthusiasm: she will hesitate with the construction of the Danube–Black Sea Canal conceived by Stalin). This Bashkir avant-garde would not be complete without the Bulgarian convoy: Dimitrov and the inevitable Kolarov, accompanied by Dimitrov's deputy in charge of Western Europe, the Italian Stalinist Togliatti.

The Comintern and Dimitrov's bunch are not exactly very busy in Ufa. As Dimitrov's diary tells us, the only thing that raises dust in discussions are Tito and his Partisans.

The Comintern was soon to be dissolved. It expired in the summer of 1943. Fascist Italy collapsed between July and September of the same year. Tito's Partisans disarmed some 200,000 Italian troops and got hold of huge quantities of war materiel. The Oberkommando der Wehrmacht (OKW) will not stay on the sidelines. Here is the account of General Milorad "Mića" Janković, the commander of Tito's Escort Battalion:

> As early as on 6 August 1943, immediately after our forces had managed to break out of encirclement in the 5th Offensive, Hitler summoned Rendulic to his headquarters. Anticipating an Italian surrender within months, or even weeks, he gave him two orders: first, eliminate Tito as soon as possible and, second, disarm the Italian forces in Yugoslavia. Our strength was estimated at 100,000 and the Italian strength was estimated at 300,000 troops.

The OKW had to consolidate its line of defense along the Adriatic coast because the Allies reached Naples and Bari in late September and would be able to land in the Balkans next. Hitler's personal bodyguard, the 1st Panzer Regiment of the Leibstandarte SS Adolf Hitler Division (LSSAH), was sent to retake Istria and Dalmatia. Crushed at Kursk in the crucial battle of July 1943, the unit first rests and replenishes its ranks in northern Italy and then, as the most important unit of the 2nd SS Panzer Corps in Operation Istria (Unternehmen Istrien), bursts into the eastern Adriatic and takes Trieste, Pula, and Rijeka. At the same time, the 3rd SS Panzer Corps takes Slovenia and secures communications with Greece, where Army Corps F is still deployed. The central massif is in the Partisans' hands, and Tito has gotten hold of substantial quantities of Italian arms. He sends Krstulović and Ribar to retake Dalmatia. Deakin accompanies them. Ribar is predestined for big things—he is running this operation of decisive political and military repercussions. He controls the volatile Krstulović, who adores him, and manipulates the Oxford don who fell from the sky—he persuades him to make a speech at the central square in the temporarily liberated Split as a representative of the Western Allies while he translates it consecutively. After that, Tito decides to send Ribar to Cairo and London as a plenipotentiary representative to the Western Allies. But, while boarding a plane in Glamočko Polje field, two days before the second session of the AVNOJ in the Bosnian town of Jajce, a German Storch comes out of nowhere and drops a bomb. Ribar is killed at the age of twenty-seven. His younger brother Jurica, a lawyer and painter of some fame, was also killed a month earlier, while fighting in a Montenegrin brigade sided with the Italian division "Venezia" that had joined the Partisans. Tito would not convey the terrible news to their father Ivan

Ribar, the "speaker" of the AVNOJ—the Partisan parliament in the woods—before the session was over. The whole thing was too important.

Tito himself chose the delegates for the second session of the AVNOJ. No more excuses for the Slovenes—they will attend it in large numbers. Acclaimed painter Božidar Jakac, the author of Tito's semi-official portrait,[1] remembers:

> There was this incredible moment at the session, when our president of the Liberation Front, Comrade Jože Vidmar, proposed on behalf of our Slovene delegation that the rank of marshal be introduced and that Comrade Tito become the first marshal of Yugoslavia.

Antun Augustinčić was summoned to sculpt a bust of his fellow countryman and old buddy from the Zagreb days. Here is Augustinčić's account:

> There was one particular moment at the session when one could see the extraordinary cleverness and a huge talent of our Marshal. All the delegates underlined in their speeches that we should demand from the Allies to recognize the AVNOJ. After all of them had said their piece, the Marshal stood up and said: "No! We shall not demand the recognition of the AVNOJ from the Allies because they cannot give it to us. For them, there is still the king and the royal embassies and they cannot give it to us at the moment. And if they cannot give it to us, it would be a slap in our face. And if you let them slap you, they will keep slapping you. We will therefore demand that our army be recognized as an equal Allied force—a war ally!" And indeed, we won this recognition immediately.

The statesman-in-the-making needs statesman's paraphernalia. Actually, an entire image design. If he was not all spruced up, he would look like just another one of the dirty, unshaved, and crumpled men around him, and it would be impossible to present the whole thing as a heroic saga. He was always cleanly shaven and properly attired, out of his manly pride, but the future statesman's PR requires some basic elements: an elegant uniform sewn by a bespoke tailor from Zagreb, a flattering portrait by a Vienna-educated painter from Slovenia, and a statue by a renowned European master who routinely renders immortality to European leaders by sculpting them in bronze, mounted or not. Vladimir Nazor, a well-known poet who joined the Partisans despite his advanced age, wrote a few poems that were instantly set to music by composer Oskar Danon in such a way to be fit for the Partisan choirs singing in the glory of the newly minted Marshal Tito.

As he cannot be just Walter, or Comrade Tito, or general secretary any more—and it is too early to even think about a presidential title—the title of marshal will do for the time being. It will be proposed by the Slovenians—in other words, with Kardelj's support. But instead of Kardelj himself, who would have to disobey the Comintern directives on two separate communist parties, the formal proponent will be Josip Vidmar, president of Osvobodilna Fronta (Slovenian National Front) and the future president of the Slovenian Academy of Sciences. No improvisation here. Everyone is playing by the notes.

In November 1943, a US delegation arrives in Tehran for the Allied conference codenamed "Eureka," with a bundle of raw estimates and worst-case scenarios of the realistic Harry Hopkins, Roosevelt's special advisor, who anticipates Soviet domination in postwar Europe. On the first day of the conference, 28 November, Tito sends a telegram to Stalin, notifying him of the decision he is to make in Jajce the next day, 29 November. The message includes a sentence crucial for the fate of King Peter II: "A British general has already informed us that the British government would not insist on assisting the king and Yugoslav government in London." The only "British general" around was Brigadier Maclean.

On 29 November, the second day of the first meeting of the Big Three (when Roosevelt and Churchill first met Stalin), the AVNOJ was recognized as an Allied force. The same date was included in new Yugoslavia's coat of arms, created by Kun and Augustinčić. On the same day, the AVNOJ was "constituted as the supreme legislative and executive representative body of Yugoslavia and the supreme representative of the sovereignty of the peoples of Yugoslavia and the entire state of Yugoslavia." As a result of this *fait accompli*, a new state was created in the Bosnian woods.

The AVNOJ presidency was also elected, but Tito has to be cautious and create the new government in accordance with the national front format. The AVNOJ's government cabinet—the so-called National Committee for the Liberation of Yugoslavia (NKOJ)—is also formed, but its political capacity is nil. AVNOJ is merely a front for the revolution carried out by the party. Marshal Tito is the prime minister of the NKOJ (which means that his transformation from an underground fighter to a statesman has been completed). The deputy prime ministers are Kardelj, Vladimir Ribnikar (a Soviet resident in Belgrade), Božidar Magovac, and Franjo Gaži (bourgeois politicians from the Croatian Peasant Party—HSS—transported here from Zagreb by the reliable "Stevo" Krajačić), and Frane Frol from the same, "left" faction of HSS (appointed commissioner for justice). Dr Josip Smodlaka, a prewar politician and a member of the Yugoslav Committee in the First World War, who in the 1920s had proposed that the Kingdom SHS be renamed Yugoslavia, was appointed commissioner for external relations. Slovenian Christian socialist

Edvard Kocbek became commissioner for education, and the Orthodox priest Vlada Zečević became commissioner for internal affairs. Nominally, of course, Comrade Marko—Aleksandar Ranković—is the one who runs these things, although he has no visible function in the government. Other communists participating in the government include Politburo member Ivan Milutinović, Sreten "Black" Žujović, Hebrang, and Nikola Petrović as commissioners for trade. So, the leaders of all the phantom national front parties included to fit Moscow's combinations (Tito, Kardelj, Hebrang) are here, as well as Moscow's confidants (Ribnikar, Žujović, Petrović) and a number of decorative members with a bourgeois political background. Tito does not put his own men into the first row—Bakarić, for instance, is Smodlaka's discreet deputy, and Ranković is not mentioned at all. Formally, this is a perfect national front government, but one left without any power after it has performed its designated role—providing Tito and his communist apparatus with the façade of legitimacy.

After the Tehran Conference, all of the Allied logistics, arms, and media support are redirected to the Partisans. General Mihailović, who was glorified as a leader of resistance for almost three years and about whose heroic fight a film was made in the United States,[2] has now been shelved. The British will try to keep some capacity of the government-in-exile by exerting pressure on Tito through Moscow. Tito's telegram on the self-proclamation of the sovereignty of AVNOJ was a nasty surprise for Stalin and enraged him. But Tito had already arrived where he had wanted to be—at the intersection of two spheres of interest. He will be perfecting this kind of positioning for the rest of his life. But he cannot show it yet, and for the moment it is only implicit.

23

EAGLE

BARI 1944

A large Soviet air force squadron took off from Moscow's Central Airport on 17 January 1944. Twelve C-47 transport aircraft were escorted by two fighter squadrons of long-range Yak-9DD aircraft. They flew to Astrakhan and then proceeded to Baku, Tehran, Baghdad, Tripoli, and Tunis. From there, they flew over the Mediterranean Sea and finally landed at the airport near Bari on Italy's Adriatic coast. At that moment, on the Eastern Front, fighting is going on at the Dnieper. The Germans are still holding Crimea and Leningrad is still under siege. In Italy, 300 kilometers north of Bari, the battle for Monte Cassino on the German Gustav Line has begun.

The Soviet expedition is headed by General Lieutenant Nikolai Vasilyevich Korneyev, former commander of the 11th Army in the Battle of Kursk, who now works for the GRU. Korneyev is a decorated Stalingrad veteran, but—what is more important for this mission—he also did two perilous shifts in China in the 1920s and '30s—the man is a specialist in communist insurrections in exotic destinations.

Operation Bari is a Soviet special operation of the largest scale, second only to the Red Army's General Staff endeavors in China in the 1930s. With a sophisticated and intelligent intervention via Bari, the STAVKA (in other words, Stalin) intends to exercise control over the guerrillas from Athens to Marseille and then land the role of the key political factor in the new, fascism-free Europe.

The Soviet mission left Moscow as soon as a suitable airport was arranged in Bari. The base is given over to the Soviets after lengthy negotiations with the Western Allies. The Italian government of Marshal Badoglio, who had been entrusted by the Italian king with forming a new government after the capitulation, was the most inclined to accept the Soviets. His government agreed to make the base available to the Soviets in exchange for Stalin's recognition.

Bari thus became the Red Army's Mediterranean headquarters. But instead of their troops, the personnel gathering there includes large numbers of high-ranking staff officers, special GRU units, intelligence operatives, radio operators, code clerks, analysts, and NKVD operatives. It is actually the headquarters of a Soviet Partisan army, which, according to staff manuals, is formed behind the enemy lines for every "front" (Army Group) of RKKA. So this is the headquarters—but where are the troops? The troops are Tito's Partisans, organized in line with the Soviet military doctrine found in the textbooks that their commander had studied in the special schools in Moscow. So, when they make connection with Tito's Supreme HQ, the Partisan army will become an advance component of the Red Army. Officially, however, General Korneyev is only the head of a Soviet mission at the Supreme Command of the Yugoslav Partisans of Marshal Tito. He landed near Bosanski Petrovac on 23 February 1944. Tito's political capacity as the president of NKOJ is ignored for the time being, because Stalin will not recognize the AVNOJ without political considerations, but the army—Tito's army—is a completely different matter. Integrated in the Soviet communication and agent networks, it will become a strategic formation deep behind enemy lines on his European Western Front.

Korneyev is a high-ranking officer. The Soviet representative in the Allied Mediterranean Command in Caserta is Major General A. A. Kislenko, who is of a lower rank. Clearly, Kislenko's function is less important, much the same as the function of the Soviet military attaché in London, a mere colonel, who cooperates with the heads of the intelligence services of Belgium, Denmark, Netherlands, Poland, Czechoslovakia, Norway, France, and the Kingdom of Yugoslavia. This shows the real status of the mission in Moscow's eyes.

Korneyev thus arrives in Drvar, where the Supreme Command moved from Jajce in early January, shifting the focus of its operations from central Bosnia to Croatia. Here is the invaluable testimony given by General Korneyev shortly before his death:

> Having flown 9,000 kilometers above Asia and Africa, the Soviet military mission landed in Bari. But our Anglo-American allies were taking their time in

organizing our transport to the liberated territory in Yugoslavia. They had various excuses: fighting is going on near Rome; no planes can be used for the transport; there is no airfield, etc. I was forced to send a telegram to Marshal Tito, inquiring if landing of our aircraft on the liberated territory was possible. We had been in Bari for three weeks and had become tired of waiting, when we received Marshal Tito's telegram. He says—we eagerly look forward to seeing you here; thousands of our heroic youth and soldiers have prepared a landing strip for you and are guarding it. The message thrilled us and I strongly insisted to the Allies to transfer us to the liberated territory in Yugoslavia as part of any air operation. And so, on 23 February—Red Army day—we flew to Yugoslavia under protection of a few fighter planes.

We landed on Jezdino polje field near Bosanski Petrovac. From there, we immediately proceeded to the NOV Supreme Command. Marshal Tito greeted us the first day. I greeted him on behalf of the mission. When I turned to the translator, Marshal Tito said in perfect Russian: "Mister Korneyev, why don't we talk in Russian!" I was thrilled and impressed.

Korneyev claims that he did not know who Tito was and that he was surprised to hear him speak Russian—in other words, that he had not been briefed about this old Moscow cadre, who had been working for the center for sixteen years and had been in continuous radio contact with Comintern since the beginning of the war four years earlier. Korneyev gave the above testimony in different political circumstances, not to compromise Tito's statesman position. At the formal supper, Brigadier Maclean, head of the British military mission at the Supreme Command of the National Liberation Army (NOV) and Partisan Detachments of Yugoslavia (POJ), joins Tito's welcome with the following words:

Here in Yugoslavia, General Korneyev will have an opportunity to see what I have seen—the beginning of a new Europe. I am convinced that what he is about to see will fill him with enthusiasm and confidence in the future ... But the consequences of this movement are not confined to the Yugoslav borders. The National Liberation Army has tied down numerous enemy divisions that would otherwise be deployed on the Eastern or Italian Fronts, or as a defense against the large-scale Allied landing that will soon begin in Western Europe. It is a very tangible and important contribution to the Allied war efforts. Let us hope that the glorious example of Yugoslavia will encourage other oppressed nations of Europe to rise against the common enemy and that the loathsome forces of fascism will soon be crushed by the force of the United Nations.

There is no doubt that the Soviet envoys were impressed with what they saw in Bosnia, miles from anywhere. Like the Partisans on the Eastern Front, Tito's units are created from "detachments," but he soon turns them into mobile brigades, divisions, and, eventually (in October 1943), into corps—military prefectures used for establishing his power on liberated territories and for carrying out operations on occupied territories. Drvar has become a true capital of the European guerrillas.

The importance of Drvar cannot be overestimated. It did not escape Hitler's attention. It is a place where high-ranking officers of major Allied armies have gathered for the first time. Tito is actually holding a separate front in the Mediterranean; it may be stretched and less important in military terms, but it has significant strategic potential because it connects the Anglo-American and Soviet forces. After all, it prefigures the Stalin–Churchill agreement on equal distribution of influence in Yugoslavia, which is to be achieved in Yalta. The origins of that arrangement can be traced to this small town in Bosnia. Also, this redoubt of Tito's has symbolic importance as the center of resistance in Hitler's Fortress Europe. No wonder Churchill also sends to Drvar a strong British political mission—the people who will provide reliable information about the character of this protagonist who came out of nowhere and set up an army that has great strategic potential, provided it becomes integrated in the Allied operations. The mission is headed by Britain's best secret agent, Brigadier Maclean. Joining it will be the premier's own son, Randolph Churchill, famous writer and commando Evelyn Waugh, and Colonel Valentine Vivian, vice-chief of SIS, the British secret service (better known as MI6). There is yet another "celeb"—later a famous actor, Christopher Lee. Before becoming an actor, he joined the paratroopers as a nineteen-year-old volunteer. In the adventure of his life, he was dropped into Bosnia, where he met Tito.

On 18 March 1944, Brigadier Maclean sent a note to Churchill, informing him that Tito, while realizing that guerrilla warfare is the best option under the existing circumstances, is eagerly awaiting the moment when the National Liberation Army will become capable of becoming a regular army. At the end of the note, Maclean says that the Partisans are opening to the Anglo-Americans and are trying to establish friendly relations with them. If this judgment is correct, concludes Maclean, there is nothing contrary to British interests there. A strong, independent, democratic Yugoslavia should be established that would maintain friendly relations with its neighbors and would not fall under the exclusive influence of any major power. Crucial here is the logistics for the support to the Partisans that will turn this guerrilla movement into a maneuvering army. His propositions were instantly met. Maclean says in his testimony: "A special branch of the Royal Air Force was established with only one task: supplying the National Liberation Army. They also provided air support."

The Balkan Air Force (BAF) was formed on 7 June 1944, a day after the Normandy landings. It consisted of six squadrons of light bombers, attack and transport aircraft, and night fighters. Their crew members were American, British, Italian, Polish, South African, and Yugoslav. A mixed Soviet transport-fighter air regiment was attached to it. BAF carried out 38,340 runs, dropped almost 7,000 tons of bombs, and transported 22,000 people. It was formed as Tito's air umbrella and it now provides reliable air transport in the Mediterranean. Under this umbrella, Tito operates as the supreme commander of the Balkan Front, supported by an air force component equal to an air division. The airfield is under the control of the British army, but it constitutes part of the 15 AAF (the 15th American Air Fleet).

The Partisan army in Yugoslavia is no longer an isolated guerrilla force in the woods. The airlifts and the sophisticated and extended Soviet radio network connect it rather well with the Allies. Escorted by fighters from the advanced base in Bari, transport aircraft are flying operatives to various destinations in the Balkans: Yugoslavia, Albania, and Greece.

To ensure communication logistics for Tito's Yugoslav, Albanian, and Greek Partisans and establish a Soviet presence in the Mediterranean in the process, a special radio unit under the command of Colonel S. V. Sokolov has joined the Soviet air force contingent in Bari. Its duty is to set up a radio network in the Balkans. It consists of fourteen radio relay devices, two radio centers—Groza-1 and Purga ("Blizzard")—and twelve individual radio stations distributed to the general staffs of larger Partisan units. Groza-1 is in the Bari base and Purga is with Tito's Supreme Command. The detached officers and their radio stations are located in Serbia, Croatia, Slovenia, Macedonia, Montenegro, Bosnia, and Vojvodina. They are also located in the guerrilla units in Italy, Albania, and Greece—in all the places included in the secret empire of Marshal Tito, who now has the communication structure, in addition to the political and cadre structures. The codename for Walter, or Comrade Tito, T. T., has now changed in Moscow. He has become Eagle (Orel).[1]

With the Purga station at his disposal, Drvar communications are organized like a standard Soviet Partisan army command communications knot. This helped the Germans locate Tito's Supreme Command by using radio reconnaissance and prepare a surprise attack. Korneyev recalls:

> The English warned the NOV Supreme Command and Josip Broz Tito about the possible airborne landing on the liberated territory. But there were no specif-

ics as regards the exact time and place of the landing. Marshal Tito notified me of the whole thing. We decided to prepare a reserve command post. Marshal Tito took me with him to inspect this place in Potoci near Drvar. I studied it. We agreed that the place was very convenient, in a thick forest with very few access paths and with a nearby field that could be used as an airstrip. We waited and waited, but there was no raid ... And, our vigilance started to diminish.

24

PANTHER'S JUMP

DRVAR 1944

A week before the German raid, Randolph Churchill left Drvar. A plane came for Brigadier Maclean and Major Churchill, the prime minister's son, and they discreetly left the European guerrilla capital. According to Korneyev's account, the British mission had informed Tito's Supreme Command about a possible German raid, but they could not be specific in order to avoid compromising the source. Obviously, it was the intelligence obtained by breaking the radio communications encrypted by the Enigma cipher machine. The British realized from the intercepted messages that the Germans were preparing a raid.

Captain Franz Kraigher, member of Abwehr, the German military intelligence service, was the first to inform the German command about Tito's relocation from Jajce to Drvar. The intel was given to Colonel General Lothar von Rendulic, commander of the 2nd Panzer Army, and SS General Otto Kumm, commander of the 7th SS Division Prinz Eugen, who were in Bihać. With them was Captain Kurt Rybka, commander of the 500th SS Parachute Battalion assigned with the mission of raiding Tito's headquarters. Kraigher was well informed because he had his agents and scouts from the Brandenburg special units on the ground.

All his life, General Janković, the commander of Tito's Escort Battalion in Drvar, studied the operation. He says:

When giving orders to the commander of the southeast, Field Marshal von Weichs, Hitler underlined: "Remember, von Weichs, remember, Tito must be

159

captured alive; that also goes for the officers of all Allied missions. And he must be brought here without anyone knowing it." Until these April conversations in the OKW, the plan had been to physically destroy the Supreme Command and Comrade Tito. Somewhat later, Hitler gave the same order to Rendulic—that Tito should be captured alive and taken to Berlin in deep secrecy.

Some 900 troops participated in the airborne assault. There were six glider groups and three parachute groups. They came in two waves. The focus was on the first wave, with around 720 troops. Panther Group was to carry out the most important task. It was supposed to land at the suspected location of Tito's Supreme Command, Šobića groblje—the local cemetery. The Germans expected the Supreme Command would be there. Using goniometry and intelligence, the Germans had obtained reliable information that the Supreme Command's radio center was there.

Mića Janković remembers everything very accurately:

On the morning of 25 May 1944, I was in Drvar as battalion commander. I was a young man, twenty-five-and-a-half years old, and recently promoted to captain. As one of the last of the many things we had done to maintain combat readiness, the night before, around midnight, we had been ordered to have the entire battalion and the whole town up at five o'clock in the morning. The battalion's headquarters was in the houses, some 200 meters from the cave where Tito was quartered. After 6 a.m., we heard the sound of airplanes.

We watched the bombardment, thinking it was one of the usual bombing raids, but then the gliders came. The sky became crowded with paratroopers from transport aircraft. We jumped out of the trench. I rushed to the headquarters building, found three submachine guns and plenty of ammunition there and hurried to the cave. One group landed less than 100 meters away. I opened fire on these paratroopers. At the same time, our comrades on the positions around the cave also opened intensive fire on the Germans. The whole of Drvar was boiling. The paratroopers who had landed were firing at us and our anti-aircraft machineguns were firing back.

I had to run in short breaks between the bursts to reach the cave. Comrade Tito, Comrade Kardelj, and a few other comrades were there. Around 9 a.m., the firing became more intense. We saw a German skirmish line, some thirty to forty men, trying to approach closer. The Germans were advancing by charging in alternation, first one flank, then the center, then the other flank—textbook tactics. Sharp orders could be heard. Nested in the bell tower of the Orthodox church, a light or heavy machinegun opened fire on the cabin Tito was in. The bullets clattered on it as if someone threw a handful of pebbles on the roof. The tension sustained for quite a while, perhaps thirty to forty minutes.

Then, the fire quieted down a little. Probably it was that psychological moment in the battle when both sides assess the results. Comrade Tito got out of the cave and stepped on the terrace by the cabin. I was lying a few meters from him. I did not know what to do—do I stand up when approached by the Supreme Commander and thus become a target, or do I keep lying? Confused as I was, I chose a half-way solution—I sat up. He kept standing there, exposed to enemy fire. He wanted me to explain the situation to him right there, to show him where the Germans were. I showed him where the Germans were, what they were doing, where had they come from, where they were going—everything I saw, or guessed based on the intensity of fire. At that moment, the fight started again in earnest, but the shots were individual. Such fire is the most dangerous one, because it means that those who are firing have enough time to take their aim.

When observing Drvar Valley, Comrade Tito noticed several groups of Germans in the orchard on the slopes leading to Šobića groblje. He realized they were moving rather casually—they did not move like one should on a battlefield. He ordered his adjutant to bring him his sniper. It was the sniper rifle presented to him by the Soviet delegation. When the adjutant brought him the rifle, he grabbed it with one hand and—as the telescope was not attached to the rifle—he started mounting it. Then he started loading the rifle. He did all that while standing totally exposed, as if he was on some peacetime shooting range. Then he would aim at Germans, fire at them, and then analyze the result. He is known as a great shot. He would adjust range and aim again, and then fire again ...

To me, these moments during which he laid himself open to the enemy fire looked like eternity. I did not know what to do. At one moment, Comrade Kardelj himself got out of the cave. When he saw Tito standing between the rock face and cabin, shooting at the Germans, he was taken aback. With a voice imploring and fearful at the same time, he started begging Comrade Tito to stop exposing himself and return to the cave.

Carried away with shooting, Comrade Tito paid no attention to his pleas or did not hear him at all. Kardelj approached Comrade Tito from the back and begged him again. Then he pulled his sleeve. When that didn't help, he enclosed him with his arms from the back and told him—I can't remember the exact words, but the meaning was this: "Comrade Old Man, do you remember who you answer to?"

I had been with the Supreme Command—as fighter, deputy commander, and commander of the battalion—since 1942, since the days in Foča. I had known all the members of the Supreme Command and all the people who had contacts with the Command and the Central Committee but, being a young man and a young party member, I had no idea who could be senior to Comrade Tito ...

Maybe Comrade Stalin? Janković was not particularly proficient in things political, which was good for him—he would later be steadily promoted and have a career as a general:

> Upon hearing those words, I saw Comrade Tito lowering his rifle. They exchanged a few more words—Comrade Kardelj was probably convincing him a bit more—and then, arm in arm, they went back to the cave. They entered the cave and that was when the preparations for the departure began.

The commander of the Escort Battalion highlights the stubborn resistance:

> When Rendulic was explaining the idea behind the raid on Drvar in a 1966 interview, he could not understand why it failed.

> All around Drvar, the members of the Supreme Command, party, headquarters of local and regional units, field hospitals, and parts of the 6th Division of the NOVJ were stationed. All in all, there were several hundred people. It was the fourth year of the war and they were all battle-hardened fighters, party, and SKOJ members, strongly attached to the Communist Party, Central Committee, and Supreme Command. They engaged the enemy as our elite units would, although they did not belong to any special company, battalion, brigade etc. They bore the brunt of defense in the first moments of the fight. An airborne assault has an advantage in the first twenty to forty minutes. And it was these people, who made up the "hedgehog" of defense points in the town, that bore the brunt of the fight, together with the units of the Escort Battalion.

> Between 11:15 and 11:50, the German air force was preparing for the second wave of the assault. In the meantime, Comrade Tito had left the cave and gone up the hill, toward the point right above the cave. Battalion of the 6th Lika Division arrived at around 11 o'clock and engaged the enemy after a short preparation. The fight for encirclement of the German paratroopers and their destruction thus began.

> Since the arrival of the first Lika fighters, Tito had observed the whole situation from Gradina Hill above the cave. After an unstoppable assault, the units of the 6th Lika Division pushed the Germans to a very narrow space around Šobića groblje, despite the fact that, unlike the Germans, they had very little ammunition, and they suffered heavy casualties.

> Only the next day, 26 May, around 8 a.m., a German motorized column from Petrovac arrived in Drvar, joined the paratroopers, and saved them from destruction.

Actually, the casualties of the 500th SS Fallschirmjäger Battalion included exactly sixty-one killed (including one officer) and 205 wounded (two officers). Eleven paratroopers were missing in action. A total of one-third of the entire force was put out of action. Other German and Croatian forces advancing to Drvar simultaneously with the parachute drop suffered minor losses—some thirty of them were killed. The paratroopers counted 421 dead enemies. They captured "136 bandits, two Englishmen, and one American." And it was not over yet. Korneyev says:

> The paratroopers were almost completely destroyed, but the fascists then launched attacks supported by tanks, armored vehicles, and motorized infantry from north, south, and west. They began to tighten the grip. In fact, the Supreme Command was now surrounded. We were forced to leave Potoci for the Veliki Šator mountain. There we came under aircraft fire and bombing again and we had to proceed to Veliki Klekovac peak. The fascist aircraft and infantry thus pursued the Supreme Command and everyone with it for about ten days.

Besides the 6th Lika Division, it was the Royal Air Force that saved Tito in Drvar. The British mission radioed an alarming message to London, and Churchill ordered his air force based in Italy to attack immediately the German troops moving in to close the pincers. The rapid advance of German troops could have been fatal were it not for the more than 1,000 runs of the RAF aircraft in the wider area around Drvar.

Upon breaking out of the encirclement, Tito had to make a pivotal decision about the following stage of his "revolution in motion." Obviously, he does not need to defend the territory as long as his guerrilla army controls the space. The only irreplaceable resource is himself—and the freedom of action of his Supreme Command. As long as he is on the territory controlled by his own army, Tito is independent, but as soon as he steps onto a territory controlled by the Allied forces, he comes under control of the ally who controls that safe haven. On the other hand, this has become a serious war now, and he cannot command his forces from some forest hideout. Besides, the war in Europe has been won—in the east, the German Central Front was crushed in Operation Bagration; in the west, the Anglo-Americans landed in Normandy; in Italy, Rome fell. It is now crucial that, in addition to the recognition of the status of an Allied force, won with arms, sovereignty be recognized by way of diplomacy. And diplomacy cannot be pursued from the bush. But if he makes a mistake and, having escaped an enemy, falls into the hands of a friend who will reduce his freedom of political maneuvering ... However, urged by Korneyev, Tito agrees that he and the members of the Supreme Command should be flown to the Russian base in Bari.

Three days after the arrival in Bari, the British navy destroyer HMS *Blackmore* will transfer Tito and his retinue to Yugoslav territory—the island of Vis. There, in a cave once again, the operational command for the Balkans and Mediterranean will be created around him. Americans are also coming to the island, now represented by Roosevelt's men. This is the first time that the political representatives and operational commands of four Allied armies in the European theater of operations—Tito's Partisans and the British, Soviet, and American armies—have established direct contact. They are jockeying for positions for the Cold War that will follow in Europe after the hot one is resolved. Actually, it has already started, albeit secretly.

III

THE SECRET EMPIRE

25

THE PURGA ARCHIPELAGO

VIS 1944

The raid on Drvar was the final attempt to use military means to eliminate the Partisan movement and its Supreme Command. After that, the forces of the Axis powers were thrown onto the defensive in the Balkans. But the attempt was almost successful. If the German paratroops succeeded in eliminating Tito, some Anglo-American units would probably enter Yugoslavia in accordance with the plan for landings on Krk and in Rijeka (Operation Gelignite). Instead of the landing on the French Côte d'Azur (Operation Dragoon, undertaken in the summer of 1944), the landing logistics would be used in the Adriatic, as was proposed by the British General Staff. But the operations in France, where fighting for the Normandy bridgehead has been going on for three months, could drag on, increasing the Red Army's chances of capturing a larger chunk of Germany and reaching the Atlantic Ocean, which was Stalin's strategic goal in the Second World War. Faced with the choice between losing Western or Eastern Europe, Western political strategists did not have to think twice.

On the island of Vis, Tito's liberated territory once again offered a neutral ground and ideal conditions for special warfare. In the Balkans, intelligence operatives are more important than Russian tank armies or a US strategic air force. A stage has been set on which adventurous secret operatives of a magnificent empire past its prime—writers, Scottish aristocrats, and men of the world—will have an opportunity to excel. Joining them will be the Moscow-trained Yugoslav technocrats of the dictatorship of the proletariat and brigand captains disciplined and organized by Tito in order to carry out feats on a European scale.

In addition to daily communication with Moscow, Tito uses his Purga radio station for contacts with the headquarters and units of his multinational guerrilla army operating in the areas between Greece and northern Italy. He has become "Eagle," Stalin's marshal in the Red Army's vanguard. However, for turning his secret empire into an autonomous franchise of world communism—an ambition clearly manifested by Tito since 1937—he must first ensure a balance between his Allied patrons. Velebit, his closest confidant, describes establishing this second line—the one Tito needs because the German force separating him from the Soviet force is now declining. Velebit met Tito in Bari and joined him on his trip to Vis:

> British destroyer HMS *Blackmore* transported us from Bari to Vis. Soon afterward, president of the new Yugoslav government in London, Mr Šubašić, requested to meet Tito. Tito agreed immediately. And so, the first meeting took place on the island of Vis in the early summer of 1944. Our relations with the Western Allies improved in this period. Churchill expressed his wish to meet Comrade Tito in person. This wish was camouflaged as Field Marshal Wilson's invitation to Tito to visit the headquarters of the Allied forces in Italy.

Brigadier Maclean gives his account of the meeting:

> I think the meeting of Mr Churchill and Marshal Tito was one of the most important meetings of the Second World War. Mr Churchill had been fascinated with Yugoslavia, its resistance during the war, and the personality of Marshal Tito. The fact that, for security reasons, we could not tell Tito why we wanted him to stay for a few more days, made it a bit harder to organize the meeting. We kept saying: "It would be good if you could stay a couple of days more." I remember well, Tito and I took a swim on Capri. I thought he had no idea why we were holding him up. Then he glanced up at the sky and, seeing a large transport aircraft escorted by fighters, he said: "Here comes Mr Churchill." Then I realized nothing slipped his attention. But then again, I had already known that ... There was no initial restraint. They had a useful and far-reaching conversation. They immediately developed a genuine affinity for each other.

> When you speak with Tito, you realize you're speaking with someone who knows human weaknesses and has a sense of humor; with someone who cares about others. It is very easy to establish a personal relationship with him. I am glad to say that such a relationship still exists between us. Of course, he has various other virtues. As a soldier, a commander, he was a synonym for composure in the most difficult situations. He never hesitated. He could lead his troops and the people around him in such a way that they were willing to sacrifice for the

goal that both him and all of them believed in. As a politician, a statesman, he certainly sees far ahead. There are not many people in this century who could compare with him.

The meeting between Churchill and Tito will change the history of Europe. At first, the consequences will be limited to the war in the Balkans, but ten years later it will have much wider repercussions. From the outset, Tito wanted to establish a close personal relationship with Churchill because it was immensely important for him. The US intelligence service has an almost negligible capacity for observing the players and their motives in the political game. James Jesus Angleton, future head of CIA operations, works at the Office of Strategic Services's (OSS) Italian desk in London (Section X-2). Only in November 1944 will he come to Italy. It will take the Americans years to acquire anti-communist expertise—and even that they will manage only when they obtain (through Tito's apparatus in the 1950s) a deep insight into the hidden communist cosmos of the "world behind the Iron Curtain." At this moment, however, the West is in the Mediterranean theater of operations represented only by the British government and Churchill. In order to create the balance with Stalin, Tito, who always thinks one step ahead, needs to have the support of the British premier. He is going to charm him, show flexibility, and prove he is willing to make compromises. That would give Churchill hope that the UK, as a colonial power that persistently supports the king in Greece, will retain some influence here as well and maintain overall domination in the Mediterranean. Maclean will play an important role. He is fascinated with Tito. He saw him in action, in combat; he understood his dominant nature, grasped his energy and total self-confidence. He already knows that Tito is not in Stalin's pocket and that he has no other priorities but to achieve military victory and establish his own, independent authority.

Neither Churchill nor Maclean are democrats; someone's integrity and personality are more important to them than the liberal values of a political system—and they do not really believe that it is possible to introduce them to the barbaric Balkans by means of constitutional decrees. They are aware that the achievements of British political culture and fair play cannot be adopted here in less than 1,000 years. Churchill's political goal is to restore the monarchy, if possible, and install King Peter. However, the twenty-two-year-old is currently studying in Cambridge, cycling, rowing, and not caring very much about returning home and joining Uncle Draža in his shepherd's cabin in the mountains.

Even today, seventy years later, the reports submitted to Churchill by Maclean offer a brilliant insight into Tito's domain. He described a self-organized army consisting of regiment-like formations and fighting in line with the rules of regular warfare. The Partisans created a system of government. Besides, Churchill judged Tito perfectly. So, if we disregard the system, what remains is the man. And the man, while obviously a communist, has left a favorable impression on Churchill. Like Maclean, he concluded that Tito was not Stalin's man, but his own. And so he will be given British recognition, support, and a protected base on Vis, where he will arrange his guerrilla headquarters and establish his exterritorial state without territory—well functioning, if virtual. What Western Allies did not realize, however, was that it was also a component of the Soviet subversive penetration of the West. Stalin will officially recognize this strategic role of Tito by awarding him the Order of Victory on 9 September 1945. Only twenty pieces of this highest Soviet decoration were minted for sixty people who were crucial for victory over Hitler in the Second World War. Bakarić casts some more light on the Vis mystery of the "secret Mediterranean headquarters":

> I was mostly preparing reports on the situation in Italy for Tito, with special reference to the viewpoints of the Italian Communist Party and to the Allies' attitudes about the resistance. Tito was also sending his views about the situation in Italy to the Comintern. An Albanian delegation was also on Vis at the time and we had comprehensive talks with them. We were also in position to establish stronger links with some units in the field. For example, Comrade Tempo came from Macedonia. He told us about the situation in the northern part of Greece, in Macedonia, in Bulgaria, and in the whole area. As a result, Tito had much better control over the things than he could have in Jajce.

Unintentionally, Bakarić confirms that Tito's area of operations extended from northern Italy to the gates of Istanbul. The operations were taking place in Italy, Albania, and Greece and with the mixed Soviet–Yugoslav agent network in France, Spain, and Algeria. In Italy, Tito's own undisguised troops start forming in the autumn of 1944. The 4th Overseas Brigade of the National Liberation Army of Yugoslavia (NOVJ) was formed in Brindisi on 7 September. It consists of dispersed "flying companies" on special missions, responsible for logistics and sea and air transport of troops to destinations in Italy, Yugoslavia, Greece, and Albania.

Bari has become a Partisan capital. In addition to GRU operatives, their main Mediterranean relay station Groza, and the Partisan garrison protecting it, British operatives are also located here.

The Naples-based "Intelligence Unit No. 1" of the British SIS was entrusted with gathering intelligence about the situation in Italy behind enemy lines.

Attempts at planting its own agents were totally unsuccessful. Information started flowing only when it relied on communists, to whom they started issuing radio stations in Naples. Togliatti, secretary of the PCI, who had arrived in Naples from Moscow via Ufa, tolerated it until early 1945 and then he threw the English liaison officer out of the communist headquarters. However, in the meantime, Section 2 of SIS had developed very successfully in Bari. It was run by Major James Miller, a Cambridge graduate who had worked for the service in Berlin and Zagreb until the beginning of the war. His Italian network made up of Tito's communists started flowing in to such an extent that, at one moment in early 1945, the British headquarters realized that "in planning their operations, the army and the air force are fully dependent on the information obtained from agent 35600 [Miller]."

The Yugoslav military presence in the Apennines and Sicily will soon become substantial. Four out of five of the NOVJ's Overseas Brigades were formed in Italy (the fifth one, made up of POWs—Slovene conscripts in the Italian units that had surrendered during the Allied invasion of Normandy— was formed in London). They are made up of Slovene, Croatian, and Montenegrin internees in Italian prison camps. A tank unit and two artillery units were also established. Meanwhile, within reach of the 9th Slovenian– Friulian–Italian Corps and through the Milan section of the 1st Section of OZNA for Slovenia, guerrilla units are formed to put Friuli and northern Italy under control. The Milan section is run by Dr Anton Vratuša, "Head of the NKOJ Delegation at the Committee of National Liberation for Northern Italy (CLNAI)."[1]

The CLNAI forces were divided into three camps. There were communist Garibaldi Brigades, the liberal-anarchist Brigate Giustizia e Libertà connected with Partito d'Azione, and the socialist Brigate Matteotti, controlled by the Italian Socialist Party (PSI). There were between 15,000 and 20,000 armed communist guerrilla in the Alps, Apennines, and River Po Valley. In addition, Tito has military bases on the Adriatic coast, in Carbonara di Bari and the nearby Gravina di Puglia, where a few thousand Partisans are stationed in Italian barracks at all times. Logically, it is these forces that could be identified as the phantom "6th Army" mentioned in the documents found in Belgrade archives.

On New Year's Day, 1945, four Yugoslav armies were formed. The 1st, 2nd, and 3rd Armies were operating in the central massif in Bosnia and in the Pannonian Valley, and the 4th Army was engaged on the Adriatic coast and in its hinterland. As the 5th Army was also left hanging in the air and was not exactly visible, it could—also logically—be described as belonging to the secret empire. It included the forces deployed in the south—in Greece and Albania. In addition to the thirty-three Macedonian and Kosovo brigades under the command of Lieutenant General Mihajlo Apostolski, the Albanian army and Greek divisions under the direct control of Tito's commissars and military instructors should be included here, too. Not more than ten days after the liberation of Belgrade, these forces will take the deserted Thessalonica.

In Albania, Tito's forces had been active since September 1941. In September 1943, the Albanian Supreme Command was established, headed by Hadji-Captain Leshi, Tempo's Partisan commander from Macedonia. At the same time, in Greece, Tito's commander Tempo founded three divisions—the 9th, 10th, and 11th Divisions of ELAS (Greek People's Liberation Army).

In early 1945, a large offensive will be launched on the entire front of the secret empire. But the most important thing must be resolved first—Tito must renew the mandate he was given in Moscow in 1940 as a secret operative. In the meantime, he proclaimed himself a marshal and head of a non-existent, unrecognized state. How will Comrade Stalin look at it? Tito established relations with the British, and was receiving their military and logistic support for his operations on a grand scale. But that came with a price. Bakarić explains:

> It was clear after the Churchill–Tito meeting that the Allies would try to keep as much influence on Yugoslavia as possible.

> Eventually, Šubašić came to talk to the national committee. Ralph Stevenson, British ambassador at the royal government-in-exile, came to Vis with him. Šubašić required that a joint government be formed, but we refused it and proposed three men in our confidence who would join his government. What was the Comintern's view of it? Our talks were very public and complied with the Comintern's general line. In other words, all the missions were informed about every detail of the talks. But we began to feel somewhat uncomfortable on Vis. Tito decided to visit the Soviet front. He went there one night, not informing us in advance about his departure ...

But that was preceded by another very important episode—the political elimination of the hapless Hebrang.

26

A RENDEZVOUS WITH STALIN

MOSCOW 1944

Tito is getting ready to flit away from his Adriatic "eagle's nest." After four months spent there, he flew to Bari and went to Caserta, where he met Churchill. From there, he even took a short tourist trip to the only just liberated Rome, where he visited St Peter's Church. An incident happened at the entrance—the priests wanted to prevent armed men from entering. The whole thing ended up in such a way that the bodyguard with a submachine-gun with a safety catch off stayed in the portico and the Marshal entered with a gun at his belt.

The departure from the Vis base is being prepared in utmost secrecy. Not even Tito's closest associates have been informed about it. Here is Vladimir Bakarić's account:

> We didn't know Tito was gone either. We found it out when we came to the room where we would usually stay in the evening. Upon seeing Đilas behaving mysteriously, we realized something unusual must have happened. So we pressed him a little and he told us Tito had gone. And it was my unpleasant duty as a man from external relations to receive various people who came to Vis, often unannounced ...

> Murphy came a day after Tito's departure, also unannounced. So they instructed me to talk to him. Obviously, he had already been appointed Eisenhower's political advisor for Europe, so he came to inspect the situation in the area they had considered more or less their own, so they could come and go as they pleased.

This is the prehistory of containment, the Cold War, and the Berlin Wall, all in one place. Robert Murphy and Frank Wiesner who accompanied him were the main US experts for Europe—the former for political affairs, the latter for intelligence issues. Murphy divided Germany and Wiesner dug the famous tunnel under the Berlin Wall:

> So Murphy came with his team—five or six men—unannounced. And he came to talk to me. Of course, I had nothing to talk to him about. He kept asking where is Tito, and I kept replying—on the front. Where on the front? Well, the Yugoslav front stretches a long way ...

In his long account about the events on Vis, Dr Bakarić, a young thirty-two-year-old bookish communist, reveals the most important information almost as an aside: "Of course, when Tito left, Vis became less important. Two or three days later, I went to Croatia via Bari. I went to Topusko, where I took over as the new secretary of the Central Committee of the Croatian Communist Party."

It is perfectly clear that, even before his trip to Craiova and Moscow, Tito had appointed him to replace Hebrang, briefing him beforehand. Although inadvertently, Comrade Krajačić explains why the replacement was being prepared:

> In 1944, Comrade Tito ordered that Ozna be established. He summoned me to report on it. And not just on that, but on the overall situation up there. I managed to reach Vis via Bari. I was supposed to explain what was going on in northern Croatia. I was presenting the report for two hours. Comrade Kardelj was present, too. I think I explained the problems we had up there rather well. Tito agreed and kept us on Vis for a couple of days—me and Rade Žigić. Then we came back.

Žigić was the political commissar of the 6th Lika Division, which excelled during the raid on Drvar. These are Tito's most reliable men. Krajačić continues:

> We traveled back via Bari. When we took off the first time, we could not land, so we had to return to Bari. We set out again, this time from Brindisi. Churchill's son and a Russian delegation on its way to Croatian headquarters were with us. When we reached the airstrip, the plane could not land, although the pilots were very good. There were six crewmen because they were transporting Churchill's son, who was lying in the back of the plane, drunk. There was another high-ranking British officer with him ...[1] After the failed landing, the plane started taking off again. It reached some 300 feet and then the engine failed. So we crashed and the plane caught fire. The whole crew was killed. The tail had separated from the rest of the plane. Since Churchill's son had been sleeping in the

tail, drunk, nothing had happened to him. One of our comrades who accompanied me was killed, too. A few of us survived, but we were all burnt. ...

That happened in August 1944. Comrade Moša Pijade was waiting for me by the airstrip. He wanted to give me his message for Comrade Tito. He was in a very, very strange situation then ... Although a member of the Supreme Command and Central Committee, he had nothing to do ... But this is a different story that should not be discussed here.

What is going on in Topusko? At a session of the ZAVNOH, the national front government of Croatia, Hebrang runs the show. Appointed by Moscow, he has been the head of the Croatian party since 1928. He presided over the Eighth Conference of the Zagreb party organization,[2] where he appeared together with the organizing secretary and head of the apparatus, "Proletarian Georgijević," recruited by Štajner from the OMS and Sakun from the Comintern Executive Committee. When Hebrang was arrested in Zagreb in 1942, he was temporarily replaced by Bakarić, but only in Tito's hierarchy. It is not valid in the Comintern, which is in charge of the Croatian Communist Party. Stalin has recognized Tito's authority of the supreme commander of the NOV and POJ on the whole territory, but the party relations are something completely different. As the general secretary of the CPY, even the Marshal is formally not superior to the leadership of the Croatian Communist Party, to say nothing of Pijade, merely a member of the CPY Politburo. This is why Moša "has nothing to do" in Topusko, where the anomalous "situation" that Krajačić mentions has started to develop.

The third session of the ZAVNOH in Topusko took place on 8 May 1944. Tito came to Vis on 7 June and, a week later, on 16 June, signed an agreement with Šubašić. The day before, on 15 June, he ordered the founding of the OZNA (Department for People's Protection). It is now the backbone of his authority, because he does not have clear political authority any more—he shares it with the Slovenian and Croatian national front formations backed by Stalin, and with the government arising from the agreement with the London cabinet, which keeps the Chetnik General Mihailović in the field as minister of war. This compromise-based government is backed by the Western Allies and, inevitably, by Stalin, a master of all double schemes. Save for the proletarian brigades, not even the army consists solely of communist cadres anymore—mass mobilization on the liberated territories and the integration of Macedonian, Albanian, Greek, and Italian units have changed its composition. As for the party, Tito has his clique and the men he can trust, but many of them—even the closest ones—still adhere to the Moscow line, as the 1948 break-up with Stalin will show. Thus, the only real support of his authority is OZNA, a secret service, an organization formed by the trustworthy Ranković, assisted by Croatian *silovik* Krajačić and his Slovenian counterpart Ivan "Matija" Maček. OZNA was like NKVD and SMERSH (Smert Shpionam, counterintelligence directorate of RKKA) fused together.

When he agreed to cooperate with Šubašić—not yet to form a joint government with him—Tito acquired the diplomatic legitimacy required for the 15 August meeting with Churchill in Caserta. This gave him a huge amount of prestige. But he first founded the OZNA and was about to use it for striking the national front structures in Slovenia and Croatia.

The VOS of the Slovenian Liberation Front was disbanded in May 1943.[3] As of that moment, the OZNA runs the apparatus in Slovenia. In Slovenia, that means Comrade Maček and that, in turn, means Tito.

Tito sends his executioner Krajačić to Croatia with the same task and with corresponding instructions. He is to help Pijade, the special commissar for errors and political deviations, and the high priest of the Marshal's personality cult. Before flying to Craiova and Moscow, Tito briefed Bakarić. He instructed him to take over Hebrang's function as soon as Hebrang is replaced. Tito departed on 19 September. Two days earlier, on 17 September, he had set in motion the whole party coup by sending a telegram to Hebrang.

In the telegram, Tito criticizes two decisions made by the ZAVNOH at its third session. First, the decision to establish the Telegraph Agency of Croatia (TAH), "although every country has only one official telegraph agency," so this, therefore, suggests there will be two of them. Second, he dismisses the ZAVNOH's alleged decision to "introduce compulsory religious instruction to schools," a decision that is nowhere to be found in the ZAVNOH's conclusions (merely "equality before law, regardless of national origin, race or religion" is mentioned in the declaration on the rights of the peoples and citizens of the Federal State of Croatia).

This is the pretext. Besides, the ZAVNOH conclusions, passed in May— four months earlier—challenge Tito, as a communist autocrat in more fundamental ways. The first conclusion in Topusko was that the ZAVNOH would become the "supreme legislative and executive authority of the Federal State of Croatia." Next, it is promised that "every citizen shall be guaranteed the safety of his/her person and property and freedom of private initiative (entrepreneurship)." But what will the OZNA do then? How will the expropriation and collectivization be carried out, how will the planned economy be introduced, and heavy and military industries built? In short, how will Stalinist socialism be introduced—which, as one would expect, has been the goal of the entire bunch who have been working on it with dedication since 1928? Not to mention that the declaration proscribes the very thing that must be done first—cleansing the space from unwanted ethnic groups: Germans, Italians, and Turks, while eliminating local quislings and all class enemies. The party does not need a purge—when created in Lisca, it was created "pure," as a Stalinist hierarchy, but an extensive purge of the entire population is required.

In short, the illusory ZAVNOH government would be constituted on national front principles, or what was called a "people's democracy government" in Stalin's bloc. In such a federal Croatian state—which is actually a separate, independent state, fully constitutional—communists are merely a "moral majority" or a disguised senior partner (who always controls security, the army, and other "enforcement departments"). And if Croatia is a federal state with still undefined borders, the other states that are to form this new Yugoslavia will have to be similar, so a set of "people's democracy" statelets will be created, possibly—but not necessarily—with a joint federal administration and joint head of state. And if a compromise with the government-in-exile headed by Soviet agent Šubašić is reached under pressure of the British and Soviets, then it is really not clear what function Comrade Tito could have in such an awkward arrangement.

The head of the "anomalous" Croatia created in Topusko is Comrade Hebrang. He has his separate contacts with Moscow, and he is a true communist, solid as a rock. He is a true believer, but in the church in which he prays, Comrade Tito is not God, just a priest of the Moscow cult. Hebrang is also honest, ascetic, and has no ego. Early in the war, when he was offered an opportunity to play his own game through the Zagreb party committee, he bluntly refused it, although it would be legitimate because the Croatian Communist Party was a separate party that could have direct contact with the Comintern. In theory, Hebrang (and Kardelj) always had an opportunity to manifest dissent.

Moscow wants and allows the creation of national front/people's democracy states in Eastern Europe. First, it does not want to antagonize the Western Allies with premature moves (the Allies are providing crucial military and economic assistance to the Soviet Union). Moscow does not want to leave the impression that it encroaches upon territories in Europe, although Harry Hopkins, Roosevelt's foreign policy advisor, sees clearly that this is exactly what is going on. But Stalin acts stealthily, not obtrusively. He is being cunning. Tito, his best student from the Comintern's secret apparatus, will prove up to this "indirect approach strategy." Nothing is explicit yet, perhaps not even planned, but the great rivals in this game, Stalin and Tito, think in advance, aware of various possibilities. While the former wants to leave some possibilities open, the latter is determined to close them.

Comrade Tito trusts Comrade Kardelj because he himself chose him and installed him. He also controls him by means of the OZNA apparatus that has replaced the disbanded Slovenian VOS. Unfortunately, Comrade Tito does not trust Comrade Hebrang. Having sent him a telegram about the all-too-important issue of the non-existent Croatian news agency, Tito sends a telegram to Kardelj the very next day (18 September 1944), instructing him to travel to Croatia at once and replace Hebrang with Bakarić. The replacement (Bakarić) was notified in advance, in mid-September, as he unintentionally reveals in his account. Bakarić had no idea that Tito was going to Moscow and that he was making arrangements in such a way that Moscow could not be an arbiter in the whole thing. The following day (19 September), Tito flies to Craiova, and on 20 September he is in Moscow. The replacement will take place exactly at the moment when he is in the Kremlin. It will seem as if it was made jointly, in Moscow, and not beforehand, on Vis. What perfect timing! Tito could not abolish the Communist Party of Croatia, but he could appoint his yes-man as its head. So now he has his Kardelj–Bakarić dream team in Slovenia and Croatia. The task of replacing Hebrang was given to Kardelj, the second "autonomous" co-chairman from the Fifth Land Conference, and not—for instance— to Pijade, widely known as Tito's personal executioner. Thus, having consolidated his clique in power in advance, Tito leaves for Moscow.

When he was invited to Moscow in 1944, Tito was not formally the secretary of the Central Committees of the Slovenian and Croatian parties (those were Kardelj and Ribar, respectively), but only of the unrecognized and undefined Central Committee of the CPY—a party whose future is uncertain if the other two continue to exist. So, Tito goes to Moscow only as an army commander (which is—politically—of secondary importance) and president of the NKOJ, the government the Allies want to fuse with the royal cabinet chaired by Šubašić, a Moscow mole in the London-based government-in-exile. No state or party status is guaranteed to Tito in his own backyard. But he has real power in his hands—a substantial Partisan army, OZNA, and a balanced position between Stalin and Churchill. And they have already made a deal for Yugoslavia. In Yalta in 1945, they will agree to divide their influence in the country on a fifty-fifty basis. But what is this half of an abstraction that both of them would have?

In his speech to the commanding officers of German military districts and higher military schools, Reichsführer-SS Heinrich Himmler judges Tito this way:

> Unfortunately he is our enemy, but is a man of strong character. He really has earned his title of Marshal ... He is our enemy, but I wish we had a dozen Titos in Germany, men with such leader's qualities [*Führerqualitäten*] and with such resolution. He may be on the side of the Russians, British, and Americans, but is brave enough to oppose them. With the British and Americans, he even goes as far as to humiliate them ...[4]

While Himmler is making his speech to German officers, Tito—a Soviet marshal of the Mediterranean and Comintern's agent with long experience on Europe's secret frontlines—is entering the Kremlin because he has an audience with Stalin. This is the first time he will meet him in person.

Tito arrived in Moscow on 20 September 1944, but it seems Stalin received him only on 27 September. Stalin immediately expressed his willingness to engage the Red Army in the liberation of Belgrade. This would enable the Partisans to conquer Serbia, from which they had withdrawn after their defeat in Užice in late 1941. Serbia was practically pacified over the next two and a half years. Unlike the British government, which wanted the Partisans to remain on the "guerrilla" level, Stalin is willing to give NOVJ the heavy weapons; in return, he wants a national front-based government according to the Russian recipe. In this government, Stalin will have Šubašić. At the helm of the army, he will have Lieutenant-General Arso Jovanović, the chief of the General Staff and a Montenegrin Russophile who will indeed side against Tito in 1948. Stalin has given the arms, but he hopes that the army will side with him. Also, he would want his man as the head of government—when Tito came to meet him in the Kremlin, he proposed that he yield the leading position to Šubašić, under the pretense of not provoking the West. Here is Petrović's account:

> As soon as he arrived from Moscow, Tito called Mitar Bakić [his secretary] and me to his cabinet and told us, briefly, about the talks he had had in Moscow. The most important issue discussed there was the issue of forming a joint government with the royal government in London. Comrade Tito had discussed this thing primarily with Stalin and Comrade Meldev from the foreign ministry.[5] They insisted on the joint government. I must say, Comrade Tito was in a bad mood and rather angry. He said something like this: "The royal government has lost the battle both militarily and politically. Its credibility among the people has been destroyed. And now we are supposed to make a joint government with them? But if some higher interests so demand—so be it, we will make it."

However, I had a strong impression that Comrade Tito was against the idea that Yugoslavia should become a puppet on the string of great powers and that its fate should be decided upon.

So, no autonomous position in the areas controlled by his political operatives is guaranteed to Tito. Before going to Moscow, Tito sends a dispatch to Ranković on 5 September from Craiova, urging the liquidation of the ZAVNOH: "Bevc [Kardelj] and Đido [Đilas] with Bakarić to go to Croatia. Secretariat to be formed of comrades you suggested. Do everything to correct the errors made. Andrija [Hebrang] to come with Bevc and Đido. Upon return from Croatia, they should secretly meet Ercoli."[6]

Tito will keep Hebrang close and never let him out of sight. Kardelj and Đilas, who carried out this all-too-important task for him, must then go to Rome via Bari. In Rome, they meet Comrade Togliatti—on 18 October, and have a four-hour conversation with him. They discuss Trieste and the Slovenian Littoral—the province of Friuli that Tito has claims on, just like he plans to take Carinthia after he takes Istria, Rijeka, the whole of Dalmatia, Albania, and Macedonia. But right now, the most important thing is to liberate the capital.

27

THE BELGRADE OPERATION

CRAIOVA 1944

There are no minutes of Tito's September 1944 talks with Stalin in Moscow. The self-styled Marshal is very impressed with the fourteen-year older generalissimo, who is now at the peak of his power—his word moves armies of millions. Stalin was willing to give Tito arms for building a real army and to send two Soviet strategic formations to the Balkan theater of operations. In addition to Soviet troops, he would also send others—the representatives of the Bulgarian Fatherland Front will thus come to Craiova in Romania to sign an agreement with Tito on the engagement of their army against the German forces on the Yugoslav front. Although he did not get political satisfaction in Moscow, Tito ensured unlimited military support. Promising this military assistance, the unquestionable leader of world communism knows that the Yugoslav army, with all those Comintern cadres and equipped with Soviet arms, and relying on the Soviet communication network, will be just another Soviet army. At the moment, Tito has no choice. His guerrilla army is not strong enough for the kinds of operations crucial for achieving distant objectives in the final stage of the war. In Moscow, he made an arrangement with Stalin that the Red Army enter Yugoslavia, liberate Belgrade, and simultaneously cut the German Army Group E withdrawal route from Greece along the Morava Valley. NOVJ will participate in the operation with its forces that have been crossing from Bosnia into Serbia since the autumn.

On 12 July, Lieutenant General Koča Popović, commander of the 1st Proletarian Corps, was appointed commander of the headquarters of the National Liberation Army and Partisan Detachments of Serbia. Koča was flown to Kuršumlija, in southern Serbia. As there were no Partisan forces on the ground there, paratroopers landed first in order to mark the airstrip. The 50,000 fighters that have arrived in Serbia across the Drina are now under Koča's command. His most important task is to destroy the Chetnik forces, gain control over the territory, and introduce the bodies of the revolutionary government there.

The Stalin–Tito agreement reached in Moscow will have important international repercussions. The Red Army's Supreme Command will officially and formally request from the Supreme Command of the NOVJ to allow it to carry out its operations on sovereign Yugoslav territory. Why such a precedent?

In Eastern Europe, Stalin makes his moves by respecting legitimate frameworks, because he is preparing for the Yalta Conference. There, peacefully and in agreement with the Western Allies, he intends to consolidate his sphere of interest in Europe. But in addition to this formal reason for a public agreement on the Soviet army's temporary access to the Yugoslav territory, there is a much more important strategic and political one.

If the Soviet army requests permission to send its troops to Yugoslav territory, the Western Allies—who have constantly been trying to penetrate the eastern Adriatic, even by sending small units—will also be obliged to do so. A British detachment made up of two marine battalions (45th and 46th Commando), the 2nd Brigade of the Special Air Service (SAS), and a light brigade from the 51st Highlander Division (the elite unit of Montgomery's 8th Army) is operating from the island of Vis. But they land sporadically on the occupied islands in small groups, mixed with the Partisans of the 26th Division of NOVJ. A minor autonomous British landing near Mostar ended fatally. It was thus clear from the very beginning that there is no chance of arbitrary access to the operational area controlled by Tito. So, with Stalin's help, Tito will manage to impose restrictions on the Anglo-Americans. At the same time, their vicinity helps him take a stand in Moscow as someone with options. After all, he has a substantial autonomous military force at his disposal, separated from the Soviet army by German forces and logistically dependent on the Western Allied bases in Italy. *Your adversary is your best protection from dangerous allies.* This is Tito's main military and political strategic doctrine, one that he applies in all situations.

Emerging on the Danube near Turnu Severin, the Soviet army established contact with Yugoslav forces on 12 September 1944. By that time, the NOVJ already had some 450,000 fighters, but not on the Serbian front. Only the 1st Army Corps of the NOVJ and 14th Serbian Corps of the NOVJ (the latter established only four days earlier) operate here. The 14th Serbian Corps consists of three divisions (the Serbian 23rd, 25th, and 45th Divisions) formed of local detachments a month earlier. As such, the fighting value of these units is purely symbolic. And the 1st Proletarian Corps that Peko Dapčević took over from Koča Popović has only 21,000 fighters—slightly more than a regular German division.

The Battle of Belgrade began on 14 October and lasted until 20 October 1944. Contrary to the general perception—resulting from decades of official propaganda—the Yugoslav capital was not liberated by the Partisans with the assistance of the Red Army. The analysis of troop movements and strength of forces clearly shows that the real NOVJ–Red Army ratio was around 1:10. Some 300,000 Soviet troops directly participated in the Belgrade Operation. The NOVJ had fourteen divisions at this front, but those were not "real" divisions, but in fact some forty Partisan brigades—each having 950 fighters on average, without heavy weapons. The following is an account of Marshal Vladimir Aleksandrovich Sudets:[1]

> The Third Ukrainian Front under command of Marshal Tolbukhin concentrated its forces in Bulgaria, while the units of the Second Ukrainian Front under command of Marshal Malinovsky reached the left bank of the Danube near the Romanian city of Turnu Severin. They prepared to liberate eastern Serbia, Macedonia, Vojvodina, and Belgrade—the capital of the fraternal Yugoslavia—in the joint operations with the National Liberation Army of Yugoslavia.

> According to the agreement, the Soviet government handed over to the National Liberation Army of Yugoslavia two aviation divisions—a fighter and an assault aviation division under command of General A. N. Vitruk, fully equipped and manned, as well as the arms for Yugoslav infantry divisions and artillery.

> The Soviet units assigned for the Belgrade Operation included the 57th Army of Marshal Tolbukhin and the 10th Guard Rifle Corps of Marshal Malinovsky's Second Ukrainian Front—a total of thirteen rifle divisions, five autonomous motorized rifle brigades, and General Zhdanov's 4th Guard Mechanized Corps, three more artillery divisions, five artillery battalions, fifty autonomous artillery and mortar regiments, engineer units and signal units.

> On the Third Ukrainian Front's advance line alone there were more than 3,000 cannons and mortars, 150 pieces of reactive artillery ordnance,[2] and some 500 tanks and self-propelled guns.[3]

The 17th Air Army of the Third Ukrainian Front (then under my command) also took part in the operation, with approximately 2,000 combat aircraft.

On 5 October 1944, the representatives of the Bulgarian Fatherland Front arrived in the city of Craiova, where Marshal Tito was located. The agreement on military cooperation in the fight against Hitler's Germany was signed, envisaging participation of three Bulgarian armies consisting of thirteen regular divisions and brigades in the Belgrade Operation—specifically, in southern Serbia and Macedonia.

The combat activities of our armies on the Belgrade route began in the late September. They were carried out very dynamically.

According to the agreement with Stalin, by the end of 1944 the NOVJ was supposed to receive 96,515 rifles, 68,423 light and heavy machineguns, 3,797 anti-tank guns, 712 anti-aircraft machineguns, 3,364 mortars of various calibers, 170 anti-aircraft cannons, 895 other pieces of ordnance of various calibers, 1,329 radio stations, 491 combat (assault and fighter) aircraft, seven evacuation hospitals and four surgical hospitals, and other materiel required for equipping twelve fully manned infantry divisions (10,000 troops each) and two aviation divisions. However, most of this materiel was received only after the Belgrade Operation, so it was used for the rearmament of the 1st Proletarian and 12th Shock Corps (as of 1 January 1945 renamed the 1st and 3rd Army, respectively), the 2nd Army, and some other units. The 4th Army in Dalmatia relied on British and American supplies.

Maclean was following the fighting closely, and wherever he went, he kept shocking everyone around with the Order of Suvorov on his Scottish uniform, awarded to him for his services in Iran. Thanks to his reports, Churchill had a reliable insight into the political situation in the Balkans. These analyses made him realize there was no way of splitting Yugoslavia into separate states after the war. Tito's "brotherhood and unity" format was cemented in advance. And something else—Tito outlined the future borders of his state, investing in these areas his political and military capital. But these borders stretched much farther than the ones of the first Yugoslavia. He built a resistance movement and extended his power to the territories he planned to annex by means of the National Liberation Committees (NOO). For example, the annexation of Istria was called "returning Istria to its motherland," although this slogan did not correspond with the peninsula's demographic reality and its political history.

Tito promised to achieve the goals of the national programs of all the small South Slavic nations obsessively preoccupied with the creation of their own nation states in the process they had joined a century too late. He will help them achieve their main territorial claims. While doing so, he will award his satraps fiefdoms that would later be turned into parastates (and eventually into internationally recognized states). But as long as he was alive, assigning a separate territory to each nation was out of the question. The territorial spread of nations was not the criterion by which socialist republics and socialist autonomous provinces were formed.

If Yugoslavia was no longer divisible, and if the future of its peoples could not be secured separately—as Maclean realized, estimating that a Yugoslav nation (or, more precisely, Tito's personal New Yugoslavia) had been forged in the struggle—one would have to talk to the one who possesses the "software" for managing the whole entity. This is why Mihailović and his Yugoslav Army in the Fatherland are immediately out. Not only because they never really fought—at least not on the Allied side; the major problem of Mihailović's Chetnik movement, which rarely moved, was its inability to generate any realistic political platform for an integrated Yugoslavia. No force could ever impose the renewal of the unitarist Serbian kingdom based on royalist anti-democratic ideas. King Peter II had inherited the dictatorship of his father Alexander and the collaborationist regency of his uncle Prince Paul. The program of a unitary, Serb-dominated state was out of the question. Although Tito's brotherhood-unity formula did not allow "negative" stock-taking, everyone was fully aware that the war in the eastern part of Yugoslavia, particularly in Serbia, was of the lowest intensity.

In his book based on research of the German order of battle carried out in the military archives in Karlsruhe, former JNA officer Nikola Anić established that the Wehrmacht's highest-ranking officers who were deployed—not on a permanent basis, of course—in the operations against the Partisans in the Greater Croatia (NDH) were three field marshals, four colonel generals, seventeen technical branch generals, forty-two lieutenant generals, twenty-three major generals, four Luftwaffe generals, one SS gruppenfuehrer, and one vice-admiral. On the other hand, in 1945, the National Liberation Army of Croatia, where most of the battles were taking place (the territory of the quisling Independent State of Croatia that incorporated the whole of Bosnia), had only five generals. At the Tehran Conference, Churchill said to Roosevelt and Stalin: "The Partisan army of Josip Broz Tito has tied down in the Balkans no less than twenty-one German divisions ..."[4] That was not an exaggeration: fourteen divisions were deployed in present-day Croatia, three in Bosnia–Herzegovina, three in Slovenia, one in Montenegro, and none in Serbia.

However, anti-Axis forces under Tito's control are also fighting in Albania, northern Greece, and Friuli. Between January 1942 and the beginning of the Belgrade Operation in September 1944, not one German division was stationed in Serbia proper. There were only Bulgarian garrisons there. As for the Axis (Hungarian) and quisling forces (Slovenian White Guard, Ustashe and Croatian Home Guard, Nedić's and Ljotić's troops), they were only occasionally used as auxiliaries under the command of German headquarters.

So, at the moment when global combinations are being made, General Mihailović does not have any trump card to play—neither an army nor a convincing political program—for the plot that is about to develop. As a result, despite London, Moscow, and Washington recognizing his government and him as its minister of war, he will finally be dropped and conveniently forgotten.

When twenty Russian armies reached the Danube, Mihailović was instructed by the German political commissar in the Balkans, Neubacher, to participate in the creation of a joint anti-communist army with Ljotić and Nedić. However, Hitler soon rejected the idea. He said to his overenthusiastic Balkans' expert: "I have no intention of creating an English fifth column!" Anyway, General Mihailović was then fantasizing that the outcome of the war would be determined by Turkey entering the war, so he withdrew to his starting position—the Bosnian mountain of Ozren. Those who wanted to join the German army on its retreat received his permission to do so. He rejected Ljotić's last offer to jointly form a front on the Isonzo River in Slovenia. Mihailović gathered 1,000 to 2,000 men and led them in the opposite direction, to Serbia, on 10 May, one day after the great parade on the Red Square that had marked victory in the Second World War. They were soon crushed and dispersed by the Yugoslav Army. The general would later hide in mountain houses. In March 1946, he would be captured, put on trial, shot, and buried in an unmarked grave. He would be rehabilitated at a 2015 trial in Belgrade. The sentence of the communist court may have been reversed, but the sentence of the court of history will probably remain unchanged when it comes to his ideas and their realization.

28

CONQUERING THE BALKANS, ACT 1

ALBANIA

TIRANA 1944

On 25 October 1944, Tito leaves Vršac for Belgrade. He has with him the Purga radio station, now renamed Alpha. It has a much stronger transmitter, now under the competence of the Soviet embassy in Yugoslavia. By this point, the defeated German troops have crossed the Danube and retreated to Hungary. They were chased by the Soviet 57th Army. On the dark night of 8 September, they secured the bridgehead at Batinska Skela, defended by the 31st SS Division consisting of Volksdeutsche volunteers and NDH police units. The Soviet thrust across the Danube failed—after fierce fighting that dragged on until early December, it ended with an unsuccessful attempt of a combined landing at Vukovar, where the members of the NOVJ 51st Division and Soviet marines tried to form a bridgehead with the support of the Danube River flotilla of Admiral Sergey Georgyevich Gorshkov, future commander of the Soviet navy. The entire landing force had to be evacuated and the front stabilized on the banks. It stayed like that until late April 1945. For almost five months, the NOVJ did not attempt a westward thrust on the Slavonian front. Why?

Tito and Stalin had their own priorities. Together with the three Bulgarian armies incorporated into its own forces, the Soviet army crossed over to the Danube's left bank again and started its advance through the Pannonian Valley toward Budapest. At the same time, Tito's army attacked Thessalonica and Trieste. Simultaneously, the NOVJ is trying to stop the Army Group E on their withdrawal from Greece. This army group has in the meantime integrated with the units commanded by Field Marshal von Weichs's Army Group F. There are three German army corps and two two-division corps (of the eastern Aegean and Crete), a total of almost 350,000 soldiers who are desperately pushing west. After heavy fighting in Macedonia, where they were also attacked by the Bulgarian Fatherland Front units, they could not continue their withdrawal along the Morava Valley, now held by the Soviet and NOVJ units participating in the Belgrade Operation. They had to retreat to Kosovo, where they came under attack from the 2nd Bulgarian Army and two NOVJ Albanian divisions. In western Serbia, the German 34th Army Corps managed to hold their positions near Kraljevo while awaiting one marching column of Army Group E. Then they pulled out together toward Čačak and Slavonia. The NOVJ Operational Group commanded by Koča Popović is chasing this German echelon, reinforcing its troops with conscripts mobilized in Serbia.

At the same time, the elite German units in Montenegro, the 1st Mountain Division of the Wehrmacht and the 7th SS Division are beginning to pull out. Only a year ago, the same units bracketed the Partisan Main Operational Group on this territory and had them crammed on the Sutjeska. Now they are but a miserable remnant withdrawing from the superior NOVJ and the former Italian division of Taurinense, renamed Garibaldi under its operational control. Within a year, the tide of the battle was turned.

Four scattered divisions of the 8th Dalmatian Shock Corps of the NOVJ liberated Dubrovnik on 18 October. In the Knin Operation in late November 1944, they utterly destroyed the Wehrmacht's 264th Division and liberated all of Dalmatia.

Tito entered Belgrade on 20 October, five days after the city had been liberated. On 30 October, Yugoslav–Greek troops captured Thessalonica. Two out of three of Tito's objectives were thus achieved—he consolidated the core of his new state, including its capital, and he emerged on his projected southern borders.

Having been pacified for two and a half years, Serbia will now become an economic and demographic base for a real, regular army. Tito has established a front in Srem, but his forces there are still on the defensive. The regular army is just being organized and equipped with Soviet arms. Active operations are being carried out in Dalmatia by the 8th Shock Corps, where Tito is focused on the offensive toward Friuli–Venezia Giulia and Carinthia—the regions he intends to capture in accordance with the maximalist claims of the Slovenian Liberation Front. Belgrade was the main focus of his operations, with the 1st Proletarian Corps and 50,000 troops. Auxiliary lines of advance are pursued by the 8th Corps with 35,000 fighters, and the Aegean front of General Apostolski, with some 20,000 fighters of the NOVJ, and three divisions of ELAS commanded by Tito's Greek commander Markos Vafiadis.

An unbelievable turn of events took place in December 1944—the communists captured Athens. It was not done by Tito's cadres. However, the Athens adventure—although carried out by other communists—will have fatal consequences for Tito's Balkan plans. But how did he manage to create such a superiority on the southern front in the first place? How did he practically occupy Albania and most of mainland Greece?

Since Moscow entrusted him with founding the Albanian Communist Party, Tito sent two delegates there—Dušan Mugoša, a military organizer, and Miladin Popović, the future governor of Albania. The founding conference of the Albanian Communist Party (ACP) takes place in Tirana on 8 November 1941 and the Temporary Central Committee is elected. Mugoša came to report to Tito in May 1942, and in September, Tito sends a radio dispatch to IKKI in Moscow stating: "There are no political parties in Albania. There are only individuals without political traditions, principles, and national feelings and everyone cares about their own interests only. There are various factions there and money matters a lot to all of them."[1]

Tito gave Mugoša a letter to the "fraternal Central Committee of the Albanian Communist Party," the same formula he uses in communications with the Central Committee of the Croatian Communist Party. In his letter, he informs that Grandpapa, at his request, gave permission for organizing a conference of the ACP and electing a permanent Central Committee. In Albania, almost at the same time, on 16 September 1942, the National Liberation Conference of Albania was held in Peza, in order to unite all patriotic forces in the fight against the invader. The Main National Liberation Committee was elected (an equivalent of the Croatian ZAVNOH), but this is a parallel, national front-based structure that the Titoites will ignore. The First Land Conference of the ACP took place in Labinot on 17 March 1943. The Central Committee was elected, with Enver Hoxha as its secretary.

The party is actually organized as a chapter of the CPY—like the Slovenian Communist Party. In addition to other evidence, the party documents that fell into the hands of the Italian authorities in the summer of 1943 clearly show that Mugoša is the real head of the ACP.

Tito's military delegate, the commander of the southern fronts, Vukmanović, goes to Albania in March 1943 and then again in the August of the same year. A real army had to be organized. The Supreme Command of the National Liberation Army of Albania was formed on 10 July 1943, and Hohxa was appointed its political commissar.

A military mission of the NOV and POJ pays them a visit, but this is in fact an OZNA team that has come to assume executive power. At the Second Plenum of the Central Committee of the ACP that took place in Berat on 23 November 1944, Hoxha was strongly criticized and Koci Xoxe was proposed as a more appropriate replacement.[2] Hoxha survived, but he became Tito's secret enemy, his renegade—the same as Tito to Stalin.

The final battles are in progress in Albania. The German army is leaving the country. Tirana is liberated on 28 November 1944. The true power in Albania lies in the hands of Veljo Stojnić, the OZNA representative, who reports on a daily basis to his boss, Ranković. Tito will thus control Albania through OZNA and two divisions of KNOJ under its command. Regular units of the Yugoslav army will also be sent to Albania soon. As Tito now holds power and full control in the country, just like in Slovenia, Albania can now become a base for the next stage of his strategic combinations. Promising Greek and Italian cadres are now sent there for training. For example, a set of dispatches on the events in Albania and drafts for ideological and political work from 1944 to 1945 include the information that Renato Bianchi has come to Tirana. He is now in Valona and "wants to see Kocho."[3] The Kocho mentioned here is Xoxe, and Bianchi is in fact Renato Alessandrini, the man who will lead the uprising in Florence only days before the arrival of the Anglo-Americans. The excessively venturous Renato will be killed on 11 August 1944.[4] At that moment, in late 1944, Tito and his men are still in firm control of the liberated territories and liberation movements on both sides of the Straits of Otranto.

29

CONQUERING THE BALKANS, ACT 2

GREECE

THESSALONICA 1944

Tito's plan to take the whole of the Balkans failed before it even started to materialize. The reason was the Athens catastrophe—the Dekemvriana—caused by the disintegration of the KKE. The party barely survived the repression carried out by dictator Ioannis Metaxas between 1936 and 1941 and fell apart completely in 1940, when Italy invaded Greece from Albanian soil. The party instantly disintegrated into its ethnic components. The Hellenes were now in the most difficult position. As for the Bulgarians, their faction became dominant in the KKE when the German armies entered Greece after having overrun Yugoslavia in their Balkan onslaught. The Molotov–Ribbentrop Pact secured the position of the Bulgarian communists—they were collaborationists. Šatorov, a man installed into the CPY leadership for Macedonia by Dimitrov, detached the Skopje-based Regional Committee from the CPY and attached it to the Bulgarian Communist Party, which broke all connections with the party organization in western Macedonia, occupied by Italy. In short, a chapter of a Greater Bulgarian Communist Party was created in Greece—a party that would placidly collaborate with the German occupying forces with the approval of Dimitrov and the Comintern.

Not everyone was happy with this arrangement. The remaining parts of the Greek communist organizations are suffering under Nazi repression—particularly the Hellenes, who, of their own initiative, have decided to put up resistance. In order to survive, the activists flee from the occupied territories and—on 22 May 1941—form a communist insurgent committee in Karditsa, Thessaly, much before the National Liberation Front (EAM) is formed on 27 September 1941.

The German aggression on the "first country of socialism" affected the Bulgarians' position and gave rise to a new leadership. It is headed by Georgios "Geros" (Old Man) Sianthos. There are probably a number of organizations operating (if operating at all) at the same time. In February 1942, Moscow certainly has better things to do than think about the composition of the Greek Central Committee.

The Greek resistance was stimulated by British SOE operatives Eddie Myers and Chris Woodhouse, who supported the royalist renegades of Napoleon Zervas. He blew up the railway bridge on the Gorgopotamos River, splitting the country in half and separating Attica and the Peloponnese from Macedonia. As for the communists in Macedonia and Attica, they are led by Aris Velouchiotis. He cooperates with Zervas and his National Republican Greek League (EDES) movement, in accordance with the national front concept prescribed for a national liberation struggle by the Comintern. What failed in Užice succeeded in Greece—an alliance between combative communists (ELAS) and royalists (EDES), in line with the alliance of the big powers—the United States, Great Britain, and the Soviet Union. A Yalta-style idyll under Mount Olympus.

Velouchiotis organized Partisan detachments and, on 16 February 1942, established the Greek National Liberation Army—ELAS. Having started from scratch, the army soon grew into a 50,000-strong force of fighters-fugitives, most of whom joined this communist archduke because he, like Tito in Bosnia, helped them survive on the liberated territory.

The uprising in Albania has taken root, but the one in Greece is spreading much slower. Everything is going to change when the god of war—Tito's Montenegrin delegate Vukmanović—comes here in the summer of 1943, via Albania. He has finally managed to organize a Partisan detachment in Vardar Macedonia, appointing Apostolski as its commander. He appointed Malinska secretary of the Local Committee of the CPY in Skopje in place of the two-faced Metodija Šatorov.[1] The new, Titoist Macedonian party organization was founded in Tetovo on 19 March 1943. In Tito's perception, Macedonia is a space, not the national territory of a Balkan tribe. It also includes Aegean Macedonia, Epirus, and Thessalonica, with all those mixed ethnic groups of the Balkans.

In the summer of 1944, major events are imminent—Bulgaria is switching to the Soviet side. Three Bulgarian armies (the 1st, 2nd, and 4th) will enter Macedonia and Kosovo. The political situation for Tito's detachments on the ground will thus become critical—all of Vukmanović's efforts could come to nothing. However, fortunately for Tito's Partisan forces, the Bulgarian armies are a regular military force and they follow the Soviet armies toward Hungary and Vienna. Thus, the entire southern Balkans from which the last German forces have withdrawn is now empty.

Vukmanović's organizational efforts will finally pay off. Three ELAS divisions (the 9th, 10th, and 11th) are being formed in Macedonia under Yugoslav control. At the beginning of the war, Vafiadis led guerrilla groups in Crete. In 1943, he was transferred to Macedonia, where he became the *kapetanios* of the 9th Division. The division included a company of Yugoslavs (4th Company of the 3rd Battalion of the 31st Regiment). In the autumn of 1944, Vafiadis commanded a corps consisting of the 6th, 9th, and 11th Divisions that undertook the most important action of the Greek Partisans— the capturing of Thessalonica. In May 1944, after the Lebanon agreement, ELAS recognized the Greek government in London. Under the technical agreement signed in Caserta, British General Sir Ronald MacKenzie Scobie, former commander of Tobruk and Malta, practically became the supreme commander of the Greek resistance. The agreement also defined the zones within which ELAS could operate. Epirus was given to Zervas, Athens was left to the English, and Vafiadis's group of divisions was allowed to advance only toward Thessalonica. Vafiadis entered Thessalonica on 16 October 1944, at the same time as the Belgrade Operation was taking place (12– 20 October). Despite the agreement, they defeated Zervas's security battalions, which had fallen behind. The battalions withdrew to Demir Kapija in Macedonia in order to reach Kosovo and join the rearguard of the German Army Group F. But they did not make it farther than Kilkis (Kukush), 50 kilometers from Thessalonica. They were surrounded and destroyed in the main Second World War battle of the Greek Partisans.

News about the success of the Thessalonica Operation reverberated powerfully across Greece. Vafiadis became a true star that overshadowed various party committee stars, Sianthos and Velouchiotis in particular. What exactly happened in those dramatic days was never really established. Be it as it may, the communist guerrillas, encouraged by the victory at Thessalonica, suddenly gained control of Athens, before major British units entered the city. As soon as the British arrived, fighting broke out. In the street fights that lasted from

December 1944 to January 1945, the British lost 210 dead and their Greek supporters around 1,000. The insurgents lost around 2,000 combatants. There were 3,000 civilian casualties, too. The December events in Athens—the Dekemvriana—were a turning point in the history of the twentieth century. It was the first armed confrontation between the communist East and capitalist West, and the first conflict in the struggle for emancipation from colonial powers in the Mediterranean. Dekemvriana had anticipated the conflicts that characterized the second half of the twentieth century in Asia and Africa. These events also meant the final defeat of the authentic Greek communists. Velouchiotis, by all accounts the main instigator of the rebellion, was killed under unexplained circumstances six months later. Sianthos, the second political sponsor of the rebellion, was pushed off the stage. Vafiadis never supported the Athens operation, which means Tito did not want it either. Dekemvriana was a spectacular debacle. It failed because poor tactics were used. But its failure will also have a negative impact on Tito's operations within his secret empire. The British are now very much aware of the communist penetration into Italy, Albania, and Greece.

30

ROME'S STALINISTS VERSUS MILAN'S TITOISTS

MILAN 1944

January 1944 saw the beginning of bitter fighting for the hilltop abbey of Monte Cassino in the Apennines. This crucial German stronghold on the Gustav Line will hold off the Allied advance for almost half a year. Meanwhile, in Italy, behind enemy lines, deserters who have found shelter in the woods in the inaccessible mountains of the central massif of Gran Sasso, on the Alpine slopes of Savoy and Friuli, and in some pockets in the Po River Valley, form the resistance groups. But the true, combative Partisan units will be formed only when Tito's delegate Vratuša arrives in Milan, when the Soviet–Yugoslav base opens in Bari and when Tito's Command is installed on Vis and starts to coordinate the intelligence and guerrilla activities in the Western Mediterranean.

In early 1944, Vratuša came to Udine and then to Bologna. In perfect sync, three operatives of the Fifth Section of the NKVD responsible for contacts and secret operations arrived there at the same time. The trio left Moscow in January 1944. They took a 1,300-kilometer-long route via Tehran, Cairo, and Bari. In April, they reached Drvar, went to Slovenia, and, with the help of Tito's 9th Slovenian–Italian Corps, arrived in Milan. Using Groza and Purga relay stations to send their dispatches, they will establish contact with Moscow. This team of Italians from Moscow consisted of Teresa "Marushka" Mondini, Vincenzo "Bianco" Vittorio, and Andrea "Nicio Eritreo" Marabini. On 8 January, before their departure from Moscow, they were politically briefed by Dimitrov himself, in Togliatti's presence. The meeting took place in the AUCP(b) Central Committee building in Moscow. Dimitrov's personal archive contains documents indicating that Mondini was sent as a radio operator responsible for radio contacts with the main Soviet communication headquarters. The group, codenamed "the Correspondents of the 100th Institute," was also instructed to recruit an agent network, a separate group within the Central Committee of the PCI.

The trio arrived in Milan, the capital of the Italian resistance, and established contact with the PCI headquarters led by the "insurgents' triumvirate" composed of Pietro Secchia (organizing secretary, intelligence), Luigi Longo (political commissar), and Vincenzo "Cino" Moscatelli (military activities). Mondini will marry Cino and will have a son with him. At the rally on the occasion of the liberation of Milan on 26 April 1945, she greeted the crowd in Russian, although she was from Imola in Emilia Romagna. She conveyed the "fiery greetings of the Red Army." Comrade Longo was translating her words from Russian. Secchia, a party hardliner, commanded Moscatelli's unit, which entered Milan. It was then that Cino's wife addressed the thrilled crowd in Russian. It is all one army—Stalin's and Tito's secret "Front" in the West.

When all the young code clerks are identified, one can reconstruct the GRU and NKVD radio networks in the West. In Istanbul, we have Natalia Nikolayevna Smolnikova, working for the Istanbul resident Mikhail Matveyevich Baturin (whom she will marry soon). Josip Kopinič brought to Zagreb his wife Stella Bamiadzidos, trained in the Comintern's special technical school. Srebrnjak also has his wife with him—Franciška "Beba" Klinc, also a trained code clerk. Tito's adept, Martini, has Maria "the Italian," and Marabini has Teresa Mondini. In Greece, the pro-Bulgarian (and pro-Soviet) party leader Petros Russos will have as his travel companion and code clerk Chrysa Hatzivassiliou, while the Spanish leader Jesús Monzón will be escorted by the radio operator and party secretary Carmen del Pedro.

Comrade Tito, who is more ambitious than any other member of this group made up of Moscow's progeny, leaves enciphering to a more serious person, to Pavle Savić, a prewar scientific associate of atomic physicist Irène Joliot-Curie.

It may not be visible yet, but a certain differentiation is already in place: two lines are being established, and this will lead to the first major schism in the world's communist empire, creating the Stalin–Tito conflict. How did this breakup in the PCI happen?

Until the surrender of Italy in the summer of 1943, the leadership of the Italian party was confined to the Ventotene island in the Tyrrhenian Sea, which Mussolini had been using as his Siberia. The entire party leadership was exiled here. After Badoglio's overthrow of Mussolini in 1943, the communists were evacuated. In Milan, Italy's main industrial center, the top party brass formed an umbrella political organization, the National Liberation Committee for Northern Italy (CLNAI).[1] Vratuša joined them. He was sent by the commander of the Slovenian–Friulian 9th Corps, Ivan "Matija" Maček. At first, he was in charge of the headquarters of the Garibaldi Detachments and Italian Volunteer Corps in Gorizia. The Garibaldi Brigades in that area would soon formally join the NOVJ.[2] Thus, the communist military units formed in northern Italy came under the direct control of Tito, not of the National Liberation Committee (CLN) in Rome.

Founded on 9 September 1943, the Rome-based CLN brings together communists and other insurgents, guerrillas, and underground fighters in the cities. It is a typical national front body in which all parties except fascists are represented and is therefore recognized and assisted by the Anglo-Americans. In the late spring of 1944, the CLN will form the national provisional government. It will substitute Badoglio's cabinet. Ivanoe Bonomi, president of the CLN, is an eminent prewar bourgeois politician, a democrat who will form a republican government that will liquidate the monarchy, sign peace treaties, and organize parliamentary elections. Unexpectedly—and sensationally—Togliatti joins this "governo Bonomi secondo" ("Bonomi primo" was in 1921) formed in June 1944. Togliatti's participation has ensured the government's legitimacy on the left, as well as the background support of Stalin himself. However, on the other side of the country, there is that other committee, founded underground in Milan even earlier, in September 1943, as the National Liberation Committee for Northern Italy (CLNAI). Stalin now has two players on the Apennine Peninsula. In the south—in the visible spectrum—communists have accepted the parliamentary format, hoping they will win the general election. At the same time, cities in the north are swarming with the conspirators of Tito's clandestine empire. CLNAI is the umbrella organization of the Partisan army, run by Tito's communists. If the former have Moscow's support for peaceful and political activities, it does not mean that the latter will be denied support for military and subversive activities. Besides, Stalin is holding Milan by means of two lines—one is Tito's and the second is Mondini's direct line with Dimitrov in the Central Committee of the AUCP(b) in Moscow.

Tensions will inevitably appear between the communist Partisans of CLNAI and the Rome-based CLN. The political monopoly is at stake here—

the very authority in the military formations and on the liberated territories from which the postwar system will arise.

Operations on the Partisan front are developing very slowly. Simply, there are no eager fighters in Italy. The country has been at war for ten years, ever since the Ethiopian intervention. The nation's energy has been exhausted. The first combat detachments on the Apennine Peninsula were therefore formed by the Yugoslavs one year before the end of the war. At the helm of the first of these brigades is the National Hero Vida "Lenka" Tomšič, the wife of the fallen National Hero and organizing secretary of the Slovenian Communist Party, Tone "Gašpar" Tomšič. Five overseas brigades of NOVJ, 27,000-strong, have been formed. They are deployed in Italy and North Africa (their members are recruited from the internment camps and Allied units in Kenya, Sudan, Egypt, and Algeria). One of the brigades—with almost 3,000 fighters—was formed in London. Of course, it was Velebit who negotiated it. It is made up of the Slovenes from the regions annexed to the German Reich, mobilized in the Wehrmacht and captured after the Normandy landings. Now they have joined the NOVJ. Two royal Yugoslav fighter squadrons of the Allied air force in the Middle East have also joined Tito.

As for the Italians, they just do not want to fight. Even if they join the Partisans, they do so in order to avoid being drafted into Mussolini's Esercito Nazionale Repubblicano (RSI) or deported to Germany as forced laborers. The war in Greece did not stop even after the fall of Berlin because the arch-enemies of Tito's anti-fascists there were not fascists but the bourgeois parties that could seize power after the liberation. This is why the Partisan movement in the mountains of Macedonia and Epirus spread again. In Italy, it is different: the Partisans returned to their homes in 1945. Actually, they did so even in the winter of 1944 by order of British Marshal Harold Alexander, which was broadcast in November after the first armed conflicts had taken place in Athens. The incident in Florence, where "Bianco" Alessandrini, trained by OZNA in Albania, tried to seize power for the communists before the British forces occupied the city, led to British concerns of a possible Italian Dekemvriana in the north. Longo, the communist leader in Milan, is in close contact with Tito, and he will become a National Hero of Yugoslavia. But he is not Tito, and Italy is not in the Balkans.

31

THE CASTLE OF LEAD

BLEIBURG 1945

In February 1945, Churchill sends to Belgrade Field Marshal Alexander, Supreme Allied commander of the Mediterranean Theater of Operations. He is to discuss with Marshal Tito the coordination of support to the spring offensive of the Yugoslav army. This is of course a pretext. The true purpose of Alexander's visit is to assess Tito's intentions in Italy. Tito shows him the dispositions on the stationary Srem Front while concealing his far-reaching initiative on both sides of the Adriatic, and in the south, in Greece and Albania. He has just ordered that the 4th Army be formed of the 8th Corps units in Dalmatia. While three armies are currently passive on the Srem Front, the 4th Army, established on 1 March, should launch its lightning Trieste campaign.

At the two meetings with Tito, held on 21 and 24 February 1945, Alexander explains that he would need a land corridor for advancing from Trieste to Vienna. He suggests it would mean Anglo-American "occupation of all the areas west of the Italian–Yugoslav prewar border." He points out that he is not authorized to accept changes to this border because it is to be resolved at a postwar peace conference. Tito replies that he sees no reason for the Allies to occupy the whole of Istria only to secure a corridor to Austria. He offers them use of the "Ljubljana Gate," passing across Yugoslav territory. In return, he wants his own occupation zone in Austria. Alexander does not want to discuss it—he realizes he has been outmaneuvered politically. He will get verbal guarantees of cooperation along the demarcation line—something that neither side takes very seriously. Tito is hard to out-bluff—he is never impressed with force unless an imminent threat is involved.

If the war went on, Tito would place even more territories under his control. This is why he is not in a hurry to finish it. At first, the Anglo-Americans count on his troops: in the last months of the war, they are concerned that Nazi guerrilla units will be formed and organize a final stand in the Alpine redoubt. Engaging Tito's forces against them could be very useful. However, in return for using his 200,000 fighters to take on the Germans in Tirol, Tito modestly requires his own occupation sector in Vienna and Berlin. In other words, instead of the four victorious great powers, there should be a round table of five powers at which he would sit. Indeed, in terms of its military might, Tito's army is stronger than the French army, but Yugoslavia is but a provisory country that no one takes seriously yet.

In April, jitters can be felt in Alexander's headquarters in Caserta because of the massive redeployment of enemy forces on the routes to Upper Austria. The remnants of the 6th SS Panzer Army commanded by Oberst-Gruppenfuehrer Josef Sepp Dietrich, vanquished in the last major German offensive, "Spring Awakening" (Fruehlingerswachen), are retreating to Vienna and Upper Austria. This explains the British willingness to get rid of the Croatian troops amassed on the Slovenian border with Carinthia. These troops have arrived there in order to avoid surrendering to Tito's Yugoslav army. Moving toward Carinthia are members of the "Croatian Armed Forces" (HOS), comprising the Ustashe and Home Guard units, amalgamated since the autumn of 1944. Their withdrawing units are mixed with the remaining members of Nedić's State Guard, Ljotić's Volunteer Corps, Chetnik detachments from Bosnia, Serbia, and Montenegro, and Slovenian Home Guards (who collaborated with the Germans, unlike the White Guards, who collaborated with the Italians). Joining them in the retreat are the massive units of the 15th Cossack Cavalry SS Corps, the strongest Axis formation in the Balkans. None of them wants to surrender to their fellow countrymen.

British air reconnaissance has established that more than 400,000 German troops from various formations are moving toward the Austrian border, together with some 200,000 members of the armed forces of the NDH followed by numerous fleeing civilians.[1]

The information about the movements and plans of the defeated armies gathered by Anglo-American military intelligence has caused hysteria in the Allied headquarters. The end of the war in Europe had been expected way back in late 1944. However, the German counteroffensive in the Ardennes disrupted them, and Eisenhower, anticipating resistance in the Alps, changed the strategic priorities and shifted the focus of the operations from Berlin farther south. Despite the pessimistic predictions and fears in the Allied head-quarters, the Germans ended their war neatly: after the capitulation on 7 May 1945, there were no more combat operations on Greater Germany's soil.

Supreme Headquarters Allied Expeditionary Force (SHAEF) studied the reprisal techniques used by the Germans on occupied territories since they were considered rather successful. Indeed, resistance movements in Europe spread only on the territories occupied by the Italians or by other Axis allies to which the task of occupation had been "outsourced." SHAEF issued instructions that gave each Allied occupation army substantial freedom of action when it came to reprisals and hostage-taking. Only the British signaled at the outset that they would have a problem with measures that would involve bloodshed. And all together there were only a few incidents and casualties.

On the Balkan Front, where the Red Army and Tito's army are operating, things are totally different. However, the British leaders are still hoping some combination with the Yugoslavs is possible. They are not ready to give up their investment in Tito, NOVJ, and the Tito–Šubašić provisional government (NKOJ). Intensive talks continue even after Alexander's mission and, because of political opportunities, a fatal decision is made to leave the quisling forces in Austria at the mercy of Tito and Stalin. The British will do so although it is now clear that this is not an army trying to move from one mountain redoubt to another and organize a new front there, since the German army strictly observes the capitulation it has signed.

As the British have the leading role in the Mediterranean theater of opera-tions, they send to this delicate mission Harold Macmillan, a member of the wartime cabinet, minister resident in the Mediterranean, and a future Conservative prime minister. Macmillan orders General Sir Charles Keightley, commander of the 5th Corps, to carry out Operation Keelhaul—handing over to the Red Army and Tito's army some 70,000 quisling troops, POWs who have already surrendered to the Western Allies in Austria. Smaller groups of them will be returning across the border for weeks after the German capitula-tion, so this number will increase. In the general confusion thus created, 4,000 White Russians and 11,000 of their family members, who had never even been Soviet citizens, were also delivered to the Soviets to disappear without a trace. Their handover was not even in accordance with the Yalta Agreement.

In the Austrian woods, the Soviet army organizes mass executions of the Cossacks who have fallen into their hands, while Tito's army eradicates the members of Yugoslav quisling formations. German POWs also perish on a massive scale—entire divisions are being executed. Civilians are also being shot—the Yugoslav army is not willing to take over so many people, and a general massacre will be the most efficient solution. After all, Tito has won the war, but the power he holds is still shaky. Having captured so many enemy troops, he must neutralize them without a military or civilian organization that would deal with the problem in a civilized way. He only has the instruments for the final solution. In the rear, his political power is not consolidated yet. He does have a few proletarian brigades, OZNA, and specialized military repression organs (KNOJ), but he has not legitimized his authority—he is merely the prime minister of a provisional government and its defense commissioner. Tito is also aware that Stalin's support depends exclusively on how Moscow perceives his power on the ground—if he himself cannot control his own territory and annihilate his opponents and has to ask for the assistance of the Soviet army to do so (as all the leaders of "people's democracies" do), he will become replaceable like everyone else in this East European choir. This is why Tito will have no mercy. But these are merely the circumstances in which he implements his decisions; the general plan and intentions can be seen behind the military movements. Understanding the whole thing is easier if the Rijeka Operation is taken as a case study.

Having suffered heavy losses, the Yugoslav army captured Rijeka on 3 May. The operation's strategic goal was to capture Trieste and reach the Monfalcone–Duino–Gorizia–Tarvisio–Villach–Klagenfurt line. Tito notified Field Marshal Alexander of it in advance, explaining that his civilian authority (the "people's authority") would be installed on these territories—Friuli and Carinthia—regardless of the Allied troops stationed there, and that all detachments of the Yugoslav army would loyally cooperate with these troops.

The Yugoslav army units entered Trieste on 1 May. Street fighting ensued because the enemy decided to fight to the very last, awaiting the British troops to whom they wanted to surrender. They did not make it and had to lay down arms to the Yugoslav 4th Army. However, the British contingent entered the city immediately afterward and protected them. The discussions on the joint administration of the city then took place.

The city of Rijeka is a "pocket" populated by the "wrong" people, also marked with a cultural memory that is not to communists' liking. Just like Königsberg, which was razed to the ground by the Red Army somewhat earlier (9 April), Rijeka will be taken by brute military force and ethnically cleansed.

"Four brigades of the 19th and 26th Divisions participated in the destruction of the Rijeka group," says the report of the operations officer of the 4th Army headquarters. "The enemy's advance toward Trieste is being blocked by the 9th, 17th, and 43rd Divisions and by one brigade of the 29th Division." Now that the goals in the West have been attained, these substantial forces could have been engaged in breaking the resistance. The report continues: "The fighting with the enemy group in Rijeka is particularly bitter and violent because their soldiers have been ordered to fight to the last man ..." Such orders are always easy to give, but why would the soldiers obey them? What could the war objective of both sides possibly be, when one is sparing no troops to win the last battle in a war that is already won and the other is fighting bitterly to delay the defeat? The answer can be seen from what happened after the Yugoslav army took Rijeka on 3 May, receiving a special commendation from Marshal Tito for this success.

Who was defending it? After Italy's surrender in 1943, General Ludwig Kübler and the German 97th Corps captured Istria and Dalmatia. The soldiers under his command treated the population very brutally. Kübler closely cooperated with the notorious SS General Odilo Globočnik, an Eichmann associate, later stationed in Trieste. Wounded in that last battle in Rijeka, Kübler was captured. He was hanged in Ljubljana in 1947. His younger brother, Lieutenant General Joseph Kübler, who commanded the forces on the Neretva and then the German defense of Belgrade, was also hanged in 1947, but in Belgrade.

As for the troops—the German 188th Reserve Mountain Division was not an elite unit. It was a garrison unit, a reserve "Home Guard" division from Innsbruck formed from the 718th Division half spent on the Neretva and some elder reservists. In 1943, it was sent to Istria to take the positions abandoned by the Italians. It was commanded by Hans von Hösslin, also hung in Ljubljana together with Kübler. What happened to his troops? There were eight infantry battalions. A preserved photograph shows the members of the divisional 1088th Artillery Regiment surrendering in good order in Pula's Musil fortification on 6 May 1945. They held out the longest, hoping to be rescued. Where did they end up?

The units of the 188th Division had to split up. The main force tried to break out of the encirclement and reach Trieste, but they were stopped at Ilirska Bistrica and surrendered there on 7 May. They were all shot in the woods of Kočevski Rog—a former Partisan base—and buried in shallow graves with no markings. The soldiers of the divisional 1088th Artillery

Regiment and the 1047th Infantry Regiment who surrendered in Musil in Pula were shot and thrown into the pits in the Istrian Karst region.

The remaining members of the German army captured in Rijeka were executed in Zaprešić near Zagreb after a "death march." Around 4,500 corpses of the members of the 392nd (Croatian) Infantry Division of the Wehrmacht were found there. They were mostly mobilized members of the Croatian Home Guard units under the command of German officers and non-commissioned officers, also liquidated.

When Rijeka was captured, OZNA began a systematic ethnic cleansing campaign. Almost all Italian citizens were expelled and many were killed. While the 1936 census put the number of Rijeka Italians at 53,896,[2] the one in 1948 recorded only a few thousand of them. The emptied city was then populated by migrants from all over Yugoslavia.

The year of victory over the Axis powers saw the beginning of retaliation and Stalinization in the half of Europe that had ended up in the Soviet sphere of influence. The Potsdam Agreement of August 1945 authorized resettlement of the population and pacification of hostile elements. Roosevelt's successor Harry S. Truman attended the meeting of the Big Three for the first time, and so did Clement Attlee, who had replaced Churchill after the Conservative Party lost the election of 5 July 1945. Stalin will have a much easier job imposing himself on his new partners than on their predecessors. Underlining his authority are the 264 Soviet divisions (thirty-six of which are armored) deployed in Europe.

Tito has four armies, too. It is a force that guarantees his full domination over the captured territories after the war. He uses the time-tested Stalinist technique of large-scale repression. It has two components: political purges and ethnic cleansing. They are carried out simultaneously, so the mass slaughter of various troops and civilians is camouflaged as being unplanned. In fact, these are well-prepared and well-studied processes with a clear political purpose.

The quislings and class enemies are being wiped out systematically. OZNA takes care of it, using cadres trained by the NKVD in Moscow and by Soviet specialists in Yugoslavia. The executions are carried out by special military units of the KNOJ, almost the most numerous formation in the Yugoslav army (it had 113,858 soldiers at the end of 1945).[3]

Ethnic cleansing of entire ethnic groups—the populations collectively perceived by the regime as dangerous—is being carried out at the same time as the executions of the captured troops. The Germans and Italians will disappear from postwar Yugoslavia. Local Germans (Volksdeutsche) could not join the

Wehrmacht because they were not German citizens. They therefore had to serve in SS units, where recruitment was done on the basis of racial criteria. Their liquidation is also part of the policy of ethnic cleansing of the undesirable groups. Of 499,969 Germans recorded in the census of 1931 who had specified German as their mother tongue (of that number some 10,000 are Jews), only 55,337 remained in 1948. Of this prewar population, 240,000 were evacuated to Germany to avoid the advancing Red Army and Yugoslav army. Not counting the captured troops, the remaining 200,000 or more Volksdeutsche civilians ended up under Tito's regime. According to the available evidence, 48,687 of them—including 6,000 children below the age of fourteen—died in prison camps between 1944 and 1948.[4] Proportionally, this exceeds the crimes committed on the territories occupied by Stalin's troops. This is another domain where Tito was an avant-gardist. The systematic extermination of the entire German population in Yugoslavia has all the characteristics of a genocide.[5]

As for the POWs from the Home Guard, Slovenian White Guard, and Chetnik units, a simple criterion was used: all officers were executed. Since, for example, all students and educated members of the middle class who wanted to avoid being sent to a frontline enrolled in Home Guard officers' schools, their execution would also mean eliminating the class enemies of the elite of a nation—thus facilitating such nation's future integration into the new society. The NKVD used the same methodology in the Katyn Massacre, when thousands of Polish reserve officers—the country's intelligentsia—were executed.

The 40 to 60 kilometer-long refugee column leaving Croatia for Austria contained hundreds of thousands of people. Mixed groups of soldiers and civilians were turned around and forced to march to faraway destinations. The marches ended in prison camps in Vojvodina or in mass graves. Some 1,500 mass graves have been identified so far along these death roads, most of them in Slovenia. While the total figures are hard to determine, the following dispatch sent from the headquarters to the head of OZNA for Croatia on 3 July 1945 is rather illustrative:

> As for the number of officers in the NDH in the last months of the war, the estimates range around 5,000–6,000 active and 8,000 reserve Home Guard officers and 2,500–3,000 Ustashe officers. Most of them were captured in Slovenia and, unless dealt with immediately, were transported to Srijem ... In Zagreb, 2,882 Home Guard officers were registered in May—1,607 active ones and 1,275 reserve ones. Half of them have been dealt with; quite a lot have been

sent to camps. Others included non-commissioned officers, various gendarmes, police officers, Ustashe etc.—17,000 of them. Most of them have also been dealt with, and the rest are currently being processed.[6]

In some places, systematic executions are turning into arbitrary massacres. This, of course, would arouse fear among the population—and outbursts of discontent. That is something the authorities do not want because they are not as consolidated as they would like the people to believe. This is why, at the first conference of the highest-ranking OZNA officers for Croatia in July 1945, formidable Comrade Krajačić gives instructions for the future *modus operandi*. He says:

> Some members have been carrying out or ordering executions arbitrarily ... The reason for the executions was the attitude adopted in Slavonia not just by OZNA but also by other institutions, which comes down to this: all those who are known to be our enemies and who would turn against us tomorrow must be liquidated without much scruples. Comrades, stop with these executions! It's not that I feel sorry for the enemy—I wouldn't feel sorry for my own father—but because people have started to grumble. We must find a new way of eliminating this enemy. We have courts, the court of national honor. There are ways of tracking down the enemies, infiltrating their ranks, and eliminating them legally ...[7]

At the beginning of the conference, a representative of the Central Committee of the Croatian Communist Party said: "The instructions that you receive from OZNA's Croatian Section are not just the instructions of Comrade Stevo [Krajačić]. They are also the instructions of the Central Committees of the Croatian and Yugoslav Communist Parties." In other words, they are Comrade Tito's instructions.

To legalize the repression and turn it from chaotic violence into a controlled retaliation carried out by the authorities, a system of prison camps has been introduced. Besides the POWs, civilians are also sent to them on the basis of racial criteria. The ethnic Germans, prewar citizens of Yugoslavia, are summarily executed or evicted from their houses and apartments and sent to the camps.[8] The legal basis for the repression was found in the AVNOJ's decision on confiscation, passed at its Third Session on 21 November 1944. It is a racial law. All enemy property, including "all the property of ethnic Germans, with the exception of the property of the Germans who fought in the ranks of the NOV and POJ or who are subjects of neutral countries and did not act in a hostile manner during the occupation," will become government property.[9] A total of 97,720 land plots (637,939 hectares) were confiscated, mostly in Vojvodina (389,256 hectares) and in Croatia (120,977 hectares).

In June 1945, exactly 96,769 Germans (including 24,435 children and 19,953 persons above sixty-five years of age) were interned in camps in Vojvodina. Half of the internees were able to work and the rest were left to die.[10] In early May 1945, Tito signed an order entitled "Using the Labor Force from Ethnic German Camps." The order introduced the same regime that was in effect in the labor camps of the Third Reich:

> In order to make the best and most rational use of the interned male and female Germans for farming works, I hereby order that the German labor force be used as much as possible on the state-owned land in Vojvodina. The treatment in the camps must be such that it stimulates the Germans to agree to go to work by offering them privileges ... Prison commanders will report to me once a month about the distribution of the camp labor force and the type of work that such labor force is performing.[11]

This "Siberia of the Balkans" is a system of "slave-driving kolkhozes [collective farms]" where the labor force is mercilessly exploited on their own confiscated land. Poor nourishment, miserable accommodation, and lack of hygiene, medicines, and medical assistance cause outbreaks of diseases like dysentery and typhus. Starvation and the exhausting work in harsh weather conditions are also taking their toll. The first ones to suffer are the children, the elderly, and the frail. The typhus epidemic that began in the autumn/winter of 1945 will reach frightening proportions the following winter.[12]

The extensive elimination of the people's enemies is not confined by the state's borders because they have not yet been defined. Tito's elite formation—the intelligence service developed from the OZNA—carries out operations outside the borders. Section 2 (which used to deal with the internal enemy) has been transferred to the Foreign Ministry now that the "internal enemy" has emigrated and become "external." The State Security Administration (UDBA), military intelligence agency, and military counterintelligence agency (KOS) have been formed from the remaining parts of OZNA. UDBA had become the political police for internal repression and elimination of the "enemies of the people."

The experienced Vratuša becomes head of the elite part of the OZNA that has now become part of the Ministry of Foreign Affairs. This "Yugoslav CIA" will later be named Information and Documentation Service (SID). Immediately after the war, the service carried out aggressive operations against quislings and political opponents on the territories under Anglo-American occupation—in other words, in Austria and Italy. An assassination attempt against Ustashe leader Ante Pavelić's deputy Mate Frković took place in

Salzburg in 1945. Dr Ivo Protulipac, president of the clerical Croatian Eagle Alliance, who was involved in smuggling Ustashe members and sympathizers across the "soft" Yugoslav–Italian border, was killed in Trieste in 1946. Drago Jilek, former head of the "Ustashe Supervisory Service" (UNS), was abducted in Rome in 1949.[13] Temistocle Testa, the Italian prefect of Kvarner and special commissar for Sicily, committed suicide under suspicious circumstances in the remote Terme Poretti in 1949.[14] This was just the beginning of the decades-long global campaign of Tito's secret operatives abroad that would culminate in the 1970s and reach New York, Stockholm, and Sydney.

32

LOS CUATRO GENERALES

TOULOUSE 1945

Tito's power in the secret sphere was based on the revolutionary cadres from the Spanish Civil War. The generals mentioned in the most famous Spanish war ballade, *Los cuatro generales*, are the four Nationalist commanders who laid siege to Madrid. Tito had his own four Spanish generals too, mentioned in another, no less famous revolutionary ballade, *El quinto regimiento*— Enrique Líster Forján, Juan Modesto, Antonio Cordon, and José Manuel Tagüeña Lacorte.

General Líster was born in Cuba but joined the Spanish Communist Party (PCE) at the age of eighteen. In 1932, he went to the Soviet Union to receive military training. In the Spanish Civil War, he commanded the predominantly communist 11th Division. He excelled as a commander and won fame as a war hero. After the defeat, he went to Moscow and fought as a Soviet general in the Battle of Leningrad in the Great Patriotic War.

In his memoirs, Dimitrov describes the conversation he had with Líster in mid-October 1944 discussing the future of the Iberian Peninsula.[1] He summarizes Stalin's general line for Spain: (a) spoiling the plans of the Western imperialists who support Franco; (b) forcing the leaders of the Spanish socialists, anarchists, and republicans to drop the policy of passively waiting for external assistance; (c) forming a government that would represent Spanish people; and (d) only guerrilla warfare can give rise to such a national movement.

After the defeat of the Republican army, some 440,000 people crossed the Pyrenees. Moscow charged Tito with repatriating important cadres. In France, numerous communists are being interned because they have refused to take an oath of allegiance to France. However, the Molotov–Ribbentrop Pact has made Moscow desert them, just like the communists in Greek and Yugoslav camps and prisons (Acronafplia, Mitrovica, Kerestinec). In Spain, *maquisards* (so-called *huidos*), the fugitives, were hiding in the mountains from 1939 to 1943 to avoid repression.

When France was occupied, the Central Committee of the PCE moved to Moscow. The infighting that ensued was won by Santiago Carrillo, head of the party's youth organization. But one of the party leaders did remain in the field. It was Monzón. After hiding in the French Pyrenees, he managed to slip across into Spain in the spring of 1943. Like Tito, he wants to fight the enemy in his own country, not in the refugee committees or behind a desk in Moscow. A few months later, in September 1943, he founded the Junta Suprema de Unión Nacional (JSUN) and became its president.

After the Wehrmacht's retreat and liberation of Toulouse, the Working Commission of the PCE (Comisión de Trabajo del PCE) was established in order to carry out *Operación reconquista de España*. The decision on the military operation was made by Monzón.

The Valley of Arán was chosen as the target of the attack. The idea was to create a liberated territory there. In winter, the snow-bound valley is cut off from the rest of Spain, but the passes leading to France can still be used. By blocking the Bonaigua Pass, the insurgents could defend the free territory, the center of which was supposed to be in the fortified town of Vielha, with a population of 821. To carry out the operation, Monzón transforms the 14th Corps, a guerrilla unit, into the operational group Agrupación de Guerrilleros Españoles (AGE)— equivalent to an army brigade or a Partisan proletarian division (8,000 to 9,000 guerrillas). They will move to Spain from the base in Toulouse.[2]

These activities aroused concern in the Moscow-based Central Committee of the PCE, so they sent Gabriel León Trilla from Spain to France. Officially, he was sent to help Monzón's insurgency, but the real intention was that he, as a loyal cadre, would help other loyal cadres to renew Moscow's direct control over the PCE in the country. Having realized that he was politically isolated and that time was working against him, Monzón launched the invasion of Vall d'Aran.

In October 1944, a few thousand men entered the Valley of Aran in order to establish a front in northern Catalonia. A major town was supposed to be taken where a government would be formed, demanding recognition from the anti-Hitlerite coalition. The insurgents also hoped that their operations would incite masses across the country and result in a general uprising. The hopes were in vain. Besides, the crucial military and political aspects of the Aran Valley operation were poorly planned, resulting in a crushing defeat of the guerrilla corps. What was left of it, withdrew to France.[3]

While the Vall d'Aran operation was still in progress, Moscow ordered Carrillo to leave North Africa where he was based for southern France. In Toulouse, he joined the leading group in the Communist Party. He sent his emissary Agustín Zoro to eliminate the Monzonite faction and regain control over the party. Monzón was ordered back to France. As Líster later wrote, the only reason Monzón avoided assassination was because he had been captured and imprisoned in Barcelona. His associates were executed by a group of communist *pistoleros*.[4]

The 1944 Churchill–Stalin Agreement sealed the fate of revolution in Europe. The Soviet leader ordered all the guerrillas to demobilize. He strictly adhered to the agreement because he was aware that Europe's postwar map would depend primarily on the frontline operations and titanic effort of the Soviet army and state. Way back in 1943, when he dissolved the Comintern, Stalin gave up exporting revolution. The communist network in the field is, of course, a useful clandestine asset for the secret service, but as a revolutionary device it is not worth the efforts invested in it. Nowhere will revolutionaries win in Europe, except in the anomalous Balkans, in Yugoslavia, and they are going to create huge damage to the united communist front run by Stalin from Moscow.

In the meantime, Spanish guerrilla groups in southern France continued with their activities because they were in line with Tito's tentative conspiratorial military and political command in the Mediterranean. Dimitrov informed Stalin that he had conveyed to Tito the request of Ibarruri: "As regards possible dispatching of Spanish comrades—Modesto, Lister, and Cordon—to Yugoslavia and their temporary engagement in the National Liberation Army, Tito gave the go-ahead ..."[5]

In the Spanish Civil War, Juan Modesto (real name: Juan Guilloto León), once a Spanish legionary in Morocco, became commander of the legendary 5th Regiment, of which the ballade *El quinto regimiento* was composed. He kept his rank in the Red Army while fighting in the Great Patriotic War. Then he went to Tito's Yugoslavia. Having spent a few months in Belgrade, Líster and Modesto came to Paris in February 1945. The city had been liberated only six months earlier. Republican General Antonio Cordón García stayed in Yugoslavia as a liaison officer for more than a year—which means that the operations in Spain in 1945 and 1946 were coordinated from Belgrade.[6] When the repression increased in 1947, the PCE explicitly requested Yugoslav assistance and expertise, knowing that Tito's regime was also supporting the Greek insurgents. Tagüeña came to Yugoslavia as head of the expert Spanish team that was supposed to be turned into the field command when a new stage of the fighting in Spain began. In addition to the Spaniards, many other former members of the International Brigades started coming from Russia to the Belgrade military academy as of 1946.

Tagüeña was based in the city of Niš, as an expert assistant at the Yugoslav army's headquarters. In early 1948, the Yugoslav and Albanian armies are preparing a joint operation (Operation Lakes), a thrust into Greece via Lakes Ohrid and Prespa.[7] Tagüeña is promoted to lieutenant general of the Yugoslav army, the same rank as the chief of the General Staff. At the same time, Carrillo and Líster visit Tito as representatives of the Politburo of the Central Committee of the PCE, requesting that the Yugoslav air force carry out an airborne landing to support the guerrillas of Levante (Catalonia and Andalusia). Tito refused, on the grounds of the insufficient range of Yugoslav aircraft and the high risk involved. As a token of support, he gave them USD30,000.

When the open conflict broke out between Tito and Stalin, Tagüeña took refuge in Czechoslovakia. He later declared himself a Titoist. He died in Mexico. Cordón died in Rome. Líster lived to return to Spain. There is no doubt that the Belgrade group within the PCE existed and operated until 1948 and even later. The PCE leadership was summoned to Moscow in October 1948, and Stalin, Molotov, Kliment Voroshilov, and Mikhail Suslov explicitly told them to abandon their heretical revolutionary goals and Titoist ideas. The Spanish leadership meekly acquiesced. Still, some guerrilla corps continued to fight—Agrupación de Guerrillero de Levante-Aragón (AGLA) and Agrupación de Guerrillero de Granada (AGG) fought all the way up to 1952.

33

THREE TITOIST EVANGELISTS

TRIESTE 1945

In less than four months spent on Vis, Tito managed to consolidate his secret network in the Mediterranean, based on the communist cadres from the Spanish Civil War. A great many of them will also fight in the Partisan units of the French resistance. During the occupation, Yugoslavs spearheaded the combat groups in the whole of southern France—in Marseille, Lyon, Toulouse, and Bordeaux. The most prominent among them is Ljubomir Ilić, also known as "Boris," "Conti," "Louis," or "Cdt Brunetto."

After his studies at the University of Paris, Ilić went to Spain in 1936 and joined the Dombrowski Battalion of the 12th International Brigade "Giuseppe Garibaldi" as political commissar and then a company commander. After an impressive career in the Republican army (he worked up to commander of the 14th Guerrilla Corps), he will end up interned in Saint-Cyprien prison camp in France. In February 1941, he and some other Yugoslav comrades were transferred to a special prison in Toulouse. Soon afterward, Petain's police moved them to Castres prison as a transit stop on the way to German death camps. Italian communist Longo was there, too. In September 1943, a group of thirty-six of them managed to escape and join the French resistance.

Ilić became commander of the French Zone South. In January 1944, he was invited to the French National Military Committee and was appointed commander-in-chief of the FTP-MOI (Francs-tireurs et partisans—main-d'œuvre immigrée, Irregulars and Partisans—Immigrant Movement) for the whole country. He was then promoted to a French army general. In October 1944, he was sent to SHAEF.

Dimitrij "Cot" Koturović, a former Yugoslav member of the International Brigades, organized the uprising in Marseille, where he led the first FTP-MOI group, until he was killed by the bomb he was trying to plant. He was succeeded by Vlajko Begović, a major in the Republican army who would become a member of the headquarters of Operational Zone South.

By late 1944, the FTP had grown to 100,000 combatants. This Partisan movement was dominated by communists and commanded by Yugoslavs. In the final months of the war, the Gaullists "nationalized" the French resistance—the twenty-nine-year-old Brigadier Jean-Jacques Chaban-Delmas was sent to Paris to improvise an uprising there. Soon afterward, the 2nd Armored Division commanded by General Philippe Leclerc will enter the city in the vanguard of George S. Patton's Third Army. That will help Charles de Gaulle establish the myth of self-liberation and the heroic role of the French resistance.

The other large theater of operations in the Western Mediterranean where Stalin's marshal of the secret empire is gaining the upper hand is Italy. On 2 May 1945, a day after the units of the National Liberation Army of Yugoslavia had entered Trieste, Lord Halifax, British ambassador to Washington, notified the Foreign Office that, at the suggestion of Sir Alexander Cadogan, permanent undersecretary for foreign affairs, he spoke with James C. Dunn, head of the State Department's Office of European Affairs, about the cessation of British supplies to Yugoslavia. It simply made no sense any more. Obviously, Tito could neither be counted on nor manipulated. But it was too late.

Northern Italy is already in Tito's hands. Genoa was liberated by the Garibaldi units. The local garrison surrendered to Anton "Miro" Ukmar, a Slovene commander of the Sixth Operational Zone (Liguria). Ukmar liberated Genoa on 25 April, despite the resistance of the Decima Flottiglia MAS fascist volunteers from the neighboring military port of La Spezia. The Slovenian 9th Corps acted as a superior command and a rear echelon of the communist Partisans in the north and even of the Garibaldi units that captured and executed Mussolini on 28 April. Caught in the village of Dongo on the road to Switzerland, he was shot the next day together with his entourage and his mistress Clara Petacci by order from Colonel Valerio, who had arrived from Milan. According to the official version, that was the *nom de guerre* of the Partisan commander Walter Audisio. He bragged about his deed when he became a communist senator in the Italian Parliament. However, Urbano

Lazzaro, commissar of the 52nd Garibaldi Brigade, who recognized and captured the disguised Mussolini, published his memoirs in 1962, identifying Colonel Valerio as Longo, the future general secretary of the PCI, decorated with the Order of the National Hero of Yugoslavia.

At the end of the war, Tito's forces occupying Friuli–Venezia Giulia dealt brutally not only with the enemy but also with those who did not sympathize with their cause. The entire Italian Garibaldi Natisone Division, carrying out the execution of the members of the rival national-democratic partisan unit from Osoppo Partisan Division near Porzus in Friuli, was incorporated into the 9th Corps of the Yugoslav army.

With the mandate received from Dimitrov in 1940, Tito practically controls the PCI (its cadres, not the rank and file). He has a special relationship with Longo and Ilio Barontini, probably the most significant Italian revolutionary with war experience. In the 1920s, Barontini attended the Frunze Academy and acquired the rank of major. He was sent to China, to Spain, and then to Abyssinia, where Negus (King) Haile Selassie would promote him to the position of vice-emperor of Ethiopia in recognition of his role in the resistance. Barontini came to Selassie's aid together with his fellow countryman Domenico Rolla and the Trieste Slovenian Ukmar. The *noms de guerre* of the three communist evangelists on the Comintern's mission were Paul, Peter, and John. After the Italian victory, the elusive Barontini escaped to Sudan, and, together with Ukmar, to France in 1940. During the war, the two of them will be among the chief organizers of the communist guerrillas on the French territory occupied by the Italian army after the fall of the Vichy quisling government. Their superior officer in the FTP was, of course, Ilić. In 1943, Barontini became the commander of all Partisan units in the Emilia-Romagna military district (Comando Unificato Militare Emilia-Romagna, CUMER). Partisan resistance in Piedmont was under the command of Ukmar. Clearly, these Abyssinian internationalists held the whole of northern Italy—all three military districts there: Barontini was in charge in Bologna, Rolla in Tuscany, and Ukmar in Genoa. Giulia–Venezia and Friuli is covered by the 9th Corps of NOVJ. Ukmar's corps was the only Italian Partisan unit that won a battle against an equivalent German unit—he captured the arms and equipment of the German garrison of more than 20,000 troops in Genoa.

In the south, there is a large garrison of Tito's military personnel, headed by Montenegrin delegate Nikola Kovačević. OZNA is recruiting Italian POWs from the expeditionary forces in Dalmatia and Albania and repatriating them in the Bari zone.

At the top of the pyramid are Longo, Secchia, and other communist leaders at the Partisan headquarters in Milan, together with Tito's delegate Vratuša.

It was only on the River Tagliamento outside Venice in 1945 that the communist army of the north was stopped. *Captain* Valerio deserves credit for that.

Captain Junio Valerio Scipione Borghese, the fascist "Black Prince," formed a volunteer quisling division based in the navy port of La Spezia near Livorno during the period of Mussolini's Italian Social Republic. It was former commando unit Decima Flottiglia MAS (X MAS) that under his command damaged two British battleships in the port of Alexandria. When the US headquarters in Italy realized that, based on some obscure arrangements with the British, Tito would occupy all of northern Italy, perhaps even Venice, the X MAS was urgently deployed at positions on the Tagliamento, 90 kilometers from Venice. Borghese was led by Angleton of the X-2 American counterintelligence section, the future head of CIA's counterintelligence staff.[1] Although most of the soldiers of X MAS were killed in the battle, they managed to hold their positions until the arrival of the British troops. Angleton dressed Borghese up in an American uniform and personally drove him to Rome. The Italian court sentenced him to twelve years' imprisonment for his collaboration with the occupying forces and the innumerable war crimes his black-shirt fanatics committed against the civilian population. However, due to his heroic deed at Tagliamento, the prison sentence would be reduced to four years.

After the war, Tito's secret army controls the region between Mount Olympus and the Pyrenees. The places where its troops are deployed include the Gramos Mountain, Albanian ports, Bari and Duino (where the 1st Proletarian Division of the Yugoslav army is stationed), Friuli and Carinthia, and the large military base at the Hopital Varsovia (Warsaw Hospital) in Toulouse, France. Yugoslav ships were smuggling arms to the communist cells of the Spanish war veterans based in Toulouse, in that huge complex. Some 150,000 combatants were trained there between 1944 and 1948.

Tito's army includes troops of some dozen nationalities and uses their respective languages as the command languages. This powerful army has not been demobilized yet; it is still fighting or threatening on all fronts. What they failed to achieve in the war, the Yugoslavs will try to achieve subsequently, but the global constellation of forces will prevent them from affecting the postwar order agreed on in Yalta and Versailles.

Churchill, the last British imperialist, will lose the General Election, and Great Britain, economically devastated by the war, will lose the status of a major power. Infallibly assessing the constellation of forces, Tito realizes that this former master of the Mediterranean will not be able to confront the ambitions that he has in the region under his direct control or incorporated in his secret empire. Tito's entire expansionist project had clearly been planned long in advance: as the Americans introduced their (blue) occupation dollars in Italy and Germany, Yugoslavia introduced its Yugoslav lira in the Free Territory of Trieste in 1946. The same year, parity between the Albanian lek and Yugoslav dinar was introduced. A special dinar—the Buljkes dinar (named after the village of Buljkes in Serbian Vojvodina, where the Greek People's Liberation Army had its headquarters)—was introduced in Greece. It was a legal tender of Vafiadis's Partisan units in Greece.

The 1st Proletarian Division in Duino will stay there until 1953. Yugoslav troops will leave Bari only after the direct intervention of the Carabinieri. The condominium in the city-state of Trieste has the same function as the Albanian territory—it is a base behind the lines used for distribution of propaganda material, weapons, and money in northern Italy, including Milan and Turin. In Pula, under the joint occupation like Trieste but controlled by OZNA, the ammunition depot on the Vergarola docks blew up on 18 August 1946. There is no doubt it was an act of sabotage—it coincided with the swimming tournament organized by the last Italians who remained in Istria after thorough ethnic cleansing. Around seventy people were killed, including two British soldiers. It was a clear sign for the remaining members of the unwanted ethnic group to pack up and embark the passenger ship transporting refugees to the camps across the Adriatic every Sunday.

Three days after the Vergarola explosion, Yugoslav Yak aircraft shot down an unarmed US Army transporter C-47 near Bled, flying over unannounced en route from Naples to Vienna. Five crew members were killed.

Meanwhile, a civil war is raging in Greece. The Greek government seeks the UN Security Council's protection from the aggression of Yugoslavia, Albania, and Bulgaria. Bulgarians are innocent in this respect, as their army is under Soviet control.

However, insurrection and guerrilla groups cannot overthrow a government unless a country has been weakened by war—if an international war is not available, a civil war will do.

The civil war in Italy will begin on 27 November 1947. Prime Minister Alcide De Gasperi replaced the socialist prefect of Milan, Ettore Troilo,[2] and appointed a city junta composed of Christian democrats, liberals, and independents. De Gasperi, the founder of the Christian Democratic Party (DC) and a man who would lead the country into peacetime with the ardent support of Stalin-backed Togliatti, is trying to do away with the communist den in Italy's most important city, thus throwing down the gauntlet to the leftist combatants who bore the brunt of resistance and were supported by Tito through his clandestine network. All the militants left will mobilize. Communist paramilitary detachments took over the city prefecture. They were commanded by Giancarlo Pajetta, once Longo's deputy in the CLNAI wartime headquarters and now commander of the Red Flying Squads (Volante rosse). If this is not a reprise of the October Revolution, then what is it? The Petrograd uprising also began in November (New Style calendar), exactly thirty years earlier. But where is Lenin here? Instead of Lenin, they only have Tito.

34

PLAN MAXIMUM

GRAMOS 1947

Strategic weapon systems have now become a priority, so Stalin puts his most capable man, the unscrupulous Lavrentiy Beria, at the helm of the Soviet nuclear program. At the same time, spacecraft designer Sergei Pavlovich Korolev has been released from exile in Kolyma and appointed head of NII-88 Institute to develop the first intercontinental ballistic missile 8K71, based on the German V-2 (Aggregat 4; A4).

The efforts invested in the development of these critical technologies almost exceed the industrial war efforts, so the Soviet Union cannot waste its energy on pointless local wars on its borders, particularly not in Europe, where it could risk direct confrontation with American and British troops. Anyway, integrating the already occupied countries into a new "socialist bloc" is the political priority. If expanding the sphere of communist influence requires some wars, they can be conducted in China and Korea as proxy wars. As for Europe, there must be peace there. Stalin's policy is in contrast to Tito's policy.

Tito has established his power in Yugoslavia and relinquished the Yalta arrangement obliging him to share power and cooperate with non-communists. He has terminated the provisional wartime government of national unity—a fusion of the royal government and the puppet parliament, the AVNOJ. By discarding the combination with the king and the premier of the government-in-exile unsuccessfully imposed on him by Churchill and, with much more success, by his second, more important protector, Stalin, Tito won himself a state; the party may not be entirely his yet, but the OZNA that controls the party and the army is. Consequently, he has no use for the provisional national front government any more. As a result, on 31 January 1946, the Constitutional Assembly proclaims a new constitution for the Federal People's Republic of Yugoslavia (FNRJ) and forbids the king's return. Tito has been the prime minister of the NKOJ since 29 November 1943 and of the FNRJ government since 7 March 1945. In April 1946, the US government establishes diplomatic relations with his new Yugoslavia. However, Tito is fully oriented toward the East because it is the only way for him to ensure his absolute power. He replicates the Soviet communist system instead of using the "transitional" form of a national front-based "people's democracy" that is being introduced in other countries under direct Soviet control. In these countries, communists cooperate with bourgeois parties, although the latter are being deprived of any real political capacity. On the other hand, Tito's monolithic regime undisguisedly eliminates all political opponents and fellow-travelers.

OZNA controls everything and answers only to Tito. In the spring of 1946, they capture Mihailović; in June, they will shoot him and bury him in an unknown place. The bishop of Ljubljana is sentenced in his absence. The bishop of Zagreb is arrested and sentenced to sixteen years in prison. The Ustashe guerrillas—the "crusaders"—are captured and publicly hung. Dr Dragoljub Jovanović, president of the People's Peasant Party that joined the national front and entered the FNRJ Constitutional Assembly, is arrested, too. In the National Assembly, he criticized the luxurious uniforms of army officers, which was (correctly) understood as criticism of Russophile militarism.

In late 1946, the Presidium of the National Assembly instructed the navy commander-in-chief to launch a fleet-development program and build 140 submarines, four cruisers, twenty destroyers, and 116 patrol and torpedo boats. By that time, the intelligence service had managed to obtain in Germany the original drawings of the Mauser MG 42 machinegun, which was later to be produced in Yugoslavia as the Zastava M53. It took the Western Allies reverse engineering to make their own copy, MG 1, for NATO. Everything suggested that Tito was not demobilizing his army but preparing it for new campaigns. Along Yugoslavia's borders with the former Axis countries, there are no armed forces that would be worth mentioning. They have been replaced by the weak occupational forces of the Western Allies (they only have nine divisions in all of Europe). With the superior Soviet conventional forces along the western border of the Soviet sphere of interest, this imbalance of forces is of almost fantastic proportions. Still, in view of Stalin's strategic priorities, the Soviet army is taking up defensive positions in Europe. So what is Tito going to do? He will try to achieve political gains with help from his secret forces in the Mediterranean, because that is where his real power lies.

Insurgency bases are being established on the provisionally governed territories, so that secret and proxy wars could be conducted from them without international sanctions. The most important among these territories is Albania because it enables operations in southern Italy and northern Greece. Yugoslavia will do anything to protect this free zone. In 1946, after an attempted landing of Albanian anti-communist commandos transported to the country's shores from Malta aboard British ships, the Yugoslavian minelayers *Mljet* and *Meljine* came from the port of Šibenik and laid mines off Albania's coast. On 22 October, two large British warships struck mines and their crews sustained casualties. Albania was officially held responsible for the incident. For this reason, the country was banned from joining the United Nations until 1955.

Tito took possession of Albania with two infantry divisions. The instructors from the CPY's Central Committee installed a Tito man in the Albanian Politburo. It was Koci Xoxe, a shoemaker from Florina. Albania was supposed to become Yugoslavia's "seventh republic," together with Kosovo. At its session of 27 March 1946, the CPY Central Committee Politburo decided that Hoxha should be invited to Belgrade to sign a cooperation treaty. The visit had been put off twice, until Tito was given the green light for it at a meeting with Stalin and Soviet party leaders on 27 May 1946. At the occasion, Stalin practically allowed Tito to take over the ACP, telling him to "swallow Albania." But at the same time he instructed him to form a Balkan Federation with Bulgaria. The Balkan Federation is a Comintern format from the 1920s—it cancels the independence of the petty, always belligerent statelets in the Balkans and, as perceived by Stalin, includes all the Slavic population between Vienna and Thessalonica. Imperial perceptions never change, be it under the Turkish crescent or in Moscow under the communist red star.

The Yugoslav leaders have also made territorial claims in northern Greece, where local CPY committees are being established in regions with a sizable Macedonian population. Opposing this Yugoslav intrusion is Great Britain. As far back as 1944, it managed to prevent the EAM and its predominantly communist military wing ELAS from taking all of Greece. In Dekemvriana—the five week-long armed conflict that broke out in Athens in late December 1944—the British army at first lost all of its strongholds except the port of Piraeus and the Athens airport, but then it deployed two fresh divisions, transported from Italy aboard US aircraft. At the same time, they carried out airstrikes to prevent communist reinforcements from Macedonia reaching Attica. As a result, the Treaty of Varkiza, backed by Stalin, was signed. Thenceforth, through KKE General Secretary Nikos Zachariadis, a policy of cooperation with bourgeois parties in the West will be sanctioned by Stalin, the same one Togliatti has been trying to apply in Italy. Zachariadis spent the war in German captivity. He returned to Greece from the Dachau concentration camp in May 1945, reassuming the leadership of the KKE from Georgios Siantos, who had led the party to the ill-fated Dekemvriana adventure.

Tito discussed his Aegean ambitions with Stalin during their third—and final—meeting in Moscow on 27 May 1946. Here is an excerpt from the official minutes: "Yugoslav prime minister said that he had claims from them [the Greeks]: Aegean Macedonia and Thessalonica."

Molotov, who attended the meeting, remarked that Thessalonica was "an old Slavic city." He also mentioned the need to have "access to the Aegean Sea."[1] Stalin is still avoiding confrontation with his hyperactive minion because the balance of forces on the ground is not quite clear yet. However, his global policy is thoroughly defined.

Tito tried to create a political framework for the annexation of Macedonian territories. In August 1947, he signed the Bled Agreement with Dimitrov. Under the agreement, a federal Balkan republic would be created. Yugoslavia and Bulgaria would enter a customs union like Benelux and back each other's claims in Macedonia, including Aegean Macedonia. The Bulgarians also recognized the Macedonians as a separate ethnicity—something they had denied in the past. Stalin's fierce reaction ensued immediately. He sent a telegram warning the leaderships of both countries about the "technical mistake." They were later summoned to Moscow to receive an earful, of which there are a number of accounts.[2] Tito did not come, on account of health problems. He sent Kardelj. Stalin first explained to Kardelj that Yugoslavia's Albanian policy was unacceptable because it was provoking the Western Allies. Also, said he, it is not a smart idea to start a civil war in Greece and provide the Americans and British with an excuse for an intervention. An uprising should not be supported if it did not stand a chance of succeeding, he said, adding that "I kind of doubt that the Partisans stand a chance of winning." He asked Kardelj directly: "Do you think the uprising in Greece can succeed?" According to his later account, Kardelj said that the Greeks themselves had organized the uprising, not the Yugoslavs. "As for us, we share the same border with them and could not avoid extending them assistance that any revolutionary movement would extend to another revolutionary movement." Stalin commented: "The idea that the Western powers would leave Greece to communists is wishful thinking!" Then he gave a short philosophy lecture to Kardelj and Kolarov, the Bulgarian representative who was also there:

> You are afraid to address the issue bluntly. The "moral debt" has left an impression on you. If you cannot lift the burden, you must admit it. You seem to be afraid of some "categorical imperative" and "moral debt." We are not concerned with such a "categorical imperative." It all comes down to the balance of power. If you are strong—strike! If you're not, don't fight!

Despite everything, the fighting in northern Greece has continued. The operations are run by the Yugoslav army headquarters. It provides logistics to Vafiadis, the ELAS commander in Macedonia, and it also sends regular Yugoslav troops there. However, not even Eastern Bloc governments recognize the Greek Provisional Democratic Government (PDK)—"the government in the mountains"—with General Vafiadis as premier and defense minister. When the Yugoslavs proposed that representatives of the KKE be invited to the first, preparatory Cominform ("a little Comintern") conference, held in Poland in 1947, Moscow "opposed sending the Greek party the invitation to participate."

At the Cominform (Communist Information Bureau, or Informburo; IB) founding conference in Szklarska Poręba, Poland, the Greek question was not discussed at first. As it was avoided by the Soviet representatives, Yugoslav delegates Kardelj and Đilas played along. However, at the seventh session, on 26 September 1947, Kardelj did open the subject. He attacked French and—particularly—Italian communists for "avoiding radicalization and use of arms to seize power" under the pretense that they do not want to create "the Greek situation."[3] Exalted, Kardelj says that Greek comrades "are leading their people in the fight, arms in their hands," while the French and Italian communists are "exaggerating the importance of parliamentary maneuvers in their countries." His discontent is really directed at Moscow, which controls these processes. Kardelj is particularly disappointed because, ever since 1945, he and other Slovene comrades can clearly see that the Soviet Union does not support Slovenian territorial claims in Carinthia, although they were given assurances that Moscow would support them at the Paris Peace Conference. In fact, at the conference, Soviet diplomats told their Western partners in confidence that they had no intention of challenging Austria's pre-Anschluss borders.

In September 1947, the Central Committee of the KKE openly rejected the Treaty of Varkiza and called for an uprising. The decision was made by the part of the Politburo that was on "liberated territory and abroad" (in Yugoslavia), and the members of the Athens-based leadership were practically ignored.[4] Fighting and large-scale war operations began. It is a somewhat unknown war—a European equivalent of the Korean War—that raged on until 1949. Indeed, in the autumn of 1947, the Yugoslav army was mobilized for Operation Lakes with Thessalonica as its strategic goal. Driven by unlimited ambition and utterly aggressive, Tito openly opposed Great Britain in Albania and Stalin in Thessalonica. He was ready to go to war with everyone, on all borders.

As support for the offensive preparations, the 113th Fighter Aviation Regiment was redeployed from Slovenia to Tirana airport on 18 June 1947. It was supposed to provide support to the thrust toward Thessalonica. True, there were no large Yugoslav army units deployed in Greece (no brigades or divisions, that is). There was some artillery support, and some instructors and small commando units were sent down there, but that was it for the time being. The Yugoslav army headquarters prepared the war plan Maximum, based on the idea of a "strategic defensive approach, which is to develop into a counteroffensive when the operational situation so allows." The plan was based on the assumption that the "aggressor will attack from Austrian and Italian territories and, possibly, advance from Hungarian territory, too." A counteroffensive on the western front was planned, toward Klagenfurt and the central part of the Julian Alps, with Trieste and Venice as the main goals. As for the southern front, the options included advancing toward central Greece along the main line of advance and toward Thessalonica along the auxiliary line of advance, as well as from Albania into Epirus, with Ioannina as the main goal. As no serious resistance was to be met on the main lines of advance, the above mentioned war goals would be reached and Tito's secret empire would become a real state with a much larger territory.

The basic idea is clear—a federation will be created, consisting of Greater Slovenia with its planned ethnic borders and with Trieste as its capital or biggest city; Greater Croatia with annexed Istria; a new composite state of Bosnia–Herzegovina in the central massif where the Partisans had won the war; Serbia with an ethnically cleansed Vojvodina; Montenegro with the addition of a Catholic Boka Kotorska; Albania with Kosovo; and all of Macedonia—Vardar, Aegean, and Pirin provinces—with Thessalonica as its capital.

With a population of around 30 million, Tito's imperial Balkania would be the most populous country in Eastern Europe—even among the most populous ones in the whole of Europe, next to Great Britain, Germany, France, and Italy. Only a final military effort was required and the plan would be realized—a communist empire would be established and he would dominate the Mediterranean. It was within reach—or at least Tito thought so. But Stalin had completely different plans.

35

STALIN'S HISTORIC "NYET"

DEDINJE 1948

In February 1948, a very high-ranking delegation arrives in Moscow. Again, Tito is not in it. Geoffrey Arnold Wallinger, British envoy to Hungary, is the first to realize that something unusual is going on. His aide sent him a report from Bucharest noticing that a chill in the relations with the Yugoslavs could be felt in Romania after Stalin's Moscow meeting with Kardelj and Đilas.[1] This led Wallinger to conclude: "There is something wrong about Tito ..." However, these early judgments were non-actionable—in other words, they were hard to translate into a concrete assessment and policy. Simply, in 1948 no one yet understood what kind of game Tito had been playing.

According to Đilas, Stalin was urging integration with Bulgaria because the "swallowing of Albania" had already begun. He would sanction it provided the "Balkan Federation" was created at the same time. If the Balkan Federation is realized under Stalin's auspices, Tito and his apparatus will not survive. Moscow controls Bulgaria and its army, and the top brass of the Bulgarian Communist Party were imported to the country from Ufa in Dimitrov's convoy. For Stalin, the union with Bulgaria is an unconditional requirement. "The first land of socialism" is the only country entitled to create "composite states" in the imperial manner. All other countries in its zone of interest are either dependent national states or Soviet republics and regions. This makes no big difference—for instance, how independent really is, say, Mongolia? This Yugoslav military-political operation in the Balkans follows the same imperialist pattern. Stalin has no intention of tolerating it; he did allow Tito to control the secret network in the West, but just as long as Tito did so as Moscow's resident, first underground, then legal, in the visible spectrum. But Stalin would never allow him to control it as a sovereign fiefdom, part of his own empire.

The Yugoslav delegation arriving in Moscow consists of Kardelj, Bakarić, and Đilas. Its composition reflects Moscow's fictional arrangement with three separate communist parties (the Slovenian, Croatian, and Yugoslav parties). When they arrived in the Kremlin, Stalin warned them to stop inciting the war in Greece. There is no point in doing it, he says, because the United States will never let this pivotal Mediterranean country slip under communist control. So Tito has been conducting his operations in Greece, Albania, and Italy, confronting the US and British military and intelligence structures without Stalin's approval. Stalin needs an arrangement that will help him keep his territorial gains without new conflicts. He has no intention of initiating a fight as long as he is weaker, because he does not have an atomic bomb. This is his categorical imperative.

According to Đilas, in the margins of the dramatic Moscow meeting announcing a large conflict and a schism, Molotov and Zhdanov gave them a hint about Stalin's working solution for reorganizing the people's democracies into a Soviet-superstate monolith. It would be a final solution for taking over the whole of Eastern Europe. Molotov tells them: first the union with Bulgaria and then with Albania, not the other way round. Zhdanov then mentions the plans for the unification of Byelorussia, Poland, and Czechoslovakia on the one hand and Ukraine, Hungary, and Romania on the other. So, the three-times-three formation is to be implemented. A typical army structure. This would resolve the minority issues arising from the Versailles demarcation. Stalin would thus put his half of Europe in his pocket. As for the eastern halves of Germany and Austria, he has occupied them together with their capitals. Only the Mediterranean is still undefined, and this is where Tito is enjoying his excessive autonomy.

The priorities of Soviet European policy include military disengagement and creation of a *cordon sanitaire* against the West. In Scandinavia, this was done via the "Finlandization" of Finland. That country was forced to give up the Karelian Isthmus, disarm, and become neutral. In Germany and Austria, a demarcation line defines the zones of occupation, with the Berlin "island" within the Soviet zone. Stalin will try to eliminate this discontinuity by imposing a blockade on the city in the summer of 1948. However, he raised the blockade in less than a year because it had failed to yield the expected results. Although the West's defense of the Berlin enclave was illusory in a tactical sense, Stalin yet again decided to avoid any military escalation. His policy of self-isolation of the Eastern Bloc is taking shape. Austria has been "Finlandized," too. It is now a buffer state. The only remaining potential crisis spot is the volatile territory between Austria and the Adriatic Sea—the Free Territory of Trieste, where Tito's troops mingle with the Allied soldiers. This is why Soviet diplomacy has discreetly been trying—ever since the Paris Peace Conference—to turn Trieste into a free port, an autonomous territory, thus completely separating the communist East (including Yugoslavia) from the West with another buffer zone. Tito opposes this with all his might because he is still trying to realize the Greater Slovenia in which all the Slovenes would live. Also—perhaps even more importantly—he does not want a buffer zone and a free port separating him from Italy, where he has big ambitions. Stalin is on the contrary trying to isolate Tito's influence in Italy and monopolize his influence among communists through Togliatti and the legal Italian party, which participates in the parliamentary process.

The same disguised conflict can be found in Greece: Zachariadis recognizes the Treaty of Varkiza, Vafiadis rejects it. Nobody understands that. To the US intelligence services, all the communists are the same: their loyalty is only to Moscow and they are working on the goals set there. The only differences can be found on the personal level between various communist strongmen.

Observing the European space from the Kremlin, Stalin sees that only Yugoslavia and Albania are still outside the Eastern Bloc. They can join the bloc or not. One way or another, Yugoslavia will function as a buffer zone and this is what matters. It is in line with the general Soviet containment project— self-isolation in Europe. This also corresponds with the US containment doctrine—they want to encircle the Communist Bloc. Whereas the US initiative is offensive in both military and political terms, the Soviet initiative is defensive in military terms, in accordance with the Kremlin's general European strategy. Stalin's offensiveness manifests itself only through the regular parliamentary competition of the Moscow-backed Western European communist parties, popular movements with numerous followers. While the West cannot intervene legally in the closed societies of the occupied Eastern states, Stalin can do so in the West owing to the very nature of the pluralist and democratic system imposed on Europe by the United States.

Indeed, without the global supremacy and economic strength of the United States, everything would have been lost way back in the 1940s. Still, it will take fifteen years and huge expense to accomplish the German

Wirtschaftswunder and Italian *Il miracolo economico* and to ensure the success of the European democracies. All this will change the overall political configuration of the continent.

At the same time, in March 1948, on the other side of the Iron Curtain, the Soviet Union announced the withdrawal of its experts from Yugoslavia. They were supposed to assist in the reconstruction of heavy industry, creation of large state-owned weapons factories, and building an Adriatic fleet with dozens of cruisers and destroyers. A month earlier, during Ðilas's visit, Stalin criticized the Yugoslavs for occupying Albania without consulting Moscow. Somewhat earlier, Tito paid a visit to Poland, Bulgaria, and Romania. He was welcomed there as an independent statesman, not like someone from the Communist Bloc hierarchy. Such anomalies cannot be tolerated. The autonomy of the Yugoslav regime must be reduced.

On 1 March 1948, Tito summons his aides for an enlarged session of the Politburo. He tells them openly that "Bulgaria could be a Trojan horse in the new Balkan federation demanded by Stalin." These words were conveyed to Moscow immediately and, as early as 27 March, they received the "Letter from Central Committee of Communist Party of Soviet Union to Comrade Tito and Other Members of Central Committee of Communist Party of Yugoslavia." Specifying the reasons for its having been sent, the letter mentions ("first") the alleged "anti-Soviet statements" and "leftist phrases" (Trotskyite excesses) of the highest-ranking Yugoslav leaders—Ðilas, Vukmanović, Kidrič, Ranković, "and others." Significantly, Kardelj and Hebrang (the latter one has fallen from grace) are not mentioned.

After having been relieved as head of the Croatian party in 1944, Hebrang was sent to Belgrade where he became minister of industry and head of the Federal Planning Commission in charge of five-year plans. For communists, economy-related departments are always second-rate political functions. Isolated among the top-ranking leaders, Hebrang is constantly under suspicion. In his 1946 letter to Kardelj, he complains about Tito's autocracy. Comrade Kardelj immediately forwards the letter to Tito. According to the diehard Stalinist Vlado Dapčević, this was a death sentence for Hebrang.[2] But it was not before January 1948 that Hebrang was totally marginalized, when he was appointed minister of (non-existent) light industry.

From the Kremlin's perspective, neither Comrade Hebrang nor Comrade Kardelj have necessarily become lost causes. Hebrang could turn renegade, and Kardelj, the secretary of the autonomous Slovenian party that once fitted so nicely into the Stalinist format of the Liberation Front (Osvobodilna

Fronta, OF), is adaptable and shows an aversion to speaking his mind, unlike Đilas, Tito's "ideologue," who is always more zealous than anybody else. Particularly dangerous is Ranković, Comrade Marko, head of OZNA and the party apparatus, the key man in the Yugoslav *nomenklatura*. They are all listed in the letter as bad guys.

The most important item in this epistle ("second") is the direct delegitimization of the CPY leadership. They are declared "self-appointed"—indeed, the members of the Politburo were coopted into this highest party body. The criticism is devastating because it is based on facts. The CPY leadership was indeed formed by Tito's appointments, since the party did not have its congresses—because the Comintern's Ispolkom would not let it. And it would not let it because it never really recognized the CPY after 1928. As a result, the Yugoslav party developed from the apparatus, not from the political practice of "class agitation," as postulated in Leninist doctrine. Almost all general secretaries of communist parties were political cadres, Marxists, theoreticians, or—at least—authors of enthusiastic reports like Kardelj. Organizing secretaries are merely liaison officers for communication with the Soviet apparatus. For Moscow, legalizing one of its agents and organizing secretaries as a real general secretary is a huge step in an unwanted direction. So when Tito installed himself in that position, his arrangement broke in a fundamental way. The integrated apparatus of Stalin's global conspiracy makes it impossible for national communist parties to become truly autonomous. As Tito established his own, separate apparatus, he gained autonomy—and thus true sovereignty. The same thing happened in China—simply because it is too big to be run from Moscow.

The third most important item in Stalin's letter is identifying Velebit as an English spy. In fact, it is an indirect denouncement of Tito's foreign policy—balancing between the two Allied poles and keeping the door open to every single opportunity that comes along.

Tito and the Politburo responded with a letter in which they rejected the accusations. At the same time, the CPY leadership distanced itself from Hebrang and Politburo member Sreten "Black" Žujović for failing to unequivocally support Tito. Both were then arrested. Tito dared not convene the Politburo immediately because he was not certain if he could count on a majority of votes at the plenum. The members were being "prepared" individually. But his men at the helm of the apparatus remained loyal to him—they are not political figures but *siloviki*: Ranković, Krajačić, and Maček. These three aides of Tito who run the OZNA, all with a psychological profile and intellectual range comparable with his own, have no other future but the one guaranteed by his charisma and protection. From this solid nucleus and from the rest of the apparatus cleansed by purges, a renewed and consolidated party will emerge.

In late June, at its meeting in Bucharest, the Cominform passed a resolution concerning the situation in the CPY, which was accused of "pursuing an incorrect rural policy" and "lack of party democracy." The "healthy elements" in the party were urged to replace the Yugoslav party leadership.[3] *Borba*, a Belgrade daily with a mass circulation, printed the resolution. Wise tactics. The Yugoslav party is a cadre-based organization (the Soviets estimated its membership at around 450,000), and Stalin has a stature in its *nomenklatura* and, to a lesser extent, in its ranks. The general masses, on the other hand, feel strongly opposed to the Soviet Union, communism, and—in western, Catholic regions—Orthodox Russia. Like Stalin, who resorted to national values and great historical figures in the perilous days of 1941, Tito has now mobilized the middle class and national sentiments. Communist-internationalists will thus find themselves between a rock and a hard place, or between the people and OZNA. They won't stand a chance.

Meanwhile, the UN Security Council has accused both Yugoslavia and Albania of "assisting guerrillas in Greece." Hoxha expelled all the Yugoslav personnel from his country—he barely managed to hold on to his position as party leader after their attempts to replace him. He would not succeed if it was not for his own contact with Moscow through the Soviet ambassador in Tirana.

Upon receiving Stalin's letter, Tito immediately went to Zagreb, where he surrounded himself with the most loyal members of his personal network (Krajačić, Augustinčić, and Miroslav Krleža—a leftist writer and ideologist who had spoken against Stalinism—and Tito—even before the war). Ranković and Ivan "Matija" Maček are making sure everything is under control in Belgrade and Ljubljana. In July 1948, Tito convenes the Fifth Congress. Montenegrin Russophile Arso Jovanović, chief of staff of the Yugoslav army, was killed "while trying to escape across the border." Ranković becomes deputy prime minister and Kardelj foreign minister. At the same time, organized repression against disloyal cadres begins—Goli Otok prison camp is opened. More than 15,000 people—3 percent of all party members—will be sent there.

Meanwhile, Vafiadis is in the Pindus Mountains, fighting at the head of his Greek Democratic Army—ELAS has become a regular army of his irregular, unrecognized state. In the summer of 1948, putting up fierce resistance, Greek

Titoist Partisans manage to fend off an attack of the superior forces loyal to the government in Athens. The government forces will win in their next offensive, Operation Pyrsos (Torch), in 1949, with substantial US assistance and with US instructors in all battalion units. Operation Torch was carried out in three stages throughout August 1949. Clearly, Tito would not yield until the last moment; he never gives up his plans until he is forced to. His loyal forces retreated into the Greek mountains, but his subversive operatives in Italy tried to launch an offensive and hit the politically most sensitive spot. There is ample evidence, albeit circumstantial, for this conclusion. No other logical explanation can be found for what happened in Rome on 14 July 1948.

36

THE EXCOMMUNICATION

BUCHAREST 1948

Italian parliamentary elections were held in April 1948. De Gasperi and his Christian Democrats won a clean victory, receiving more than 12 million votes. Adhering to the united front model, Togliatti's PCI coalesced with Pietro Nenni's left-wing faction of the Socialist Party (PSI). The coalition won them 8 million votes; they came first in Tuscany and Turin. However, the electoral system was arranged in such a way that the leftist opposition could not win more than 216 seats in the Chamber of Deputies. The Christian Democrats won control of the Camera dei deputati with 305 seats.

The electoral defeat dramatically damaged Togliatti's authority. In Milan, before the elections, he kept promising certain victory in order to appease the "maximalists" who claimed that the founding of the Cominform in the autumn of 1947 meant a call to communists in the West to begin the armed stage of the class struggle and start a revolution. There is no doubt that the Italian party cadres linked with Tito's secret apparatus indeed wanted that. They still did not understand that Tito's policy was formulated independently of Moscow. After all, was it not Belgrade that was chosen as the Cominform headquarters after the preparatory meeting in Poland? At that meeting, it was Kardelj who openly supported the radical line in front of the Italian leaders, urging them to start an uprising like the Greeks. Longo showed his support for this line when he replied to the Yugoslav representative that the mobilization of the Yugoslav army and its concentration on the border were a precondition for the success of a revolution in northern Italy.

Back in November 1947, the communist Red Flying Squads took the Prefecture Building in Milan. They tried to keep communist Troilo as head of the Milan department of the Ministry of Interior. The leaders of the communist Partisan movement clearly saw that a new, civil society was being born and they were trying to maintain their revolutionary base in Lombardy. When Togliatti found out about this, he was infuriated.

According to a contemporary historian of the Italian postwar years, "Togliatti feared a division in the party because he might become isolated and lose his influence on the party members."[1] He was aware that:

> if the hardliners like Secchia took over, they would call [the members] to arms, bringing about grave consequences for the party and for the whole of Italy. Would some militant leader like Secchia, a battle-hardened veteran of the resistance, really be able to start the long-awaited uprising? Did the Soviet comrades really expect their Italian comrades to engage in that? The wave of protests and violence that engulfed parts of Italy and France in the autumn and winter of 1947 suggests that the answer to both questions is affirmative.

Nobody realized that there were two conflicting political lines here. Not Togliatti's and Secchia's, not even Togliatti's and Longo's, but Tito's and Stalin's. Togliatti is merely the Kremlin's commissioner in Italy transplanted from Ufa, still adhering to the national front policy that he helped concoct in Moscow's ideological laboratories. Even in April 1945, at the Second Plenum of the National Council of the PCI, he rejected the "Greek scenario" for Italy.[2] He canceled the Italian Dekemvriana that could have happened in May of the last year of the war, when Tito's troops emerged on the border. This is why Tito used his "delegates" like Nikola Kovačević to create a parallel leadership in Milan, an underground faction of the Italian party headed by Organizing Secretary Secchia. It was Belgrade, not Moscow, that Secchia was receiving money from—tranches of 30 million lira each, collected by the taxation of retail in Trieste.[3] At the same time, the 6th Army was established in Yugoslavia.[4] It was probably a "paper army" supposed to be reinforced with the Italian POWs who were being repatriated en masse to the Apennine Peninsula. After appropriate agitation, the POWs would become the internationalist avant-garde of the revolution—similar to what Tito himself had been part of thirty years earlier in Siberia.

US intelligence keeps a vigilant eye on it and notices—correctly—that there are two apparatuses operating in Italy. However, to them, they are all various emissaries of Stalin with the same task.[5] Instead of Togliatti, referred to by Yugoslav sources as the "secretary of the dissolved Comintern" and called by his Moscow nickname Ercoli, Tito wants Longo as head of the PCI.[6] At the same time, more and more "delegations" of Italian Partisans are visiting Yugoslavia in 1947. The country has clearly become the base for the next Mediterranean revolution. Troops and aircraft are deployed in Albania. The greatest generals of the Spanish Civil War are taking part in the realization of Plan Maximum, the Yugoslav army's invasion of Thessalonica. The wave of protests and violence that has engulfed southern France and Italy has nothing to do with Stalin—Tito's agent network is behind it all. Yugoslav ships are transporting weapons for the "reconquistadors" in the Hopital Varsovia base near Toulouse. According to US intelligence, some 40,000 members of Garibaldi units, armed with submachine guns, have already gathered in Italy, with a logistics corridor via Ljubljana made available to them.

While making these fantastic designs for conquering the Western Mediterranean, Tito is paying no attention to the clear instructions from Moscow. He has turned the task of establishing a Balkan Federation into a farce. The Bled pact he signed with Dimitrov on 1 August 1947 envisages the "inclusion of Pirin Macedonia into the Federal Yugoslavia as part of the Federal People's Republic of Macedonia (Vardar Macedonia)."[7] Pirin Macedonia would retain its "cultural autonomy," whatever that means. So, instead of enabling Stalin to gain control over the Balkans by annexing Bulgaria to Yugoslavia and Albania, Tito would bite off half of Bulgaria and introduce a customs union instead. Of course, such a combination was out of the question and Stalin immediately castigated Comrade Dimitrov. If he had not been fatally ill (he died in 1949) or if he had any political relevance, Stalin would probably have had him arrested.

At the same time, Comrade Togliatti was almost overthrown at the Sixth Congress of the PCI held in Milan in the first week of January 1948, just before the parliamentary elections. The Yugoslav delegation was given a cool reception by the Roman leadership. Unlike them, the delegates of the congress—representatives of 1,009 Italian party committees—gave them an enthusiastic welcome.

After the communists' electoral defeat, Togliatti will become totally discredited, so the idea of his replacement seems very realistic. The party would be taken over by Tito's men, Longo and Secchia. Longo did succeed Togliatti, but not before 1964. If Tito managed to gain control over the Italian party, then nothing could stop his revolutionary offensive: he was fighting his war in Greece, he had taken Albania, he had almost split Bulgaria, and now he was very close to bringing under his control the territory of the strongest communist party of the West (it had more members than any other European party, even in the 1960s and '70s, save for the German SPD). This large European political organization led by the supposedly moderate Togliatti, who is remote-controlled from Moscow, is now being wrecked by a subversive network created from the remains of the CPY from the Balkan backwater, the same CPY that Togliatti himself had dissolved in Vienna way back in 1928.

Moscow is not concerned with what Tito is doing in his own country because Yugoslavia has been an exemplary Stalinist state. It has adopted even more than is required from the countries of "people's democracy." Indeed, Tito is Stalin's best disciple, a straight-A student. He has carried out the genocidal ethnic cleansing of politically unsuitable ethnic groups and large-scale reprisals against class enemies, introduced a centrally planned economy, started building heavy industry, and ordered collectivization. Only Soviet films are screened in theaters. The party still operates in secrecy, and the social climate is characterized by fear, optimism, and hunger. If it were not for the American assistance through UNRRA, the people would starve.

Consequently, the real reason for bringing Tito and his Politburo to heel are not ideological differences; none exist, for Tito has no ideology at all; he only saw *Das Kapital* from a distance, when Pijade was translating it in the power plant of the Lepoglava penitentiary. The real reason is strategy: either Stalin's isolationistic policy of containment will be pursued, or Tito's subversive policy that generates insurgencies in the Mediterranean littoral and does not allow states to consolidate in times of peace.

Stalin therefore sends a letter reprimanding Tito and the CPY's Politburo. The letter was sent through party channels because it was supposed to shake Tito's authority, as a warning, and change the course of Yugoslav politics. Stalin did not aim to initiate a public conflict. The first letter was sent on 27 March, accusing Yugoslav leaders of claiming that "socialism in the Soviet Union is not revolutionary any more." At the same time, the CPY cannot be considered a true Marxist–Leninist and Bolshevik party of democratic centralism, claims Moscow, because its leadership was not elected at a congress. The CPY replies defensively on 13 April, denying a lack of Bolshevism among the Yugoslavs and reaffirming their deep appreciation of the Soviet Union— Tito is still looking for an exit strategy.

Five days later, on 18 April, there followed the elections in Italy, which saw a crushing defeat for Togliatti. As the most important thing for Togliatti at the moment was to retain the Kremlin's patronage, at the 30 April meeting of the PCI Secretariat he discussed international affairs instead of the electoral defeat.

His discussion was in line with the later verdicts in which, in the context of the Yugoslav issue, the loyalty of Italian communists to the Soviet leadership was confirmed and the "leading role of the Soviet Union" demanded.[8]

Stalin sends a new letter on 4 May, criticizing the CPY leadership for their unwillingness to correct their mistakes and for insisting too much on their achievements in the national liberation war. Indeed, claims Moscow, the Red Army saved the Yugoslav Partisans from defeat. This was a huge tactical mistake on the part of the Soviet leadership because, regardless of the substantial engagement of the Red Army in the Belgrade Operation, this was a lie: all of those who had fought in the five-year war and were now holding positions on the basis of these merits knew it very well. This is why, in its response of 17 May, the CPY concentrated on this attempt at belittling the Yugoslav resistance, suggesting that everything be discussed at the Cominform session planned for June. But Tito now had in his hands something that would win him the support of the masses as soon as the letter was published. Too certain in his power, Stalin made a wrong move.

French communist leader Maurice Thorez who, like Togliatti, entered the postwar national front government as a deputy prime minister and supported the occupation of Indochina, is an obedient follower of the line—he immediately sends a confidential message of support to Zhdanov on 4 May. The French party's Secretariat also passed an appropriate resolution on 27 May. The Italian party passed a similar resolution on 20 May. Then, on 19–23 June 1948, the Second Conference of the Cominform takes place—not in Belgrade, but in Bucharest. A communique is published, ousting Yugoslavia from the communist club. This was the famous Cominform Resolution, edited by a commission presided over by Togliatti.

The true nature of the conflict between Tito and Stalin can be discerned from the communication of well-informed insiders, such as dispatch no. 516 from Rome to Belgrade of 23 September 1948. Its source is designated as no. 27—either the Yugoslav ambassador to Italy Mladen Iveković or, more likely, Rudi Janhuba, the main intelligence operative and Ranković's correspondent. The dispatch describes the split that occurred in the ranks of the Italian communists after their two superior headquarters had come into conflict. Source no. 27 reports that there are "two groups: one group thinks that the Cominform's accusations are accurate and the other that they are not, but that the anti-fascist front led by Moscow should not be divided." The outlines of the confidential conversations with Togliatti, Secchia, and Longo are also given. The Italian comrades said:

Tito's nationalism, which is contrary to the interests of the international proletariat headed by the AUCP(b), rests on the questions of Trieste, Carinthia, Greece, Bulgaria, and Albania. This is the real reason [for the conflict], not the internal affairs of the FNRY. This is why the Cominform has chosen this form, in order not to show the weakness of the anti-imperialist bloc when it comes to international politics. The conflict will be resolved either if the CPY leadership capitulates to Moscow due to economic sanctions or if [Yugoslavia] joins the imperialist bloc and thus finally takes off its mask.

So it is not about communist doctrine but about the strategy for the communist revolution in Europe. Everybody has taken positions in accordance with their primary interests, which means that an invincible force will encounter an invincible obstacle. Tito is not letting go of Italy, Greece, Albania, and the bases in southern France. Stalin is rendering him irrelevant, and European communists are acting opportunistically, regardless of their own opinions, which they keep to themselves. To everyone in the West, this is all too confusing. A deadlock occurred that would need to be broken.

37

TARGET

TOGLIATTI

ROME 1948

Palmiro *Togliatti*, Italy's no. 1 communist, was shot and gravely wounded on 14 July. Riots engulfed the whole country. Communist-led unions called general strikes in Rome and Milan. Communist press howled for the resignation of Catholic Prime Minister Alcide De Gasperi. Violent strikes began in many parts of the country.

This Associated Press report was printed on the same day as the news that Vafiadis, the communist rebel, sent a radio message to the authorities in Athens, offering negotiations on equal terms. But the developments in Italy are something more than just a series of spontaneous strikes provoked by the workers' wrath—a revolution is spreading, visible to all those who know where to look ... A union leader from Genoa gave this account:

> At a meeting in the Workers' Chamber, we decided to declare a forty-eight-hour general strike as a protest. We were just about to write down the instructions, when the news came that crowds in the square overpowered the police and captured their armored car. We were on the brink of a civil war. The people took control of Genoa that night. I remember, the chief of police called the veteran Partisans' association and requested: "Send me a group of Partisans to defend the police headquarters! I am totally isolated here!" All the police dispersed, all of them, it was a terrifying situation ...[1]

Was it possible that revolution could flare up in Italy at that very moment? All the communist leaders denied it then and later. Indeed, the riots in the north did not spread everywhere; the south remained quiet, save for an incident or two. Secchia, the party's organizing secretary, estimated that an uprising might have been successful solely in three big cities—Genoa, Turin, and Venice. But what if Tito and his secret organization had not been officially ousted from the communist movement by the Cominform Resolution three days earlier? What if his cadres, organizers, and agents were not being forced to hide their intentions and plans? If the Yugoslav army was waiting on the border to intervene in the areas where it was stationed in the joint occupation zone? Although the minister of interior mobilized 180,000 police officers upon the news of the attempt on Togliatti's life, this demoralized force would not stand much chance against the Garibaldi veterans and revolutionary communists—as it showed in Genoa. However, it all still hung by a slender thread—and so did Togliatti's life.

Antonio Pallante, a twenty-five-year-old Sicilian student, admitted to the police that he had arrived in Rome in order to kill Togliatti. He waited for him in front of the Chamber of Deputies building and fired four shots. Gravely wounded, Togliatti was taken to hospital. Urgent surgery saved his life. As soon as the shock was over, the fifty-five-year-old communist leader started to recover. But no one believed the official reports about his stable condition. The streets were full of protesters. Around 20,000 people gathered in front of the hospital, where Longo read Stalin's telegram of support. Labor unionists captured the whole of Genoa and the Fiat plants in Turin, taking the management hostage. In some smaller cities and towns, "crisis committees" took power. The headquarters of bourgeois parties were set ablaze in many places. De Gasperi summoned his government for a secret session. Beforehand, he told the press that the shooting was "the worst thing that could happen." In the Vatican, they were praying for Togliatti's life. Stalin was sad and angry. In a great essay written a few days after the attempted assassination, the special correspondent of the US liberal-left magazine *the New Republic* explained that "no one in Italy is praying more ardently for Palmiro Togliatti's recovery than his own worst enemies."

"Wherever the blame may lie," explains the well-informed *New Republic* correspondent,

> there is little doubt where the benefits of Antonio Pallante's act will accrue. Whether Togliatti lives or dies, they are unquestionably on the communist side. For in either case the party not only will have acquired a dramatic spur to its

activities, but may also find at least a partial solution to its delicate problem of leadership. It is an open secret that, following the disastrous defeat of the leftist forces last spring, Togliatti's standing with his party was severely shaken.

In short, if Togliatti died, either the Italian uprising would begin and things would go the desired way, toward the "Greek scenario," or—at least—the much hated Togliatti would disappear, punished for his part in the declaration of the Cominform Resolution, which would change the political course he had dictated from Rome to communist cadres in the north. Reliable men from Tito's network would then have their turn.

The *New Republic* goes on to describe Togliatti's potential successors. One is Eugenio Reale, a forty-two-year-old Neapolitan physician who is now on the Central Committee, not a very convincing candidate for national leadership; he is a Togliatti man. The second candidate is Longo, "tough as armor plating," a military cadre "who could fit the Soviet war plans in Western Europe," as the American magazine wrongly believes. And the third is Secchia, the "organizing genius of the party" and a man totally devoid of the so-called "humanist" and cultural interests that shaded Togliatti's background—a clear Titoesque cadre, with "NKVD" written all over him. Togliatti is described by the foreign press as a strikingly modest, nondescript man, more like some petty professor than a revolutionary, always wearing dark, double-breasted suits. A bureaucrat who leads a secluded life. He is married to an old-school left-wing feminist. She met her husband in the editorial offices of Antonio Gramsci's paper and then she followed him to Moscow and to the Spanish Civil War. A moving love story of a couple of steadfast Stalinists. When they returned to Italy, she wrote the book *La famiglia, il divorzio, l'amore (nel pensiero delle donne comuniste)* (Family, divorce, and love (in the eyes of a woman communist); 1945). Indeed, Togliatti is a true antipode of the master of the secret empire.

Although Pallante was a liberal, the communist press wrongly claimed after the shooting that he had been active in the fascist movement, substantiating it with the discovery of *Mein Kampf* in his suitcase during the police search of his property. He did declare himself as an anti-communist; he even said that he had perceived Togliatti as "an enemy of the homeland, *a Cominform member* [our italics] who entered the service of a foreign power." However, politically, by his attitudes and real affiliation, Pallante was close to minor Italian postwar centrist parties, mostly liberal ones. There was no visible trace of any connection with rightists.

Upon turning eighty-six in 2009, Pallante gave an interview to *Corriere della sera*, in which he tried to explain that he was not a hitman and that his act was not against the man he had shot but against his ideals. What ideals? According to the impartial analysis of the *New Republic* in 1948, Togliatti was the principal designer of the project of demobilizing the Italian left. He joined the coalition government and aligned with Nenni's socialists. He and his "softcore communists" then swallowed the socialists. He popularized the party, sent conciliatory signals to the church, and, generally, implemented the post-revolutionary "ballot instead of bullet" strategy. In Bucharest, heading the party commission that imposed sanctions on Tito, he personally condemned Yugoslavia, the main exporter of revolutions in the region. It was really Stalin's message. Did T. T. reply to the master of the Kremlin through the pistol muzzle?

After the attempted assassination, there was media speculation that "it was Togliatti himself who ordered the execution of Benito Mussolini." Clearly, it was a suggestion that the shooting had been the fascists' revenge for Togliatti's murder of their leader. However, nothing really supports this theory. Why would the fascists assassinate him? All of them had been pacified, with the exception of some extremists—the exhibitionists used mostly by the CIA. The US government strongly supported De Gasperi and his project of renewing Italian society with the help of the Marshall Plan. Togliatti himself participated in it—when he did not have to feign revolutionary fervor in front of the northern party members. All this was in line with Stalin's intentions to peacefully define the spheres of interest in Europe and hermetically close the Eastern Bloc.

Despite the lost elections, the Cominform Resolution, and possible attempted assassination of the PCI's general secretary, the Yugoslav secret service maintains regular contact with Togliatti's potential successor, Secchia. On the first day of the Cominform Conference in Bucharest, where the CPY would be removed from the communist kabala of the world, the Yugoslav operative in contact with the Italian party in Rome sends a message with a technical question:

> Terracini[2] came to me today and told me that he is about to raise the question—in Togliatti's name—of the Greek communists and other patriots who want to leave Italy for Yugoslavia and then further to Markos, on the instructions of the Greek party. Terracini gave me a telegram signed ... on behalf of the Central Committee of the Greek Communist Party. It is about groups of Greek seamen and other refugees. Terracini also says that these are well known Spanish war veterans and that the Italian party vouches for them. Eight others are to arrive from Egypt with regular passports. Some are located in Italian camps because they have no papers, and some—also without papers—live illegally in Genoa and other Italian ports (19 June 1948).

The prominent "anti-fascist" and "framer of the constitution" Terracini is clearly on a secret mission here: cadres, weapons. A united revolutionary command, from which the PCI will gradually distance itself. But contacts will be maintained, without Togliatti's consent and despite all the temptations and changes in the political course of the Italian party. Iveković, the Yugoslav ambassador to Rome, sends a very important telegram early the following year:

> 2/79 report of Ambassador Mladen Iveković to Marshal Tito concerning Italian Communist Party, 25 March 1949
>
> Strictly confidential, no. 28/49
>
> TO: COMRADE MARSHAL TITO
>
> COMRADE EDVARD KARDELJ[3]
>
> 5. ... Longo openly told the undersigned that turning the general strike of 14 July 1948 (the attempted assassination of T. [Togliatti]) into a revolution had not been possible due to the unreliable conduct of the "Trotskyist" Yugoslavia, which could stab the Italian revolution in the back! The Italian party's leadership had verbally instructed its organizations to interpret the failure of the general strike of 14 July along these lines. Italian party leaders keep saying that the Italian proletariat had always counted on the direct armed assistance of the new Yugoslavia at the moment of the Italian uprising. Now, there is no alliance with the CPY anymore, but chances are that Tito's clique would play its counterrevolutionary role and help the Italian ruling clique to crush the uprising.

At this level of the strategic game, Comrade Stalin brilliantly outplayed Comrade Tito. True, he did not manage to topple him with the assistance of "internal forces," and he did not use military force due to unfavorable conditions. Indeed, why did Stalin not intervene in Yugoslavia in 1948?

Marshal Rodion Yakovlevich Malinovsky,[4] a Soviet military expert from the Spanish Civil War and later the commander of the Don Front who triumphed over Field Marshal Erich von Manstein, said that, on Stalin's orders, he deployed eight Soviet armored divisions along Yugoslavia's borders in 1948, awaiting the order to intervene. However, in the political situation of the day it could not be done. Stalin knew he would have to count on stubborn resistance (in the "Bosnian redoubt") and on massive assistance to Tito's forces from the West. The CIA's original assessment was the same: the agency believed that the Yugoslavs would be able to put up resistance for three to six months, so it considered the risk of aggression to be rather low.[5] Nevertheless, it was decided that massive supplies of materiel be stored near Trieste so that they could be swiftly shipped to Yugoslavia, if necessary. If the war in the Balkans spread, with foreseeable complications in Greece, thus turning into a conflict between the East and West, it would inevitably escalate into a nuclear war, given the Western Allies' huge inferiority in conventional weapons. Such a nuclear war would be devastating for the Soviet Union. In 1948—the year of Tito's schism—Stalin still does not have an A-bomb. The first test was carried out in Semipalatinsk only in August 1949. By that time, the Americans already had some fifty operational bombs and thirty-five "Silverplate" B-29 bombers for delivering them. By 1950, the USSR also began serial production of the Tu-4 strategic bomber (an exact copy of the B-29), but the Americans had already developed an H-bomb, some thousand times more powerful than the atomic bomb. The "Ivy Mike" ten-megaton bomb was detonated on Eniwetok Atoll on 1 November 1952. Stalin died four months later—not for one moment did he have a window of opportunity to threaten a war in Europe. Besides, for him, Tito's Yugoslavia was not of any particular geostrategic importance because, even with its "outside-the-blocs" status, it fitted both the US interventionist and Soviet isolationist concepts of containment.

For Tito's regime, the threat of a collapse loomed larger than the threat of military intervention. And not because of the internal enemy. The internal enemy had been efficiently crushed in the first years after the war, and the local "reactionaries" were more afraid of Stalin than Tito. As for the local Stalinists—the supporters of the Cominform (*informbiroovci*)—radical cuts and cauterizations were carried out against them. Hebrang and his wife were arrested, together with everyone close to them or likely to be associated with them. As the trial never took place, because Hebrang allegedly hung himself, most of those who had been arrested died in prison during the investigation or were sentenced to long terms in prison. Some 20 percent of party members suffered one sanction or another. The guilty ones, the less guilty, the unwary, those who could deviate, members of their families, and those who made a slip of the tongue while drinking or joking—they all ended up in the concentration camp on the Adriatic island of Goli Otok. Tito was as meticulous as he always was when his very survival was threatened. Now there was only one more miracle left for him to make—to feed the hungry multitude with but a few fish, in a country completely devastated by the war and postwar repression.

38

THE MAHARAJA OF THE BALKANS

LONDON 1954

In 1946, Ambassador George Kennan, director of policy planning at the US State Department and architect of the US containment policy, outlined in his so-called "long telegram" the need for "patient but firm and vigilant containment of Russian expansive tendencies." He helped define the Marshall Plan as an instrument of US European policy. And then the solution for the most acute problem presented itself: the main European exporters of the communist revolution came knocking on the State Department's door. Immediately after the public split with Stalin, Tito sent his people to Western capitals to establish political relations. On 29 June, a day after the Bucharest communique—the Cominform Resolution—was published, the US military attaché in Belgrade sent two recommendations with the following guidelines:

> B. We recommend the boldest possible exploitation of this defection in the keystone of the Soviet satellite structure. In withstanding Soviet pressure, Tito would have good prospect of success if given full support from the West. This would help solve our problems in Europe.
>
> C. We recommend that the US take action only through propaganda until approached by the Yugoslavs. In such case, swift and positive action should be taken.[1]

Kennan developed a visionary strategy—the West should capitalize on Tito's betrayal, and Germany should be united by fusing the Western zones of occupation. After that, a lengthy process of deconstructing Soviet domination in Eastern Europe would ensue.[2] It soon became clear that Tito's split with Stalin was absolute and that Yugoslavia was leaving the Soviet bloc. On the other hand, there were no indications that Tito would change his ideological course. However, he had to change his political position because his regime was in a critical state and had very little maneuvering room left. The CIA made a devastating assessment of the Yugoslavian economic situation, particularly of its agricultural production, concluding that the 1947 harvest was far from the prewar results. Three indicators were particularly alarming: shortage of staple foods, growing inflation, and decreasing industrial production due to obsolete equipment. Not much had been obtained from the Soviet Union, although contracts on USD232 million of loans had been signed in 1946/7. Only USD87.8 million were actually withdrawn by 1948, USD73.6 million of which were used to pay for the purchase of Soviet weapons.[3]

In early 1943, the United States approves the alleviation of import regulations and allows the financing of private and public loans for Yugoslav imports. However, the economic situation is deteriorating and, in 1950, Yugoslav Ambassador Vlado Popović requests urgent assistance to the tune of USD100 million, half of that in food. President Truman joins in, explaining in his letter to Congress that the support to Yugoslavia is important for US national interests. Truman will also issue his crucial directive for the approach, defined with the sentence *Keeping Tito afloat*. What is more, this cruel Stalinist dictator is to be redesigned into the captivating figure of a true freedom fighter, for he is an "erosive and disintegrating force in the Soviet sphere." Over a period of fourteen years (1948–62), the United States will send more than USD700 million of military assistance to Yugoslavia, grant USD1.5 billion of non-repayable government loans, and help with USD500 million drawn from other sources.

To qualify for this funding, Tito closed the border with Greece in 1949, putting an immediate end to the civil war there.[4] Yugoslavia joins the Western alliance:

> After the ideological conflict with Stalin in 1948 and the ensuing isolation of almost three years, Yugoslavia definitely turned to the West and, upon intensive negotiations with the United States, joined the Mutual Defense Assistance Program (MDAP). The accession document was signed on 14 November 1951. By joining the program, Yugoslavia practically became a member of the North Atlantic Treaty Organization, because the program also included NATO members facing the risk of possible Soviet aggression. The Yugoslav People's Army (JNA) received large quantities of weapons and military equipment—its first jet aircraft, second-generation tanks, and large-caliber guns

were obtained in 1953, the first radar network was installed in 1955, the sound barrier was broken in 1956 ... and all that for free, on the grounds of being part of the program. Until the Trieste Crisis of 1953, the JNA was even involved in NATO military planning.[5]

It was Velebit who played the crucial role here. In early 1951, he toured the United States and had unofficial talks with leading American politicians. They gave a positive response to the Yugoslav offer.[6] He was given a list of the military equipment to be delivered. General Eisenhower, commander-in-chief of Allied forces in Europe, started planning coordinated military action in case of a Soviet attack. Neither the US ambassador to Belgrade nor Great Britain and France was notified of it—clearly it was assessed that the information would be immediately forwarded from these European capitals to Moscow. On 22 February 1951 (three weeks before the first shipment of US equipment was made on 12 March), Tito gave a commitment that "Yugoslavia will fight on NATO's side if the Red Army attacks Greece, West Germany, or Italy through Austria."[7]

Having seen the strength of US conventional forces after Douglas MacArthur's Inchon counteroffensive in September 1950, Stalin soon withdraws his directive on a "total, intensive, and aggressive war" against Yugoslavia with Hungarian, Romanian, and Bulgarian troops attacking the country in the first wave and Soviet troops in the second, with a massive airborne landing in Yugoslavia's central massif. These staff plans had to be discarded given the reality of US strategic superiority in military and political terms. In January 1951, Stalin was still discussing with the defense ministers of the satellite countries an offensive allegedly planned by Zhukov, but that was probably just Eastern Bloc propaganda. Meanwhile, Koča Popović, appointed chief of staff of the JNA—the most reliable military cadre in the most difficult situations—visits the Pentagon. Before that, he spoke with Eisenhower in Paris. The US Joint Chiefs of Staff proposed that the atomic bomb be used against the satellite countries if they attacked Yugoslavia, based on the assessment that the Soviet Union would respond with nuclear weapons only if its own territory came under such an attack. In their opinion, suitable targets could be found in Romania and Czechoslovakia.[8]

Yugoslavia had been receiving massive military assistance since early 1951. The most urgent were the shipments of wheat (25,000 tons), oat (13,000 tons), beans (6,000 tons), peas (10,000 tons), and 8,000 tons of fat and sugar for its army. They were followed by war materiel—1,200 machineguns, 100 howitzers (105mm), and seventy cannons (155mm) were sent in that first year alone.[9] Pilots were sent abroad to train to fly on the F-84G Thunderjet and F-86 Sabre jet fighters. As many as 12,500 various non-combat vehicles were also sent in. And that was only the beginning. The JNA will soon supply eight divisions and form sixty artillery regiments with the US weapons, including the largest calibers. Allied ships entered Adriatic ports—aircraft supercarrier USS *Coral Sea*, escorted by a Sixth Fleet squadron, came to Split on 11 September 1952.

The JNA headquarters has established contacts with the highest-ranking commanders of the Greek and Turkish armies, negotiating joint defense with them. Since both Greece and Turkey are members of NATO, the commitment to fight on their side in case of a conflict means operative involvement in the strategic planning of NATO. Protected by such a wall, Tito could sleep peacefully. It was then that his diplomatic offensive in the Mediterranean began, with goals completely opposite to those from the previous period. With a newly acquired style, he now concentrated on the most important crowned heads.

The first spectacular diplomatic *demarche* was organized in the summer of 1952 on the Brijuni Islands, the Mediterranean archipelago Tito had turned into his summer residence. Aboard the heavy cruiser HMS *Glasgow*, the commander-in-chief of the British Mediterranean Fleet, Admiral Louis Mountbatten, who had just lowered the flag of the British Raj in New Delhi, came to visit him.

The visit received orchestrated media coverage, showing Marshal Tito as a man of destiny and courage, a freedom fighter, a champion of national independence. His apprenticeship as Stalin's disciple would be forgotten, and the West would make huge investments in crafting his image.

But there was a price for it, not agreed in advance. At the beginning of the year, in April, Tito swore to the Federal Assembly that he would "never accept the Anglo-American occupation of Trieste and the conclusions made at the London Conference without Yugoslav participation." However, at the end of the month, with his back against the wall, he would have to sacrifice that vital corridor to his underground networks in Italy and thus cut the path used by various "armed men" without papers. In London, Churchill's Conservative government had returned to power in October 1951, with Maclean as deputy defense minister. The socialists Clement Attlee and Aneurin Bevan are no longer here. Like before, Churchill and Maclean are ready for wholesale trade, but the status of Trieste is non-negotiable. Strengthening the democratic parliamentary process in Italy is a first-order goal in Europe, and the Trieste

Agreement will strengthen the position of the De Gasperi government in Rome, and that of Togliatti, a cooperative Roman communist "confirmed" in Moscow, but also loyal to the new Italian Republic.

On the Brijuni Islands, Mountbatten met JNA Chief of Staff Koča Popović in order to discuss the question that Koča had raised, first with General Eisenhower in Paris and then with General Matthew Ridgway, who replaced Ike when he started working on his presidential ambitions.

The crucial question was this: Where could the Soviet forces be stopped on their westward advance? Turkey agreed to redeploy eight of its fifteen divisions from Anatolia to Thrace. With these divisions, together with Greek forces and Tito's thirty-five divisions armed with US weapons, the configuration of the Balkan Front on NATO's right flank had been enhanced substantially.

In addition to the military purpose, the Brijuni meeting is also important in terms of propaganda—the press has already started presenting Tito as a "wise statesman." But this is only the beginning. As King George VI died a few months earlier and Queen Elizabeth II—married to Mountbatten's nephew Prince Philip—succeeded the throne, Tito's future visit to Great Britain is certainly discussed. When it takes place, Tito must be presented as a major acquisition, and his image must be improved significantly so that all the horrors committed after the war in Yugoslavia, Greece, and Italy could be forgotten. This is why Foreign Secretary Eden comes to Belgrade and Bled less than two months after Mountbatten's visit. Tito used the opportunity to introduce his young bride. Thirty-two years younger than her husband, twenty-eight-year-old Comrade Jovanka Budisavljević is a medical corps major; she had fought German commandos at Drvar with the 6th Lika Division. She nursed Tito after his gallbladder surgery in 1951. Five years earlier, twenty-five-year-old Comrade Zdenka had died of tuberculosis and, Tito being Tito, he became close with the even younger Jovanka.

As agreed on the Brijuni Islands, Yugoslavia signed an agreement on friendship and cooperation in Ankara with its enemies of yesterday, the Greek royal government and the equally anti-communist Turkey, both fresh NATO members. Two weeks later, on 6 March 1953, the news of Stalin's death was announced. A period of uncertainty began in Moscow. Tito can peacefully go to London now, in his first official visit to the capital of a state on the velvet side of the Iron Curtain. He sailed on 7 March 1953, two days after Stalin's death. It was his first departure from the country after the Bucharest communique. He was more than cautious, aware of the power of the master of the

Kremlin and his network of operatives because he himself had belonged to it until recently.

Tito's ship, *Galeb*, landed at the Thames Embankment and an admiral's launch boat took Tito from there to Westminster, where the queen's consort Prince Philip, the Duke of Edinburgh, Prime Minister Churchill, and Foreign Secretary Eden were awaiting him. After reviewing the navy guard of honor, he went to his official residence by car, escorted by two gentlemen in top hats and tails—the trusty Velebit and Koča Popović, who had no problems acting like gentlemen. Koča had become foreign minister on 15 January 1953 and Tito was proclaimed president of the republic, succeeding Ribar, a sound figurehead in all postwar arrangements. As a result, Tito is officially visiting the queen, not Churchill who welcomes him humbly at the Embankment.

The talks he had with Churchill defined the joint Balkan strategy. The British prime minister used the opportunity to warn him: "In war, for strategic reasons, one should not keep one's enemy behind one's back." Tito understood the hint and replied: "In case of an aggression, preventive measures should be taken. Since we have a treaty with the Greeks and Turks, solving this problem would not be difficult." He quoted this exchange in his message to the conference of the chiefs of staff of the three military headquarters of the Balkan Pact countries in Athens when they requested instructions on how to treat Albania. Greece then committed to deploy two divisions on the Albanian border and so did Yugoslavia.[10] The first time Tito planned to "swallow Albania" was with Stalin in 1946 and now, seven years later, with Churchill, too.

As the queen received Tito in a plain black silk dress, he, too, refrained from parading this time—he had an olive-drab uniform with his Order of the National Hero on the left pocket. There will yet be opportunities for flashing in gala uniforms Göring-style.

The US government armed Tito and fed his army, and the British government was now redesigning him for devastating political actions behind enemy lines. If Tito remains afloat, the West's border in Europe will be protected. It is not really in danger, given the Kremlin's isolationist strategy, but the effect would be much more impressive if Tito showed the public in the satellite states of the East that the *nomenklatura* could stay in power outside the protective cocoon of the Communist Bloc and even keep the dogma. This is why Tito's tour of European courts continues with British assistance. His stance is a clear message to other ambitious leaders on the wrong side of the Iron Curtain.

In the next diplomatic season, *Galeb* reached Istanbul on 8 April 1954. Marshal Tito was guarded like the Koh-i-Noor. When he left Istanbul for Ankara in a convoy of three trains, 4,000 guards were lined along the entire railroad. A visit to Greece followed on 31 May 1954. It was a true spectacle. A squadron of four destroyers escorted *Galeb* to the port of Piraeus. A motorcade of convertible limousines followed the one carrying Greek King Paul, young Queen Consort Frederica of Hanover, and the swaggering Croatian metal worker and his very young bride, all of them dressed in white. Then, continuing his peace-keeping offensive, he sailed to Thessalonica. A military parade awaits him there while squadrons of Thunderjets are flying above their heads. He has the same ones, but more of them.

The bill for all this splendor was now sent to him. On 20 May, Tito had to respond to the Allied note demanding withdrawal of his troops from Italian and Austrian territory. He replied that "Yugoslavia would not be humiliated or double-crossed" when it came to its territorial claims—Carinthia, Trieste, Gorizia, and Friuli–Venezia Giulia. Marshal Alexander, commander-in-chief of the Mediterranean, replied that the Yugoslav military encroachment of these territories would "resemble the actions of Hitler and Mussolini." So much for the earlier accolades of his "wise statesmanship." The crisis from 1945 was being repeated, but it was clear this time that Tito had a weak hand and was playing on his own.

Upon returning from Greece, Tito went on a Yugoslav tour. He made a series of bellicose speeches in the crowded main squares of Yugoslav cities. Besides sending a message to the world public, he also wanted to send some reassuring signals to the Slovenians—like de Gaulle promising support to the French in Algeria. He mobilized the army. The 1st Proletarian was put in combat readiness. Leftist demonstrations started in Trieste. However, at the end of the day, he had to back down. President Eisenhower sent him a kind and conciliatory letter on 10 September 1954. He offered the mediation of "mine and your friend Robert Murphy," authorized to consider certain "economic events and extraordinary moments."[11] It seems that the consideration of the "extraordinary moments" yielded positive results because, immediately after the memorandum of understanding solving the Trieste question for good was signed by Yugoslavia, Italy, Great Britain, and the United States, the deputy prime minister for the economy, Vukmanović, traveled to Washington, DC, and negotiated a shipment of 1.3 millon tons of wheat, which was to be sold in the domestic market but with the money being kept by the Yugoslavs. This was the equivalent of around 200 million of today's dollars. Instead of

American control of the distribution of the money thus earned, it was agreed that the money would be used for the construction of the Adriatic Highway that would open the country's seaside to European tourists with motorcars.[12]

The irreplaceable Velebit, the real foreign minister in charge of the Western countries, then goes to London and signs a memorandum on the border demarcation lines. Yugoslavia kept Zone B (northern Istria), while Zone A with the city of Trieste remained in Italy. As Tito had annexed Istria, Rijeka, Zadar, and the Kvarner islands to Yugoslavia, he fared well in terms of territorial gains, but he lost all the momentum in terms of foreign politics. It was clear he had been kicked out of the world league into a lower, Balkan league. It was not something he could accept. He came too close to his friends, so his enemies could not protect him from them. But after the Trieste debacle, new combinations started to open. A message came from Moscow, sent by Nikita Sergeyevich Khrushchev.

39

L'HOMME NIKITA

BELGRADE 1954

In November 1952, two months after the Sixth Fleet's visit to Split, the Sixth Congress of the CPY takes place in Zagreb, where the party will be renamed the League of Communists of Yugoslavia (LCY). It is now modernized and federalized as the umbrella organization of six separate territorial parties. Nevertheless, the federal Central Committee with 109 members and its Executive Committee of thirteen members still wield full authority. And yet, a cautious change of the political course can be felt. Before the party congress, a "writers' congress" was held in Ljubljana. It was a typical communist conference, where Krleža, Tito's ideologue for cultural issues, spoke against the "Zhdanovite aesthetics" of socialist realism. Comrade Đilas, chief of agitprop, went much further in the iconoclasm. In his articles, he argued that Stalin's ideas had nothing to do with Marxism and that they were much closer to Hitler's. It was Comrade "Đido," as his fellow party-members call him with a certain awe, who criticized Krleža at the preceding Fifth Congress in 1948 for his prewar "Trotskyism" (in fact, anti-Stalinism), claiming he had "denied the dialectic materialism as the working class' philosophy." Now he went to the opposite extreme, proclaiming Stalinism to be fascist by its nature, with Stalin still alive and well in the Kremlin and Stalin's best disciple ruling Yugoslavia (as an apostate, but always ready for a sudden shift if it could yield a favorable outcome). Tito listens to this condemnation of Stalinism, yet it could just as easily apply to him.

In the days of the split with the Soviet Union, Moscow singled out Đilas as the most dangerous enemy—he was supposed to be used as a scapegoat for "deviations" in ideology, like Velebit in foreign policy, should Tito finally decide to change course and return to the Soviet bloc. But in 1952, Đilas's sharp anti-Soviet criticism is still very much needed. Goli Otok prison camp operates in top gear, too. At the Sixth Congress, Comrade Đido is elected to the six-member Secretariat of the party's Executive Committee (the Politburo). In charge of agitation and propaganda, he joins the team of Tito's closest confidants, together with Ranković (cadres and state security), Ivan Gošnjak (the army), Kardelj, and Kidrič (Tito's Slovenian party cell). A Montenegrin, a Serb, a Croat, and two Slovenians—even the national key has finally been tuned.

The following year, in the national daily *Borba*, Đilas begins publishing a series of his essays on the political aspects of destalinization. As the chief of agitprop is officially the party ideologist, his views carry a certain weight; they determine the party line and are "discussed" at party meetings. However, the things Comrade Đilas is writing are about to cause widespread dismay. He daringly argues that the party should strive to be a democracy, but not a "socialist democracy." Everybody knows that "socialist democracy" is nothing but a means to ensure the dominance of the party. He says that UDBA, the secret police, should give up its party links and become normal police. And there is no point continuing with the class struggle because it leads to "deviations and bureaucratism." According to Đilas, the LCY leadership has "degenerated into a selfish bureaucratic caste."

How could it happen that Comrade Đilas suddenly "saw the light" and realized that the communism they had all invested so much in by serving time in the king's jails and fighting in the woods for it, first dying for Stalin and then betraying him, then discarding it for some even more radical revolutionary agenda, was a used up concept and that they should now try something completely different? The most interesting theory about it was given by Dragoljub Jovanović, that Serbian democrat who joined the communists in the postwar Constitutional Assembly, only to be sentenced to nine years' hard labor in 1947 because of a comment made during a speech in the assembly. He had intimate knowledge of all the actors on the Belgrade political scene. He served time in Sremska Mitrovica, where Đilas soon joined him. While in prison, he wrote an extraordinary collection of portraits of his contemporaries.[1] They were all there, in their countless interrelations, including Đilas and his sudden political twist. Jovanović explains that it was Dedijer and the

British Labour Party that influenced Đilas. He visited London in 1951 and was dumbstruck with what he saw there. Born in the town of Kolašin in the Montenegrin backwoods, with a population of only 2,000, by that time he had only seen the Balkan metropolis Belgrade and the gloomy communist capital Moscow. So when he first saw the West, it was a cultural shock for him. When he visited London in the company of Dedijer, he realized that this highly civilized country was ruled by socialists—revolutionary labor unions. Dedijer was Tito's official biographer and *Life* had just begun publishing his serialized exclusive story about the Marshal, a Balkan freedom fighter and "wise statesman," with Tito's flattering portrait on the cover of the magazine. In those days of the Yugoslav twist, the Yugoslav leader's photo also appeared on the covers of *Time* and *Newsweek*. Maclean had just published his *Eastern Approaches* (1949), a bestseller creating a narrative that would pave the way for a favorable Western perception of the transformed Yugoslav leader. But how far will Tito go in this metamorphosis of his? Not far enough, whispers Dedijer in the ear of the volatile Đilas—according to Jovanović, who knew both of them quite well. Would it not be useful if another socialist party were founded as a corrective and with a younger and more elastic leadership? As Tito has already shown that he is not an inflexible doctrinaire, but is always ready to experiment with communist formats, he might not necessarily be opposed to this approach.

In the final article published in *Borba* on 7 January 1954, Đilas concludes: "Today, revolution means reforms, peacetime progress. Today it makes no sense to seize power in a revolutionary way, not only because it is unrealistic but because it is counterrevolutionary." Togliatti would sign this any time. Tito, of course, would not. Two days later, a denial was issued—the articles in *Borba* are the personal opinion of Comrade Đilas, and the Executive Committee of the Central Committee of the LCY—the Politburo—disagrees with it. Tito, of course, intends to continue with revolutions; if he cannot do so on the European rim of the Mediterranean, he will transfer the initiative to its other coasts.

Despite Đilas's attempts to push the regime in a more liberal direction, as a result of which he became increasingly popular in the West—something that eventually hurt him more than the hatred he had triggered in Moscow—he neither disappeared without a trace nor ended up in Goli Otok prison camp. Tito and Ranković summoned him to Tito's residence. Đilas defended himself by saying he merely wanted to "improve socialism." Ranković suggested he should resign the position of speaker of the National Assembly, because his ousting would bring discredit on the party.

Following the customs of "socialist democracy," the Third (extraordinary) Plenum of the Central Committee then took place and Tito accused Đilas of revisionism. All party bigwigs agreed, with only Dedijer trying to defend him. Pijade told Dedijer from the first row that he was stupid and that it would be much better if he shut up. Đilas then resigned his party membership and returned his jeep and limousine. However, instead of keeping quiet, in 1955 he gave an interview to *The New York Times*, as a result of which he was sentenced to three years in prison for enemy propaganda. He was sent to Sremska Mitrovica to serve his sentence. However, as his book *The New Class: An Analysis of the Communist System* (1957)—a compilation of his *Borba* articles—was published in the West while he was serving time, his sentence was later extended to nine years. When he finally got out in 1961, he published another book, *Conversations with Stalin* (1962), and was promptly sentenced for disclosing a state secret (Tito's arrangements with Stalin on "swallowing" Albania). They gave him four more years. Dedijer got off lightly, sentenced to six months on probation. They treated him as a fool, not an enemy.

Thus the issue of Đilas was shelved in January 1954. This gave Khrushchev a perfect opportunity for making the first step—sending a letter to the Central Committee of the LCY and Tito on 22 June 1954. After the introductory phrases about the damaging effects of the conflict between the two parties and the need to improve their relationship, he offers a symmetrical explanation of the conflict's causes. During the investigation of the imperialist agent Beria and his men in the secret service apparatus, writes Khrushchev, it turned out that they had done something unthinkable: "Without knowledge of the Central Committee and Soviet government, they had recruited certain Yugoslav citizens for intelligence activities." This hostile provocation has now been unmasked, says Khrushchev, but not before it had inflicted huge damage to the relations of two parties and two countries. On the other hand, "the Central Committee of the AUCP(b) is of the opinion that the CPY leadership also failed to undertake all the available steps to avoid the conflict, which was particularly manifested in the anti-Soviet excesses of Đilas, a pseudo-Marxist who had alienated himself from the communist cause ..." And so, concludes Khrushchev after a few more pages full of bureaucratic prose, we think it would be good if a meeting of our top leaders took place as soon as possible, in Moscow or in Yugoslavia, "at your convenience."[2]

Comrade Tito replies to Comrade Khrushchev on 11 August 1954, at the peak of the Trieste Crisis. Although the letter from Moscow came at the perfect moment, he pretends he is not particularly interested in the offer that will enable him to rejoin in the strategic game he was just kicked out of. Normalization of relations would be a good thing, he writes, but we cannot expect that this alone would eliminate the differences in our views on international problems and their solutions. Tito did not swallow the "Đilas bait": he points out that it was not Đilas who caused the conflict, regardless of his "unbalanced approach and tendency to extremes." As for Beria's responsibility, "you know his role in the whole affair the best, so there is no reason for us to challenge your claims." This is almost impertinent. "As for the meeting, we are not against it, but first we must neutralize the political and material damage standing in the way of normalization."[3] Khrushchev replies very soon, in September, saying he accepts everything. Why does he need Tito so badly that he is insistent like an impatient child?

The Yugoslav communist leader's transfer to the enemy camp has created unbearable pressure on the architecture of the Soviet bloc. Though the East European countries are not abandoning communist dogma, they are trying to maintain their own identities. In Poland, for instance, this is particularly manifested among the supporters of Władysław Gomułka. This ill-concealed anti-Semite was eliminated from politics for a period of eight years, but his ideas on the communist national renaissance have remained. At the same time, in East Germany, massive protests took place in 500 cities and were brutally crushed by Soviet tanks. In Hungary, Imre Nagy became prime minister in 1953, promoting a new course. Everybody realized that Tito was backing him from behind in some way. When Murphy came to Tito for a *tête-à-tête* conversation, he gave the Marshal some tit-for-tat proposals—among other things, would Yugoslavia assist Hungary economically, if the United States provided the funds?[4] All such emissaries underestimated Tito because they perceived him as the dictator of a small, poor country on Europe's periphery. They did not realize the nature and extent of his secret empire. Khrushchev, who had been an insider in Stalin's communist system, knew very well the power of Tito's kabala and its impact on the communist cadres, politics, and secret operations. The Soviet bloc would lose its cohesion if every country went its own way, and then the Soviet Union's influence in Asia would also disappear. The revolutionary project must keep renewing itself and permanently expand, and no one does it better—and with minimal resources—than the renegade "devil's disciple," Marshal Tito. And so, having met his every requirement and overcoming the (false) skepticism of the Yugoslav leader, Khrushchev got on the plane and flew to Belgrade. It was a very risky move for him, but, given the situation he was in, it was a necessary and inevitable one.

When Stalin died, Khrushchev was not a particularly important member of the Politburo. His name was on the last, tenth place on the list of the members of the leadership that had succeeded Stalin. Bureaucrat Malenkov became the chairman and Beria, head of the nuclear program who had distributed his and Stalin's Georgian fellow countrymen throughout the security apparatus, became interior minister. It was clear that Beria had the best chances of succeeding Stalin by gradually eliminating all the other members of the Politburo, just like Stalin had done by making temporary alliances in Lenin's cabinet. This was Khrushchev's advantage—as he was so weak, he was able to work on those ranked in the middle; they had reason to fear the highest-ranking ones more than the lowest-ranking one.

After Beria's liquidation, Khrushchev takes over as the chairman of the Politburo in February 1954. His letter to Tito marks the beginning of the destalinization process—a daring and immense undertaking. Before taking any action to atone for Stalin's and his own sins, one of the biggest Soviet Stalinists must consult the biggest Stalinist outside the Soviet Union. Both of them carried out genocidal repressions, but it seems that Comrade Tito has found a magic formula—despite leaving Stalin and giving up Stalin's brutal repression, he has managed to hold on to power. Indeed, he travels around the world and is received by kings; political leaders of the free world are coming to visit him, they respect him and finance him. This is why Khrushchev and Nikolai Alexandrovich Bulganin board a plane and fly to Belgrade. Awaiting them in Beli Dvor (Prince Paul's White Palace) is Marshal Tito, dressed in his impeccable white double-breasted suit without any medals or similar paraphernalia. His appearance is sending a clear message to the brutes from Moscow who have come in their loose-fitting trousers and horrible ties, decorated with medals of the Hero of the Soviet Union. Tito has an Order of Victory—something they never qualified for—but he decides to leave it in a drawer for the occasion.

40

A NEW MEDITERRANEAN OFFENSIVE

SUEZ 1955

By the time he received Khrushchev in Belgrade, Tito had already activated a new subversive network. His bases on the northern Mediterranean shore had been closed in the meantime. In the *Boléro-Paprika* operation, launched on 7 September 1950, émigré activists, guerrillas, and communists were forced out of Saint-Cyprien camp near Toulouse. Fifty of them were imprisoned after having been arrested in the Hopital Varsovia.[1] Spanish cadres then moved to North Africa—Morocco and Algeria. A new base would be set up there. Italy closed its border after Tito's excommunication in 1948, and the members of Garibaldi units who had been attacking other resistance groups fled to Yugoslavia. In Italy, the entire underground network has gone even deeper underground—the PCI cadres are keeping their contacts with the Yugoslavs in great secrecy. But the two-way political and financial channel for the exchange of information and money has remained.

The career of communist Jesús Hernández says a lot about the influence Tito has maintained among Spanish cadres. After the military defeat in Spain, the NKVD sent him to Mexico in 1943 under the codename Pedro, as head of the Soviet illegal residency there. After the war, Pavel Fitin, head of the NKVD's Foreign Department, ordered that all Soviet operatives should distance themselves from Hernández. In 1951, Hernández would come to Zagreb and attend the Peace Conference, where a pacifist-communist international front would be founded. Like Eurocommunism, its role was to strengthen Tito's line among the outcasts from Moscow. Finally, in October 1956, with a group of Spanish veterans, he comes to the large congress of the International Brigades of the Spanish Civil War taking place in Belgrade marking their twentieth anniversary.

What happened with other Spanish communist cadres exiled in Mexico? Together with Hernández, the party expelled from its ranks Enrique Castro Delgado, who had formed the famous Fifth Republican Regiment (El Quinto regimento) in the Civil War. Trained by the NKVD, the regiment was used to carry out repression against cadres. It entered legend and a poem was written about it: *Líster y Campesino, / con Galán y con Modesto, / con el comandante Carlos, / no hay milicano con mideo ... / Anda jaleo, jaleo!* (With Líster and Campesino / With Galán, and with Modesto / With the commander, Carlos, / There isn't a militiaman with fear).

Líster and Modesto are also Tito's generals, and Galán a Spanish Soviet cadre, the same as "Commander Carlos," a big shot in this communist pantheon who deserves his own biography.[2] But regardless of Hernández, Delgado, and all these famous Spanish warriors, Tito does not have a single rifle he can count on in the Catalonian Levante in the early 1950s. The same also applies to the Levant. In Albania, Hoxha carried out a purge of Yugoslav cadres in 1948. As the minister of interior and the party's organizing secretary, Xoxe had the principal support of Tito's operatives, the same as Comrade Secchia in Italy. Xoxe was executed by Hoxha in early 1949. Hoxha's position was even tougher than Tito's position against the superior forces of the Soviets and their satellites: in addition to domestic Titoists and the Yugoslav and Greek armies on Albania's borders, the British were also trying to topple Hoxha. When they tried to do so before the Conminform split in 1947, they parachuted a group of commandos into Albania. At the time, Tito's forces and Yugoslav ships laying mines in the Corfu Channel still opposed the intrusion. But Tito then went over to the other camp, and infiltrations of saboteurs (Operation Valuable) in Albania continued until 1952. The operation was also supported by the CIA. The agency had just been established, so it was its first subversive action. This sneak preview of the Bay of Pigs ended up just like the Cuban adventure nine years later. At that time, "Kim" Philby was coordinating British and American subversive activities against Albania in the UK embassy in Washington. Having lost that base, Tito no longer has armed men he can count on in his sphere of influence in the Balkans.

In May 1954, Tito received an aide-mémoire demanding withdrawal of his troops from Trieste, the largest urban center in the Eastern Adriatic and

Balkans in the final years of the nineteenth century. The city had a significant Slav minority. It was the western focus of his secret empire. But he will have to sacrifice it, even if it was one of his most important wartime goals. Driven out from Trieste in such a humiliating way and thwarted in Italy and southern France after the excommunication from the Cominform, Tito will hit British and French vital interests in the Mediterranean with a vengeance. For Great Britain, it is primarily Suez in Egypt; for France, it is Algeria—almost a home-land territory in the French national perception. Tito's new project was initi-ated in the summer of 1954, six months after the London memorandum on the withdrawal from Trieste had been sent to him. Great Britain, France, and Italy lost their strength in the war, and he is confident that the United States would not support European colonial powers in their attempts to maintain or renew their overseas empires. That was the same assessment he had formed at the end of the war when he launched his offensive on the European shores of the Mediterranean. He was dead wrong then—Great Britain was still strong enough to stop him in Greece, and Truman was supporting the building of a *cordon sanitaire* around the communist world. But now, Comrade Tito is not carrying the burden of the global communist project on his shoulders, and the British and French Empires are bankrupt. After the Bretton Woods Conference in 1944, the American dollar substituted the British pound ster-ling and the Americans terminated their presence in the Mediterranean. It is the right time to start a new global revolution.

In June, Tito returned from Thessalonica and his Aegean tour, and in July he received in Belgrade the dwarfish Amharic Emperor Haile Selassie I, a symbol of the anticolonial struggle, supported by Comintern a year before the showdown in Spain. Tito welcomes the emperor as an old friend, equally luxu-riously attired and decorated with symbols of power. No one yet understands the purpose of this show and the role to be played by this bit-part actor. However, Tito received Khrushchev's first telegram in August and he sailed from Rijeka to Africa in late November 1954. His voyage will take him to Port Said, Bombay, Calcutta, Rangoon, and Madras. In Asia, he will seek a magical act for his political makeover. Until that time, his foreign policy kept shifting from the East to the West, depending on circumstances. Now, with this new global approach he has intuitively invented, he will be able to adopt a seem-ingly neutral but shifting and active position; it will enable him to pursue principled diplomacy in his international relations, while at the same time enabling his underground operatives to instigate revolutionary regime-chang-ing all over the world.

The first country Tito visited on his maiden trip to Asia in late 1954 was India. He wanted to explore the country supposed to become a key support for the implementation of his strategy. It was big and important, yet economically weak. Despite its poor resources, this country seemed to be an ideal partner for a new foreign policy round, this time with ambitious, yet fundamentally weak countries. Bringing together the Third World countries was originally Sukarno's idea, not Tito's. However, Tito took it and radicalized on a global scale.

Tito appeared in the waters of the Indian Ocean like an unexpected guest, six months before the large African–Asian conference in Bandung. He had a phenomenal feeling for global processes in international politics. Sukarno's vision was an anti-Western one, while Tito and Indian Prime Minister Jawaharlal Nehru, who met in Delhi before the Bandung Conference, conceived a policy of maintaining equidistance between the two major global systems. Their joint declaration was released a day before Nehru's departure to Jakarta to attend the preparatory meeting for Sukarno's Bandung Conference, where the Indonesian leader would unleash his uncompromising anticolonial and anti-Western rhetoric.

Immediately after India, Tito traveled to Burma. In Rangoon, he explained to Prime Minister U Nu that "I will never trust any great power because every one of them has its imperialist appetite, both the Western countries and Russia; we cannot ignore the fact that China might also become such a country someday, as has happened many times in history ..." Burma was trying to isolate itself from China and Vietnam because Burmese communists were receiving arms supplies from both of these countries. Also, the members of Chiang Kai-shek's Kuomintang, armed by the CIA, were active along the Burmese–Thai border. The Burmese government decided to acquire weapons from Yugoslavia. By that time, Yugoslav arms production had increased due to US assistance and technology, and the country had started exporting weapons.[3] Export of urgently needed weapons and ammunition worth USD2.5 million was agreed with Burma back in 1953. This enabled the Burmese government to launch a massive, victorious offensive against the Kuomintang on 2 March 1954. A French military attaché notes: "The Burmese success against the Kuomintang can be attributed to Yugoslav weapons!"[4]

On the return trip from the Indian Ocean, a pivotal meeting took place— while passing through the Suez Canal on his ship *Galeb*, Tito met Lieutenant Colonel Abdel Nasser, who had led a military coup in 1952. When the two met aboard *Galeb* on 2 February 1955, Nasser was in the middle of his revolutionary takeover of power. He placed General Mohamed Naguib, the president, under house arrest, and he would later round up all of his opponents—middle-class politicians, members of the Muslim Brotherhood, and the army officers loyal to the conservative Naguib. Then, supported by the masses, he would begin creating an Arab republic, a single state supposed to gather all Arabian nationalists of North Africa around a socialist program, something strikingly similar to Tito's own Balkan project. The impatient thirty-six-year-old lieutenant colonel was impressed by the sixty-two-year-old Marshal in a dark blue *grossadmiral* uniform who hosted him on his cruiser and explained to him the benefits of his latest invention—the non-alignment and equidistance policy—while promising him Yugoslav infantry weapons. This export line would also be important for the uprising in Algeria, which would begin on 1 November 1954—the fateful "Toussaint Rouge." Weapons would be shipped via Egypt and Tunisia to the Algerian National Liberation Front (FLN), founded that same revolutionary year of 1954.

The two conspirators aboard *Galeb* are aware that the time is ripe for decisive action, because the whole of the Mediterranean is already boiling and the anticolonial fever that started in Greece is now spreading everywhere. Marshal Tito assists the insurgents regardless of their race or creed. While he single-handedly fought the royal Greek army commanded by the British and supported by the Americans, he also supported Haganah, the Israeli paramilitaries fighting British rule in Mandatory Palestine. In May 1948, two months after Stalin's letter to Tito, Yugoslavia and the Cominform countries were still cooperating in providing assistance to the Israelis. At Žatec Airport in Czechoslovakia, near the former Messerschmitt aircraft factory (where the Bf-109 model was still being produced under the Czech name Avia S-199), the Israeli 1st Squadron (or the 101st Kheil HaAvir Squadron) was formed. Eighty-one pilots were trained there, and eighteen of these Avia aircraft were put in working order and flown from Kunovice, Czechoslovakia, to Nikšić, Montenegro, in two waves, in September and December of 1948. In Nikšić, Yugoslav identification marks were painted on them so that they could fly across the Mediterranean (Operation Velvetta 1 and 2).

The 1950s started with demonstrations against Europeans in the streets of the French–Spanish condominium of Morocco, which joined the modern world after the American landing in 1942. Eventually, the authorities were forced to allow Sultan Mohammed V, supported by the nationalist movement Istiqlal, to return from his Madagascar exile. With discreet American support, Muhammad V arrived in the country in 1955 and began the negotiations on independence that would be successfully completed the following year. After that, Moroccan ports would be used to supply the FLN in Algeria with Yugoslav weapons.

In Tunisia, Habib Bourguiba takes over the Constitutional Liberal Party (Neo-Destour). Having won the support of the French labor union federation UGTT, he approached the Paris government with a request for gradual independence for Tunisia. He promised that, in return, the French colonists in the country would have half the seats in the parliament. The colonial administration responded by throwing him in a desert prison. He managed to escape and reach Cairo, where he started to proselytize the idea of national emancipation. Finally, in 1954, facing defeat in Indochina, the Pierre Mendès France government allowed him to return home. He would soon become president, and Yugoslav weapons would be reaching Algeria from Egypt via Tunisia.

Only Libya remained quiet. From 1943 to 1951, the country was occupied by Anglo-American troops. It was later under their control as a kingdom, with Idris I, from the Bedouin tribe of Senussi, as its sovereign. But the chief engineer of the secret empire had different plans and supported other people. However, in order for his ambitious North African plans to materialize, Tito must first ensure a strategic backup. He will have to win over Khrushchev.

41

A PSYCHODRAMA IN TITO'S WHITE PALACE

BELGRADE 1955

In Belgrade, on 26 November 1954—four days before departing to India—Tito convened the Fifth Plenum of the Central Committee of the LCY. The general circumstances could not have been better. Stalin is dead, and Yugoslavia is receiving huge amounts of Western financial and military support. Đilas has been eliminated, and Comrade Khrushchev has sent Tito an "indecent proposal." At first, Khrushchev was misperceived by Yugoslav diplomats as a neo-Stalinist, and bureaucrat Georgy Malenkov was believed to be the man of change. This is why they tactically procrastinated in replying to the first message from Moscow, awaiting the outcome of the power struggle in the Soviet Politburo. But there is no reason to wait any longer: Khrushchev is firmly clutching the helm; he is winning local party secretaries and has just installed a man of his choice as head of the security service—now renamed "Committee for State Security attached to the Council of Ministers." A reply should be sent to him, with the future—not the past—in mind.

Tito explains why discretion is required—as you know, comrades, the West is carefully monitoring the normalization of our relations. For the Yugoslavs, the Soviet representatives in Belgrade are radioactive at the moment. Tito's Soviet policy is still characterized by his hardline stance. He must also keep in mind his image in the eyes of the West, which is financing him. Back in 1950, with GDP of USD1,500 per capita, Yugoslavia was the poorest and most backward country in Europe, save for Albania and Romania. Now that the United

267

States is filling up its budget, life is different from that in other Eastern Bloc countries. The 1950s are characterized by zero growth in the country's centrally planned economy, but the political climate is thawing and there is liberalization, which is very dangerous for the Yugoslav leadership. The country is living at someone else's expense—and relatively well, too (compared with other postwar victims behind the Iron Curtain). However, this could give rise to calls to change the character of the regime, which should be dealt with in an uncompromising manner. All potential enemies—middle class and intellectuals of the old stamp and clergy—have been either physically destroyed or disempowered and placed under the ruthless control of the political police. For this reason, the forces of the old regime do not represent any relevant danger, but it is important that the new regime *nomenklatura* does not evolve in the wrong direction. This is why Tito needs a middle, independent position in his foreign policy. He can balance then, suppressing spontaneous processes of democratization, or allowing them to an extent in case of external, "hegemonic" pressure from the Communist Bloc. But the Trieste Crisis was a turning point—it became clear that initiative and independence in foreign policy are easy to lose—which might lead to a loss of initiative in domestic policy, too. This means he has to redefine his role in the world.

Until Stalin's death, Yugoslavia was a bulwark of the West, important because of its pivotal position in the Balkans. From a military point of view, the situation was now clear—the Truman doctrine had stopped communists in Greece, on Turkey's and Iran's borders and in Korea, and communist revolutionary expansionism in Europe had been contained. But the West is now on the counteroffensive. Tito still has a crucial role in it. He has broken the monolith. It turned out that revolution did not work as a global concept. In future, any revolutionary will be able to tear a piece of the red flag and decorate it with his own national insignia. Tito did this in Yugoslavia, as the first country to fulfill such an ambition. Others will do the same if they manage to wrest themselves free from Moscow's control. If this line of communist pluralism were tolerated in the Kremlin, Tito could be much more useful to the West than he had ever been as a military deterrent in the Levant. So, the next stage will involve cautious probing in Moscow.

Having agreed to meet Khrushchev, Tito travels to Delhi first, for a prolonged visit. At the same time, Mijalko Todorović, former commissar of the 1st Proletarian Brigade, now deputy prime minister and a special envoy at Comrade Khrushchev's court, is taken to dinner in Molotov's diplomatic residence, together with the highest-ranking Soviet leaders. Malenkov is still here, although he is about to be replaced. He will fall from grace weeks after this intimate party. At the dinner, Khrushchev comments on Tito's and Nehru's Delhi declaration, as though it is merely an attempt to cool the global conflict between the military and political blocs. As for Nehru, Khrushchev says "that's all one could get from him" when criticism of the West is concerned. The merry company then indulge in typical Stalinist jokes—they make fun of Kardelj's ideas about "democratic socialism." Todorović, who obtained a degree from Belgrade University and lived in Paris, tries to explain to these communist troglodytes the meaning of "workers' self-management," another sophisticated Yugoslav concept. They make ironic comments and compare it with the ideas of Christian socialist and proto-Marxist Henri de Saint-Simon. But in the end, their conclusion is that it is all Yugoslav business and not their concern. It does not stand in the way of normalization of relations. As for Đilas and Dedijer, the Soviets like a lot of what Todorović tells them. The sacrifice of a bishop and a pawn will be very important in the Kremlin gambit.

At the 1955 New Year party in Moscow, Veljko Mićunović was introduced as a person of Tito's confidence. He would become a pivotal link between Tito and Khrushchev.[1] As part of preparations for Khrushchev's visit to Belgrade, some trade agreements were signed. Regular diplomatic relations were established, too. Various current issues of European politics were being discussed. In a separate note, Yugoslavia was offered membership in the Warsaw Pact, which was to be founded on 14 May 1955. Almost at the same time, on 15 May, the State Treaty was signed in the Viennese Schloss Belvedere that restored Austria's status as an independent country. Some ten days later, at the end of Khrushchev's great diplomatic offensive, he will meet Tito in Belgrade.

Khrushchev will do his best to sweet-talk Tito back to the Eastern Bloc. He must prove himself by pursuing an energetic and successful foreign policy while giving concessions to his subjects in domestic policy. The die-hard Stalinists, party, and the general bureaucracy of the *nomenklatura* are not happy with his efforts to modernize Soviet society and humanize the communist dictatorship. While trying to gain the upper hand in the Politburo, Khrushchev subdued Malenkov early in the year (by accusing him of "friendship with Beria"), but he would manage to oust him from the Politburo only in 1957, together with the rest of the "anti-party group" (actually, a majority in the Politburo), which opposed destalinization.

Khrushchev has stopped insisting that Yugoslavia should leave the Balkan Pact, but Tito will leave it himself, because military confrontation is of no use to him anymore. New political dynamics are being created. Khrushchev showed great political skill—he won Tito over by flattering his endless vanity and recognizing his role as being of global importance. Doing so did not really cost Khrushchev anything, except the painful trip to Belgrade. This signals a change in the political line, but it is something Khrushchev already decided to do because he can only fight the Stalinists if he shakes the apparatus and makes the riskiest moves.

The Soviet delegation arrives in Belgrade. The pomp. The protocol. Two delegations are conducting talks in the White Palace, Tito's residence built by King Karađorđević. Shorthand minutes are being taken. Khrushchev blames Beria for the entire odium of broken relations: "Comrades, you have no idea how hard that period was and the role that Beria played ..."[2] He then explains that nothing stands in the way of cooperation—they do not mind the Americans giving money to Yugoslavia ("Money cannot buy us," Tito interrupts him). They, too, would like to trade with the Americans, but the relations between Yugoslavia and the Soviet Union should be on a much broader basis, because there is an ideological relationship after all. After this improvised introduction by Khrushchev, Tito—perfectly focused—expounds the genesis of the deterioration of the relations as he sees it. It all comes down to foreign policy issues, in other words, Yugoslavia's sovereign rights that the Soviet Union denied, particularly as regards "our interests in Carinthia and Trieste" and as regards war reparations. He is trying to say that Stalin's tutelage was not beneficial to him, only detrimental. Yugoslavia gave up reparations from Hungary, while Poland and Czechoslovakia never delivered the machines that were ordered from them and paid for. At the same time, he says, Yugoslavia was choked by the West. As it did not turn to America at first, the smaller countries it entered into deals with were imposing unfavorable terms. "This is still killing us," says Comrade Tito to Comrade Khrushchev confidentially, not mentioning all the humanitarian assistance received by the UNRRA, all the food, shoes, and clothes that helped the nation make it through the hungry Stalinist years, until shipments of beans and modern weapons for the army and billions of dollars of assistance in money and wheat started coming from the United States. He does not mention that, but he explains that Yugoslavia, left at the mercy of evil capitalists, had to compensate foreign owners of nationalized factories, adding that "approximately half of the amount has been paid so far." By the way, no one ever heard anything about this compensation, either before or since. He wants to be completely frank: "I can say that, in the period between 1950 and 1955, we received

USD576,307,000-worth of assistance ..." Khrushchev reacts here, because he is not a fool or some third-rate bit actor but the head of an organized superpower. He says, mildly: "The Americans said various things, that you had received one billion, or a billion and a half." Caught in a lie, Tito explains that 600 million was given in money,

and then we received some [assistance] for the JNA, around one and a half billion dollars. This is how the Americans count. Since the assistance for JNA accounts for approximately USD400 million, and the military and economic assistance account for one billion and 150 million dollars, the total amount is one billion and a half. We have no problem saying this openly.

That is, when you confront us with the numbers. Bulganin then explains that the Soviet Union did offer its support on the Trieste question although it had no interests of its own there, just like in the case of Austria.

Then followed a lengthy and fruitless discussion about postwar mixed companies that were supposed to boost the development of the Yugoslav economy. After that, Khrushchev once again returns to Beria, and talks, at great length, about Stalin's last moments, about how he was dying and Beria was preparing men who would take key positions after his death. Beria integrated the Ministry of Interior and state security service in order to monopolize the surveillance infrastructure and use it to wiretap all the other members of the Politburo. Khrushchev also described how they had managed to stop him with help from Zhukov and the army, how they threw him in a cell, and how he wrote letters from the cell in order to divide them until he was banned from using pencil and paper. It was now Tito's turn to speak frankly:

I would like to tell you about an episode I had with Beria. As for him, I never ... [Khrushchev interrupts: "He was a cynic."] Yes, a cynic. To me, he was ... there was something repulsive in him. I met him when Ranković and I visited Stalin, it was during my first or second visit. We stayed in Stalin's villa and he escorted me to the car [An interruption: "Beria?"]. Yes, Beria. And he kept saying: "Beware, Comrade Tito, beware." And I said: "The war is over now. What should I be afraid of?" Then he said: "Beware, don't trust Ranković or anyone else." I found that appalling. In the beginning, I didn't want to say it to anyone. But after the dispute, I said that to Ranković and some close associates.[3]

Anyone who takes the time to study Tito's narratives will immediately realize this is a confabulation. The conversation gradually turns into a form of collective therapy for molested members of the communist family. Comrade Khrushchev, who is a gifted story-teller, continues the psychodrama in Tito's Belgrade residence with yet another episode from the anti-Beria cycle, another example of Beria's numerous schemes. He goes into details of a military committee affair that was launched by Beria in order to compromise Bulganin in Stalin's eyes. Stalin saw Bulganin as his successor, so Khrushchev himself spread some gossip about one of the generals in Bulganin's retinue (Bulganin was then defense minister). Khrushchev did not want Bulganin to gain points in the Politburo, so he falsely informed on the general to Beria ("I don't know what devil tempted me to do that ..."). He now openly admits all this in front of Bulganin and Tito. To Bulganin, it was certainly nothing new. All the other Soviets in the room were probably not shocked either. They had all made it through the Stalinist period, in which millions of communist idealists lost their lives on frontlines, in prisons, and in camps. Only these hardened committee assassins, who had schemed against each other, accused each other at congresses, and smeared each other in the papers, managed to survive. Khrushchev's openness served a purpose—they came to trust each other. In Yugoslav eyes, he is no longer a Stalinist who is trying to impose Soviet dominance on them. Tito briefly confirms there is room for an agreement and invites them to continue the meeting on the Brijuni Islands.

In this Belgrade episode, one can feel Tito's laser eyes scanning half-quarrelling protagonists of this Bolshoi Theater, both character and supporting actors—he has been in the trade longer than any one of them and will politically outlive the last of them by fifteen years. The curtain has fallen on the stage, and they will all go to the Brijuni. But our hero is already turning to new challenges: backed by the Soviets, he will immediately launch a secret war against France and Great Britain.

42

A SECRET WAR IN THE MEDITERRANEAN

ALGIERS 1956

On 1 November 1954, All Saints' Day, thirty coordinated attacks and bombings took place in Algiers. Seven people were killed, five of them white colonists (*pied-noir*). French Prime Minister Mendes France said in parliament that there could be no compromise when it came to the integrity of the sovereign territory of the republic. Only six months earlier, France had suffered a terrible defeat in Indochina. After the fall of Dien Bien Phu, the peasant army of the brilliant Vietnamese General Vo Nguyen Giap captured 11,000 French troops.

In three French "overseas departments" in Algeria, there are almost 1.3 million white colonists, making up 13 percent of the total inhabitants there. In the city of Algiers, the two francophone populations are equal in numbers. Clearly, there can be no compromise or negotiations with the terrorists. The insurgents led by the FLN are in for a cruel, bitter winter of 1954.

Standing out among the top leaders of FLN, a socialist party founded in Switzerland several months earlier, is the thirty-eight-year-old Ahmed Ben Bella. Before the Second World War, he joined the French army as a volunteer. He played football for Olympique Marseille, and he even scored in the finals of the national cup. In the war, he fought in the Battle of Monte Cassino, where his unit was decorated with the order of *Croix de guerre*. He was arrested in 1951, after he and the members of the Special Organization—a group of militants later to form FLN—robbed a post office in Oran to finance their subversive activities. Sentenced to eight years, he will escape from the notorious prison in Blida, spend two years underground, and reappear in Cairo in 1954 as the undisputed leader of the FLN and a liaison officer for contacts with Nasser's "Young Officers."[1]

After the first skirmishes with law enforcement officers, Algeria becomes radicalized because of the merciless French repression. The insurgents managed to survive the first winter of persecution in Casbah and maintain the initiative in their terrorist fight. In the meantime, their fight and the Algerian question had gained international attention, and his group in Cairo was seeking support. However, in the beginning they were bitterly disappointed. Despite the support Nasser was giving them in his fiery speeches, the badly needed arms supplies were negligible. Tito cooperated with Nasser, but he still hesitated to encourage the insurgency in Algeria with direct shipments of arms because of the influence he still had in French leftist circles. At first, he considered the possibility of Yugoslavia mediating in reaching a peace agreement between the government and insurgents. Before he went to Paris for a state visit in May 1956, he received a telegram from the president of the Algerian National Movement (MNA), a nationalist organization, requesting his mediation. But none of the suggestions was acceptable to the socialist government of Guy Mollet, who nevertheless received the destalinized and born-again Yugoslav Marshal with full honor.[2]

French counterintelligence and the executive illegal groups it uses will try to solve the Algerian question with counterterror all over Europe. What little weapons the Algerians managed to smuggle from Cairo via Morocco will not be enough for fighting the real war against the massive intervention of the French army, which has started deploying its troops in Africa. The mountain campaign in the first winter was a horrible experience for the French infantry. As a result, the army resorted to a repressive strategy, which usually proves disastrous in such circumstances. They took no prisoners and adopted a scorched-earth policy. They shot hostages.[3] In the first ten days, they crushed the guerrilla movement in Casbah and other urban centers of Maghreb. Nevertheless, the shaken Mendes France government decided to replace the governor and send Jacques Soustelle, de Gaulle's wartime head of intelligence, on an impossible mission.

In the coastal mountains of Kabylia and the Aurès (Awras) Range on the Tunisian border, the lands of the Berber tribes, FLN created its free territory, but the visible struggle—covered by the mass media—was taking place in Casbah of Algiers. However, in 1955, when the guerrillas massacred 123 people (seventy-one of whom were French) in Philippeville (present-day Skikda), a shocked Soustelle demanded even tougher military measures. The ensuing French offensive was followed by a terrorist attack in Algiers: carried out by three Algerian middle-class female students, it shattered the myth about the cultural and political integration of the overseas departments.

Guerrillas in the mountains, terrorism in the Muslim parts of cities—this is no longer a job for police and gendarmerie forces. Leading his 10th Airborne Division, General Jacques Massu arrives in Algiers. This war hero will crush the FLN in Casbah and win "the Battle of Algiers" but will lose the Algerian war, because the partisan movement in the mountains will in the meantime grow into a respectable force armed with weapons from abroad.

French agents organized the abduction of Ben Bella and his closest associates who were on their way from Rabat to Tunis aboard a Moroccan plane. After Ben Bella's arrest, Colonel Houari Boumédiène, a member of the FLN's military wing, took charge of FLN. He concentrated his forces close to the Tunisian and Moroccan borders. The French army responded—inefficiently— by installing a mini-Maginot Line, a barbed-wire fence along the borders. It cannot stop the fighters crossing, but the new Algerian leader will also need weapons and the assistance of the countries that will recognize his government. Besides Egypt, the decisive support in this critical stage of the resistance will come from Tito.

When he first met Nasser in Suez in early 1953, the agile old Marshal encouraged the young Egyptian officer to nationalize the Suez Canal.[4] In December 1955 and January 1956, Tito visits Ethiopia and then Egypt again, where he stays for ten days, for talks with Nasser. They reach a general agreement on the "non-aligned position" of their countries and on "distancing from the military pacts." For Tito, this means pulling away from NATO, but for Nasser, the step is an even bigger and more dangerous one—British troops are still stationed on his territory, in the Canal Zone. Egypt's non-aligned position would mean their forced departure.

If the Egyptian agreement with Britain and France were canceled unilaterally and the Anglo-French company running the Suez Canal were nationalized— regardless of the promise of full financial compensation—symbolically and strategically it would mean the end of the British Empire. Nasser would of course never dare do this on his own, even with the help of this prodigious seafarer in a white dress uniform. To engage in a conflict with the European colonialists in their own vital zone, Nasser will need a stronger patron. But Tito guarantees that such a patron could be provided as soon as the two of them spread their conspiracy a bit farther, making it global, and involving the super-powers of the day. Having gained success with such maneuvers in the Second World War, the Marshal immediately saw in Nasser a man of the same stamp, a fiery populist unencumbered by ideology. Algeria is a sideshow, where the weaker of the two colonial powers in the Mediterranean will be stabbed in the heart. When Morocco and Tunisia became fully independent in 1956, these new countries became bases on the gun-smuggling routes to Algeria. As for the internationalization of the Algerian uprising, Yugoslavia supported Saudi Arabia's 1955 motion in the United Nations calling for the issue to be submitted to the Security Council. But this was not even remotely enough political sup-port at such a historical turning point. Tito's assistance will be crucial, and the reconfiguration of the constellation of powers in the Mediterranean will indeed happen only when he wins the Kremlin's support for his policy.

Tito went to Moscow in June 1956. The entire Soviet leadership headed by the nominal head of state, chairman of the Presidium of the Supreme Soviet Marshal Voroshilov, welcomed Tito on Moscow's railway station. One million citizens waving small flags were on the streets to salute his motorcade. The first meeting of the two government delegations took place in the Kremlin on 5 June 1956.[5] On the Russian side, the whole team from the Brijuni is here— Bulganin, Khrushchev, Anastas Mikoyan, plus Voroshilov, a mustachioed member of the old guard who will act as head of state for some time. Comrade Dmitri Shepilov is attending, too—he is Khrushchev's sycophantic rising star and foreign minister, appointed during Tito's visit in order to substitute the obsolete Comrade Molotov. Tito brought along his Kardelj, and also Koča Popović, Todorović, and Mićunović—the whole commanding staff of the 1st Proletarian Division.

Tito is given the floor to set up the framework for the talks. After address-ing some bilateral and economic issues (construction of copper smelting works in Majdanpek and aluminum works in Montenegro), he concentrates on the world scene and Algeria.

As regards Egypt, Tito says:

> The Arabs have very little confidence in the Europeans. I would like the Soviet Union to help Nasser. He is in a difficult situation. Some Western countries want Nasser toppled. Nasser told me that the Western countries were frighten-ing him with the Soviet Union, but that the Arabs and Egypt were aware that the West wanted to use the Soviet Union as a scarecrow.

Then they switch to European and bloc-related matters. When it comes to the East European satellites, they are not a problem—being satellites, they will remain in the orbit. Tito says: "Our relations with all socialist countries have improved, except with Albania. Rákosi is a different story, too. I have no idea what he thinks." Khrushchev replies that Comrade Rákosi supports the improvement of relations with Yugoslavia. So too do the Albanians. Tito responds: "They were saying that we wanted to incorporate Albania into Yugoslavia. But, it's nonsense. We don't need to incorporate a couple of million hungry mouths into Yugoslavia."

Khrushchev makes no comment. Why bring up the past? After all, Beria is to blame for everything, and so is Stalin, buried by Khrushchev in his secret speech at the Twentieth Congress held four months earlier. Analyzing all the points, Khrushchev agrees with what was said, but he observes: "It is, however, important that you recognize the German Democratic Republic."

Tito replies: "We have been considering that." In 1955, the Federal Republic of Germany—Western Germany—proclaimed its Hallstein doctrine, according to which the recognition of the Deutsche Demokratische Republik (DDR)—East Germany—will be considered a hostile act of any country except the Soviet Union, which is one of the occupation forces and a guarantor of the peace treaty. In accordance with this protocol, diplomatic relations between West Germany and Yugoslavia will be suspended if Yugoslavia recognizes the DDR.

While sitting with Khrushchev in the Kremlin in 1956, Tito is ready to sacrifice his relations with all European countries. He is preparing to enter an undeclared war with Great Britain and France. He already has a conflict with Italy over Trieste and is about to make a move that will lead to a deterioration in relations with West Germany because of an insignificant East German Soviet colony in its zone of occupation. But he has decided to leave Europe and concentrate on his ambitions in the emerging Third World nations of the South Mediterranean and worldwide. Why would he settle for leading a small, relatively irrelevant European country when he can play a global role, worthy of his ambition? For that, he needs the support of Moscow.

While Tito is driven solely by his vanity, for Khrushchev playing a prominent diplomatic role is a necessity because the people and *nomenklatura* must perceive his strength. This is why he and his delegation visited London flying on board one of the first three prototypes of the new passenger jet plane Tu-104, causing a sensation there.[6] It was a very important message, because the rate of the production of its military equivalent—the nuclear bomber Tu-16—is ten aircraft per month. Comrade Khrushchev may look somewhat comical in his baggy trousers, but his planes are impressive;

besides, he has just added Andrei Sakharov's hydrogen bomb to his arsenal. Having been shown a film about the atomic and hydrogen bombs, Comrade Tito is also impressed, and he feels good in the company of his Kremlin partner. All he needs now is to drag him into his Third World plans. Their first talks end up with mutual compliments and oaths of eternal loyalty and friendship between the two nations.

This was the end of round one. The second round follows after a short trip across the Soviet Union. France's Algerian policy—both internal and foreign—is discussed in great detail again, as if it were the main topic of the meeting. Italy is also discussed and the divisions on the left there (between the communists and Nenni's socialists). "I don't trust him too much," says Tito about Nenni. They are hesitant to tackle the pivotal issue of defining the new joint communist "general line." When Khrushchev mentioned the "socialist bloc" in this context, Tito energetically replied:

> We don't like the word "bloc"; we don't like it when the socialist and capitalist blocs are mentioned. It is not the socialist countries being surrounded by capitalist countries now; it is the other way around ... The expression "socialist bloc" can be somewhat disturbing, particularly in countries like India. It's better to discuss the essence; the form is not that important. The capitalist encirclement has already been broken. Socialism has established itself. We should reconsider this new situation.

Voroshilov finds it too abstract: "In the particular case of Yugoslavia, the bloc should not be mentioned. But in general, the socialist bloc does exist." Khrushchev interrupts like an arbiter:

> We will not insist on the word "bloc." What matters is the essence, and the essence is that we must support the harmony between the socialist countries. It is our moral obligation toward each other. The capitalists want to divide the socialist countries and destroy them one by one. Now they are talking about Poland, Hungary, Czechoslovakia ...

Khrushchev is not naïve; otherwise, he would not hold the position he is holding. He sees what is afoot and realizes the danger of vague doctrinal wording in this sensitive political issue. Tito makes the following argument: "There is the NATO pact. It must be broken somehow. Not just diplomatically, but also politically. The division into two blocs hinders it to an extent."

Khrushchev does not back down. He says he will reiterate what he has already said. When the countries of people's democracy sided with the Soviet Union, it was a positive, progressive step, although its anti-Yugoslav aspect was not fair toward Yugoslavia. He wraps it up firmly and pragmatically:

If we, for instance, gave up the term "socialist bloc," what does that mean? Does it not mean that we should then let all communist parties do as they please without coordination with other communist parties? We would have to give up our basic principles, developed by Lenin ... That would mean the end of our achievements.

"You misunderstood us," says Tito, but he is wrong. Khrushchev has understood him perfectly. However, the Marshal does not give up: "And what if we call it 'the socialist world' and 'the capitalist world'?"

Khrushchev: "A very broad and vague term. Nehru is also a socialist. But we want more from Nehru the socialist ... With Nehru we cannot nurture the same relations that exist between us—socialists."

In the end, a communique was signed that did not include other communist parties in order to avoid any ideas about the "bloc." However, at the end of the day, Tito managed to impose global issues in the Kremlin. Naturally, he did not manage to loosen the bloc, but the architecture of Soviet foreign policy would indeed change. Relations with the Yugoslav party would be based on equal footing, provided that Yugoslavia distanced itself from the West and canceled its pact with NATO. As for the Third World, Yugoslavia and the Soviet Union would approach it together and try to draw national movements in the developing world into the socialist community. As for China, no one can rule it or negotiate with it. As soon as Mao realizes that the communist monolith has burst, China will declare itself a great power—which it really is—and will pursue an independent, albeit very unsuccessful, foreign policy.

Having achieved all this—nothing is yet written in stone, but it seems very probable—Tito invites a small company from the future non-aligned countries to the Brijuni Islands. On 18 July, no later than three weeks after his return from Moscow, he receives Nasser and Nehru. Observers fail to understand what it is that connects them, because they cannot grasp the pragmatic essence of the new world politics being born here. Nasser and Nehru are nationalists who want to get rid of their colonial legacy. As for Comrade Tito, he wants to install himself here among them and sell the whole package to Moscow, thus gaining a dominant position in the Mediterranean once he pushes out Great Britain and France with his "light" revolution without communism. It would also be his payback for the Trieste humiliation and for his failed ambitions in Italy, southern France, and the Catalonian Levante.

The talks begin with confirmation of the "ten principles of the Bandung Conference"—a general anticolonial agenda adopted the year before. They agree that the great powers are complicating the situation in the Middle East; however, Tito and Nehru do not share Nasser's perception of Israel, which received arms shipments from Yugoslavia not so long ago.[7] The situation in Algeria was "assessed as very important and specific, both in terms of the fundamental rights of the Algerian people and in terms of securing peace in that region. It was agreed that colonial domination was totally undesirable and offensive." This reflects the agenda of the group Tito is trying to form. Yes, it all began in Bandung, where the Algerian FLN was also represented; but no gun came to them from there, so that the Third World jungle concerto was as relevant to the Western capitals as the distant sound of tam-tam drums. But everything was going to change now because Tito managed to fire up Nasser—which, given his temperament, egoism, and ambition to become a charismatic pan-Arab leader, was not a particularly hard thing to do. In 1955, Nasser managed to obtain weapons from Czechoslovakia and Yugoslavia.[8] Only a week after returning from the Brijuni Islands and three days after proclaiming himself president of Egypt, Nasser nationalized the Suez Canal. The same day, the Egyptian navy closed the Gulf of Aqaba and blocked Eilat, Israel's only Red Sea port. The reaction of the British and the French is unanimous. On 29 July, the French government decides to intervene militarily, first and foremost because of Nasser's intolerable involvement in the Algerian war. The French navy chief of staff goes to London to plan a coordinated operation that will be followed by the Israeli invasion of Sinai.

At the same time, the French socialist government entered into secret negotiations with the FLN, represented by Mohamed Yazid (one of the FLN representatives in New York) and Ferhat Abbas (who later became the president of the provisional Algerian government). The Algerian emissaries were first officially received by Tito on the Brijuni Islands and then they met the French prime minister's envoy in Belgrade. All this took place only days before the French abduction of Ben Bella, precisely at the moment when an agreement on military intervention in Egypt was reached with the Israeli and British governments in Sèvres. Obviously, it was but a maneuver to cover up the preparations for the intervention.

Two days before the landing, the French navy captured a ship named *Athos* off the Algerian coast. The ship sailed under the Sudanese flag and had a Greek captain. It was transporting weapons for the Algerians from Alexandria to Morocco. The weapons were paid for with Egyptian money. A total of seventy-two mortars, some 350 machineguns, and some 2,300 rifles were confiscated. This was not much for waging a real war, but it was the biggest arms shipment that Ben Bella had managed to get via Cairo by that time. It illustrated the limited capabilities of the insurgent forces in the Maghreb during this period. The occupation of Egypt would cut their logistic lines.

The Israeli army launched an attack on Sinai on 29 October. The Israelis took the entire peninsula in four days. Then followed the Anglo-French invasion, supported by seven aircraft carriers. Divisions of parachutists, commandos, Foreign Legion, and an entire mechanized brigade landed in Suez. It all took place in dramatic, very unfavorable political circumstances—exactly six days before the landing, Soviet tanks entered Hungary.

43

THE DOUBLE CONSPIRACY

BUDAPEST 1956

Khrushchev's project of peaceful destalinization failed in Budapest. Nagy, an old Comintern cadre from Hotel Lux, became Hungarian prime minister for the second time. After the war, he was minister of agriculture in the provisional national front government of Béla Miklós.[1] Nothing at the time indicated that he would lead an anti-Stalinist revolution.

At the first postwar elections, held in 1945, the Hungarian Communist Party won a mere 17 percent of the votes. The communists formed a coalition government with the Independent Smallholders, Agrarian Workers, and Civic Party (FKgP), which won 57 percent of the vote. In line with Stalin's national front recipe, the communists installed László Rajk as minister of interior. He would also be in charge of foreign affairs, while Rákosi, an old communist leader from Ufa, would become an omnipotent deputy prime minister. Having returned to the country after fifteen years spent in the isolation of a Hungarian prison and after five years in Soviet exile, he definitely felt marginalized and had to prove himself. Rajk, on the other hand, had a perfect record: he was the political commissar of the Rákosi Battalion of the 13th International Brigade Dabrowski in Spain. Upon returning to Budapest, he reassumed his underground party activities and became secretary of the Central Committee of the Hungarian Communist Party.

After the war, as minister of interior, Rajk founded the party-controlled secret police AVO (Magyar Államrendőrség Államvédelmi Osztálya, State

283

Police State Protection Department). Like Nagy and Tito, Rajk was a brutal Stalinist. But—he stood in Rákosi's way.

Another protagonist was involved in this Hungarian intrigue. He would turn out to be an amazing survivor. János Kádár (real name János József Csermanek) was born in Rijeka in 1912 as an illegitimate son of a maidservant who lived in abject poverty like a character from *Les misérables*. He joined a secret labor union in Budapest, and when police arrested him, they beat him up and he admitted everything. He only got two years, but he was expelled from the organization on grounds of treason. While serving time, he met Rákosi and they became very, very close friends.

When the Soviet army arrived in Budapest in 1945, Csermanek was head of the party's military committee, which was largely inactive during the occupation. His postwar career would suffer from his decision to dissolve the party in the middle of the war. Rákosi's group in Moscow found itself in the very awkward position of being a party leadership without a party. With the communists safely in power in Budapest after the war, Ernö Gerö—Rákosi's number two—tried to use the decision to disband the party to discredit Kádár. Nevertheless, when Rákosi was elected the party's general secretary in 1945, Kádár, who had assumed this name during the war, was appointed one of his two deputies. With his trade union worker's background and not being a Jew, he was a rare gem.

The AVO did a thorough job preparing a conflict with Tito and the Titoists. The Yugoslav *chargé d'affaires* Lazar Brankov was arrested as head of the Yugoslav spy network. Brankov admitted the crime and became a witness for the prosecution against Rajk, accused of being part of a conspiracy with the Yugoslavs.[2] But there was no need to waste too much time on the presentation of evidence and cross-examination—Rajk voluntarily admitted everything, explaining that he and the other accused had indeed tried to "wrench Hungary away from the peace-defenders' bloc, which is the only guarantee of freedom and happiness for our people and nail it to the imperialist front, thus making it a satellite and toy of imperialists."

Rajk could not avoid hanging, but at least he saved his family. Kádár himself took part in the early phase of Rajk's investigation. Also, it was Kádár who replaced Rajk as minister of the interior. Subsequently, he was told that one of Rajk's "accomplices," a Social Democratic leader, had accused him of being a British agent and police informer who in 1943 dissolved the party by order of Hungarian Regent Admiral Horthy's secret police. While it is a thankless task to try to tell the truth from lies in the cacophony of mutual accusations by these party members who were settling scores with each other, one has to conclude that, in Kádár's case, there must have been some truth in those charges, given his supernatural survivability. Rákosi, who was aspiring to confirm the status of "Stalin's best disciple," was about to politically liquidate his former fellow-inmate and close friend. He visited him in prison and suggested he should admit to all the accusations. Kádár admitted his mistake—dissolving the party—but he denied he was a traitor. He underwent an intense investigation but suffered no physical torture.[3]

After the liquidation of the Hungarian Titoists—in reality, those communists who had not gone into Soviet exile during the war—the very last of Stalin's massive purges spread across Hungary. In the Soviet Union, the remaining Jews among the party top brass were being purged. Being incurable revolutionaries, dangerous internationalists, "Trotskyites," and leading professionals in various fields, they were not suitable for Stalin's monolithic Greater Russian state apparatus. The purge was dubbed the "physicians' plot." By default, the campaign had to be extended to Hungary. However, the Hungarian party's top brass were practically all Jews. At one of the first meetings of the Politburo, Gerö, born in Slovakia as Ernö Singer, sarcastically noted: "Now that we have all gathered here, we have a *minyan*!" *Minyan* is the quorum of ten adult Jewish men required for religious rituals. But the joke will be on them.

Stalin's death probably stopped the liquidation of Rákosi, whom Beria had called the "Jewish king of Hungary" (the family name of Mátyás's father was Rosenfeld). Indeed, Jews accounted for many leading cadres of the Hungarian Communist Party, but now an ethnic Hungarian—Nagy—became prime minister and Kádár was released from prison. At a session of the Central Committee, Nagy announced his "new course," which included abandoning collectivization, abolishing compulsory sales quotas for peasants, increasing private land plots, reducing investments in heavy industry (which had reached 41 percent of GDP), and investing in the production of consumer goods. These reformist ambitions seemed quite radical, and Hungary was in for dramatic political repercussions.

When the Belgrade Declaration was signed on 2 June 1955, at the end of Khrushchev's visit to Yugoslavia, allowing each communist party its own path to socialism—except, of course, the parties under the effective control of the Soviet apparatus and army (although it is not specified anywhere)—hopes arose that even the Eastern Bloc countries would witness a true turning point. Also, news of Khrushchev's speech at the Twentieth Congress of the CPSU in February 1956 soon spread through the party ranks. Khrushchev held his secret speech at the very end of the congress, News about it leaked to the West immediately. It was probably Khrushchev's own doing: after the Warsaw Pact had been established and Yugoslavia had been drawn back to the global communist community (if only to its outer orbit), he announced he was about to go on a world tour to manifest the newly acquired self-confidence of the Soviet state as a society of industrial modernization and of relaxed socialism with a human face. Thus announced, he was well received everywhere. However, within the Eastern Bloc, tectonic movements began. Khrushchev immediately identified them as a severe danger. This is why he told Tito in Moscow that they should be very clear and specific about the definition of the "bloc" because otherwise everything would go down the drain. Having received his advance training in Stalin's classroom, Khrushchev perfectly understood realpolitik.

Less than a week after Tito's departure from Moscow, massive workers' protests began in the Polish city of Poznań. Some 100,000 people rallied in these anti-regime demonstrations. The revolt was crushed. Some 100 protesters were killed and 600 wounded. A crisis of leadership occurred. Khrushchev made a wise political move—he appointed Władysław Gomułka as the new Polish party leader. Gomułka was an old Leninist cadre—he resided in the Hotel Lux in 1934, at the same time as Tito. In occupied Warsaw, he organized the illegal parliament. After the war, Gomułka led the communist faction that was well established in Polish society: it was popular due to the distribution of German lands and properties. *Nomenklatura* and masses supported him because of his national program, which included anti-German and anti-Semitic agendas. The other, Stalinist faction was led by Bolesław Bierut, who had the military support of Marshal Konstantin Rokossovsky and "Walter" Świerczewski. The Stalinists accused Gomułka of "rightist deviations" and he ended up in prison, at the same time as the archbishop of Warsaw, Stefan Wyszynski.

After the Poznań riots, Khrushchev and the entire Soviet leadership flew to Warsaw to interview Gomułka for the leading position. Gomułka explained to them that, if the Soviet army tried to occupy Poland, the Polish army would inevitably resist. He insisted that Rokossovsky, a Soviet marshal of Polish origin who was now Polish defense minister, be removed from the post, but he guaranteed that Poland would remain in the "bloc" and that the Soviet Army (as the Workers' and Peasants' Red Army, RKKA, had been renamed in 1946) would remain in Poland. It would be welcomed and needed for the defense of the country's new western border on the Vistula and Oder. The Adenauer government was not ready to recognize this border because Germany had lost Prussia and Silesia. The destalinization in Poland was thus carried out successfully.

Hungary was a whole different case. In the Second World War, the Hungarians collaborated on a massive scale, fought wholeheartedly on the Eastern Front, and carried out a genocide of the Jews and Roma, so postwar denazification would not make much sense. Instead, communists ventured into social engineering and retorting against enemy classes. But the party carrying out all this had no legitimacy at all, and the Soviet presence was perceived as occupation. Also, that the party leadership was dominated by Jews certainly did not help suppress Hungarian racism. Therefore, although it was a sincere communist like Nagy who launched the anti-Stalinist reform, as soon as the first crack appeared, the deluge poured into the streets of Budapest and the dams started bursting.

It began with Rákosi's removal from the position of general secretary in 1956. Khrushchev decapitated him a month after Tito had made his comment in Moscow—"I have no idea what he [Rákosi] thinks." Nagy dismissed him a month before Khrushchev's visit to Yugoslavia and the signing of the Belgrade Declaration. But after Nagy's reformist government proclaimed its "new course," the masses took to the streets. Students in Budapest, and then citizens in smaller cities and towns, started organizing oppositionist "Petőfi circles," named after Sándor Petőfi, the leader of the nineteenth-century liberal revolution crushed by the imperial Russian army. The Americans instantly offered more extensive trade relations; Radio Free Europe started broadcasting news and information in the Hungarian language. The atmosphere in Budapest became galvanized on 6 October, when Rajk, a victim of Rákosi's regime, was posthumously rehabilitated and formally buried. And then, on 23 October, the Hungarian counterrevolution began.

At a mass rally in Budapest, the president of the Writers' Association read a proclamation demanding a truly independent Hungary and a form of democratic socialism that allows private property. The protesters then went to the parliament building. Gerö was quick to reject the demands of the students and other protesters. The infuriated crowd then rushed at the 9-meter-high bronze statue of Stalin and knocked it down—ironically, only Stalin's boots remained on the monument's base. Fighting soon broke out at the national radio building. The protesters started to single out and attack the much-hated members of the AVH (AVO had been renamed Allamvédelmi Hatóság, State

Protection Authority). They hanged them on the trees in boulevards. They firebombed police vehicles and stole guns from police stations. Gerö called for the intervention of the Soviet Army. Defense Minister Zhukov sent tanks immediately. They entered Budapest the very next day. The following five days saw seventy armed conflicts throughout Hungary. After the protesters' attack on the parliament building, the communist government was toppled and Gerö escaped to the Soviet Union.

Sporadic until then, the resistance reached serious proportions. Béla Király, a General Staff captain who had fought with the Hungarian army on the Don, took nominal command of the newly formed National Guard. He gathered men, broke into the Central Committee building, and started summarily executing party and government officials. The insurgents threw Molotov cocktails at Soviet tanks. Hundreds of party officials were lynched. Revolutionary committees were formed throughout the country. Nagy did not back down even when the protests turned into a counterrevolution. In a broadcast to the nation on 28 October, he announced a truce and an amnesty and demanded negotiations, dissolution of the AVH, the formation of a proper National Guard, withdrawal of Soviet troops from the capital and negotiations on their departure from Hungary.

Meanwhile, a very interesting Yugoslav observer came to Budapest. It was Comrade Dobrica Ćosić, who arrived on 23 October, the same day that the riots began, as if he knew they would take place in front of the parliament building and that the first victims would fall there. He stayed in Budapest until the last day of the uprising—29 October—when Ranković sent a plane for him. Ćosić was a Partisan writer, Đilas's associate in the Ministry of Propaganda, and the closest associate of Ranković. The best Yugoslav foreign correspondents were also there, based in the Yugoslav embassy. They gathered there as if they were expecting some important developments. Later on, they would be accused of being "Nagy's conspirators," who helped him and his "dissident clique" establish contacts with the US radio station Free Europe, which indeed played a very important role in the Hungarian events.

The Soviet Politburo met on 1 November and decided to proclaim a new Hungarian "provisional revolutionary government" with a new leader. Yuri Andropov, the Soviet ambassador to Budapest, thought that Kádár would be the best man for the job. There was not much time to choose given that news of the Anglo-French landings in Suez had just arrived. The international crisis was escalating beyond imagination. Khrushchev would soon remain with nothing but the hydrogen bomb in his hands. Immediately after the Politburo meeting, he flew to Poland, accompanied by Malenkov and Molotov. There he met Gomułka, who had just survived his own drama with the Poznań workers' revolt. Khrushchev and Malenkov then flew to Bucharest, where they discussed the situation with the Romanian and Czechoslovak leaders, and then they immediately proceeded to Yugoslavia, to meet Tito.[4] They arrived in Pula late on the evening of 2 November. It was not a diplomatic mission and was thus not entered into the otherwise meticulously kept protocol of Tito's official activities. The Soviet leaders landed in a terrible storm. Their plane almost crashed.

Khrushchev was experiencing the most dramatic moments of his career— Soviet tanks were burning in Budapest and the ongoing invasion of Suez was about to consolidate the position of the colonial powers in the Middle East and intimidate the countries that, as Tito had claimed, would be willing to join some kind of a wider socialist bloc. Stalin had bequeathed him the most powerful country in the world, and if he now suffered defeat on the international scene, everything he had achieved so far would clearly be perceived as a failure.

No direct testimony of that conversation in Tito's White Villa on the beach of Brijuni Island remains. No shorthand minutes were taken. There are, however, secondary sources, the most interesting one being the diary of Comrade Shepilov, Khrushchev's foreign minister. The entry dated 7 November is about his Moscow conversation with Ambassador Mićunović:

> Khrushchev and Malenkov have informed the party leadership and the Soviet government that Comrade Tito and other Yugoslav leaders fully agreed with the Soviet comrades' conclusion that Nagy and his helpers had not only been bankrupted politically but had themselves become accomplices of reactionaries and imperialist forces. For instance, I know that, during the discussion, Comrade Tito said: "What kind of a revolutionary is Nagy? What kind of a communist would allow hanging and shooting of leading workers, communists, and prominent public figures?" In light of these facts, we are truly amazed that the Yugoslav leadership has given refuge in their Budapest embassy to the antipeople elements around Nagy![5]

Accompanied by forty-two persons, including his family members, Nagy indeed found shelter in the Yugoslav embassy. If only he had gone to the Americans, moaned Khrushchev, he would have been exposed as an imperialist servant. On 7 November, Zhukov reported that the situation in Hungary was under control. Only the problem of Nagy remained. Khrushchev personally sent a message to Tito that extending Nagy's exile in the embassy could cause "irreparable damage in Soviet–Yugoslav relations." Of course, Tito cared about Soviet–Yugoslav relations, not about Nagy. After all, Tito himself had been told—according to Shepilov—that Nagy was "bankrupt." But that he was looking for shelter in the Yugoslav embassy implied that the Yugoslavs were involved in the conspiracy. And all that during the peak of the Suez Crisis, which was coming to an end without Tito's participation, after he had invested so much energy there.

Tito offered to receive Nagy and keep him out of politics. Kádár, head of the provisional government, was also looking for a bearable solution. In the end, Kádár and Tito's envoy Dobrivoje Vidić signed an agreement, which, however, did not oblige Khrushchev. The Soviets had lost 650 troops in the fighting, including eighty-five officers. There were 1,215 wounded.[6] As soon as Nagy left the embassy, he was arrested and taken to Romania.

Practically at the same time, on 7 November, the UN General Assembly votes in favor of Resolution 1001 on ceasefire in the Middle East. Nasser asked President Eisenhower if he would accept a peacemaking mission. Eisenhower agreed. Vice-President Nixon later explained: "We could not protest against the Soviet intervention in Hungary while England and France were intervening against Nasser!" Besides, Eisenhower was concerned that all the Arabs would switch to the Soviet side because Moscow had given unstinting support to the Arab revolutionary command in Cairo. Bulganin threatened that the Soviet Union would intervene in Egypt and Syria and launch nuclear ballistic missiles at British, French, and Israeli cities. Earlier on, Khrushchev had boasted of a huge arsenal of intercontinental missiles. Concerned, Eisenhower even approved reconnaissance flights of U-2 aircraft stationed in an airbase in Turkey. That was the decision that would bring about the Francis Gary Powers affair. Only much later would it turn out that Khrushchev was exaggerating—at that moment, he had at his disposal only four nuclear missiles 8K71, or Semyorkas, stationed near Arkhangelsk.

Despite the superiority and easy gains of the interventionists, the Anglo-French campaign fell apart under Soviet threats and American pressure. Massive peace protests began in Great Britain; the entire left was protesting. As the Suez Canal was closed and British oil supplies were threatened, the Bank of England suffered substantial losses in a period of only three days and was forced to apply for an emergency loan from the IMF. However, the United States blocked the approval. As a result, the expeditionary corps withdrew on 22 November. It was replaced by the UNEF, an international contingent of "blue helmets." At the same time, the UN and the United States confirmed Egypt's sovereignty over the canal. In December, a Yugoslav peace-keeping battalion joined the UN troops in Sinai. It would stay there for eleven years, and a total of 15,000 Yugoslav troops would rotate there in twenty-two shifts. All in all, it was Nasser's triumph. Great Britain suffered a total defeat and lost its relevance in the Mediterranean. It would only retain its bases on Malta and Cyprus. It was a loss of face and a loss of empire. And without controlling the canal, all British possessions "east of Suez" became untenable. Less than a year after the debacle, British troops and authorities would withdraw from Malaya, Kenya, and Rhodesia.

Churchill, who had withdrawn from active politicking, witnessed a full-scale collapse of the British colonial empire and of British power in the Mediterranean. He himself had made the enemy who destroyed what was most sacred to him—he had made Tito, who brought together Nasser and Khrushchev and destroyed British colonial power in the Mediterranean while creating his invisible secret empire. The Marshal was now going to concentrate his attention on Algeria.

44

THE ARSENAL OF THE
MEDITERRANEAN REVOLUTION

CASABLANCA 1958

On 7 August 1957, the French navy captured the Yugoslav ship *Srbija* off the Algerian coast. The 12,000-ton ship was escorted to the military port of Mers-el-Kebir. When they searched it, they found 70 tons of arms and ammunition on its way to Casablanca in order to be delivered to the Algerian insurgents. Morocco had gained independence a year before, and Sultan Mohammed had just been crowned King Mohammed V. He provides strong support to those fighting against French and Spanish colonialism and, to this end, has established contacts with a couple of unusual individuals on the Levant. They include a young Egyptian officer, pan-Arab-oriented socialist Nasser and a communist renegade Marshal Tito. This is why the port of Casablanca is very busy—days before the announced arrival of *Srbija*, the Russian ship *Cherkasky* unloaded some 700 tons of guns for the Algerians; a month before that, a Bulgarian freight unloaded as many as 1,800 tons of guns in Tangier. The guns are mostly Czechoslovakian. When the Politburo of the Czechoslovak party approved direct shipments in February 1957, the FLN started receiving war materiel via Alexandria—or Casablanca—where police officers, according to an agreed procedure, confiscate it and then secretly distribute it to the Algerian insurgents.

Before this well-organized activity would begin, a Warsaw Pact summit took place in Budapest from 1 to 4 January 1957. Renewed communist unity under the leadership of Comrade Khrushchev was demonstrated there, only two months after the Hungarian revolution had been crushed. Tito also had to attend and give his public support to the renewed Cominform. He had to redeem himself for the secret support he had been giving to Nagy, who was now languishing in a Romanian prison, waiting to be hanged.

Tito will have to explain his presence at the Budapest conference to US diplomats, because America does not like this rapprochement. On 26 August 1956, he had written to President Eisenhower, explaining his almost month-long visit to Moscow and Bucharest. Thanking the United States for the assistance received earlier, he says: "Our visit to the Soviet Union is often completely misinterpreted in the West. Again there is talk that we have risked our independence, that the Soviet Union will swallow us and the like ..."

Khrushchev has of course been trying to bring Tito back to the Soviet orbit, but what everyone has failed to realize is that Tito is trying to steer him in a specific direction and use him as an instrument of his foreign policy goals. So he is offended when the leading world media claim he is willing to subdue himself, when he, in fact, has always sought to attain a dominant position. In a letter to Eisenhower, he explains he does not need the new US military assistance program because the international situation has improved substantially.

Tito adds that, being a soldier, President Eisenhower will understand that an army must develop even in peacetime; however, for years, the West has had no sympathy for Yugoslavia's requests for purchase of jet engine licenses. Yugoslavia will have to solve the problem somehow—he did not explicitly mention Soviet licenses, but he suggested it as a possibility.[1]

Eisenhower's long confidential answer came on 12 November 1956, after the Hungarian events. The US president praises Tito:

> I am certain that many favorable developments could be attributed to your personal efforts, made—as I have learned—in Belgrade 1955 and Moscow 1956 to convince the Soviet leaders to engage in non-interference in the internal affairs of other countries. It seemed that this course of action was opening a possibility for improvement of the conditions in Eastern Europe and there were no setbacks after the Soviet merciless full-scale intervention in Hungary.

Eisenhower understands that Tito's influence over Khrushchev was greater than Khrushchev's over Tito:

> While truly regretting that Yugoslavia was not in a position to take an attitude in some stages concerning the repression against the Hungarian people, we salute Your Government's support to the United Nation's motion demanding immediate withdrawal of the Soviet troops from Hungary. I also think you can

be satisfied with the fact that Your efforts have been consistently directed toward a wider independence of the Eastern European countries.

Eisenhower understands how far Tito can go. He commended him for the meaningless diplomatic parade in the UN. He also knows that Tito cooperated with the CIA on the Hungarian issue, that a solution with a relatively moderate Kádár was agreed on the Brijuni Islands, and that Gomułka was chosen for Poland, not some Stalinist fossil. Khrushchev barely survived a challenge that would soon lead to a differentiation in the Politburo, where everyone saw all these moves as his weakness. That Khrushchev managed to keep his presence of mind after all, rather than adopting a more extreme position, can partly be attributed to the influence of his only anti-Stalinist ally, an opportunistic dictator who does not care much about communism and is merely trying to help stabilize the situation in Europe so that he can devote his attention to his new hobby—revolutionary activities in the Third World.

The Suez Crisis showed that the conflict between the East and the West had moved away from Europe; the war in Korea had been over for some time, and the new one in Vietnam had yet to start. The expansion of communism to neighboring Eurasian destinations had been stopped by the Truman doctrine, later expanded by the Eisenhower doctrine, with the United States committing itself to defend Iran, Pakistan, and Afghanistan from communist intrusion. The Soviet Union is currently preoccupied with strengthening the Eastern Bloc and its own post-Stalinist regime, and China is facing internal political and economic problems. Meanwhile, the process of decolonization in African and Asian countries is taking place to the detriment of the European colonial powers. The United States denied these powers its support in maintaining their positions and their sterile domination in the Third World, where the superpowers had yet to confront each other.

The superpowers will collide in 1957, but in the earth's orbit, after the Sputnik satellite was successfully launched on an R-7 rocket. While everyone was watching the sky, no one noticed what was going on in Africa. A nuclear balance between the United States and Soviet Union was established in 1949 when a Russian A-bomb was detonated near Semipalatinsk. It was not much of a mass destruction weapon—one could destroy a city with it, but if one planned destruction on a continental scale, a much stronger bomb would be needed, like the thermonuclear one the Americans detonated at Eniwetok Island in 1952. The Soviet megaton thermonuclear weapon RDS-37, built in ten secret "atomic cities," was detonated on 22 November 1955. Then, in late August 1957, days after the "directive conference" of the Warsaw Pact countries in Budapest, the Telegraph Agency of the Soviet Union (TASS) triumphantly announced that the USSR possessed intercontinental ballistic rockets. Soon afterward, on 4 October, Russian chief spacecraft designer Sergei Pavlovich Korolev launched Sputnik.

America has entered the space race with the Soviet Union already some distance ahead. Together with fear of nuclear war, it will cause national mass hysteria. Who cares for the situation in Maghreb now? This will create room for Tito and Nasser. They will also get assistance from Khrushchev who, having strengthened the bloc, finally accepted the concept of an expansionist policy in the Third World. The assistance being sent to Algeria is growing.

In January 1958, the French navy intercepted the Yugoslav ship *Slovenija* 45 miles off the Algerian coast and confiscated 148 tons of Yugoslav and Czechoslovakian weapons—12,000 rifles and 95 tons of ammunition. In mid-July 1959, the freighter *Makedonija* was stopped. It carried 10,000 machine-guns and 200 mortars—enough to equip an entire partisan army. More than fifty Yugoslav ships will be intercepted and searched because Belgrade has practically recognized FLN: a delegation of the movement was present at the Seventh Congress of the LCY in Ljubljana in April 1958.

Military assistance to Algeria is sent via all available smuggling channels. The French intelligence agency, SDECE, operates throughout Europe in order to prevent it. But the weapons still keep coming, despite the tight control in the Mediterranean. In 1959 alone, the French navy followed 41,300 ships, stopped and searched 2,565 of them in the open seas, and escorted forty-eight of those to ports for a detailed checkup. Almost 300 battalions, strengthened with armored units, were deployed in Algeria. Helicopters were used on a massive scale, for the first time in the history of warfare. However, the saboteurs in kasbahs and the guerrillas in the mountains were impossible to stop for good.

General de Gaulle then appears on the scene. Everyone sees him as a man of destiny who can deal with the Algerian Crisis that has revealed the impotence of the Fourth Republic. On 1 June 1958, fearing a coup in France, the parliament accepted de Gaulle's ultimatum—he will return the dictatorial powers vested in him. He will amend the constitution and introduce a presidential system instead of the current parliamentary system, thus establishing the Fifth Republic. He himself will appoint the members of the executive branch. As soon as he was elected in the parliament, de Gaulle went to Algeria aboard the prototype of a passenger jet plane. He was welcomed there as a savior. But in the speech in the city of Constantine, he would offer an "integration package," a vision of an undivided country "from Dunkirk to

Tamanrasset" in the Sahara. But the Algerians are no longer willing to accept anything other than full independence. On the other side of the divide, white colonists, represented by the Public Salvation Committee, walk away in protest from every rally where the general directly addresses the FLN. They did not bring him to power in order to convince the insurgents that coexistence is possible, but to destroy them. They were wrong about this man, for they did not understand his vision of France.

The opponents of de Gaulle's policy, led by the dissident right-wing paramilitary organization Organisation Armée Secrète (OAS), launched a terrorist campaign in France. At least 2,000 people were killed and twice more wounded. And the chef who had cooked this broth, Yugoslav President Tito, decorated with the Golden Medal of the FLN the year before—where is he at that moment?[2] Escorted by a squadron of ships, he is sailing on his ship *Galeb*, visiting the countries of Africa and Maghreb and weaving a new regional political network that will provide crucial assistance to the Algerian insurgents in their struggle for independence.

45

FROM DESERT TO WILDERNESS

GOLD COAST 1961

In February 1961, accompanied by numerous state officials aboard his 4,000-ton cruiser *Galeb*, Tito went on his great African tour. The convoy is made up of a navy squadron of destroyers and troop-carrier ships, with more than 1,000 sailors and troops. His Rolls-Royce was loaded, too. Everybody took with them tailor-made evening dresses, a number of silken shirts, and matching underwear. Preparations were thorough: a book on the geography, population, economy, and politics of every country on the itinerary was published for internal use.

While today it may seem like some irrelevant historical event, the eccentric expedition of an idle dictator, it was a political adventure that only this unique character was capable of. He shows ambition to become the major player in Africa, and rival to Western interests, although the United States is financing his peculiar regime.[1] Until then, it was practically inconceivable that the president of a small European country would go on a global diplomatic mission. Visiting neighbors, appearing at a session of the UN General Assembly in New York—that would be expected, but the moves of this elderly gentleman with a controversial biography could not be predicted.

When he set forth on his famous "voyage of peace" that would last almost four months, Tito wanted to make sure no unpleasant surprises would be awaiting him back home. A fleet of Douglas DC-6b four-motor aircraft would land in every port where *Galeb*, escorted by Yugoslav navy ships, would sail in.

299

The planes would bring classified dispatches and newspapers from Belgrade. Ranković—Comrade Marko—is house-sitting for Comrade Tito. The borders are quiet, the JNA is well equipped with American weapons. Headlines are reporting on the itinerary of the president's African trip. The regime runs like clockwork.

Ever since the West gave him huge amounts of money for breaking the monolith of world communism, Tito has seemingly maintained equidistance between the big powers and has modified the centralized economy with some limited competition between state-owned companies. This model is lavishly financed from abroad, where they are still interested in "keeping Tito afloat." It is not based on the dialectical materialism learned in Moscow; instead, it was refined in practice, in Tito's own political laboratory—Balkania. This is where he cooked his stew of "brotherhood and unity" and "communism with a human face." Only some exotic spice was missing. Tito would find it in the non-aligned policy that emerged in Bandung and would then adapt it to fit his secret interventionism in the Mediterranean and, later, throughout the Third World.

In Accra, the capital of the newly independent country of Ghana, Tito is welcomed by Dr Kwame Nkrumah, a professor of philosophy who obtained his MA in Pennsylvania and his PhD from the London School of Economics. There he got in touch with especially contagious Marxists, exiled Russian Trotskyites and English Stalinists, so he became an ardent leftist. Nkrumah will nationalize cocoa-tree plantations, ban strikes, introduce a one-party system, proclaim himself president for life, heavily encumber his country with debt, and launch a program of industrialization that will soon fail. During his 1966 visit to North Vietnam and China, the CIA will help a Ghanaian general carry out a coup. Nkrumah ended up in permanent exile in Conakry, the capital of Guinea.

But that was yet to happen. Tito arrived in Accra on 28 February 1961. Having spent five days there, he proceeded to Lomé, the capital of Togo. This small country, a narrow tract of land stretching into the African hinterland, had gained independence from France a year before. Its president is a guy named Sylvanus Olympio. His sublime-sounding name would not help him: only two years later, he would be murdered by Sergeant Etienne Gnassingbé Eyadema, who will rule peacefully for the next thirty-eight years. He will be succeeded by his son, Faure Gnassingbé, despite condemnations from the entire international community with the exception of France, which kept him in power. Finally, in 2005, he allowed an election. He won it, using every possible means. A minor massacre ensued.

Nearby Liberia is easy to access by sea, so Comrade Tito comes round on 3 March 1961. The president, one William Tubman, welcomes him in the capital Monrovia. Tubman will rule until his death in 1971. He was succeeded by William Tolbert, whose nine-year rule was peaceful, with no turmoil. However, he was killed in 1980. After that, the flood. A group of young officers carried out a coup, organized an election, lost it, and started a civil war. It was not before the arrival of the USS *Iwo Jima* that democracy was restored. The UN's "blue helmets" also arrived and trials at The Hague Tribunal commenced. Later, they had an Ebola outbreak, too.

After Liberia, Comrade Tito arrived in Conakry, the large capital of Francophone Guinea, a country that had gained independence three years earlier, dividing itself into the coastal part, led by Ahmed Sékou Touré at the time of the visit (he held power for twenty-six years, until his death), and the hinterland, which became the state of Mali, with Bamako—a backwater on the banks of the Niger—as its capital. Tito entered the city in his Rolls-Royce, transported aboard *Galeb*. Mali had gained independence less than six months earlier and is led by Modibo Keita, a very tall, charismatic toga-clad figure in slippers. He will also rule for a long time—twenty-eight years. This pan-African socialist who walked around in the national costume of the sub-Saharans from the banks of the Niger will be toppled in a coup, thrown into prison for nine years, and then murdered. Today, he has a monument in Bamako.

Tito completed his African tour on 26 March 1961. He then sailed back to the Mediterranean. On the return trip, he stopped in Morocco. There he was welcomed by King Hassan II, who had been crowned a month earlier as the successor of his father Mohammed V. Five years after the French colonialists had gone, a war with the Spanish neo-colonialists was going on for Western Sahara and Mauretania. When welcoming Tito, the king is accompanied by his right-hand man, Colonel Mohammad Oufkir—his "Ranković." In charge of repression, Oufkir will become known when he organizes the murder of dissident Mehdi Ben Barka in Paris in 1965. He himself will then attempt a republican coup, backed by France, which sought revenge for Algeria. Oufkir was killed, and his wife and children will remain in a desert prison for twenty years. As for the king's children, they sought shelter in the Yugoslav embassy during the coup. This is how the present-day Moroccan King Mohammed VI survived. The ambassador in Rabat was the former OZNA major who worked on the takeover of the fabled Greek gold after the war, assisted by Commissar Neubacher.

Tito's next destination is the historical Tunis. The leader of the struggle for independence was Habib Bourguiba, who had earned his degrees in law and political science in Paris in the 1920s. After the Second World War, Bourguiba traveled to the capitals of Arab, Muslim, and European countries, as well as the United States, lobbying for Tunisian independence. Then he returned to his country and offered an agreement to the French. They turned it down and imprisoned Bourguiba for three years. Finally, the Mendes France government signed the Franco-Tunisian autonomy agreement. The road from that concession of Quai d'Orsay to full independence was a short one. As soon as he became independent, a colleague with whom he had many things in common called upon him; he would make a firm, long-lasting alliance with President Tito. Bourguiba ruled happily for thirty years. Then he was toppled in a coup. He was interned for thirteen years and died at the age of ninety-six. When the Arab Spring came in 2011, his successor, the former head of the secret service, had to flee the country on account of corruption charges.

The final leg of Tito's "voyage of peace" took him to Alexandria, where he was greeted by Nasser. After the Anglo-French landings and a Middle East war that had been stopped by the decisive intervention of US President Eisenhower, President Nasser became a new pharaoh, celebrated around the Arab world. He arrested members of the Muslim Brotherhood and communists, nationalized foreign monopolies, and then created a joint federal state with Syria—the United Arab Republic. Other Arab countries, from Iraq to Yemen, were supposed to join it soon, too. Not everything went smoothly for him, but when Tito arrived in Alexandria aboard *Galeb*, Nasser was still at the peak of his power.

Beyond doubt, the main item on the agenda of the five-day visit to Egypt is Algeria. Yugoslavia has concentrated all its diplomatic activities on this turning point, as if Tito has instinctively realized that the newly created Third World countries should be as one on this issue in order to turn their quantity into a new quality. Otherwise, it is merely "cooperation," "fostering relationships," and other regular diplomatic activities—something he has no affinity for whatsoever.

Tito's resoluteness to wring the recognition of Algeria despite all the resistance and caution can also be explained by the appearance of another serious rival in the Third World—China. The Third World is not big enough for both ambitious leaders—Comrade Mao and Comrade Tito. China developed a very active policy toward the newly created "developing countries." As regards Algeria, it become involved as early as 1957; its economic assistance to the

25. J. B. Tito and Khrushchev meet during the Fifteenth Session of the United Nations
General Assembly, New York City, October, 1960 (Tito and Khrushchev, Andrei
Gromyko).

26. Nikita Khrushchev consulting with J. B. Tito during the Fifteenth Session of the
United Nations General Assembly, New York City, October, 1960 (J. B. Tito,
Khrushchev, Leo Mates, Milan Žeželj).

27. J. B. Tito's visit to Guinea: getting to the wreath laying ceremony at the monument for the victims of colonialism, Conakry, March, 1961 (Ahmed Sékou Touré and J. B. Tito, Milan Žeželj next to driver).

28. The reception in honor of J. B. Tito during his visit to Mali. Bamako, March, 1961 (from left to right, Vojo Daković, Yugoslav ambassador to Mali, J. B. Tito, Modibo Keïta).

29. Train journey from Casablanca to Rabat during state visit to Morocco, April, 1961 (J. B. Tito and King Hassan II).

30. The reception on the occasion of accreditation of George F. Kennan as US ambassador to Yugoslavia. Brijuni Islands, May, 1961 (George Kennan, J. B. Tito, Koča Popović).

31. The Belgrade First Non-Aligned Conference, the Federal Executive Council building, Belgrade, 1961 (from left to right: J. B. Tito, Prince Hassan ibn Yahya, North Yemen; Prince Norodom Sihanouk, Cambodia, Saeb Salam, Lebanon; Aden Adde, Somalia; Ibrahim Abboud, Sudan; Sheikh Ibrahim bin Abdullah Al Suwaiyel, Saudi Arabia; Makarios III, Cyprus; King Hassan II, Morocco; Sirimavo Bandaranaike, Sri Lanka; Habib Bourgiuiba, Tunisia; Sukarno, Indonesia; Osvaldo Dorticós Torrado, Cuba; Kwame Nkrumah, Ghana; Gamal Abdel Nasser, Egypt; Mohammed Daoud Khan, Afghanistan; Modibo Keïta, Mali; Jawaharlal Nehru, India; Hashem Jawad, Iraq; Mahendra Bir Bikram, Nepal; Benyoucef Benkhedda, Algeria; Louis Lansana Beavogui, Guinea; Cyrille Adoula, Congo; Antoine Gizenga, Congo).

32. J. B. Tito's visit to Algeria, the performance of the Bedouin Fantasia, near Laghouat, April, 1965.

33. The official gift-giving in the garden of the residence during Tito's visit to Algeria. Algiers, April, 1965.

34. The October Revolution Parade on Red Square devoted to the 50th anniversary of the Great October Socialist Revolution, November 7, 1967 (from left to right, J. B. Tito, unknown, Antonin Novotny, unknown, Kliment Voroshilov, Walter Ulbricht, Nikolai Podgorny, Andrei Grechko, Leonid Brezhnev).

35. State dinner in the Niavaran Palace given by Mohammad Reza Pahlavi in honor of J. B. Tito, Tehran, April, 1968 (from left to right, Shahbanu Farah Pahlavi, J. B. Tito, Shah Reza Pahlavi, Jovanka Broz).

36. New Year's Eve Party in the White Villa, the Brijuni Islands, 1969 (left side, Mladen Iveković, Vladimir Velebit, right side, Kiro Gligorov, J. B. Tito).

37. Military parade of the Yugoslav People's Army on the occasion of Victory Day, Belgrade, May, 1970 (Kenneth Kaunda, J. B. Tito).

38. The delegation of the Socialist Party of the Federal Republic of Germany, Brijuni Islands, September, 1970 (Herbert Wehner, Stane Dolanc, J. B. Tito).

39. Richard Nixon's visit to Yugoslavia, the White Palace, Belgrade, September, 1970 (Richard Nixon, J. B. Tito).

40. Richard Nixon visits Kumrovec, J. B. Tito's birthplace, Kumrovec, September, 1970.

41. J. B. Tito visits Pope Paul VI in his private library, Vatican, March, 1971.

42. State dinner in honor of Queen Elizabeth II and Prince Philip in the White Palace, Belgrade, October, 1972 (Queen Elizabeth II, J. B. Tito, Princess Anne).

43. On the terrace of the White Villa with Chancellor Willy Brandt and his family, Brijuni Islands, April, 1973 (Matthias Brandt, Rut Brandt, J. B. Tito, Jovanka Broz, Willy Brandt).

44. State dinner in honor of Idi Amin and his wife in Villa Brionka, Brijuni Islands, April, 1976.

45. The reception for the Broz family on the occasion of J. B. Tito's 85th birthday, group photograph with the staff, Belgrade, May, 1977.

46. Visit to the People's Republic of China and the Great Wall, Beijing, September, 1977 (J. B. Tito, admiral Tihomir Vilović, Chin Peng).

47. Hua Guofeng's visit to Yugoslavia, the Old Palace, Belgrade, August, 1978 (left corner, Berislav Badurina, Marshal Tito's chief of staff, Hua Guofeng, J. B. Tito, Vidoje Žarković).

48. Hua Guofeng's state visit, dinner at the yacht Galeb, Brijuni Islands, August, 1978.

49. President Tito's funeral, largest state funeral in history with a procession passing through the streets of Belgrade, May 8, 1980.

50. The state funeral of President Tito with the auditorium for world dignitaries in the background. Among those present, Leonid Brezhnev, Hua Guofeng, Kim Il-Sung, Margaret Thatcher with Prince Philip, Gustav Husak, Mengistu Haile Mariam, Chadli Bendjedid, King Baudouin, Urho Kekkonen, Helmut Schmidt, Erich Honecker, Konstantinos D. Tsatsos and many others.

Algerians topped the Soviet assistance. As Moscow was originally hesitant because it did not want to damage its relations with France and the West, China took the initiative. China has been trying to assert itself as a logical patron of the Third World countries while also maintaining equidistance between the Western and Eastern Blocs (being in conflict with the West and increasingly distancing itself from Khrushchev's Soviet Union). The Chinese government has also given up the bloc logic and the concept of mechanical expansion of communism across its borders (efficiently suppressed by the United States).

In 1959, Mao received an Algerian delegation led by Ben Youssef Ben Khedda and granted them a USD10 million loan. That was when the competition began: the Soviet Union immediately decided to send humanitarian assistance thirty times higher than the Yugoslav assistance. Other Eastern Bloc countries also started establishing bilateral relations. However, Yugoslavia had an advantage: Tito had offered uncompromising diplomatic support to the Algerian government; he was the first one, and ready to go further than anyone else. He had created an entire "Commonwealth" of the Mediterranean states backing the Algerian struggle one way or another. Nor was this merely an ephemeral, opportunistic political maneuver or his presence in the area new. A precious Chinese diplomatic-intelligence document from 1960 reveals:

> The countries of the Soviet Bloc had already been aware that Yugoslavia had its men in the field who maintained close relations with the Algerian combatants, youth and labor unions, and were spreading Yugoslav ideological influence. Belgrade's penetration into all spheres of Algerian society was so intensive that, during the anti-Titoist campaign of the Soviet Bloc, the Algerian press often supported Yugoslavia.[2]

Clearly, this source substantiates the presence of Tito's men in Algeria and dates it back to even before 1948, when the country served as a springboard for infiltration in Spain.

Competing with Khrushchev and Mao, Tito must manifest resolve and an offensive approach. But then again, he has never lacked these kinds of qualities. Immediately after returning from his "voyage of peace," he will make a decisive move in Belgrade, the capital of his imaginary global empire.

46

THE THIRD WORLD CAPITAL IN THE BALKANS

BELGRADE 1961

In September 1961, Comrade Tito welcomes in Belgrade all the promising leaders of the new world bloc that still does not have a fixed name. The First Conference of Heads of State or Government of Non-aligned Countries is taking place. Originally called a "movement of non-engaged countries," it was renamed Non-aligned Movement (NAM) in order to underline its "active and peaceful" approach—something more than mere neutralism of the countries outside the global military and political blocs. A total of twenty-five leaders and three South American observers (Bolivia, Brazil, Ecuador) are attending the conference. The heads of all African "startup states" are here: Nkrumah (Ghana), Touré (Guinea), Keita (Mali), King Hassan II (Morocco), Bourguiba (Tunisia), and Nasser (UAR—United Arab Republic).[1] The Congolese protagonists are busy with their internal power struggle and will not make it to Belgrade. But the miniature Emperor Selassie from the ancient Amharic kingdom has arrived, and so have his neighbors from the Horn of Africa. Also represented are Sudan (a five-year-old country), Somalia (a year-old country), and the Kingdom of Yemen across the Red Sea (Yemen Arab Republic) and communist South Yemen (former British Aden Protectorate). Saudi and Cambodian princes and Afghani and Nepali kings are also in Belgrade. Nepali King Mahendra abolished the parliament and put a stop to the democratic experiment in his country two years earlier. He will rule happily for another ten years. He will be succeeded by his son Birendra. The infamous Nepalese royal massacre and a coup will follow.

305

The reign of Cambodian Prince Norodom Sihanouk lasted seventeen years. He will be dethroned by the US-backed Marshal Lon Nol. The Khmer Rouge, Asian folklore Marxists, will start a revolution and carry out a genocide of their own people. This will come to a halt when Vietnam intervenes and installs its puppet regime in Cambodia. This will trigger a war between Vietnam and China. Eventually, after the fall of the Berlin Wall and the collapse of communism, Sihanouk will return to power, but this time as a king.

The first Indian president, Nehru, has also arrived. He replaced the father of Indian independence, Mahatma Gandhi. By this time, Nehru's authoritarian daughter Indira Gandhi (no relation to Mahatma) has already become head of his cabinet, the power behind the throne.

Sirimavo Rattwatte Dias Bandaranaike was the wife of the first Ceylonese (Sri Lankan) President Solomon West Ridgeway Dias Bandaranaike, assassinated by a Buddhist monk in 1959. Having entered politics, she won elections by exploiting the image of a bereft widow. The sari-clad, bespectacled lady that looked like a small-town teacher was a dedicated socialist and hardliner. Her rule was blood-stained.

Indonesian President Sukarno, a veteran anticolonial fighter, was a big star of the Belgrade summit. He was also at his peak in Belgrade: he had just launched an invasion of New Guinea, the last island held by the Dutch colonists. The Dutch had to withdraw under the pressure of the Americans who, in turn, were concerned about the growing influence of the Soviet Union, which had been shipping guns to Sukarno. Local Indonesian communists were growing stronger at the same time, and the economy was collapsing (one can always count on this side effect of socialism). Hyperinflation appeared, the private sector contracted, and the idealist doctrinarian could only come up with some new ideological formula (he was both Tito and Kardelj in a single person).

The 1961 conference in Belgrade would not be complete without one august priest. Michael Christodoulou Makarios III was the primate of the autocephalous Orthodox Church of Cyprus and the Cypriot Greek national leader during the struggle for decolonization of the island. When the British colonial authorities eventually agreed to call elections in 1959, Makarios won them. Together with Dr Fazıl Küçük, vice-president and the leader of the Turkish minority, he started making plans for true independence. The Union Jack was lowered in 1960, so Makarios came to Belgrade as an unusual, but clearly successful fighter against colonialism in Europe. This story will not have a happy ending. The Greek military junta will become involved, and a Turkish military intervention will follow.

However, the true "king" of the Belgrade summit is its host, Comrade Tito. With his hair freshly greased, he is very confident, yet somewhat sullen. One can clearly tell from his body language and his facial expression on a newsreel. Why is Comrade Tito unhappy? He has just added to his honors the title of general secretary of the Non-aligned Movement—the Third World Comintern. He is at his peak—what else could he want? Maybe he feels that his position is very fluid, just as the circumstances in the world are also fluid.

On 4 June 1961, before the Belgrade conference, Khrushchev met with President Kennedy in Vienna. At the Vienna summit, held after the failed landing in Cuba (the Bay of Pigs debacle took place in April that year), they tried to solve the issues that were affecting their relationship. Mutual trust was not established. Kennedy denied responsibility for the attempted export of counterrevolution to the Caribbean. One of the topics was also Berlin, where the building of a wall of discord would start in August 1961.

Khrushchev and Kennedy discussed the situation in Laos, too. The local communists, Pathet Lao, were fighting the US-backed royalist forces there. This was but one of the crisis spots in Indochina, where a large-scale conflict would begin soon after the American president sends massive military assistance and advisors to Vietnam. The US and Soviet leaders were obviously sliding into a conflict; it was inevitable because of their interventionist agendas. Khrushchev and Kennedy were fighting for a perception of power. The United States was superior in nuclear intercontinental missiles. Khrushchev, on the other hand, had but a few dozen missiles and a big mouth. He said that "the Soviet Union will be producing intercontinental missiles like sausages." While Cuban commandos were preparing for the Bay of Pigs operation, the Soviets sent cosmonaut Yuri Gagarin to space. After that, no one could convince the American public that there was no "missile gap," that the Soviet Union did not have the edge in missile technology, and that communism was not spreading like a plague.

The United States was forced to make aggressive moves to compensate for this non-existent weakness, imposed on the American public by Khrushchev, who was aware he was lagging behind in the armament race because he had used his resources for civilian purposes—housing and mass consumption.

The mutual intimidation threatens détente—peaceful coexistence between the two superpowers—which is good for Marshal Tito, the eternal mediator balancing between the big powers. Balancing between the two worlds is important because it also enables him to be an arbiter in internal Yugoslav affairs. As long as he can intimidate citizens and sincere moderate socialists with the Soviet military threat and win doctrinarian communists with American money, his authority will not be challenged. Bureaucrats and technocrats will not become independent and will not question the authority of this God-sent leader. As the most important state affairs are managed in the sphere they have no access to, they perceive everything through an ideological paradigm, used for stupefying the party masses. Of course, Tito is not afraid of the people but of the party—or, better, of the party elite controlled by the secret police, which, in turn, is controlled by the army and its secret service. But the authority arising from the personal apparatus and structured as a social factor is the one that could compete with his own authority if the circumstances were stable and if the permanent "state of emergency" in foreign politics was lifted. While no one is irreplaceable in a regulated system, autocrats prefer everything to depend on them. Mao, the Great Helmsman, also felt it necessary to destabilize the system, so he launched the Cultural Revolution and destroyed all the government structures he could, thus eliminating all mediators between him and the people and maintaining his limitless power for life. Unlike Mao, Tito is in no position to copy him in Europe in the 1960s, to unleash terror based on the revolutionary fanaticism of the masses. Although uneducated, he is a calculating person with acute social intelligence and has a perfect feeling for what can be achieved under existing circumstances. He understands that his rickety Yugoslavia is no China, just like his opportunistic politics do not correspond with those anticipated by Marx. Comrade Tito must therefore find something completely new, different, and original. But first he must complete this crucial stage of the anticolonial offensive in the Mediterranean. Solving the world's problems is his vocation, and he has focused his entire energy on it.

The declaration signed at the First Non-aligned Conference required the world powers to allow unhindered, independent development of the countries created after the disintegration of the large European colonial empires. While the declaration was simply empty words, Tito actually supported Khrushchev's foreign policy in his speech—at the moment when the Soviet Union was about to launch a new propaganda offensive by making a show of military strength. In 1961 alone, the Soviet Union would detonate fifty-seven nuclear bombs, including the strongest hydrogen bomb in the world, the 50-megaton RDS-202 ("Tsar") bomb.

US Secretary of State Dean Rusk sent a note of protest against Tito's speech at the Belgrade conference.[2] The US ambassador to Belgrade, Kennan, who had promoted Tito because of his balanced policy, took it hard and was professionally discredited. He would later resign and retire from diplomacy altogether.

But for Tito, the main goal of the Belgrade conference is the international recognition of the Algerian provisional government. With the help of the newly independent states, he will ensure that it receives diplomatic support at the United Nations. In Belgrade, Yugoslavia formally recognizes the FLN's provisional government, an equivalent of the Yugoslav AVNOJ. At the conference, only Ghana, Cambodia, and Afghanistan follow suit. Nehru abstained and even Nasser was too cautious. The attitude of the latter led the president of the provisional Algerian government Ben Khedda to remark that the "Yugoslavs are better Algerians even than the Algerians themselves." The recognition of Algeria resulted in the French ambassador's withdrawal from Belgrade and a break-off of diplomatic relations. But Tito is not afraid of French pressure: an uncompromising offensive has always been his tactics. And his judgment was correct again—de Gaulle would give in and begin negotiations with the (still imprisoned) FLN leader Ben Bella in Evian. Ben Bella would become the first president of independent Algeria. That pushed France into a civil war that would cause many casualties and traumas. De Gaulle miraculously survived the assassination attempted by the OAS, the white colonialist terrorist organization in Algeria.

After the British Empire, the French Empire was now also destroyed in the Mediterranean, and a civil war was raging in this great country. And who was its primary instigator if not Tito, who fanned the flames with the actions of his own Comintern—the Belgrade-based headquarters of his secret empire?

Comrade Tito achieved huge success in the Third World. He became its role model, and emperors, kings, sheiks—even one padishah—tried to imitate his style. This locksmith-in-disguise was friends with Prince Sihanouk and Ethiopian Emperor Selassie. With the exception of Tito and Selassie, no other leader who participated in the First Non-aligned Conference in Belgrade ever entered collective memory. They were all dictators, tyrants, hereditary rulers, megalomaniacs, nationalists, quasi-socialists, or half-trained Marxists with a vivid imagination. They all made up or applied some original political and philosophical doctrines. Comrade Tito had his "self-management" (he managed everything himself), Nkrumah had his "consciencism," Sukarno had numerous abbreviated formulas, and Kim Il-sung (who joined them later on) had only one idea, "juche." Mobutu will simply call it "mobutism." Although they swore they were self-sufficient, they all had to request massive foreign assistance because the visions created in their rich imagination had impoverished their subjects. Besides the negative determination of "not aligning with the blocs," one positive determination applicable to them was their common opposition to democracy—the fundamental political principle of the modern age. Never before had so many eminent anti-democrats assembled in one place like at the Belgrade conference. All of these autocrats left behind them devastated societies and political instability, which would inevitably lead to civil wars. The same thing happened in the role model country, Yugoslavia. A fragile country and a strong leader—it is a bad recipe. One does not need to be a historian to anticipate what will happen if a patched-up country is run by a God-given leader and his acolytes.

47

CUBA LIBRE

BRIJUNI ISLANDS 1962

A distinguished guest arrived in Yugoslavia in late September 1962. It was Leonid Ilyich Brezhnev, number two in the Moscow *nomenklatura*. He carried an important message for Tito and his closest associates. He would stay in Yugoslavia for two weeks and make a fiery speech to the workers of the Split shipyard, sharply criticizing the United States for its support to the Cuban counterrevolutionaries who, in April that year, were wiped out on the beaches of Bahia de Cochinos. Any further attempt on Castro's island, threatened Brezhnev, would mean the "beginning of an active war."[1] He "drew a line in the sand." And he spread the good news of the firm Yugoslav–Soviet friendship that would continue to strengthen and be beneficial not only for the two nations but also for "other countries building socialism." By that, he did not mean the countries of the Eastern Bloc but the motley crew from the Belgrade conference, strongly influenced by Tito. The Soviet Union was now going to encumber them with its heavy tutelage, as if they were a key component of international politics. This meant that Khrushchev had fully accepted "Tito's doctrine" of exporting socialism to Third World countries. Khrushchev would apply the doctrine energetically and uncompromisingly, to such an extent that the very author of the concept would probably find it excessive, because he had always been inclined to maintain a balance and "stay in the middle." Tito still needed America, because the national economy of his communist state depended on American assistance and the channels for transferring and smuggling strategic raw materials and technologies between the divided East and West. In 1962, after Tito declared his support for Khrushchev's policy, expressed in his speech at the Belgrade conference, Yugoslavia was struck off the "most privileged nations" list in trade with the United States.[2] Hence the reservations about Brezhnev's aggressive speech. But what was the nature of Brezhnev's mission and what message did he bring to the Brijuni Islands?

Brezhnev is Khrushchev's old, reliable cadre, the most important member of his Politburo. In 1960, Brezhnev replaced Malenkov as chairman of the Presidium of the Supreme Soviet, thus becoming the nominal head of state— the second highest-ranking position in the *nomenklatura*, next to the head of the party.

In charge of the "atomic cities," Brezhnev built a number of industrial centers in Siberia, where missiles and nuclear devices would be produced and advanced technologies would be developed. But one of the most important plants he would build was the one in Dnipropetrovsk (present-day Dnipro). It was a huge industrial complex where, in 1954, Mikhail Kuzmich Yangel would begin serial production of the first Soviet mid-range ballistic missiles.

After the Bay of Pigs invasion, Khrushchev's heated rhetoric leads him to fall into his own trap. He is aware that he does not have at his disposal a credible number of intercontinental ballistic missiles for strategic deterrence and intimidation. He has six brigades with a total of thirty-six launchers of Yangel's 8K51 missiles (Army designation R-5, "Pobeda") and four autonomous regiments along Siberia's borders. They can only reach Eurasia, not other continents. This is why in July 1962—immediately after the failed May talks with Kennedy in Vienna—he secretly met Castro in order to agree on a joint venture. Based on their agreement, Operation Anadyr was approved on 7 July, and the installation of launch-pads for Yangel's improved ballistic missiles 8K63 (R-12) began in Cuba. With a range of 2,000 kilometers, the missiles, each carrying a 300-kiloton nuclear warhead, could reach Washington, DC, and New York City. Marshal Sergei Semyonovich Biryuzov, commander-in-chief of the Soviet Strategic Missile Force, a separate sub-branch of the Soviet Army, was in charge of the 43,000-strong contingent that arrived in Cuba in July. Decorated with five Orders of Lenin and awarded the titles of Hero of the Soviet Union and National Hero of Yugoslavia, he had been the chief of staff of the Fourth Ukrainian Front during the war, thus participating in the liberation of Belgrade. He was wounded five times. Comrade Brezhnev was his commissar, and Brezhnev's superior was Khrushchev.

Given the relations between Tito and Khrushchev and their joint subversive project of exporting a socialist revolution to the Third World, it was no wonder that Brezhnev paid a visit to Yugoslavia amid the political drama that was blazing up in the Caribbean and was about to explode, with global repercussions. This is why Khrushchev could not come to the Brijuni Islands in person. He had to stay in Moscow and keep his finger on the nuclear trigger. Comrade Brezhnev was sent in his stead.

The brutal party bureaucrat Brezhnev, former Red Army tank driver, arrives at Tito's Brijuni residence, where the Marshal awaits him in a white suit and a classy Panama hat, surrounded by mouflons like a communist nabob. Brezhnev notifies him of the upcoming confrontation in another once-fashionable destination. It is only a matter of days before US spotter planes will discover the military installations in Cuba. What happens next is hard to predict. But the participants of this Brijuni meeting are aware that Tito has invested too much in his relations with Khrushchev to be in a position to back off now. In addition, in the autumn of 1962, as they speak, a large Yugoslav army delegation is visiting the Soviet Union. The JNA is about to switch to Soviet weapons. The air force is getting MiG-21 fighters, twice faster than the speed of sound (introduced in the Soviet air force only two years ago), modern Mi-6 helicopters, and SA-2 anti-aircraft missiles (the ones that shot down Francis Gary Powers in his U-2). The navy is getting rocket gunboats and fast self-guided torpedoes. The land forces are getting T-55 tanks and 9M14 anti-tank wire-guided missiles. Most importantly, the Soviet technology comes with industrial licenses, enabling Yugoslavia to export weapons to the Third World. In time, the value of the exports will reach USD1 billion per year. Clearly, Tito is stepping deep into the Soviet military and political amalgam. Indeed, no more than ten days after the return of Khrushchev's emissaries to Moscow, the Cuban Crisis broke out.

48

A DEFEAT IN THE HIMALAYAS

NEW DELHI 1962

The Cuban Crisis ended on 21 November 1962. The US navy lifted the naval blockade when Khrushchev agreed to remove the missiles and nuclear warheads from the island. In return, the United States signed a secret agreement according to which it would remove 100 PGM-19 Jupiter ballistic missiles from their air bases in Gioia del Colle near Bari, Italy, and Çiğli near İzmir, Turkey. With their 2,400-kilometer range, the missiles could reach Moscow. After that, a direct telephone line was installed between the White House and the Kremlin.

When the crisis was over, it became clear that, even without détente, relations between the superpowers would remain under control. In the Soviet Union, this will be perceived as a sign of weakness due to the country's military inferiority. The American public's perception, on the other hand, is that communism is unstoppable, setting up its bases around the world. The American intelligence community lacks an insider view. US intelligence has failed to see the basic matrix because it had no insight into the internal dynamics of the CPSU's Politburo—a small group at the top of the Soviet apparatus. Consequently, they could not grasp that the policy of Third World interventionism was actually Tito's initiative, which Khrushchev had accepted and imposed on his Stalinist comrades, although the other members of the Politburo saw no purpose in it. Tito is the West's useful ally in Europe, and a rival in Africa and Asia. However, no one is really aware of the nature of his engagement in Moscow or of the real effects of the Yugoslav apparatus acting as the Soviet Union's vanguard in the Third World. As an extension of Soviet power, Tito's secret empire uses long-proved cadres with impressive experience. They constitute an elite political–diplomatic–intelligence network with global reach. However, Yugoslav diplomacy, arms exports, and aid to developing countries would not have any effect without the military and economic weight of the Soviet Union. But Khrushchev no longer has majority support in the Politburo.

In keeping with the management techniques used in the Soviet Union, Khrushchev will have to seize absolute power. But those he relied on in this also perceived his actions as a deviation from the politics of Stalin's era. Even among the top brass, Khrushchev could find no supporters of his impulsive interventionism and the export of socialism to the Third World—all the things advocated by Tito, an opportunistic speculator from the Balkans who always plays at someone else's expense. Besides, the Stalinists led by Khrushchev in the nominal destalinization process are not ready for a moral catharsis and for rethinking the Soviet system.

This all became clear in 1962, when a delicate question arose: Should the leading Russian literary magazine *Novy mir* publish a story by one Aleksandr Solzhenitsyn, a forty-four-year-old officer sent to a labor camp after the Second World War? In *One Day in the Life of Ivan Denisovich*, Solzhenitsyn described the everyday life of GULAG detainees, without pathos or cheap political slogans. Simply—the reality. And an unthinkable topic. A life without taboos? Truly unthinkable. The issue finally ended up on Khrushchev's desk. He opened the debate in the Politburo. Other members did not want the story published, but he told them: "There is a Stalinist in every one of you, even in me ... We must eradicate that evil!" The story was published, and a thaw began to set in everywhere. Enthusiasm could be felt in all segments of the society. In the period between 1960 and 1965, GDP grew by around 5 percent—a rate compatible with the then growth of the US economy. At the Twenty-Second Congress of the Communist Party of the Soviet Union, held in October 1961, Khrushchev announced that, in twenty years, Soviet citizens would be enjoying a higher standard of living than people in capitalist countries. He also predicted that Soviet industrial production would be twice the industrial production of the entire capitalist world. Of course, it was a fairy tale. In reality, there was a large gap between the two economies because the Soviet Union was allocating around 13 percent of its GDP to defense spending, compared with 8 percent in the United States (a figure that was to drop to 4 percent over the next ten years).[1] While the Soviet economy did grow in terms of the quantity of things it produced, its products lagged far behind the West in terms of quality.

However, what Politburo members like Brezhnev and Andropov and the entire *nomenklatura* of the Soviet party-controlled state see as the Soviet Union's greatest weakness is its military inferiority when compared with the United States.

Two weeks after the Cuban Crisis, Comrade Tito visits Moscow. This foreign policy guru and chief communist ally of Comrade Khrushchev will stay there almost a month (4–21 December 1962), much longer than is customary in intergovernmental relations. The situation had to be summarized, information exchanged, all the global political developments analyzed and Third World trends considered. As regards the current situation in the Communist Bloc, it is less than favorable for Comrade Khrushchev. True, he managed to draw Tito into his outer orbit by nominally recognizing every communist party's right to seek its own way to socialism. While this clearly does not apply to the countries of the bloc, it is officially proclaimed as such and thus legitimizes their efforts to change their submissive position.

Khrushchev's policies led to a fatal deterioration in Soviet relations with China. The Soviet Union had selflessly been sending military and industrial equipment to China, so that the country could develop and modernize. In 1957, as a collateral result of growing Soviet influence, the "Let a hundred flowers bloom; let a hundred schools of thought contend" campaign was launched. But as soon as profound changes and the revisionist project of destalinization began in the Soviet Union, Mao launched an "anti-rightist campaign." He banned all the blooming and weeded some half a million cadres, mostly intellectuals. Regardless of the Soviet loan for heavy industry development during the first Five Year Plan, Mao gave up on the whole package, deciding that European Marxism and all these Western social engineering inventions (to him, Russia is also part of the West) are of no use. Soon, in 1958, he would launch his own "Great Leap Forward," a mass collectivization and founding of people's communes. Private plots were abolished and so was all private property. The rural population was moved to cities, which resulted in a more than twofold increase in the urban population. All the staple food was in short supply. Chinese journalist Yang Jisheng,[2] who has collected some 1,200 documents, indicates that it caused around 36 million deaths. In his book *Mao's Great Famine* (2010), the acclaimed Dutch sinologist Frank Dikötter, who was given access to the state archives, puts the estimate at 45 million.[3]

In Shanghai in 1959, Mao explained the point of this policy of death: "When there is not enough to eat, people starve to death. It is better to let half of the people die so that the other half can eat their fill." Clearly, as early as the late 1950s, the leading communist visionaries had completely different concepts of the great social experiment defined by Marx in his philosophical and economic works. Khrushchev fantasized that the Soviet Union would out-industrialize the United States, Mao would resort to Malthusian methods, and Tito wanted to free the natives of Africa and lead them to a happy socialist future. Naturally, all these contradictory ideas could not be promoted under the same communist umbrella organization.

Khrushchev paid his last visit to Beijing in October 1959. Trying to patch up differences, he promised technical assistance for the development of Chinese nuclear weapons. In return, he wanted bases for Soviet submarines in Pacific ports. However, Mao refused to accept his and Tito's peaceful coexistence policy. Chinese communists saw Soviet–American détente as the two northern countries' attempt to subdue the south and the rest of the world. Having understood this and realizing that the Chinese artillery attacks on the coastal archipelago controlled by Taiwan (the Second Taiwan Strait Crisis) were not a sporadic incident but a result of Mao's confrontational policy, Khrushchev decided to withdraw his nuclear experts. They first destroyed all the atomic bomb plans and documents they had brought with them to China.

The Russo-Chinese conflict blazed up in June 1960, at the Bucharest conference of communist and workers' parties. Representatives of eighty-one communist parties of the world—all except the Yugoslav party—were there. For Tito, it is a waste of time; he has no business attending a party meeting with a bunch of exotic side characters. The purpose of the cheap theater is to show that Comrade Khrushchev has the kind of authority among world communists that he doesn't really have. As a result, he will definitely break up there with his most important global partner,

The Bucharest conference saw a conflict, too: the Albanians openly attacked Tito because of his non-aligned policy, which allegedly weakened the anti-capitalist front. In return, the Soviet delegates criticized Albania for not being willing to abandon Stalinism.[4] The discussion is not really about Tito and the non-aligned movement, but about Khrushchev and the strategy of global communist mobilization. The Soviet Union suspended its assistance to Albania, but Hoxha pledged that his people would rather eat grass than submit to Tito or receive anything from the Soviet Union under such circumstances. Albania immediately started receiving Chinese assistance. In return, the Soviet Union offered moral support to the Tibetans who had risen against China in 1959. China also aggravated its relations with India over Tibet, and Tito was giving full diplomatic support to India. Khrushchev will then attack Mao as a "nationalist and deviant adventurer," and Mao will call Khrushchev a "revisionist and patriarchal, autocratic tyrant."

Khrushchev has come under attack from all sides. He is being challenged because of the appeasement policy he has been pursuing. Challenged and humiliated among the communists, Khrushchev must display some aggression and demonstrate his power on the world scene.

Comrade Khrushchev's only remaining friend, who has done more harm to him than a dozen internal and external enemies combined, is now coming to Moscow to administer ideological first aid after the Cuban Crisis and the Sino-Indian war, both of which took place at around the same time. Four days after the blockade of Cuba had begun, China launched an offensive on the so-called McMahon Line separating Chinese and Indian positions in Tibet. While the Caribbean showdown of the superpowers was attracting the world's attention, China seized the opportunity to solve the "Tibetan question" along the 3,000-kilometer border with India by force of arms. The "question" as such did not really exist. Nehru sincerely tried to establish the best possible relations with China and create an Asian axis. India therefore had no territorial claims of any sort. However, when an uprising erupted in Tibet and the fourteenth Dalai Lama was granted asylum in India in 1959, a *casus belli* was created.

On 20 October 1962, the Chinese army attacked on two fronts. The 80,000 Chinese troops had no problem crushing 10,000 poorly prepared Indian defenders. This low-intensity war lasted around a month, with some 2,000 casualties on each side. Compared, for instance, with the Algerian war, this would be an irrelevant skirmish. However, facing the Chinese threat and its own military inferiority, India decided to abandon its policy of non-alignment. Nehru will no longer meet Tito. After the humiliating defeat against China, when his army failed to mobilize more than 14,000 troops, he turned to the Americans and the West. They instantly began sending massive military aid via the airlift organized by the US ambassador to New Delhi, John Kenneth Galbraith.

Immediately after the first Sino-Indian war of 1962, India started developing its nuclear bomb.[5] The country gradually became a global military power and resigned its membership of the union of third-class dictatorships that Tito, backed by Khrushchev, had been creating throughout the Third

World. By the end of the 1960s, the non-aligned movement will turn into an irrelevant ceremonial gathering of exotic and deviant political lowlifes and weirdos.

49

ENTER THE DRAGON

MOSCOW, 1964

"The Soviet Union produced the most effective and successful propaganda machine in the history of mankind. Mikhail Suslov was that machine, and that machine was Mikhail Suslov," explains Krzysztof Ostaszewski, professor at the University of Illinois.[1] This is how the CIA assessed Suslov's role:

> Mikhail Suslov, a member of the Politburo and the chief party ideologue, was a typical Stalinist. He managed to retain his influence and power over the distribution of information during the 1956–62 destalinization campaign and later. Khrushchev clearly believed that Suslov would mostly follow his directives. He was wrong. It turned out Suslov was too tough and resourceful. After Khrushchev's fall, he acquired almost absolute power in the Ministry of Propaganda. The next party boss, Leonid Brezhnev, was too lazy and too dependent on other people's opinions to make a serious attempt at controlling Suslov.[2]

In fact, Brezhnev left the entire ideological sphere to his party ideologue because their views on the basic political course of the regime and the strategy of the Soviet state were identical.[3] They wanted to restore Soviet military supremacy in the world and tighten control over society at home while ensuring continued domination over the Eastern Bloc countries. Expanding Soviet influence to the Third World was a less important goal for them. Although Suslov deserved most credit for toppling Khrushchev, Brezhnev outmaneuvered him in the struggle for the top position. Still, even out of the limelight—but with his grip on power—he left an indelible imprint on the Soviet politics after Stalin. The Yugoslavs perceived him as their main enemy—the broad base of party members of the LCY knew that Suslov was the principal ideological antagonist and hardliner, the personification of a pure, malign Stalinism, while Brezhnev was merely a pharaoh-style front, a manifestation of Soviet power.

How did Brezhnev and Suslov topple Khrushchev? At the 18 June 1957 meeting of the Presidium of the CPSU, presided over by Bulganin, a majority supported the motion for Khrushchev's removal. Only Mikoyan, Alexei Kirichenko, and Suslov backed Khrushchev.[4] Khrushchev immediately told Marshal Zhukov to provide army support for his silent coup, and the members of the "anti-party group" were then sent to irrelevant positions in backwater places. Zhukov entered the Politburo, which created a new problem. Zhukov was very popular but impulsive and politically inexperienced. Khrushchev was upset because Zhukov kept making unprepared speeches in front of delighted crowds welcoming him with flowers wherever he went, particularly because the marshal would now and then contradict him in his statements, probably even without premeditation.

Comrade Zhukov was an honest soldier. One of those who follow a straight line and believe in subordination. He hated political control over the army, which had caused him and countless other Soviet soldiers to suffer so much during Stalin's reign. He therefore banned criticizing superior officers at party meetings in the armed forces. He immediately came into conflict with the army's Main Political Directorate (GLAVPU)—a very important pillar of the Soviet regime. Zhukov wanted the army to become fully professional—like the armies in the West. In this, he could not count on support from the army top brass because he had separated himself from other marshals and had never consulted anyone. He also banned other generals from being elected to political bodies; as a result, none of them was elected to the Central Committee. This made them criticize him at a plenum of the Moscow party organization. Marshals Rodion Malinovsky, Ivan Konyev, Rokossovsky, Vasily Sokolovsky, Andrey Yeremenko, Semyon Timoshenko, and Biryuzov reacted as one, adopting a joint position. They were a serious bunch—not even Hitler could overpower them. And where was Zhukov when his comrades were setting an ambush for him? As if he had not antagonized Khrushchev enough in domestic politics, he set out on a diplomatic adventure and traveled to Yugoslavia, to visit the chief of staff of the JNA, General Gošnjak. He also wanted to visit the United States, but they wouldn't have him there.

Zhukov's stay in Yugoslavia extended from the planned five days to ten days, because he unexpectedly decided to visit Albania and had to wait for the trip to Tirana to be organized. It was something the Yugoslavs certainly resented, and there is no doubt that they immediately notified Moscow of this "Napoleonesque" behavior. It could have triggered a scandal. Instead of spending a single day in Tirana, as had been planned, Zhukov stayed there longer than in Yugoslavia. When he returned to Moscow, the decision on his removal was already awaiting him. No sooner had the politically shaken Khrushchev dealt with the anti-party group and Zhukov when he faced another abyss. Comrade Mao came to Moscow for the anniversary of the October Revolution and started a debate about the crucial matter of Khrushchev's "new course." Khrushchev's status in the party *nomenklatura* depended on whether or not he could impose destalinization at home and on the leaders of other communist parties in the world. It fell to the tall, authoritative Soviet ideologue Suslov to discuss with the Chinese comrades this issue of utmost importance. His opponent in the debate was the meticulous Comrade Deng Xiaoping, who accompanied Mao. Mao claimed it was Deng who won the debate. At every international occasion that would come along, Mao would not fail to humiliate Suslov, interpreting the outcome of the debate in such a way. That the Soviet Union was now engaged in destalinization was unacceptable to Mao. Suslov was not happy with that either, but he still worked for Khrushchev. As for Tito and the Titoists, in Mao's and Deng's eyes they were a "clique ... rehabilitated and forcibly dragged into the ranks of the international communist movement."[5] Suslov's opinion was almost the same—he himself had expelled them from the Comintern in Bucharest in 1948. But he was not in a position to utter it now.

The conflict between the Soviet and Chinese party leaders culminated at the Bucharest communist conference in 1960, where, as Deng put it, the Soviet Union "tried to crush everyone else with its own weight." When Deng met Suslov for the last time, in 1963, he conveyed Mao's final assessment of Stalin: "Comrade Mao Zedong pointed out it was wrong to claim that 'Stalin's mistakes and merits are equal,' because whatever happened, Stalin's merits exceed his mistakes. The proper evaluation would be that Stalin was 70 percent correct and 30 percent wrong ..."[6]

Mao despised Khrushchev and adored Stalin, yet Khrushchev had equipped China with plants for the production of supersonic jet fighters and jet bombers, helicopters, and rockets, as well as enabling the Chinese to develop their own nuclear industry. By the time Khrushchev canceled Soviet assistance to the Chinese atomic bomb project (on 20 June 1959), Chinese scientists had become capable of building the bomb on their own.

In September 1960, some 1,300 Soviet experts were withdrawn from China, and in 1962 Moscow notified Beijing that the Soviet Union and the United States were to sign a nuclear non-proliferation treaty. It was the beginning of Khrushchev's détente. But his moves were always wrongly perceived. When the American–Soviet confrontation took place in Berlin in 1961, tanks were deployed on both sides of Brandenburg Gate and the tension began to escalate. Khrushchev made a defensive move—he terminated the direct military confrontation by building the Berlin Wall and manning it with East German police. The Soviet troops withdrew to their barracks. Then he made a deal with the United States and Great Britain that they should not supply their allies with nuclear technology, thus preventing Germany and Japan from becoming nuclear powers, but also "tying China's hands," as Deng said to Suslov during their Moscow meeting. According to Deng, the Soviet Union had been cooperating with capitalists against communists while supplying India with large quantities of war materiel during the Sino-Indian border conflict in Tibet. Clearly, Deng thinks—even if he doesn't say it—that the former Soviet comrades have turned against the true Marxists–Leninists and joined forces with Nehru and his friend Tito, whom Khrushchev imitates. How could Suslov contradict Comrade Deng when he is denouncing Khrushchev as a peace-monger? Suslov did the only thing he could—he went on an official visit to Beijing, to talk directly to Mao.

But the Chinese nuclear program could no longer be stopped. In October 1964, the first Chinese A-bomb (22 kilotons) would be detonated at the Lop Nor nuclear weapons test site. It was clear from the Central Committee and Central Military Commission's instruction given to numerous scientific and party institutions in July 1961 that China would spare no effort in developing this program. The instruction demanded that experts and resources be concentrated in the machine-building ministry, which was in charge of the program. Given the top-quality performances of the Soviet secret apparatus, there was no doubt that this and other similar instructions had also found their way to Moscow. Suslov, who had personally negotiated the transfer of technology as part of the Sino-Soviet Treaty of Friendship, Alliance, and Mutual Assistance in 1950, understood what was going on. He knew, among other things, that the Chinese had received a Soviet diesel-electric submarine Project 629 (NATO's Golf class), armed with R-11FM (SS-N-1) rockets. The rockets had a range of 150 kilometers when armed with nuclear warheads. It was a Scud rocket adapted for the navy. This Golf submarine and the seven rockets delivered with it caused concern in Moscow. If a nuclear missile fell on Taiwan, everybody would know who fired it. But if it fell on Hawaii, launched from a submarine that could simply submerge and disappear, it could lead to an exchange of nuclear strikes between the two superpowers and to mutual annihilation of the United States and the USSR. Mao's alleged wishes would thus come true.[7] These phantasmagorical scenarios began proliferating due to the fragmentation that had started sweeping the communist world.[8] So Comrade Suslov went to China again, to have his final conversation with Mao. The mutual animosity would become an insurmountable barrier here, but the communist monolith as such had already fallen apart—the first time in 1948, when Tito was thrown out of the Cominform, and the second time when Khrushchev dragged him back into it as a Trojan horse. The Stalinists were simply not ready for anti-Stalinist revisionism.

From the Soviet *nomenklatura's* point of view, the overall result of Khrushchev's almost eleven-year-long rule was devastating. In their perception, Stalin's powerful state had been turned into a regime that nobody feared or respected, as a result of which it has to back away in every confrontation. Khrushchev tried to return Tito to the Moscow-controlled communist movement and integrated many of Tito's "Third World initiatives" into his policy while simultaneously breaking with the belligerent, distrustful Chinese communists, who were still hoping for a world revolution and endless class struggle. All that eventually destroyed Khrushchev's political credibility among party members. All he was left with were his insincere allies—and sincere post-Stalinists—Brezhnev and Suslov. So in October 1964, while Khrushchev was on holiday in Crimea, they won over the other members of the leadership, the new and the old ones, by assigning them the functions Khrushchev had earlier controlled himself. They invited Khrushchev to Moscow and removed him from office at the session held on 14 October 1964. He did not put up much resistance. He was tired of everything he had had to do in order to stay in power. The explanation for his removal was that he did not fit the model of a "Leninist leader." Indeed, he did not. Regardless of the numerous crimes he had committed under Stalin and all the failures, he was an almost amiable character, not some philosophical zealot—or, using the criterion of the Marxist–Confucianist relativist Comrade Mao—he was "around 70 percent good" in his last avatar.

The Chinese hoped a major twist in the Soviet politics would ensue. Zhou Enlai came to Moscow for talks, but he returned to Beijing disappointed. He reported that "Khrushchevism without Khrushchev" persisted in the Soviet Union. But only from the Chinese point of view. Suslov even intensified the criticism of Mao's Stalinist personality cult after the Chinese leader had reassumed total power, being deprived of some of it after the collapse of the failed Great Leap Forward that had caused starvation and millions of deaths. With Mao at the helm again, China set out toward the tragedy of its Cultural Revolution—in the following fifteen years, it will remain completely self-isolated, occupied with its own social catastrophe.

IV

THE BRIJUNI INTERNATIONAL

50

THE EMPEROR WITHOUT AN EMPIRE

BRIJUNI ISLANDS 1964–80

Notwithstanding the break with China, the age of destalinization is over and every aspect of Soviet policy would change under Suslov and Brezhnev. Tito understood it the best, as soon as he was notified of Khrushchev's removal while attending the Second Non-aligned Conference taking place in Cairo from 5 to 10 October. Upon hearing the news of Khrushchev's fall, the members of the Yugoslav delegation started debating whether they should return to Belgrade and possibly take some action. However, Tito decided they should stay, for the sake of appearances. Appearances are the only thing that would soon remain of his revolutionary undertakings in the Third World.[1]

The Cairo summit was seemingly more important and certainly bigger than the first one in Belgrade, three years earlier. In Cairo, there were representatives of forty-six full-member states and ten observers (nine South American countries and Finland). However, of the founding fathers, only Tito and Nasser remained; Nehru distanced himself after the bitter defeat in Tibet. At the summit, Indonesian President Sukarno criticized the Yugoslav president and his policy of equidistance, as well as the principle of "peaceful coexistence." He disagreed with Tito's claim that the 1963 Partial Nuclear Test Ban Treaty had contributed to the safety of small countries. Tito made the claim in order to support Khrushchev, who had secured the treaty and needed some sort of public recognition for it. Sukarno told Tito that the purpose of the treaty was to maintain the great powers' domination over the developing countries and that the disempowered states would not be able to emancipate themselves until given an opportunity to confront the big powers on an equal footing. Sukarno was clearly in a belligerent mood—much like Tito in 1940, when he tried to build his empire in a visible form. Now, in Cairo, Tito only managed to say a few nice words for India, attacking China as an aggressor in the Himalayas. A resolution was then drafted calling for nuclear disarmament. It was obsolete as soon as it was written and sent to the United Nations in New York, because Brezhnev and Suslov had already set in motion the huge endeavor that was to mark the following two decades—a massive armaments race and the creation of the greatest military force in human history. Russian imperialism and total militarization of state and society would become a priority.

After Cairo, non-aligned summits became less frequent. The third one took place in Lusaka in 1970. Nasser suffered a heart attack there and died soon afterward. He had been a shadow of his former self for quite a while—since the defeat in the Israeli–Arab Six-Day War of 1967. Sukarno had been deposed in 1966. Nkrumah, the Ghanaian pan-Africanist, was toppled the same year and went into exile in Conakry.

The year of the Lusaka conference also saw the fall of Prince Sihanouk, who was ousted in a military coup. Indeed, those years were fatal for all the protagonists of this Bandung–Brijuni club except for the indestructible Marshal Tito. In the capital of Zambia, decolonized in 1964, he was welcomed as an emperor of the global abstraction called the non-aligned movement. Zambian President Kenneth Kaunda—who will introduce a one-party system immediately after this non-aligned circus leaves town—will happily rule for the next twenty years. That the movement has become meaningless and has turned into an irrelevant multilateral diplomatic initiative within the United Nations will not discourage Tito or make him reduce his international travels and activities.

Khrushchev's fall meant the end of Tito's secret empire. Without Soviet help, he could not play a crucial role in the Mediterranean or in the Third World. Without US financial and political support, his country would not be able to function, and he would not be so widely admired in the Eastern Bloc and internationally. Yugoslavia as such was an insignificant country. The Eisenhower administration had been giving Yugoslavia around USD90 million every year (not including the earlier USD700 million in military assistance). By recognizing East Germany in 1957, as he had promised Khrushchev, he ensured a Soviet loan of USD285 million. Since he was getting money from both sides of the Iron Curtain, he was forced to maintain his neutrality in Europe, which was undergoing a process of pacification and integration that had started with the Treaty of Rome, signed in the luxurious Palazzo dei Conservatori—but without Yugoslavia, the country that had transplanted itself from the northern to the southern hemisphere.

Proportionally, even more money was invested in Yugoslavia to "keep Tito afloat" than in the Marshall Plan. Although the Yugoslav economy recorded sharp rates of growth, the country's development was based on uneven industrialization, mass production, and cheap rural labor migrating to the newly urbanized cities. As a result, the final products were of low quality and could not compete with those made in the Western markets. Yugoslav leaders realized that the fundamental question of productivity was the key. But how could productivity be increased in a socialist economy? They will try to answer this question in the early 1960s.

Tito is aware of his weak points. He has no answers to the challenges of modern times, primarily in the economy. The regime cannot function without foreign assistance, and he realizes that only repression keeps him in power. He entertains no illusions about it. Back in 1952, at the Sixth Congress of the LCY, he remarked about the Soviet Union: "What is the party in the USSR today? Nothing but a pendant of the NKVD." Now he sees that his own authority is moving in the same direction. He himself—not some opposition member or dissident—will make a parallel between his Yugoslav regime and Stalinism. In his speech at the Brijuni Plenum of 1966 (closed to the public), he will say that "the state security has mounted the party ... And does it not remind you a bit of what it was like in Stalin's days?"

Tito displayed almost every human weakness except fear. He was ready to deal with any problem immediately. But, typically, he would never initiate a change in the open or directly. At the closed session of the Executive Committee (Politburo) of the Central Committee of the LCY, held in March 1962, he gave the floor to the organizing secretary, Comrade Ranković. Ranković elaborated on the subject that Tito had defined with a rhetorical question: "Why could we not carry out our decisions made at plenums and congresses ... why would stagnation always ensue?"

The decentralization and liberalization of the economy, proclaimed at the congresses, was supposed to ensure growth and development, as Kardelj and Bakarić, the ideologues of reform from the Western republics of the composite Yugoslavia, had promised. However, the regime resisted changes, and Tito himself was the main limiting factor. In order to prevent reforms from taking place, Tito had to resort to his usual, underhand methods. At a covert session, Ranković fell into his trap. In his speech, he pointed out that particularism, autonomist views, and lack of unity were the principal problems in the country and that the secret service had been losing authority because people had been perceiving it as an arm-twisting body. In short, he explained, under the existing circumstances he was not able to perform the tasks of control and surveillance Tito had entrusted him with. He thus declared himself to be Tito's most loyal executive and identified himself with the approach that Tito had already abandoned, albeit without telling anyone yet. On the contrary, he supported Ranković at the session and soon in Split, in a speech in the same spirit, defending Yugoslav unity and promising more communism. Then he promoted Comrade Ranković to vice-president of the republic while depriving him of all power and removing him from the apparatus and secret service. However, he pinpointed him as his successor, thus exposing him to the hostility of the *nomenklatura*, who were totally unwilling to replace one master with another.

1963

This position of vice-president was created in the new constitution of 1963, when the country changed its name from the Federal People's Republic of Yugoslavia (FPRY) to Socialist Federal Republic of Yugoslavia (SFRY). The order of the adjectives—emphasizing the ideological aspect over the composite character of the state—was proposed by a certain Belgrade law student, one Slobodan Milošević.

The 1963 constitution nominally transferred the power to the Federal Assembly consisting of five corporatized houses (councils). Kardelj, the chief ideologue of these reforms, took the idea from the constitutional legacy of Italian fascism. The assembly elects an operative body—the government (Federal Executive Council). However, it is the president of the republic who proposes the members, signs all the laws and decrees, and can pass his own orders—*ukazi*. From a propaganda point of view, the most important innovation was the establishment of citizens as "workers-managers"—the primary social subject. The "working class," proletariat, and workers' and peasants' avant-garde were thus abolished. According to Kardelj's scholarly thesis, a "class homogenization of the working people" has taken place in Yugoslavia. The "socialist reality" has been created, so the country can set out to a happy future, peacefully and without internal conflicts. Naturally, this constitutional prose had no tangible effect whatsoever. Money mostly remained in the hands of the central government. The army even had its own financial section that would directly order money transfers regardless of the current budget. The "socio-political communities" (all territorial entities, from municipalities to republics) were declared autonomous. This meant that they were not subordinate to each other. Instead, their functionality was based on their rights and obligations. This practically meant that higher-level officials could not appoint lower-level officials as they pleased. The vertical chain of command was abolished here and in the party, just like the secret police would be decentralized after Comrade Ranković and all his retinue were removed.

1964

Brezhnev and Suslov, who came to power in the Kremlin on 14 October 1964, proved dangerous adversaries for Tito. They had no illusions about a revolution in the Third World, which was just a battlefield where the superpowers played their global game. The new Stalinists in the Kremlin were about to apply ideological repression in all of their domains. As for Yugoslav revisionism, they kept watching for the first sign of Tito's weakness in order to establish contact with some orthodox faction in the Yugoslav party leadership that could possibly be brought to power and solve this complication once and for all.

1965

The reforms supposed to snatch Yugoslavia away from the gravitational field of the Soviet bloc are continuing. In 1965, a year before the Brijuni Plenum, Tito endorsed the beginning of a program of economic reform. Zagreb lawyer Dr Bakarić added a philosophical touch to it in an article in which he included some customized formulas from Marx's *Das Kapital*. As for the practical aspect, the project was managed by Federal Finance Minister Kiro Gligorov, a Macedonian. Commercial banks were opened in order to finance the "public enterprises," industrial companies, but that was actually a control mechanism. The managing boards of the banks granting them loans for annual production cycles or for some new investments in "extended reproduction" (expansion of production capacity) were composed of the higher government officials who controlled the course within the global framework of the projected convergence to "uniform development." Still, enterprises and their managements became responsible for the immediate business results on which the jobs and wages depended. This led to mass dismissals, which were compensated by issuing passports to all those citizens who wanted to seek jobs abroad. The admission of economic immigrants had been agreed with the Western countries beforehand. A major social change.

Ranković's removal began with the scandal in Slovenia, where the UDBA was involved in the smuggling of cigarettes and other scarce goods. Tito's secret service had been engaged in such activities from the beginning. It was not some criminal anomaly but a way of exercising power and earning money. UDBA's members were the first ones to make foreign trade deals in the West; later they continued semi-legal and illegal export–import deals via Trieste, Rome, and other cities with established channels for trading with the East. The Yugoslavs were the Eastern Bloc's mediators, connected on both sides of the Iron Curtain. Inevitably, those who enjoyed confidence became rich, whether it was friendly foreigners from the political or business "gray zones" or residents of the Yugoslav secret service who would seemingly leave the *nomenklatura* and then start a company in Milan or Lugano and carry out commercial or logistical activities for Tito's regime.

Together with the UDBA corruption scandal, a story about alleged plans for Tito's forced retirement was spread.[2] Todorović was alleged to have played an important political role in it. Ranković and the top brass of the Serbian UDBA would allegedly support this Serbian cadre.

1966

With the story about this conspiracy as a pretext, the Fourth Plenum of the Central Committee of the LCY (the "Brijuni Plenum") was convened on 1 June 1966. It was much more dramatic than the Third Plenum, when Đilas had been expelled. Đilas represented no one else but himself. Comrade Ranković, on the other hand, was important: although he had been removed from any position of real authority three years ago, opening the "case" of this quiet, sphynx-like former chief of the apparatus actually meant restructuring Tito's powerbase and the entire Yugoslav political system. It was not an internal party purge; Tito's revisionist communism was preparing for an entirely new makeover. The only thing that would remain the same was the focus of the regime—Tito's autocratic position, to which all other functions were always subjected.

The reason for organizing the plenum was the "wiretapping scandal." Tito's most loyal policeman, Krajačić, had sent his technicians from Zagreb to

Belgrade, where they found bugs in the Marshal's bedroom. With this pretext, Tito eliminated Ranković at the plenum. He also separated the party from the UDBA. Allegedly, the secret police had become too powerful and started slowing down the development of socialist democracy—although no abuse of power for its own purposes had ever been established, before or after the plenum. The UDBA had always been the most reliable supporter of Tito's personality cult. He disintegrated his own, Yugoslav monolith, just like he had earlier done with the global communist monolith. In tandem with the secret service, an undivided party could compete with him for his personal power. Avoiding the party hierarchy, he ordered that the original form of Sovietization be reinstated—the direct democracy of "proletarian activists," presenting the people with "self-management" structures. In the same month of 1966, Mao did the same thing, but using a street-terror technique—he launched the Cultural Revolution. He let the Red Guards carry it out, destroying all party and state institutions.[3]

Why did Tito decide to make his own great leap forward to "alternative socialist democracy"? He could not assume total power like Mao, because he would discredit himself in the eyes of his sponsors and disqualify himself as a global peacemaker on a never-ending voyage. So, instead of strengthening his position, he began implementing radical decentralization, thus breaking up the state and party monolith—the potential adversary. He did so without dropping the reins of power—he delegated the operative governance to the lower levels, but he retained overall control.

Ranković's removal was followed by mass dismissals from the secret service. The "security organs" of each of the six republics were placed in charge of repressive activities. These security organs were not subaltern branches anymore; they became separate agencies. In 1964, the sector changed its name from the State Security Administration (UDBA) to State Security Service—it even had different names in different republics: SDB in Serbia, SDS in Croatia, SDV in Slovenia. The six Yugoslav republics thus became autonomous entities, practically states within a state, because the UDBA had not only been an organ of repression but a crucial lever in governance and personnel policy, embedded in all levels of government. By conferring the jurisdiction to the bodies in the federal republics, Tito did not deconstruct his power—he merely unmasked his position of unquestionable authority. He would retain direct control over the army, military intelligence and counterintelligence services, federal coordination of republic services, and the foreign intelligence service (SID). But he would only "guard the guardians." From that moment on, the leaderships of the different republics gained inherent power extending to all segments of social life on their respective territories. Tito started to share the power with his lieutenants and satraps, the time-tested cadres he relied on for all tasks in all situations. Each federal satrapy must maintain political balance on its territory, as well as ethnic balance between the majority and a large minority. Federal territories were tailored in such a way.

Tito retained the army for himself—it remained a federal institution, but he removed the leading generals: old-style unitarists who were too attached to the idea of the Yugoslav state and party monolith. The removed generals and top police brass will reappear on the political scene in the late 1980s—they will support Milošević. So what is Tito's big plan here? After the global offensive, he is now on the defensive. Rather than balancing between the two world blocs, his position is now protected by the balance of the republics, autonomous provinces, peoples, and institutions, and he can direct each of these components according to his needs. Heuristically, this system may be irrational, but it is very stable.

1968

Tito is on the road. He is welcomed everywhere. His reputation goes before him. A famous military leader, an anti-fascist guerrilla fighter who defied Stalin, champion of peace who ships arms to freedom fighters around the world and offers diplomatic support and provides infrastructure for the non-aligned movement.

Yugoslavia provides a European-standard of education to students from Algeria, Syria, Ethiopia, and other developing countries. In Belgrade, foreign students live in Patrice Lumumba Student Dormitory. Opened in 1961, it had 1,250 rooms. Expert teams are being sent to the friendly Third World countries: healthcare advisors open hospitals and public services in Morocco and Libya; pediatricians and agronomists go to Ethiopia; civil engineers go to Egypt; and military experts go everywhere. The latter can train entire armies and equip them with heavy weapons like jet aircraft, anti-armor guided missiles, and large warships. So Tito is in demand—it is better to have such a man as a friend than as a foe, even in the antipodes. At any rate, meetings of statesmen are always good photo opportunities. As a guest star, Tito always appears in his immaculate uniform, sprinkled with medals and gems. He does not give the impression of being a brute or a tyrant but of being a diplomat with huge experience.

The watershed year began with Tito's usual, almost endless trips to exotic destinations, which, in the political context of the international relations of the day, seem totally absurd, except for manifesting his status as a world statesman. In early January 1968, he traveled to Kabul, invited by the Afghan King Mohammed Zahir Shah. At first, the last king of the Afghans did not partake in ruling the state; he had delegated the duties to his uncle, and he himself studied in France, at the University of Montpellier, just like Hoxha. He assumed power only in 1963 and enthusiastically espoused the non-aligned movement. Tito then went to Muhammad Ayub Khan in Pakistan, and then to Prince Sihanouk. Having visited the crowned heads of Asia, he went to New Delhi, where he, the new Indian Prime Minister Indira Gandhi, and new Soviet premier Alexei N. Kosygin held a foreign affairs conference on crucial global issues. Then he followed an equatorial route to South Yemen and, across the Red Sea, to Ethiopia, to old friend Emperor Selassie. He completed the tour with a visit to the UAR, to Nasser, who was struggling to recover from the defeat in the Six-Day War with Israel, suffered a year earlier.

After this large world tour, Tito will stay at home less than a month before setting out on an even longer tour. On 6 March, on his way to the Far East, he landed in Novosibirsk, where he went down memory lane remembering his October Revolution days spent there. He then proceeded to Tokyo to visit the Japanese emperor. He will pose with him for a photograph, dressed in a fashionable silken-serge suit. After a week in Japan, he went to Mongolia, invited by Yumjaagiin Tsedenbal, the chairman of the Presidium of the State Great Khural (the Mongolian parliament). On his way back, he stopped in the Uzbek Soviet Socialist Republic. He was photographed while riding a Bactrian camel, dressed in traditional folk costume. The whole tour strongly resembles an all-inclusive tourist arrangement. In late March, he visited another emperor. He went to see the "king of kings," Shahanshah Mohammad Reza Pahlavi. Not only do they have similar tastes—the padishah sits on a replica of the golden, jewel-covered Peacock Throne—but also a similar background: his father was a semiliterate sergeant in a Cossack unit and he, too, was brought to power by British intelligence.

The almost two-month-long exotic tour ended on 1 May 1968: totally out of schedule, Tito flew from Tehran to Moscow, for a meeting with Brezhnev. They had a friendly talk there, only there was no true confidence or mutual respect. It was a cat-and-mouse game in which the mouse played the role of a statesman and historical leader, making the leader of a superpower feel like a usurper and parvenu in his presence. They immediately disagreed about

Czechoslovakia—there is no doubt that this issue was the reason for the emergency consultations. Brezhnev and Suslov suspected Tito was playing the same role in Prague that he had played in Hungary twelve years earlier.

The Prague Spring began when Alexander Dubček was elected first secretary of the Czechoslovak Communist Party on 5 January 1968. A liberal climate had prevailed in the country even during the rule of the preceding, insufficiently rigorous party boss Antonín Novotný. This climate had spread owing to the free-thinking policy of the new leadership. Dubček, a Slovakian communist, had grown up in Soviet Kirghizia. However, unlike Tito, he did not speak the Kyrgyz language. He spoke Esperanto, because his parents had belonged to an international Esperanto cooperative of workers and farmers called Interhelpo, established for the purpose of building socialism in the Central Asian steppes. This left an indelible mark of philanthropism on him—a trait reflected in the Buddha's smile that always adorned his face. Like in Yugoslavia, an "economic reform" was launched in Czechoslovakia in 1965. It was limited, though—only some state-owned enterprises were allowed to run their business operations autonomously. While it did trigger optimism, in reality it could not work. There was a joke in Prague at the time: the English have started experimenting with right-hand driving. The new traffic rule is being introduced gradually: for now, it applies to London cabs only.

When Tito was kindly summoned to report to the Kremlin leaders, he could sincerely distance himself from the "Prague developments": in April, he had rejected Prague's proposal to establish a Yugoslav–Czechoslovak pact. He tried to convince the Soviet leaders that the "Czechoslovak comrades" would deal with the negative trends accompanying liberalization.[4] Brezhnev and Suslov are not naïve like Khrushchev was. They learned their lesson in 1956. After this Moscow visit, Tito realized that things were boiling in Czechoslovakia and that crucial events were about to happen. He immediately arranged a visit to Bucharest. It was the only place in the Eastern Bloc where he could find someone of a like mind. Nicolae Ceaușescu, who had succeeded Gheorghe Gheorghiu-Dej three years earlier, was an unabashed megalomaniac who used every possible means of state terror to make Romania a great power. He began opening to the West and started following the trail blazed by Tito fifteen years earlier. In this epigone of his, Tito had found a partner for opposing Moscow. At the emergency meeting of 28 May 1968, the two agreed on joint diplomatic activities, since both of them were afraid of Brezhnev's interventionism. However, while Tito was preoccupied with the world and with the dangerous processes in his own neighborhood, the first ever large-scale demonstrations took place in Yugoslavia, in its very capital. Tito returned from Bucharest on 1 June 1968, and student protests began the following day. Like in all such riots, the trigger was totally innocuous.

At a party organized for the voluntary work brigades building New Belgrade housing projects, a fight broke out between students and work drive participants. These work drives were the last remnant of the mobilizing revolutionary folklore that had its roots in Lenin's days. In Yugoslavia, it became a central ritual of the mass youth organization that had succeeded the SKOJ. The summer work drives mostly attracted the youth from impoverished families loyal to the regime and those from underdeveloped regions who had not discovered tourism or started hitch-hiking through Europe yet. The conflict between the students and work drive participants could therefore also be interpreted as a clash of urban and rural elements, of the conservative communists and progressive westernized classes. The following day, students armed with Tito's pictures and state flags marched to the city center. They wanted to show they were not against the regime, but against the establishment, like other '68 protesters in Western Europe. But in Western Europe, the students' glorification of Che Guevara and Mao had a symbolic countercultural meaning. In Yugoslavia, however, these Third World leaders were not fashion icons—instead, they were political figures belonging to the other, antagonistic side of the communist schism initiated by Tito himself. In the international workers' movement, he had fought against their Trotskyite ideas of permanent revolution, surpassed by the Stalinist realpolitik-based statism. Tito was personally involved in all phases of this "differentiation": he took part in the purge of old Bolsheviks in Moscow; he led the repression against Trotskyites, anarchists, and unreliable communists during the Spanish Civil War; and, together with Khrushchev, he tried to export statist socialism—not revolutionary ideas—to the Third World.

The police used brute force to crush the students marching toward the center of Belgrade. A police cordon stopped them on the railroad embankment. They would not listen to the warnings to desist. The police then charged and used firearms. The number of casualties remains unknown. One vehicle was set ablaze. The protests were contained, but the peaceful "occupation" of the university then started. Downtown, students gathered at the Faculty of Philosophy. Writers and actors with dissident tendencies joined them and gave their support. The tanks of the JNA blocked the access roads to the city. The military counterintelligence service submitted to Tito its assessment that the riots had been instigated by Western agents. Limited and orthodox, the

General Staff officers would always be the first to succumb to the paranoia created by their own narrow-minded military thinking. However, a few old communist underground fighters, Spanish war veterans, visited the university and talked to the students. They later informed Tito that they were "our children," true leftists loyal to the communist idea, and that they were merely chanting slogans like "Down with the red bourgeoisie!" and "We're exporting people like frozen beef!" In short, that they actually wanted more communism. Upon realizing what it was all about, Tito gave a televised speech and told the students they were right. They started dancing in the streets and cheering him. He promised that "some irregularities would be corrected." Indeed, a protective "minimum personal income" (minimum wage) was introduced and the chief of Belgrade police—who had ordered his men to fire on the protestors—was removed (but was immediately given a much better job in the management of the football club Red Star). The leaders of the protests were ousted from the university and their passports revoked.[5]

Unlike the Belgrade students, their Prague counterparts and Czechoslovak leaders wanted *less* communism from their Soviet-style regime. This is why Tito would sincerely try to help them. He went on an official visit to Prague on 9 August. Four days later, Ceauşescu also arrived in Prague to give moral support to Dubček. But it was too late. A week after the Romanian president's departure, a multinational contingent of the Warsaw Pact marched into Czechoslovakia. Only Romania and Albania refused to take part in the intervention. Hoxha even left the pact in protest against it. As for Ceauşescu, he made a fiery speech in Bucharest's main square a day after the invasion—21 August—and strongly condemned it.

One Soviet airborne division landed at the Prague airport Ruzyně. The entire Polish 2nd Army entered the country, and so did Hungarian and Bulgarian troops—a total of 250,000 of them, with 2,000 tanks. Around 100 Czechoslovak civilians were killed and some 300,000 people emigrated to the West in several waves, some of them via Yugoslavia. Dubček's leadership was removed. An eighteen-year-long period of depression and apathy ensued. It was officially called "normalization."

This marked a dramatic change in the configuration of European politics. Now that the Brezhnev doctrine, which provides "brotherly help" to other parties and limits the sovereignty of every communist regime, had been used in practice, the left lost all its legitimacy in the West and its authority in Eastern Europe. Only brute force remained. It was the end of the communist movement in Europe—except in Italy, where its popularity actually grew, but split into two factions. Togliatti had died back in 1964 and been succeeded by Longo, who was loyal to Moscow.[6] But Longo's deputy and later successor, "Eurocommunist" Enrico Berlinguer, had had close contacts with Tito's men since the 1950s. He condemned the intervention in Czechoslovakia, describing it at the PCI congress as a "Prague tragedy."[7]

1969

Since virulent communist ideas in his own country and in its neighborhood had threatened the stability of his personal regime, Tito decided to abolish the party. He abolished it as a single organization with a pyramidal internal structure and clear vertical chain of command. At the Ninth Congress of the LCY, held in March 1969, the separate parties of the six republics and two autonomous provinces become separate political subjects. Tito had created his own little "intranational" Comintern. Instead of a sovereign Central Committee of the LCY and the principles of "democratic centralism"—a communist euphemism for strict, Leninist–Stalinist centralism—a federalized Presidency of the Central Committee of the LCY is created. As with the Central Committee itself, the Presidency consists of representatives of the eight parties. It is a large and totally irrelevant body. The real power in this representative organization that participates in the division of power in the country will be retained by Tito as president of the LCY (the position of general secretary was renamed president in 1963). Tito will exercise this power through the Executive Committee of the Presidency of the Central Committee, a small body with a few people he can rely on. Although the Executive Committee resembles a Politburo, this Executive Committee is merely Tito's transmission instrument, his political "kitchen cabinet." As he had eliminated Ranković and abolished the apparatus, he would rule indirectly and institutionally for a while after the Ninth Congress. But the practice would show that it was incompatible with his position of unquestionable power.

Czechoslovakia made Tito focus on Europe. Instead of going to Moscow to attend the conference of communist parties, held there in June 1969 in support of the intervention, he went to see Ceauşescu again, who also failed to attend that festival in the European metropolis of fastidious repression, together with the Chinese, Albanian, Vietnamese, and North Korean parties. The communist movement is falling apart, but Brezhnev does not care about it as much as Khrushchev did. For Brezhnev, and Suslov as his gray eminence, the strengthening of the Soviet military industry is the top priority. Everything else comes second. Khrushchev wanted everybody to like him, and Brezhnev wants everybody to fear him, which is much easier to achieve.

In Bucharest, Tito made arrangements for the intensification of Yugoslav–Romanian cooperation, including launching ambitious joint projects in the energy and military industries. Then he received Austrian President Franz Jonas and Italian President Giuseppe Saragat, two reliable Eurosocialists. This is so very boring, of course—all these regular bilateral relations, but it has to be done. In May, he visited Italy for the first time after the meeting with Churchill in Caserta. Pope Paul VI, who hid Ustashe leader Ante Pavelić in his residence after the war while he was a cardinal in Pius XII's curia, also receives him in the Vatican. The visit to Italy could not pass without a political farce. Borghese, the tireless Black Prince, gathered a large group of neo-fascists, supported by 187 game-wardens (members of the Corpo Forestale dello Stato). They planned to assassinate the minister of police, take the Quirinale Palace, and start street protests because of Tito's forthcoming visit to Rome. But the protests were called off because of rain. The *Paese sera* daily newspaper discovered Borghese's plot, which was codenamed *Tora, tora*. According to the daily, the plan envisaged the involvement of the US Sixth Fleet. But this combined game-wardens and marines' intervention failed to materialize. After news of the plot made the headline of the communist daily, the Italian police took vigorous action and put Borghese on a wanted list. Undisturbed, he then left Rome and Italy for Spain, where he stayed until his death in 1974.

But then, a drama ensued again in Tito's neglected backyard. It turned out that the six republics and two autonomous provinces as quasi-sovereign entities could not fly on auto-pilot, whatever Kardelj and Ranković were saying.

1971

All power in Croatia lies in the hands of Tito's satrap Bakarić. He keeps a very low profile, far from the limelight, and is inaccessible and allegedly ailing. Back in 1968, he finally managed to get rid of Krajačić, who had left high officialdom when he resigned his last position—membership of the (irrelevant) Central Committee of the LCY. There was no place among operatives for the old political policemen any more.

Bakarić is a pragmatic mandarin who believes in "objective reality" but who also knows where real power lies. He defined his credo in 1964: "Science cannot be the party's servant, but if someone opposed our social development, we would not hesitate to arrest him." In 1969, he appointed Savka Dabčević-

Kučar head of the League of Communists of Croatia. She earned her degree in economics in Leningrad and then her doctorate in Zagreb, with a PhD thesis on John Maynard Keynes. Later, as a Fulbright scholar, she took further training in the United States. A similar succession of generations took place in Belgrade, too: Koča Popović launched a young diplomat, Marko "Four Eyes" Nikezić, his comrade-in-arms from the Kosmaj Partisan Detachment. At work, in the Foreign Ministry, the two could freely speak in Nikezić's mother tongue—French. Nikezić became chairman of the League of Communists of Serbia in 1968. In Croatia, however, the liberalism of the "modernizers" stirred the same processes that had manifested in Budapest in 1956 and in Prague in 1968. Demonstrations instantly broke out. The middle class and the masses saw the relaxation of controls as an opportunity to rock Tito's communist "tyranny with a human face." The Zagreb police dispersed the protesters within days. Nightsticks and courts were put in action, and the whole thing was over very soon. The liberal modernizers in the leadership capitulated immediately, being fully aware of the nature of Tito's dictatorship—every resistance sets off tenfold retaliation. Besides, they were statist socialists. They understood that any substantial reforms were impossible while Tito was around—and Tito could not be removed. Croatian liberals were politically liquidated in Karađorđevo, a Habsburg estate that Tito used for hunting trips and diplomatic receptions, in an atmosphere much like the one of "comrade-criticism" in Stalin's dacha. Their Serbian counterparts, whose turn would come soon, in 1972, did not dare utter a sound. But the most important consequence of the purge would be another twist of the regime. Krajačić, marginalized in the visible spectrum of politics but still the maid-of-all-work in Tito's personal network, sent his two most reliable men—brothers Ivan and Milan Mišković—to Belgrade to take over the civil and military secret services. In the meantime, the left intelligentsia had become passive—after 1971, there was no one left in the *nomenklatura* who still believed in Lenin and in the road to the distant horizons of communism, except for some agitprop harlequins. True, some pro-regime Marxists still remained at colleges, particularly in less developed republics.

Tito realized that his autocracy could not rely solely on balancing and arbitrating between two centers of power. All the structures of power that had been strengthened in the meantime should clearly be disempowered, not unlike the initiatives of Comrade Mao. Comrade Tito also has at his disposal an ideologue with even more theoretical knowledge, the trustworthy Comrade Kardelj, his collaborator for the past thirty-five years. Kardelj has been given the task of creating a perfect system that will finalize the process of liberating human labor, thus bringing absolute liberty to the individual. At the same time, Tito and his lieutenants should hold onto power in this utopia for the rest of their lives. The task seemed tremendously hard, but in fact, all they had to do was continue the path Yugoslavia had taken in 1963.

1973

In the period from 1966 to 1975, Yugoslav economic growth slowed to 5.8 percent. The growth rate was still high enough, but the economy was burdened with a trade deficit, disproportional investment growth, and low productivity. In other words, in order for industry to grow at a rate of at least 6.6 percent, confirming that Yugoslav socialism works, inflation and fiscal measures should be employed to reduce wages to a Third World level and invest more in the country's capacities. It is a pyramid scheme typical of socialist economies, which project their results on the far horizons of the future. The statist management of economic resources prevents capital from transferring to propulsive sectors and enterprises. Participants of the production process are demotivated by the indiscriminate allocation of resources. Everything is sliding down to an inevitable collapse and bankruptcy, which, in Yugoslavia's case, will be postponed until Tito's death. A similar process was taking place in the Soviet Union. As it would turn out, the Brezhnev–Suslov regime was a much worse time bomb than Tito's Yugoslavia.[8]

But whenever he faced the inherent shortcomings of communism (which he could not give up because it legitimized his dictatorship), Tito would always find international sponsors and, being a wheeler-dealer without equal in foreign policy operations, he would get money to patch up the budget and lead his country to yet another development cycle.

In April 1973, young social democrat Willy Brandt came to visit him in Brijuni. A leader of great charisma and true integrity, Brandt had launched his New Eastern Policy and won the Nobel Peace Prize. He had established relations with East Germany and, as foreign minister, restored diplomatic relations with Yugoslavia in 1968.[9] Tito supported him in his rapprochement with the communist world, in which 17 million ethnic Germans had been trapped. Brandt arrived in the Brijuni paradise immediately after the British queen and the new Egyptian President Anwar el-Sadat and before new Polish party boss Edward Gierek and Shahanshah Reza Pahlavi. Using the so-called "Brijuni formula," he and Tito calculated the amount Germany should pay to

Yugoslavia as war reparations. They associated the reparations with a loan the Yugoslav regime badly needed to carry out its original experiment—introducing futurist socialism without communism. They rounded the amount to one billion marks. Compared with purchasing power, the present-day equivalent of the amount would be somewhat less than USD2 billion. With the exception of a few minor installments, Yugoslavia never repaid the loan.

1974

Now that a sponsor has been found, Tito gives Kardelj a free hand to plan their radical self-management utopia—a project that could be perfectly described with the epochal 1968 slogan "Be realistic, demand the impossible!" Kardelj will complete the job on the thirtieth anniversary of Tito's ascent to power, when New Yugoslavia was proclaimed in Jajce. The project of the "delegational system"—an attempt to rearrange society on the post-democratic basis of an imposed utopianism—was introduced as part of a new constitution proclaimed on 21 February 1974. An analysis of this project is hard to find in the literature. US political scientists who studied it descriptively, empirically, and statistically, such as Lenard J. Cohen from Simon Fraser University in Vancouver, could only identify some of its features (e.g. the "deprofessionalization" of management functions). Cohen observed that, among the delegates of more than 21,000 delegates' assemblies (formed throughout the country in all territorial entities and enterprises), there were relatively few "professional socio-political workers"—only a third of them—with the rest being amateurs. The latter did not take the whole thing very seriously, realizing that important decisions were being made elsewhere, not in the places where they assembled. It was established that as many as 41 percent of the delegates (in the observed twelve-month period of 1988–9) never attended assembly sessions and that only 13 percent of them took the floor three or more times. Of course, examples of impressive activism were also recorded. A delegate from Našice, Croatia, who had been elected to the Federal Council of the Federal Assembly, addressed the house at nine out of ten sessions. He had spirited arguments with officials and—as the impressed American professor noticed, not expecting such filibustering in an apparently totalitarian land—was altogether a true legislative workhorse.

The indescribable effects of the delegational system are perceived differently by Yugoslav scholar Zdravko Tomac. As a true Marxist with a philosophical-historical Hegelian approach, Tomac claims that Kardelj's delegational system attained the unrealized goals of the French Revolution, Paris Commune, and Lenin's soviets, because "the idea behind the delegacy is to ensure the power of the people." He goes on to explain that this experiment has been carried out in Yugoslavia since the introduction of self-management in 1953 and the constitutional declarations of 1963.[10] And what is the purpose of this social engineering? Comrade Kardelj, the very creator of the utopian project, defines it as follows: "Our assemblies are not assemblies of some general political representatives, as is the case in bourgeois parliaments; they are increasingly becoming a direct continuation of the process of social labor and self-management of the people in their work and creativity ..." Such generalities are hard to challenge. Manuals for the delegates are printed in large editions. They are discussed at local party meetings and in the army, where quizzes are organized for the conscripts: those who manage to memorize the subject will be rewarded by serving ten days less. What were the results of the social reform of 1974? The poorly managed economy was about to become totally unmanageable. But for the moment, everything was all right.

In June 1974, Tito went for a short visit to West Germany. This diplomatic mission was the crowning moment of his career. Finally, he was accepted in Europe not just as a leading communist figure but also as a statesman with significant influence on international politics. Admittedly, Brandt had been ruined—because his success was intolerable for the Soviet Union and East Germany. With Brandt's ascent to power, they had lost a precious enemy in West Germany—the rightist conservatives ("fascist reactionaries"). In order to eliminate Brandt, the East German secret service run by General Markus "Mischa" Wolf (who had attended courses in Ufa for operatives behind enemy lines together with Tito's son Žarko) tipped off its own agent Günter Guillaume, Chancellor Brandt's chief of cabinet. Brandt had to resign, but he was succeeded by Helmut Schmidt, who received Tito with equally great pomp and, at a gala occasion in Hamburg Town Hall, outside protocol, pronounced him "the greatest of the winners of the Second World War." Such praise, surpassing even that from Heinrich Himmler, had not been awarded to anyone else.

Tito was eighty-two then. He could now enjoy his achievements. But the *annus mirabilis* was about to become an *annus horribilis* on a private level. He will divorce Jovanka, leave his Dedinje residence, and move to the White Palace in Belgrade's Topčider district. This will turn into a court scandal. Some of Tito's associates have split into factions and clashed. While he is losing his vital energy, they are trying to place him under control and push out their rivals from his vicinity. The scandal is treated as a state secret and its elimination as an important state affair. Over the years, hundreds of documents, statements, and shorthand transcripts will be accumulated in the dossier of the scandal, entitled *The Unacceptable and Destructive Behavior of Jovanka Broz.*[11] The bureaucratic language used in the documents conceals the essence of the problem, which needs to be deciphered.

The whole thing became serious when "on 22 January, the president formed a special commission charged with establishing the attempts of the individuals from outside the residence who have been visiting Jovanka Broz to influence the atmosphere and relations in the residence." Jovanka has accused Lieutenant-General Ivan Mišković of being a Croatian nationalist, of surrounding her with his Slavonian relatives, of wiretapping her, and opening her letters in order to discredit her in Tito's eyes. Even if it was paranoia, there is a system to this madness—she is accusing the army of trying to take control of the people in Tito's environment. Indeed, the army is the main stronghold of Tito's personal regime. Has it accumulated enough power to emancipate itself as an independent force? These are very serious questions in every dictatorship. This is why the special commission for the marital problems of the master of Dedinje includes the vice-president of the Presidency (the collective leadership introduced by the 1974 constitution in order to replace Tito when the time comes) and five other high-ranking government officials and three generals.

The reason for the escalation of the marital scandal was an expected one: Comrade Tito started receiving daily massages from Jovanka's masseuse Darjana Grbić (who was twenty-two at the time). Her sister Radojka soon came to assist her. Jovanka later played down the whole thing, claiming she knew that nothing had happened because Tito was an old man and "even if he slaps their bottoms now and then, that is all." But she became jealous and realized that the courtiers were trying to eliminate her from the protocol and from Tito's vicinity.

Jovanka can see that Tito's strength and concentration are draining away and that he is being manipulated, for the struggle to succeed him has already begun. The denunciations against her are mostly coming from military circles. In their official statements, army officers claim that she has been seeing Krajačić and that she has a crazy idea that "the military security service has gained a dominant influence in the residence."

Who was the head of the Security Section of the president's cabinet when the scandal blazed up? Major-General Anđelko Valter, who retired in 1973.

The dossier includes his subsequent statements. He is a Croat from Slavonia, an early resistance fighter, party member since 1942, and a member of OZNA. The first head of the military intelligence service and General Ivan Mišković are from the same part of the country, where cadres for the army intelligence were selected from the ranks of the People's Defense Corps of Yugoslavia, KNOJ.

Jovanka did not quite understand the political relations and positions of the protagonists, but her instinct told her that the circle around her was tightening. She felt she would become a nuisance and dispensable, and she therefore began to fight for the prerogatives of the first lady. Having done so in this patriarchal environment, she was doomed. At every step, she was thwarted and discredited, and presented as an uncontrolled and immensely ambitious woman. As for Tito, who could have been her only ally, she started annoying him. This is why he moved to the White Palace. But the marriage was still valid—they would divorce only after the next crisis at the Marshal's court.

The "enlarged session of the Executive Bureau of the Presidency of the Central Committee of the LCY" was held in March 1974. Without Tito attending, all the top members of Tito's leadership are there. As if the regime has been hit by a cataclysm, not by the "masseuse scandal." Kardelj and Bakarić are attending, as his closest and most important associates, semi-autonomous political rulers of their respective statelets. Also present is Stane Dolanc, Tito's confidant and the coordinator of all secret services, Kardelj's protégé, and a nephew of the Second World War hero Lidija Šentjurc, the wife of the then Slovenian President Kraigher. General of the army Nikola Ljubičić, the defense minister, represents the third branch of Tito's triad (the other two being the party and intelligence services). Other important people from the republics and autonomous provinces are also here. They all take their time, carefully weighing their words, so the shorthand transcript has 106 pages in the end. Kardelj, as a true philistine, says in his opening speech that Jovanka's insubordination is undoubtedly a sign of mental disorder and that Tito would have divorced her if he wasn't "afraid of a scandal." He adds: "Tito is a good man and he does not hate her yet ..." The morality of the Dedinje residents is narrow-minded and hypocritical: when Kardelj's daughter became pregnant in the fourth grade of Dedinje high school, she was expelled and sent to live in Slovenia.

General Ljubičić stated that he had informed Tito that "Jovanka has with her a group of UDBA members who are well informed about the developments in Croatia." By that, he meant the unstable situation in Zagreb after the removal of the reformists and the repression against the participants of the "mass movement," a volatile blend of nationalists and democrats who had taken to the streets. The supreme commander then allegedly ordered him to "investigate that." Ljubičić thus notified everyone that the army had been given a mandate to investigate the civilian state security service, run by Dolanc under Kardelj's auspices. At the same time, Ljubičić discredited Bakarić, who was also present, because the street protests and counterrevolutionary movement had emerged in his sphere—and Comrade Bakarić had clearly not kept things under control there. A debate then ensued over whether Jovanka really interfered in political decisions and the nature of Krajačić's role in the whole thing. Dolanc tried to minimize the problem by saying that any conversation with Jovanka was impossible because she hated Mišković so much. "An additional question is whether this is just a pathological hatred or not," he said. It sounds as if he could not dismiss Jovanka's claims that military intelligence had gained control of the residence and monopolized all access to Tito. Clearly, the army and the civil authorities (the latter being represented by the secret police, as in every dictatorship) are sizing each other up over the conference table. They have already started fighting for the nomination of Tito's successor and for their very survival, like Tito himself, who let them use the plenum to solve their problems in his own bedroom. He told them: "She is tormenting me. And I could live well—I feel better, my blood sugar is all right, my pulse is normal. Everything's fine, but she is tormenting me."

After thirty-five years of marriage, having served the institution of the Dedinje absolutist and his pharaoh cult, Jovanka began to wonder what her real position was and what would happen when Tito was no longer around. This is the question all the members of Tito's *nomenklatura* and all the citizens of Yugoslavia will soon have to ask themselves.

Tito told his lieutenants that a single night fight with Jovanka (when he would seek shelter by locking himself up in the bathroom) was more exhausting for him than a trip to Burma. He only wanted her to leave him alone. He is spending his last peaceful days in the Igalo resort in Montenegro, while masseuse Darjana carries around in her arms a white poodle, one of the small pack of lap dogs that have replaced his loyal wartime German shepherds. Darjana has started appearing with Tito. She does not have an official role yet, but she has stopped being invisible to those around Tito.

1975

The nominal purpose of the Conference on Security and Co-operation in Europe—CSCE, later OSCE), founded in Helsinki in July–August 1975, was to facilitate communication between the blocs, their economic cooperation, and disarmament control. In fact, the accords signed in Helsinki guaranteed the sovereignty, inviolability of frontiers, and territorial integrity of all European countries while demanding that states refrain from the use of force in international relations, seeking peaceful settlement of all disputes and non-intervention in the internal affairs of other countries. Of the ten command-ments of the Helsinki Accords, six disqualify the interventionist Brezhnev doctrine, while the next two (respect for human rights and self-determination of peoples) effectively condemn the East European regimes, which have been subjugated by the Soviet Union. The final two points (cooperation among states and fulfillment of obligations under international law) were merely wishful thinking. But in general, the accords did limit Soviet influence in the Eastern Bloc countries. Everything that Moscow had earlier taken for granted was now made illegal. As the Soviet representatives co-signed the document, they had to abide by it, publicly at least. Why did they agree to sign it? The Soviet Union was weak and communism was on the defensive, so they too adopted defensive politics—or at least they were paying lip service to it. In the early 1970s, growth in Soviet GDP dropped below 1 percent—a disastrous indicator for a major economy.

Tito is a prophet of the ideas of détente and coexistence between the East and West. He is praised in Helsinki and is entrusted with organizing the next CSCE conference in Belgrade. He has become an idol of the new détente policy, which had advanced from "easing tensions" to a project of building a world order with higher ethical standards. Tito was the first in Europe to launch the rhetoric associated with détente. Everything he did before that, while creating his secret empire or serving as Stalin's disciple, faded into the background and was now forgotten. Only some crazed right-ists are protesting against the Marshal while he is preaching peace and understanding around the globe.

Tito has finally become a statesman highly regarded in the West. He had twenty meetings with heads of states in the year of the Helsinki Accords alone. He traveled only to Poland and Finland but received the prime minis-ters of Australia and New Zealand, the Finnish and Egyptian presidents, the Greek prime minister, North Korean communist ruler Kim Il-sung, Indonesian General Suharto (who had toppled the hapless Sukarno), reliable Mongol Tsedenbal, US President Gerald Ford, UN Secretary General Kurt Waldheim, Senegalese President Léopold Senghor, the president of the People's Republic of the Congo (a Marxist–Leninist state on Africa's west coast), Nepalese King Birendra, the presidents of India, Cape Verde, and Portugal, Sihanouk of Cambodia, and, finally, Austrian Chancellor Bruno Kreisky. The Brijuni Islands have become a Lourdes of world politics with powerful statesmen falling over themselves to book a room in Brijuni's White Villa in order to warm themselves on Tito's aura and take a ride in a convertible Cadillac driven by the octogenarian former test driver of Mercedes with a lifelong driver's license.

1976

Spain is undergoing a transitional period (*La transición*) after Francisco Franco, a great antagonist of Comrade Tito and the entire generation of revolutionary pistoleros, died in 1975. Democracy has come to the Iberian Peninsula. The same year, the military junta in Portugal decided to call free elections, which were held in April. As early as March 1975, a month before the elections and two months before Mário Soares, a socialist, would form the first government, Tito arrived in Lisbon. Formally, he was visiting the president of the republic, General Francisco da Costa Gomes. In fact, he was extending support to the leaders of the moderate left. The dangerous communist sect, threatening Marxists led by neo-Stalinist Álvaro Cunhal, who had returned from his longtime Moscow exile, was even planning a coup.

These sparks on the Atlantic shores announced the imminent beginning of terrorism in Europe, initiated in the communist bases of northern Italy and spy cells in West Germany. The logistical support to it will be provided by a specialized subversive organization headed by Comrade Suslov's protégé, Comrade Andropov. The connections between the Soviet intelligence apparatus and the activities of the Red Army Faction and Red Brigades will perhaps be revealed in fifty or 100 years. But the general political topography clearly indicates the motives that led to the explosion of terrorism in Western Europe in the late 1960s. It coincided with the implosion of the repressive communist system in Eastern Europe.

The Soviet economy was in a serious crisis. The Kremlin had to adopt the Helsinki Declaration that deprived it of a legal pretext for intervening in the Eastern Bloc countries, where a dissident movement had been growing. A group of Prague intellectuals had signed Charter 77, overtly demanding the resignation of the pro-Moscow government of the old reactionary Gustáv Husák. Many ended up in prison, but the charter's very existence indicated that fear—the principal ally of repressive regimes—had begun to fade.

Meanwhile, the archbishop of Kraków, Cardinal Karol Wojtyła, initiated the evangelization of workers' communities—the strongholds of industrialization and socialism, where the new man, freed from traditional Christian cults, was supposed to emerge. But that battle was lost in advance: it was the uprooted peasants that accounted for most of the population of these new housing projects springing up in all the socialist countries of Eastern Europe, including Yugoslavia. They will spontaneously return to the piousness of their ancestors and embrace the religion preached by the militant anti-communist proselytes of the renewed church of Stefan Wyszyński, Jozef Glemp, Wojtyła, and Aloysius Viktor Stepinac, ready for martyrdom and long years of underground activities from the catacombs of Eastern Europe.

The collapse of East European industry forced the satellite countries to borrow heavily from the West. The *nomenklatura* lost their temper. Dissidents were heroes of the underground. People were poor again, open to the penetration of subversive Western ideas and the attraction of Western pop culture—how can it all be countered? The only thing that remains is the export of subversive Marxist ideas and direct action—in other words, a "mirror war," the "Suslov maneuver" transferred from the domain of ideology and agitprop to the reality of the "class struggle" in the streets of Western cities. But in the visible spectrum of ideological tendencies, the Soviet Union will be forced to retreat. This clearly showed at the large communist gathering organized in East Berlin in 1976.

Tito and Jovanka broke up just before his departure for this not particularly important conference. She refused to join him, although two new Boeing 727 passenger aircraft with VIP interiors and a 3,000-kilometer range had recently been bought. She started making demands, so she stayed in Belgrade. The whole thing did not sound like fun anyway: the conference was taking place in the newly opened high-rise hotel Stadt Berlin in the gloomy Alexanderplatz, where all twenty-nine delegations would be accommodated. All European communist parties (except the Albanian party) were participating—the original idea was to make it a continental conference, but it was soon realized that it would be impossible to avoid discussions about "Eurocommunism" and the need to give up the bloc policy determined by Soviet domination. In the meantime, Europe had become more democratic and left-leaning: socialists were in power in West Germany; in Italy, the Titoist "Eurocommunist" Berlinguer, who had taken over the helm of the PCI, won the votes of a third of the electorate. Berlinguer started negotiations with Aldo Moro's left Christian Democrats and Nenni's socialists in order to form a "government of a historical compromise." The Labour Party was in power in the UK. The last strongholds of fascism on the Iberian Peninsula had fallen. Yugoslavia and Romania had introduced a policy of equidistance between the East and West, and Albania was relying on China. So what was left of the Eastern Bloc and European communism? Comrade Brezhnev's score seemed even worse than that of Comrade Khrushchev. Having realized that, Moscow decided to invite to Berlin all the relevant and irrelevant parties of the world. But the new wave of democratization of the left was impossible to stop. How did the Kremlin respond to that challenge? With secret operations and a military adventure in Asia.

1977

At the apogee of his brilliant statesman's career, Tito received perhaps the most important invitation of his life: the new Chinese leadership invited him to Beijing. He outlived Stalin and Mao, but most importantly, he beat them in terms of public perception. The same people who had once called him "leader of a clique of traitors" at international party meetings had now changed their mind after having gone through the wringer of Mao's Cultural Revolution.

Mao died on 9 September 1976, and the members of the "Gang of Four," who had been instigating the chaos and terror of the Cultural Revolution, were purged in October. The worst among them was Mao's widow Jiang Qing, a commissar who would mobilize the "cultural revolutionaries."

This former actress and an incredibly talented choreographer of the avant-garde "Beijing opera" described her role the best when she exclaimed at her trial: "I was Chairman Mao's dog. Whomever he told me to bite, I bit." But the most important for the production of this phantasmagorical play of Mao was Kang Sheng, head of the secret police, who, like Tito, had been installed by Karaivanov.

After Mao's death, the Gang of Four fell into disfavor. It was a tactical triumph for Comrade Deng. Commanding respect, he was called "the Architect" because he built the new, modern China and turned it into a global economic power after the Great Helmsman had run it aground. But in the beginning, Deng was only vice-chairman of the Central Committee, vice-chairman of the Military Commission, and chief of staff of the People's Liberation Army. Power was nominally held by Hua Guofeng, a Maoist who had replaced Zhou Enlai. Zhou was a man of the world—he had studied in Japan, where he was bitten by the Leninist bug at the Imperial University in Kyoto, then in

Marseille, Edinburgh, Paris, and Whampoa Military Academy in Taiwan, organized in 1924 by the Soviet instructors sent to Sun Yat-sen's and Chiang Kai-shek's Kuomintang.

Unlike them, Hua is a home-grown military cadre, formed in the 8th Army that went through the Long March. When Mao first met him in 1955, he was allegedly "impressed with his plainness." It was a positive recommendation for Hua as a successor because chances were he would not stand in the way of the Gang of Four and Kang Sheng. But they did not count on Deng. He started winning Hua over as well as winning all political centers of power.

In less than a year after Mao's death, while the "general line" of the Chinese communists had not yet been established, they decided to invite the only surviving anti-Stalinist in the global communist movement—Marshal Tito— for a state visit. Anti-Stalinism made sense for China at that time—neo-Stalinists were in power in the Soviet Union, their permanent antagonist.

During the preparations for Tito's trip, the story of the first couple came to an end. Jovanka insisted that she should revise the list of the members of the delegation supposed to go to Beijing (at least, so General Ljubičić claimed later on). She ended up on ice. Her last appearance in an official capacity was the reception organized for the Norwegian prime minister on 14 June 1977. Two months later, Tito went to Moscow, Beijing, and Pyongyang without her. It was his most spectacular tour. Twenty years earlier, *Renmin Ribao* (the official newspaper of the Chinese Communist Party) had described him as a "dwarf kneeling in the mud and trying with all its might to spit at a giant standing on a high mountain." But the Chinese comrades had now changed their mind, like everyone else—except, of course, the Albanian comrades, whose embassy in Beijing issued a booklet denouncing the betrayal of socialism by the "Titoist revisionist clique."

In the Square of Heavenly Peace, underneath Mao's portrait, where Tito, Chairman Hua, and both vice-chairmen arrived with a motorcade, a "small group" of 100,000 people cheered them. The official program for the visit— the talks and lengthy toasts at banquets—was crammed up. Mao's Memorial Museum was opened on Tiananmen Square at the same time. All this eclipsed the visit of US Secretary of State Cyrus Vance. He only got a few lines in the official bulletin, which was almost entirely dedicated to the miraculous Yugoslav leader.[12] That the old Marshal had turned eighty-five impressed the Chinese—a combination of old age and wisdom is irresistible to them. Besides, Tito really did beat all of his opponents in the field of communist politics. However, he glorified the merits of the late Chairman Mao and, in his speech in Mao's Museum, he explained that the Chinese people had suffered a loss beyond words—the preceding year saw the departure of three greats: Comrade Mao, Comrade Zhou, and Marshal Zhu De, commander of the Chinese Red Army who came to Mao's funeral in plain peasant footwear to show he was willing to take another Long March should Mao's principles ever be betrayed. So it was only the vigorous seventy-three-year-old little "Architect" Deng and the model Marshal Tito, still very fit while facing eternity, that the bereaving Chinese people had left. Hua could not hide his admiration for the fact that Tito had passed 15,000 kilometers to visit them.

On his Beijing trip, Tito was accompanied not only by General Ljubičić but also by another faction leader in the wars of succession, head of the federal security service Dolanc. Even before the appearance in this "Beijing opera," he made a state visit on his own in February 1977. That visit was much more important for him. He went to London to present himself as a potential successor of Yugoslav sovereignty. However, it would show that Tito never made mistakes in cadre-related decisions. As he would impeccably select capable people early in his career, in the final phase of his career he would equally select incapable people—those who would not jeopardize his authority either in his lifetime or after his death. Inevitably, he will be succeeded by a "collective leadership," since no one would have the necessary qualities to impose themselves as leader. That was obvious when the eminent successor went to Great Britain to present himself in the country traditionally in charge of king-making, producing Balkan leaders and their reputations.

The story has a short introduction. The British ambassador to Belgrade, the experienced Sir Dugald Leslie Lorn Stewart, another Scottish clan chief from the war generation of Maclean, decided that the special relationship with Yugoslavia should be extended to the whole British parliamentary spectrum. He therefore organized a visit to Belgrade for Anthony Crosland, a writer and politician and the author of the important book *The Future of Socialism* (1956). He was considered the ideologue of the revisionist wing of the Labour Party, which had distanced itself from Moscow and inevitably found itself on the road to Eurocommunism. The Yugoslavs immediately established relations with Hugh Gaitskell, who led the revisionists before becoming head of the Labour Party.[13] Unfortunately, he died in 1963 and was succeeded by the inert Harold Wilson. Crosland met Dolanc in Belgrade, and he made a rather positive impression on him. At the intervention of Sir Dugald, the head of Yugoslav secret service will travel to London in early 1977 to visit Foreign Minister (later Lord) David Owen. The ambassador had announced Dolanc as "the most impressive political operator in modern Yugoslavia, second only to Tito." But Owen formed a different, less favorable impression. Dolanc seemed to him like a typical Warsaw Pact communist. With such a character reference, his meeting with Prime Minister Callaghan could not yield any relevant results. Dolanc came back from London empty-handed. Of course, Tito had impeccably cast him as an apparatchik without political relevance. In addition, even in this socialist or "Eurocommunist" milieu, Yugoslavia was no longer that interesting to the West because it had stopped being a pivotal state in the anti-Stalinist frontline. The action had moved to Poland and Czechoslovakia. Romania had also emancipated itself. Only Bulgaria, the eternal Russian client state, had remained firmly in the bloc.

London was not impressed by Dolanc, but his trip alarmed part of the intelligence community in Belgrade.[14] However, it was not the one under his control. It was a rival intelligence service—the military one. They obtained some materials that would later be published in the United States by Duško Doder, a journalist of Serbian origin. He wrote that Dolanc had been a member of the Hitler Youth.[15] Though designed to discredit him, this information was hardly surprising. Born in 1925, he was a sixteen-year-old high school student in Ljubljana when the war broke out. When his parents left the Italian zone of occupation and moved to Graz, Austria, he continued his education there. He automatically became a member of the Nazi youth organization. But at the age of nineteen he joined the Partisans. After the war, he stayed in the JNA. In 1960, when he was thirty-five, he became colonel of the military Counterintelligence Service (KOS). Material designed to discredit someone often contains true information, not useless fabrications. However, the "revelation" did not hurt Dolanc's career while Tito and Kardelj were alive. After their deaths (in 1979 and 1980, respectively), he became federal minister of the interior in 1982, a post he held for two years.

1978

On 16 March 1978, on the way to the parliament, when he and other Christian Democrats and Berlinguer's communists were supposed to vote for the "large coalition" and government of "historical compromise," Moro ran into a Red Brigade ambush. The terrorists killed five members of his escort and abducted him. They shot him after fifty-five days of harassment. The kidnappers demanded negotiations, but the Christian Democrat government led by Giulio Andreotti, Moro's big rival, ruled it out. Pope Paul VI offered himself as a substitute hostage. But nothing could save the politician who made the greatest possible offense—he crossed the line separating Berlinguer and the Eurocommunists on the one hand and the Italian pro-Moscow communist kabala on the other.

From 1967 to 1973, members of the PCI went to East Germany for training provided by the Stasi (the GDR state security service). Their teachers there were from the KGB. Just before the 1972 election, Longo wrote to Brezhnev and asked for additional financial assistance. That year, almost USD10 million was injected into party funds through the companies that served as fronts for such transactions. The party had cadres and secret funds, but it was its own secret apparatus, not the political superstructure in which Eurocommunists will prevail when Berlinguer becomes general secretary in 1972. The change of leader triggered the ultra-leftist terrorist activities.[16] The terrorists' most important achievement was the abduction of Moro, breaking Berlinguer's "Eurocommunist" initiative to align with the liberal Christian Democrats and parties of the Socialist International. They also killed and wounded numerous activists and union agitators of the PCI. The party therefore requested that the Soviet comrades order the Czechoslovak secret services StB (Statni bezpečnost) to stop providing logistical support to the Red Brigades, for which they were responsible in the Warsaw Pact. This is verified by Vasili Mitrokhin who defected to the West with numerous documents of the KGB's First Chief Directorate.[17]

The 1970s were crucial years. The earlier Yugoslav intelligence service war against the Italian party cadres, supporters of the Moscow line, is now turning in reverse, and terrorists try to isolate the communist officials supporting Eurocommunism and exterminate all the ideas advocated by the new paragon of peace and cooperation, Marshal Tito. When he dies, the attacks on Eurocommunists will become more intense. An assassination of Berlinguer will be attempted. The technique of declining any responsibility for it bears striking likeness with the attempted murder of Togliatti.[18]

In West Germany, the Red Army Faction launched an offensive consisting of synchronized operations. The organization's doctrine was: "Anti-imperialist urban guerrilla movement engaged in armed resistance to the fascist state." It is a Soviet textbook definition from the Balashikha school for subversive activities. In 1977, a large offensive was launched—a series of attacks, after which a state of emergency was imposed, later to be called the Deutscher Herbst (German autumn). Five successive attacks were carried out on German soil that year. The first target was the US Army base in Giessen near Frankfurt, where nuclear warheads were stored. The terrorists planted a time bomb in a fuel tank, but it did not ignite. Three months later, the federal public prosecutor was assassinated. Three months after that, the chairman of the board of Germany's largest bank, Dresdner Bank, was also assassinated. Three months later again, on 5 September 1977, Hans Martin Schleyer, president of the Confederation of German Employers' Associations, was kidnapped. The Red Army Faction did not kill him immediately because they wanted to negotiate the release of their leaders Andreas Baader, Gudrun Ensslin, and Jan-Carl Raspe from Stuttgart's Stammheim prison, where they had been serving time since their arrest in 1972, after the first wave of early terrorist attacks.

The first ones to come to the rescue of the imprisoned heroes of European terrorism were the members of the Popular Front for the Liberation of Palestine (PFLP), who called themselves Commando Martyr Halima. On 13 October, they hijacked a Lufthansa plane with ninety passengers flying from Palma de Mallorca to Frankfurt. The PFLP was a Marxist–Leninist group led by George Habash. Based on the Soviet archive documents published so far, Habash can be identified as a KGB agent. The martyr-commandos demanded the release of the Red Army Faction's leaders, but the German government refused. Instead, it sent the special police group GSG 9 to Mogadishu, Somalia, where the plane had landed after leaving Cairo. The squad members stormed the plane, killing three hijackers and wounding one. After that, the Red Army Faction's leaders committed collective suicide in the prison. On the same day, 18 October 1977, Schleyer was murdered by his kidnappers after forty-three days in captivity.

In the spring of 1978, the wave of terrorism reached its climax. In Italy, Moro was murdered on 9 May 1978. A month later, the German Red Army Faction carried out its most spectacular attack in Mons, Belgium, when they tried to assassinate NATO Supreme Allied Commander General Alexander Haig by detonating a land mine hidden under a bridge as his vehicle passed over it on the way from his headquarters. It was a near miss.

After that, terrorist activities declined, but their accumulated impact would yield the desired political effects. The German right grew stronger, and the Christian Democrats (CDU) won the 1982 election. They will stay in power for sixteen years. In Italy, the right-wing faction of the Christian Democrats prevailed—a socialist government would interrupt their long rule only for a short while, in the mid-1980s. In Great Britain, the Labour Party lost to the Conservatives, who would dominate British politics for the next twenty years. Socialists did manage to return to power in France in the early 1980s, but there had been no attacks there because France had left NATO way back in 1966. So, was Comrade Suslov's European offensive successful?

Comrade Suslov had seized real power in the Soviet Union by surrounding himself with a clique consisting of Foreign Minister Andrei Gromyko, Defense Minister Dmitri Ustinov, and Suslov's protégé and heir apparent Yuri Andropov, a Don Cossack from Stavropol and director of the KGB. Brezhnev was suffering from a disease that had been degrading his central nervous system since 1975—he had heart attacks, podagral, leukemia, and emphysema. His condition resembled that of Soviet society in the terminal stage of communism. But the apparatus—this malign formation in the core of the system—was still functional and determined, carrying out well-planned operations in remote destinations. After Western Europe, an invasion of the non-aligned Afghanistan was about to be launched.

1979

That summer, Tito went on his last trip. He arrived in Cuba on 29 August in order to attend the Sixth Summit of the Non-aligned Movement. After the first summit in Belgrade in 1961, where big plans were being made, "dropouts" had already begun to appear at the second conference in Cairo in 1964. When the third conference took place in Lusaka in 1970, the non-aligned club had become largely pointless. The fourth conference was held in Algeria in 1973, bringing prestige to the young Maghreb state. The fifth one was organized in a tourist destination—in Colombo, Sri Lanka. As for the sixth one—it made sense politically: it had been announced that Castro would attempt a coup, redirecting the movement to the left and connecting the liberation and anticolonial struggle with the anti-capitalist Eastern Bloc. As there are no European countries in the non-aligned movement, they could not care less about Soviet domination of the Old Continent and about the Kremlin's expansionist policy on Soviet borders. Most of these countries consider the neocolonialists—the United States and the CIA—a bigger problem. The leftist countercultural revolution that had stirred tumultuous rhetoric in the West would certainly contribute to it, particularly when young Third World intellectuals, educated in European capitals where anti-Americanism and revolutionary ideas are *de rigeur*, bring these ideas back to their native countries. Of course, Tito sees all these things differently, from the perspective of a man who used to work inside the system now managed by Comrade Andropov. So he decided to travel to Cuba, although he did not feel well and was often distracted, being a prisoner of the clique who had been scheduling pointless meetings for him. They live in perpetual fear that he might launch an initiative they could not control—even as old and as ailing as he is, he could still eliminate all of them. Tito told his foreign affair advisors that, if Castro tried to drag the movement to the left with some declarative twist, he would break the movement up because he had more friends in it than that cheeky neophyte. While briefing the press, the Yugoslav delegation overstated the drama of the announced confrontation, trying to increase the importance of the summit, which, in fact, was completely over-shadowed internationally by SALT II—resulting, among other things, in the Protocol on the Limitation of Strategic Offensive Arms—initialed by President Carter and Chairman Brezhnev in Vienna a month earlier. Brezhnev had barely managed to come to Vienna and, compared with the youthful and slim American president, he looked like a mummy borrowed from the Red Square mausoleum. SALT II was not ratified because of the crisis in Afghanistan that took place months later, but this Vienna waltz pushed the choir in Havana into the background nevertheless. Eventually, the question of the movement's "incli-nation" was not even raised seriously.[19]

However, Tito returned from Havana triumphantly, just like Brezhnev from Vienna, but the most important decisions were now not being made by either of them—they were being made by Comrade Suslov, who was leading the Kremlin clique. It was he who decided on the intervention in Kabul with-out formally consulting the other Soviet leaders.

The Soviet intervention began the same morning, under the command of Marshal Sergey Leonidovich Sokolov. The 103rd Guard Airborne Division landed at Bagram airport near Kabul and parts of the 40th Army crossed the border—a total of 100,000 troops and almost 4,000 tanks and armored vehi-cles. Few other countries could deploy such massive forces. But the Soviet strength in numbers conceals a massive weakness. What was the point or goal of this operation, anyway?

The Soviet Union was falling apart as a society, and its economy was col-lapsing. Only the army and apparatus had retained their power, and they were now manifesting it in exotic destinations. The political results will be disas-trous, because the Soviet Union will end up completely isolated in the inter-national community, and the ten-year war will eventually lead to the collapse of its economy, society, army, and the communist system as a whole. Mass protests and uprisings began in Azerbaijan, Armenia, Georgia, Moldovia, Ukraine, and Byelorussia way back in 1988. In February 1989, the last forma-tion of the Soviet Army left Afghanistan. At the same time, Andropov's successor Mikhail Gorbachev announced that elections would take place in the first country of socialism as soon as an adequate law was passed.

The Soviet Union collapsed in the convulsions that accompanied its last attempt at exporting revolution, the epochal project in which Tito had been formed. He worked on it as a Comintern and NKVD agent, then he applied the same technology in building his own secret empire in the Balkans and Mediterranean that never became a reality. Then he started exporting anticolonial revolution to the Third World, in alliance with Khrushchev. For the rest of his life, he kept waging a war, the nature of which changed over time, until it became his diplomatic fight for abstract world peace. He tried to hold on to his global relevance, maybe to secure his place in history. But the energy of the project embarked upon in 1917 had played itself out. And so had his own, eventually. In January 1980, he was admitted to the Ljubljana University Medical Center, where he died on 4 May, three days before his eighty-eighth birthday. Suslov died in January 1982. Brezhnev, who had been out of action for a long time, died in November of the same year. Andropov, who succeeded him, died two years later. Konstantin Chernenko succeeded him in 1984, but he died the next year. In only five years, the entire generation of Stalin's disciples left the construction site of the communist utopia, which looked like Chernobyl after the nuclear accident. It was Gorbachev's turn now. He tried to relax the regime, began the transition, and has lived to the present day. Communism collapsed and the Soviet Union disintegrated, but Russia remains the biggest and one of the most powerful countries in the world. China became a major capitalist power. The Eastern Bloc countries joined the rest of Europe. And what became of Tito's Yugoslavia?

NOTES

1. A STAR IS BORN, PANTOVČAK 1928

1. Quotation from William Klinger and Denis Kuljiš, *Tito: Neispričane priče*, Zagreb: Paragon/NIGD NN, Banja Luka, 2012. This quote is from the collection of interviews made for Veljko Bulajić's 1980 TV series *Titovi memoari* (RTV Zagreb). Since 1994, they have been kept in the Yale University Library's Slavic Studies Collection: Veljko Bulajić Collection (MS 1689), Manuscripts and Archives, Yale University Library. Compiled by Andrea Feldman and Richard Szary. Subsequent quotations without a corresponding citation are from the same source.
2. Trilisser (1883–1940) became head of the Foreign Department in 1921, when it was still part of the Cheka (Chrezvychaynaya komissiya, Emergency Commission, led by Felix Dzerzhinsky). The following year, Cheka became Gosudarstvennoye politicheskoye upravlenie (GPU), then Obyedinyonnoye GPU (OGPU), and, finally, in 1934, the NKVD (Narodnyy Komissariat Vnutrennikh Del).
3. Harper & Brothers published his book *In Stalin's Secret Service: An Exposé of Russia's Secret Policies by the Former Chief of the Soviet Intelligence in Western Europe* (1939).
4. While lying in a Zagreb hospital in 1991, the aging Štajner heard the air-raid sirens wailing and, in his mental derangement, thought the behemoth of communism was coming to claim its due, which was exactly what was happening in the metaphorical sense. The air force of the Yugoslav National Army, founded by his buddy Marshal Tito, rocketed the city from which the two of them had set out on this adventure together.

2. THE SIBERIAN ODYSSEY OF A ZAGORJE CORPORAL, OMSK 1917

1. No evidence of his participation in the Serbian campaign has been found. He himself denied it, explaining he went straight from Ruma to Ukraine. Admittedly, after the disintegration of Yugoslavia, a picture would appear in the press now and then, showing an Austro-Hungarian soldier, with a striking resemblance to Tito, lying in

a trench and aiming with a rifle over the parapet. We have identified the source—
Ilustrovani list, a Zagreb weekly, which, during the First World War, regularly carried reports and photographs from the front. The photograph with the rifleman in
the foreground, claimed as a proof of Tito's presence on the Serbian front, accompanied the story "Our Troops on the Drina." The photograph in *Ilustrovani list*
lacks a caption identifying the soldier. Be it as it may, the soldier's resemblance to
Tito is striking indeed. Finally, in the Croatian State Archives, we found a convincing piece of evidence supporting the thesis that he really had fought in Serbia. In
the collection of documents entitled *Istaknute osobe radničkog i komunističkog pokreta
dvadesetog stoljeća 1900–1975* (Prominent figures of the twentieth-century workers' and communist movement 1900–75), in the *Komunisti pojedinci* (Individual
communists) file (HR HAD 1371—1), the documents classified as no. 8—*Materijal
za proces Josipu Brozu* (Minutes from the trial of Josip Broz)—include the original
statement given by Broz at the famous "Bombing Plot Trial," when he was sentenced
to five years' hard labor. For the minutes "made in Royal Police Headquarters in
Zagreb on 5 August 1928," he said: "I served the army in the 25th Home Guard
Regiment. I was conscripted in 1913. When the war broke out in 1914, *I was first
sent to the Serbian front* [our italics] and then to the Russian front, in Galicia."

2. Perm oblast, around 1,000 miles east of Moscow by the Trans-Siberian Railway,
and then through taiga to the north. Omsk is situated a further 750 miles down
the railway line to the east.

3. The Putilov Plant (Putilovski zavodi) in Petrograd was one of the biggest industrial
companies in the world at the time. It had 35,000 workers. In early 1917, the plant's
workers declared a general strike, which led to the February Revolution.

4. *Jugoslaveni u Oktobarskoj revoluciji*, Zbornik sećanja Jugoslovena učesnika
Oktobarske revolucije i građanskog rata u Rusiji, Belgrade: Institute for
Contemporary History—Narodna knjiga, 1977. Account of J. B. T., p. 15.

5. Ibid. Dimitrije Georgijević's account, p. 49.

3. THE COMBAT CELL, VELIKO TROJSTVO 1920

1. Croatian State Archives (HDA), Group: Kominterna XII. "Ministarstvu
Unutrašnjih dela, Kraljevine Srba, Hrvata i Slovenaca. Odeljenje za Državnu Zaštitu.
Pov D. Z. broj 1944, 6. marta 1922. god. u Beogradu—Pokrajinskoj Upravi Zagreb.
EČ CENTRALA ZA SVU JUŽNO-ZAPAD. EVROPU."

2. Kosta Nikolić, *Boljševizacija KPJ 1919–1929: Istorijske posledice*, Belgrade: Institut
za savremenu istoriju, 1994, p. 80.

3. "В Югославию—иметь в виду Н. Милютина, но для окончательного решения
вопроса Коларов должен поговорить с Радовановичем. В начале января 1923
г. вопрос о работе Милютина на Балканах был решен окончательно, туда же
был направлен Абрамович."

NOTES pp. [29–56]

4. The English translation of the quote is from J. V. Stalin, *WORKS Vol. 7*, Moscow: Foreign Languages Publishing House, 1954.

4. PROLETARIAN GEORGIJEVIĆ, KRALJEVICA 1925

1. HR-HDA-(fond) 1220—Ministry of Foreign Affairs of the Kingdom of SHS—Department for State Security, reg. no. 158352 of 2 November 1925.
2. Croatian State Archives HR-HDA-1371. Prominent figures of the workers' and communist movement of the twentieth century (collection). Period: 1900–75.
3. According to Belgrade police records, 85,000 golden rubles were remitted from Moscow to the Kraljevica group in April 1921.
4. Not much is known about Sakun, except that he was born in Odessa in 1902. He went to Yugoslavia in 1927 and 1928 using the pseudonyms "Milković" and "Mirković." In 1930, he wrote an article about the organizational problems of the communist parties in the Balkans for the Comintern's bulletin—clearly based on his field experience: W. Sakun: "Organisationsfragen der kommunistischen Parteien des Balkans," *Die Kommunistische Internationale*, XI, 22–23 (18 June 1930), pp. 1294–305.

7. QUEEN OF HEARTS, VIENNA 1934

1. Brigitte Timmermann, *Der Dritte Man*, Shippen Rock Publishing: n.p., 2005.
2. Kim and Litzi soon went their separate ways because their careers were incompatible. In 1944, he became head of Section IX, the anti-Soviet/anti-communist section of SIS (MI-6). In 1946, he officially divorced Litzi, who then moved to East Germany and married Georg Honigmann, a *Berliner Zeitung* journalist (also a Russian agent). They had a daughter, Barbara. When Georg died in 1982, the mother and daughter emigrated to Vienna, disappointed in Soviet communism. Litzi spent her last years in a small apartment near Belvedere Palace, in the former Soviet occupation zone, close to the site of the former delegation of the Comintern. Then she suddenly visited her daughter in Strasbourg and told her about her adventure with Philby. Barbara wrote her biography, not all of which should be taken at face value.

8. OBERKRAINER COMMUNISM, LJUBLJANA 1934

1. The Croatian and Slovenian parties were founded in 1937, the Macedonian party in 1942, the Serbian party on 8 May 1945, and the Montenegrin and Bosnian–Herzegovinian parties in 1948.
2. Pero Simić, "Šefa na gubilište," feuilleton in *Večernje novosti* daily of 23 April 2010: "On 4 March 1935, Tito spoke with NKVD agents about his colleague Adolf 'Levi' Muk, a Montenegrin communist and one of the top CPY officials. Tito smeared him in the conversation. On the upper part of this document, typed in Russian, there is a mark '-4.' On the left margin of the first section, a note in Russian is writ-

365

ten in ink: 'A conversation with c[omrade] Broz 4/III 35.'" This time, Tito was debriefed by Yakubovich, who was above Karaivanov in the NKVD *nomenklatura*.

9. THE LIGHT OF THE LUX, MOSCOW 1935

1. The most complete edition of Georgi Dimitrov's diary was published in Italian: Georgi Dimitrov, *Diario: Gli anni di Mosca (1934–1945), a cura di Silvio Pons*, Turin: Einaudi, 2002, p. 34.

2. Nikita Viktorovich Bondarev, *Misterija Tito: Moskovske godine* (Mystery Tito: The Moscow years), Belgrade: Čigoja štampa, 2013. The work by Bondarev, senior research fellow at the Center for Euro-Atlantic Research of the Russian Institute for Strategic Studies, casts some light on these years.

3. Wilhelm Reinhold Pieck (1876–1960) was a carpenter and a member of the German Social Democratic Party. He joined Rosa Luxemburg and Karl Liebknecht. In 1922, he became head of Red Aid (MOPR). He was president for life of the GDR, enjoying Stalin's full confidence.

4. Univermag (Universalni Magazin), a retail chain opened in major Soviet cities in the late 1930s.

5. Žarko Broz was twelve at the time—he was born on 2 February 1924. At first, he lived in the Soviet Union with his mother Pelagija Belousova, but he grew up in the homes for Soviet officials' children, says Tito, adding, however, that "he behaved like a stray child then," which means that he was an abandoned child. His mother went with another man. Evacuated from Moscow to Ufa in 1941, with all the Comintern cadres and their families, he attended special commando training. Yelena Bonner, later the wife of Sakharov, inventor of the Soviet A-bomb, fell in love with him. He joined the Red Army in war as an officer and lost his right arm in battle. He came to Yugoslavia for the first time in 1944, when he was twenty years old. He befriended Prince Đorđe Karađorđević, King Alexander's older brother who was kept under lock and key for twenty years after his forced abdication. The two went drinking together. Žarko married three times and had four children. He had a son, Josip Joška (b.1947), and a daughter, Zlatica (b.1949), with his first wife Tamara Veger, a Russian he had brought from the USSR. He had Edvard (b.1951) with his second wife Tereza Kujundžić, and Svetlana (b.1955) with his third wife Zlata Jelinek. He died in 1995.

6. The KUNMZ (Communist University of the National Minorities of the West) was founded in late 1921 by Lenin himself as a center for the education of cadres of the Western minorities in the Soviet Union. Its first sections included a Lithuanian–Jewish–Latvian section, a German section (for the Volga Germans), and Polish and Romanian sections. Slowly, other sections were added, including Byelorussian, Bulgarian, Italian, Moldavian, and Yugoslav sections. In the 1922 academic year, 352 candidates were enrolled. The courses took three years. Students were trained

to become professional revolutionaries. They studied party work techniques, politics, economics, and administration.

7. Stalin actually destroyed the Bolsheviks as a permanent threat to his project of turning the Soviet Union into a state; for more on this, see John Arch Getty and Oleg V. Naumov, *The Road to Terror: Stalin and the Self-destruction of the Bolsheviks, 1932–1939*, Annals of Communism, New Haven: Yale University Press, 1999.

10. WALTER IN THE COMMUNIST UNDERGROUND, PRAGUE 1936

1. Bondarev, *Misterija Tito*, p. 147.
2. *Sabrana djela, Josep Broz Tito*, vol. 6, p. 27.
3. Archive of Yugoslavia, record group MG, d. 18/121, p. 5.
4. V. Maslarić, "U zemlji borbe," *Španija 1936–1939*, Reminiscences of Yugoslav Volunteers in Spanish Civil War, vol. 2, *Vojnoizdavački zavod*, Belgrade: n.p., 1971, pp. 11–12.
5. The account of Vlajko Begović was published in Vladimir Dedijer's *New Contributions to the Biography of Josip Broz Tito*, Rijeka: Liburnija, 1981, pp. 224–32, but only after the Marshal's death.
6. From Prague, Tito went to Ljubljana and Kumrovec, and then to Zagreb, where on 16 December 1936 his father died in a hospital. Josip was in town, but he did not go to see him, nor did he contact anyone at home. In his recollections, he obfuscates dates and his itinerary, hiding his involvement in the failure of the "La Corsa" mission, the ship with volunteers for Spain.

11. COMRADE ORGSEC, ANINDOL 1937

1. Vicko Krstulović, *Memoari jugoslavenskog revolucionara 1*, Zagreb: Buybook, 2012.
2. Having a congress means having a national party, and a national party requires having a state. After Dresden, the CPY never had a congress again, as long as it depended on Moscow. The Fifth Congress of the CPY took place in Belgrade in 1948, but with an anti-Stalinist agenda, renouncing the Moscow line, as the final act in solidifying a different communist creation—Tito's Yugoslavia. At the very next congress in Ljubljana, the party will change its name to the League of Communists of Yugoslavia.
3. In Paris, Živojin Pavlović edited the party journal *Proleter* for Gorkić. In 1940, he escaped to Belgrade. Having found a job in the Central Press Bureau, he wrote a book about the purges. In 1941, Pavlović was apprehended by Tito's retinue in Serbia. He was ill-treated and shot. Sixty years later, the only preserved copy of Pavlović's book was found and republished.
4. Alenka Nedog, "O nastanku izjave treh komunističnih strank o slovenskem narodnem vprašanju," *Prispevki za zgodovino delavskega gibanja*, 1–2 (1967).
5. Arrested and sentenced in Sušak—the Yugoslav half of Rijeka—Špoljarić did

undergo some torture, but he avoided being sent to Kerestinec in 1940. Eventually, he joined the Partisans, had an impressive commissar's career, and became a delegate of ZAVNOH, the Croatian wartime parliament in the woods. In 1948, he was sent to Goli Otok prison camp and, after serving his time, changed his name and found regular employment. He died in 1991, blessed to see the end of communism.

12. THE REVOLUTIONARIES FROM BOULEVARD SAINT-GERMAIN, PARIS 1937

1. After the war, a knitwear mill in Sevnica was named after the place of this historical meeting. Even today, huge posters in all former Yugoslav countries advertise collections of women's intimate underwear under the "Lisca" brand. The Marshal would certainly find this historical reference to the Communist Victoria's Secret amusing. The CPY was born in Sevnica. So was Melania Trump, thirty-two years later.

13. THE STALINISTS, BOHINJ 1939

1. Pero Simić, *Tito, tajna veka*, Belgrade: Kompanija Novosti i Službeni glasnik, 2009.
2. The reference is to *History of the All-Union Communist Party (Bolsheviks): Short Course*. Edited by a commission of the Central Committee of the AUCP(b), it was printed in the edition *Classics of Marxism–Leninism*, translated in Yugoslavia in 1945 (Edicija Kultura).

14. T. T., ISTANBUL 1940

1. He got this new "pistol name" after Tula Tokarev—the famous "T. T."—a Soviet officers' handgun. Tito's "pistol names" reflect his double role. He is T. T. only when communicating with Yugoslav communists (when pronounced in Russian, it sounds almost like "Tito"). When contacting the Comintern, he is always Walter. Stalin calls him that, too. The reasons are not hard to fathom: T. T. is an army issue, a heavy gun fit for a military-trained operative on a subversive mission. An organizing secretary, on the other hand, is a member of the secret apparatus and therefore packs a light German Walther PPK, a small-caliber pistol suitable for concealed carry—a secret agent's weapon.
2. The role of Ivan Šubašić (1892–1955) is corroborated in two of the most authoritative sources—the decrypted messages of the Soviet embassy in Washington (Project Venona, run from 1943 to 1980 by the US Army Signals Intelligence Service, the predecessor of the NSA, declassified only in 1995) and the accounts of Vasili Mitrokhin in "The Mitrokhin Archives," published in 2005 after his death. Mitrokhin was one of the most important Soviet defectors, a senior archivist at the KGB's First Main Directorate. Both sources mention Šubašić as the Soviet asset codenamed "Seres."

15. MICKEY MOUSE IN WAR SCHOOL, DUBRAVA 1940

1. Franz Honner (1893–1964) was a member of the Central Committee of the Austrian Communist Party from 1927 and organized an Austrian battalion in the Spanish Civil War. He also organized an Austrian Partisan battalion in the Second World War, part of the National Liberation Army of Yugoslavia from 1944 to 1945. Honner was deputy minister of interior of the provisional Austrian government of 1945 and deputy head of the Austrian Communist Party from 1945 to 1951.

2. Rigoletto Martini (1907–1942) was part of the leadership of the PCI in emigration. From Moscow, he was sent to Zagreb. After the German occupation of Yugoslavia, he was arrested and thrown into a concentration camp. He escaped. While trying to cross the Italian border in Rijeka/Fiume in June 1941, he was arrested by the Italian police. He died in the prison hospital in 1942. With him was also Umberto Massola (1904–78), who in 1942 established a party organization in Milan and started publishing the paper *L'unità*. As of the autumn of 1943, he commands Italian Partisan units named "Garibaldi." See Alberto Magnani, "Umberto Massola e la riorganizzazione del Partito comunista clandestino a Milano (1941–1943)," *Storia in Lombardia*, 2 (2010).

3. J. B. T., vol. 6, "Strategija i taktika oružanog ustanka," pp. 151–81.

16. NEITHER WAR NOR PACT, ZAGREB 1941

1. David A. T. Stafford, "SOE and British Involvement in the Belgrade Coup d'État of March 1941," *Slavic Review*, 36, 3 (September 2007).

2. Ivo Banac (ed.), *Diary of Georgi Dimitrov*, New Haven: Yale University Press, 2003, p. 152.

3. Aleksej J. Timofejev, *Crveni i beli*, quote from П. Судоплатов, *Разведка и Кремль*, Moscow: n.p., 2004, pp. 88, 93.

4. Aleksandar Životić, "Jedno svedočanstvo o potpisivanju sovjetsko-jugoslovenskog pakta 5/6 aprila 1941," *Archives* (Belgrade 2010).

17. A SPY NEST IN DEDINJE, BELGRADE 1941

1. Their son Aleksandar Mišo inherited the house. He agreed to give up that property in 1979 provided a memorial museum was opened there. As that never happened, he demanded that the house be returned to him and filed a lawsuit in 2003. His claim was rejected, and the house was eventually torn down (in 2015). A community center was built there instead.

2. Velebit kept Herta Haas hidden in his small apartment, but the quisling authorities nevertheless managed to arrest her. She then went to the Reich—she was an ethnic German from Maribor—but she was arrested and imprisoned again. While in jail, she tried to commit suicide. Velebit managed to include her in the exchange of prisoners that followed the March negotiations in 1943 and he took her to Tito

in his headquarters in Bosnia. An awkward situation was thus created. Tito explained to her that he now lived with Davorjanka—"Comrade Zdenka." Embittered, Herta left, and they never saw each other again, except on one official occasion. She died in 2010. Mišo survived the war with a family that had been hiding him. Then he moved to Belgrade, and Tito's niece Marija put him up in her home. She also took care of Žarko's children from his first marriage.

3. *Dokumenti centralnih organa KPJ, NOR i revolucija (1941–1945)*, vol. 1, Belgrade: Komunist, 1985.

4. He was a GRU agent-resident in Belgrade with the codename Omega, mentioned in an authoritative work—practically the official history of the Soviet intelligence apparatus. See А. Диенко, "Разведка и контрразведка в лицах," *Энциклопедический словарь российских спецслужб*, Moscow: n.p., 2002.

5. Kopinič was attached to SS IKKI (Службы связи Исполнительный комитет Коммунистического Интернационала). Was it part of NKVD? Most probably. The NKVD's Fifth Section (Foreign Directorate) functioned separately and parallel with the military intelligence (GRU RKKA). The navy and Ministry of Foreign Affairs (NKID MID) had their own secret services. When the Comintern was abolished in 1943, the SS IKKI was abolished, too—but only administratively, as it continued to operate as "Institute no. 100," part of the International Information Section of the Central Committee of the AUCP(b). Dimitrov became head of the section, this time not as a functionary of some non-existent international communist association but as the head of a section of the Central Committee of the AUCP(b). He worked directly for the Soviet Communist Party and intelligence service. So much for the "internationalism." This is the time when Kopinič becomes an "institute man," too.

6. CPY Central Committee Politburo member Edvard Kardelj on 2 August 1941. *Dokumenta VŠ NOVJ 1941–1942*, vol. 2, book 2, collection of documents, Belgrade: Institute of Military History, 1954.

18. THE SURREALIST REVOLUTIONARIES, FRUŠKA GORA 1941

1. See Slavko Ćuruvija, *Ja, Vlado Dapčević*, Belgrade: "Filip Višnjić," 1990.

2. The order and status of National Hero was introduced as early as November 1941 by a decision published in the bulletin of the Supreme Command of the National Liberation Partisan Detachments of Yugoslavia, nos. 12–13. It was inspired by the title Hero of the Soviet Union (first awarded in 1934).

3. The Wollheim Memorial is a comprehensive online database containing information on forced laborers in Germany in the Second World War. As regards Yugoslavia (http://www.wollheim-memorial.de/en/herkunft_und_anzahl_auslaendischer_zivilarbeiterinnen_und_zwangsarbeiterinnen), it specifies that there were around 100,000 Croats working in the Reich at the end of the war (both men and women); there were also around 110,000 POWs (Serbs and Slovenes) and around 100,000

Serbian workers who had chosen to come to work in Germany in order to avoid forced recruitment for working in Serbian mines.

4. *Dokumenti centralnih organa KPJ, NOR i revolucija (1941–1945)*, vol. 1, Belgrade: Komunist, 1985, doc. no. 90, pp. 315–19.
5. Fitzroy Maclean, *The Heretic: The Life and Times of Josip Broz-Tito*, New York: Harper & Brothers, 1957.

19. THE DEFEAT, UŽICE 1941

1. *Zbornik NOR-a*, 14–1, p. 274.
2. Jože Pirjevec, *Tito i drugovi*, n.p.: n.p., n.d., pp. 118–19.
3. Since the day when the 1st Proletarian Brigade had been formed was celebrated in the former Yugoslavia as Army Day, the coincidence became rather awkward in 1948, after the split with Stalin. The date for marking the anniversary was therefore shifted to 22 December. Stalin was born on 18 December, anyway (6 December 1878 Old Style). When he seized power, he changed the date of his birth to 21 December 1879, making himself a year younger. Tito, too, allowed Youth Day to take place on 25 May, thus marking his fictitious birthday (he was born on 7 May).

20. THE LONG MARCH, BIHAĆ 1942

1. *Zbornik NOR-a*, vol. 2, "Dokumenti Vrhovnog štaba NOV i POJ," book 2, doc. no. 183: "Obaveštenje druga Tita od 16. februara 1942. godine Edvardu Kardelju i Ivi Ribaru—Loli o neuspehu druge neprijateljske ofanzive i direktiva za čišćenje tehničkog aparata pri CK KP Hrvatske i za izdavanje proglasa bugarskim vojnicima u Srbiji."
2. Vladimir Velebit, *Moj život*, Zaprešić: Fraktura, 2016, p. 268.
3. After 1945, he will be dumped in Turkey to work for the Russians. But he was not that foolish to go to Moscow. He knew he would be better off with Tito than with Stalin. Even Goli Otok prison camp was easier to survive than Kolyma. In the end, he was not arrested but appointed general manager of the large Slovenian industrial plant Litostroj.
4. Hebrang was a true rival of Tito in the Moscow hierarchy, a communist loyal to the general line. He was also very brave, resistant, almost unbreakable. He was incarcerated for decades in the Royal Prison, in the Ustashe's Stara Gradiška concentration camp, and, finally and fatally, in Glavnjača, Tito's Turkish prison in the center of Belgrade.
5. Dimitrov, *Diary*, pp. 455–7. At any rate, Dimitrov eventually conceded to Tito's line. The only thing he managed to do was send his man, Bulgarian Steriya Atanasov, to attend the first session of the AVNOJ in Bihać.
6. Due to foreign policy concerns, AVNOJ was not formally constituted as a legislative body and the highest organ of government. However, in practice, it immediately assumed the competencies of a sovereign assembly.

7. In 1945, when the main operational force of the Yugoslav army comes to Slovenian soil, the Slovenian army—until then an autonomous formation with its own command structure—will be abolished.

21. THE BRIDGE OF BLOOD, THE NERETVA RIVER 1943

1. Dr Lothar Rendulic, German colonel-general (Generaloberst) (1887–1971), Austro-Hungarian, Austrian, and German officer. He commanded the 2nd Panzer Army, the 20th Mountain Army, Army Group Courland, Army Group South, Army Group North, and Army Group Ostmark. He was awarded the Knight's Cross of the Iron Cross with Oak Leaves and Swords. His father Lukas (Luka) was a colonel (Oberst) in the Austro-Hungarian army.
2. German citizens from occupied parts of Europe or overseas could not serve in the German army. They could only volunteer for SS units. The 7th SS Volunteer Division (SS-Freiwilligen-Gebirgs-Division) Prinz Eugen mostly consisted of the Banat and Hungarian Germans. See: A. M. Wittmann, "Mutiny in the Balkans: Croat Volksdeutsche, the Waffen-SS and Motherhood," *East European Quarterly*, XXXVI, 3 (2002), p. 265.
3. Vladimir "Volodja" Smirnov, also called "Vlada the Russian" (1899–1985). Born in Tashkent. His family emigrated to Belgrade in 1917. He was the wartime head of the Engineer Section of the Supreme Command. In the film *The Battle of Neretva*, his character is played by Yul Brynner.
4. A statement of one of Krstulović's descendants given to the authors.
5. Velebit's account of the negotiations was first published posthumously, twelve years after his death (*Moj život*, 2016). Unfortunately, the editor, Croatian historian Tvrtko Jakovina, did not publish the statement on the May negotiations that Velebit, according to his own claim, wrote in 1967 in Geneva, where he worked for the UN. Vlajko Begović came to him from Belgrade to get it. Much before that, in 1950, a book entitled *Die Geheime Front* was published in Austria, describing the negotiations between the Supreme Command of the National Liberation Army of Yugoslavia and the German Command. It was written by Wilhelm Höttl (using the pseudonym Walter Hagen), a high-ranking official of the Reich Main Security Office (RSHA), who had worked for the SD (SS Security Service) in Italy, Hungary, and Croatia. See Velebit, *Moj život*, pp. 326–42.
6. Hermann Neubacher (1893–1960), first Nazi mayor of Vienna. As von Ribbentrop's flying ambassador in charge of Greece, Serbia, Albania, and Montenegro, he installed the Nedić regime in Belgrade and tried to negotiate with Mihailović and other Chetnik commanders. After the war, the Belgrade Military Tribunal sentenced him to twenty years in prison. However, he helped with the recovery of the German gold shipped to Greece, so the OZNA released him after only five years. He then worked as a consultant of Emperor Selassie in Ethiopia, where he saw Tito again—but from a distance. He wrote one of the most important accounts of the Second World War in the Balkans.

7. Sir Frederick W. D. Deakin (1913–2005), British historian and Churchill's literary secretary. In 1963, as the dean of St. Anthony College of the University of Oxford, he went to Montenegro, where, on the Durmitor Mountain, he wrote his famous bestseller *The Embattled Mountain* about the Battle of Sutjeska, which he took part in.

8. General Ivan Rukavina (1912–92), battalion commander in the Spanish Civil War and member of the Central Committee of the LCY. After the fall of the Berlin Wall, he and the former secretary of the Communist Party of Croatia, Savka Dabčević-Kučar, founded the liberal Croatian Peoples Party (HNS), a member of many government coalitions in democratic Croatia.

9. Sir Fitzroy Maclean, 1st baronet of Dunconnel (1911–96), brigadier and founder of the Special Air Service (SAS), with which he fought on the African front, in the Libyan desert and at Isfahan. He described his wartime feats in the book *Eastern Approaches*, which sold 1 million copies. He was promoted to major general and appointed junior minister in Churchill's postwar Conservative government. Upon retiring, he bought a house on the Croatian island of Korčula, where he would spend a good part of each year. He wrote around twenty books—five of which are about Tito and Yugoslavia. He was a Knight of the Most Ancient and Most Noble Order of the Thistle, Order of Kutuzov, Croix de Guerre, Yugoslav Order of Partisan Star, and, posthumously, awarded the Croatian Order of Prince Branimir.

22. MARSHAL, JAJCE 1943

1. Slovenian painter (1899–1989), symbolist, and filmmaker who lived in Paris, Tunisia, Norway, and America. Famous portraitist, a court painter of the Karađorđević dynasty, and author of Comrade Tito's showcase portrait in sepia.

2. *Chetniks! The Fighting Guerrillas*, 20th Century Fox, February 1943. Some novels were also published: George Sava, *The Chetniks*, London: Faber & Faber, 1942; Istvan Tamas, *Sergeant Nikola: A Novel of the Chetnik Brigades*, New York: L. B. Fischer Publishing Corporation, 1942.

23. EAGLE, BARI 1944

1. Major L. N. Dolgov, assistant chief of mission in Yugoslavia and an experienced radio operator, was in charge of the communications in Bari. There were around thirty GRU radio operators in the Balkans. The Purga radio station performed thirty to forty bilateral sessions daily, including six conferences, an hour of frequency control of contact with Moscow, four conferences with the Groza-1 radio center, and two to three sessions for communication with the remaining twelve stations of the mission.

25. THE PURGA ARCHIPELAGO, VIS 1944

1. After the war, Vratuša will become deputy head of the State Security Administration (UDBA), then deputy head of the 2nd (intelligence) Department of the Yugoslav

National Army (JNA) Supreme Command, and, finally, head of department and plenipotentiary minister in the State Secretariat for Foreign Affairs. This means he took part in organizing all three principal Yugoslav secret services (state security UDBA, military security KOS, and foreign intelligence, later renamed Information and Documentation Service—SID).

26. A RENDEZVOUS WITH STALIN, MOSCOW 1944

1. Famous writer Evelyn Waugh (*Brideshead Revisited*) fought in Libya and Crete as a navy commando.
2. This information can be found in a self-published book, the imprint of which only says: "Copyright dh 1978–1993, a bibliophiles' edition." It is a collection of documents printed on a mimeograph machine by Dunja Hebrang, probably with the help of Zvonko "Vonta" Ivanković. It includes articles, speeches, and documents on Andrija Hebrang. The biography contains ample information and convincing details that show that Hebrang was actually the first man of the Comintern's new network established in Yugoslavia in the 1920s, and that Tito was the second, less visible one. In his televised memoirs, he talks about organizing the May Day demonstrations in Zagreb in 1927, although they were organized by Hebrang, who was much better connected in the local communist milieu. The anonymous metal worker who had just arrived from Kraljevica and Smederevo, connected through the apparatus, played a subordinate role here. And this is something Tito could never stand or forgive. "Vonta" was a former OZNA officer who tried to rehabilitate Hebrang after Tito's death. He started sending letters to newspapers, some of which were actually printed.
3. VOS, a paramilitary formation in charge of urban guerrilla actions and armed terror in the rural areas. It was a separate Slovenian secret apparatus, led by Zdenka Armič, wife of Boris Kidrič, the first president of Osvobodilna Fronta (OF), and controlled by the commission of three members of this Slovenian "Parliament in the Woods." Tito, the Politburo, and NOVJ had no authority over them. It was later incorporated into KNOJ (People's Defense Corps of Yugoslavia). Kidrič was sent to Belgrade for an unimportant assignment, and Zdenka was substituted by Ivan "Matija" Maček, Kardelj's brother-in-law.
4. The original text reads as follows: "Leider ist er unser Gegner, aber er ist ein Mann von starkem Charakter. Dieser Mann hat fürwahr den Titel eines Marschalls verdient. Er ist unser Feind, aber ich wünschte, daß wir ein Dutzend solcher Titos in Deutschland hätten, Leute von solchen Führerqualitäten und von solcher Entschlossenheit. Er steht auf der Seite der Russen, Engländer und Amerikaner, aber er hat den Mut, sie zu verspotten und die Engländer und Amerikaner aufs peinlichste zu erniedrigen. Er nimmt es sich heraus, ein Bataillon eine Brigade zu nennen, und wir gehen dann auf diesen Leim [...]" Heinrich Himmler, "Speech to the Commanding Officers of the Wehrkreise and the Commanding Officers of the

Training Schools/Rede zu den Wehrkreisbefehlshabern und den Kommandeuren der Schulen. Jagerhohe, Sept. 21, 1944," in NARA Washington, DC (www.archives. gov/research/captured-german-records/sound-recordings.html).

5. There are no sources revealing the identity of this Meldev who tried to convince Tito to yield the leading position to Stalin's pawn Šubašić.
6. *Zbirka Vojnoistorijskog instituta*, vol. 2, book 14, doc. no. 231.

27. THE BELGRADE OPERATION, CRAIOVA 1944

1. Vladimir Aleksandrovich Sudets (1904–81), marshal of the USSR, Hero of the Soviet Union, People's Republic of Mongolia and Yugoslavia.
2. BM-8 and BM-3, rocket launchers "Katyusha" and "Andryusha."
3. The Third Ukrainian Front (army group) was one of the largest military formations ever—in 1944, it consisted of twenty-four Soviet and Bulgarian armies.
4. Winston Churchill, *Drugi svjetski rat*, vol. 5, Belgrade: Prosveta, 1964, p. 347.

28. CONQUERING THE BALKANS, ACT 1: ALBANIA, TIRANA 1944

1. *Sabrana djela, Josip Broz Tito*, vol. 12, 1982, pp. 23–4.
2. "At the November 1944 Plenum of the Central Committee of the ACP, Colonel Velimir Stojnic, the representative of Tito's Yugoslav Partisans, backed by Xoxe, challenged Enver Hoxha, the party's leader, and attempted to have him removed." See Enver Hoxha, *The Titoites*, Tirana: "8 Nëntori," 1982, p. 142. See also John Halliday, *The Artful Albanian: Memoirs of Enver Hoxha; Enver Hoxha with John Halliday*, London: Chatto & Windus, 1986, p. 69.
3. CPY Archives, IX, 1/I-10.
4. ANPI: Renato Alessandrini, https://www.anpi.it/donne-e-uomini/2136/renato-alessandrini

29. CONQUERING THE BALKANS, ACT 2: GREECE, THESSALONICA 1944

1. On 4 September 1944, a few days before the Red Army liberated Bulgaria, Šatorov was killed under unexplained circumstances in a conflict between the Bulgarian army and Yugoslav Partisans.

30. ROME'S STALINISTS VERSUS MILAN'S TITOISTS, MILAN 1944

1. In October 1943, the PCI started forming Garibaldi Shock Brigades as part of the Partisan movement. They were commanded by Longo, who was also deputy supreme commander of the Italian resistance. See Archives of the Central Committee of CPY, IX, 48/I-38.

2. The agreement between the Garibaldi Brigade headquarters and the headquarters of the 9th Corps of NOVJ of 4 April 1944.

31. THE CASTLE OF LEAD, BLEIBURG 1945

1. This is the figure used by all reliable historians, such as Z. Dizdar: *Brojidbeni pokazatelji odnosa vojničkih postrojbi na teritoriju NDH 1941–1945*, Časopis za suvremenu povijest, 1–2, Zagreb: n.p., 1996.

2. VIII Censimento Generale della Popolazione, 21 aprile 1936; XIV Fascicolo 31, PROVINCIA DEL CARNARO (FIUME)—*Tipografia Ippolito Failli*, Rome, 1937, year XV.

3. Six months after the end of the war, six of Tito's armies still had 578,708 soldiers, not counting KNOJ and the navy. See B. Dimitrijević: *Jugoslavenska armija neposredno nakon završetka rata 1945. godine*, Časopis za suvremenu povijest, 3, Zagreb: n.p., 2016, pp. 637–52.

4. Vladimir Geiger, *Josip Broz Tito i ratni zločini: Bleiburg—Folksdojčeri*, Zagreb: Croatian Institute of History, 2013.

5. Goran Beus Richenberg, *Nijemci, Austrijanci i Hrvati*, Osijek: Synopsis Zagreb—Sarajevo and the German People's Union—National Association of Danube Swabians in Croatia, 2010.

6. J. Jurčević, *Bleiburg*, Croatian State Archives, f. OZN-a, k. 39, o. 1. Single-page document of 3 July 1945.

7. Ibid., Croatian State Archives, f. OZN-a, k. 3.

8. Ivan Ivanji, "Well, You Know, There Were Killings," lecture in Buchenwald Memorial Center, Weimar, 19 September 2012.

9. Tomislav Anić, "Normativni okviri podržavljenja imovine u Hrvatskoj/Jugoslaviji 1944.–1946," *Časopis za suvremenu povijest*, 39, 1 (2007).

10. Sanja Petrović-Todosijević, "Zbrinjavanje dece nemačke nacionalnosti u domovima za decu bez roditeljskog staranja u Jugoslaviji posle Drugog svetskog rata 1946–1952," *O 'nestanku' nemačkih nacionalnih manjina*, Donauscwabisches Zentralmuseum, Ulm.

11. *Zbornik dokumenata i podataka o narodnooslobodilačkom ratu naroda Jugoslavije*, vol 2, book 15, Belgrade: n.p., 1982, pp. 442–3.

12. Vladimir Geiger, "Epidemija tifusa u logorima za folksdojčere u Slavoniji 1945/1946. i posljedice," *Časopis za suvremenu povijest*, year 39, no. 2, Zagreb, pp. 249–513.

13. Allegedly, documents incriminating Hebrang as a spy in the service of the Ustashe were found on him. This served well for the purpose of compromising Tito's rival, who was later murdered.

14. His son wrote a book: Gian Paolo Testa and Igor Taruffi, *Il compagno e la camicia nera. Istanti di storia italiana*, Rome: Editrice Compositori, 2010.

32. LOS CUATRO GENERALES, TOULOUSE 1945

1. Enrique Líster, *Asi destruyo Carrillo el PCE*, Barcelona: Planeta, 1983, p. 28; D. Arasa, *Anos 40: Los maquis y el PCE*, Barcelona: Arcos Vergara, 1984, pp. 254–5.

2. Informe de Santiago Carrillo. 30 de julio de 1945. Jacq 1–2 Dirigentes (ACCPCE) Sobre la AGE y el XIV, Cuerpo: Secundino Serrano, *La última gesta. Los republicanos que vencieron a Hitler (1939–1945)*, Barcelona: Punto de Lectura, 2006, pp. 349–59, 442–6.

3. Andres Sorel, *Guerrilla espanola del siglo XX*, Paris: Librairie du Globe, 1970, p. 56; Santiago Carrillo, *Mañana España*, Paris: Ebro, 1975, p. 123; Fernando Martínez de Baños Carrillo, *Hasta su aniquilación total: El ejército contra el maquis en el Valle Arán y el Alto Aragón, 1944–1946*, Madrid: n.p., 2002.

4. Ricardo de la Cierva, a historian of Francoism and minister of culture in the Suárez government, attributed Monzón's arrest to Carrillo's betrayal. In any case, Monzón was sentenced to thirty years in prison. As he had been expelled from the party in 1947, he was released in 1959. He then emigrated to Mexico. He spent his final years on the Baleares, where he died in 1973.

5. Juan Guilloto Leon "Modesto," general and commander-in-chief of the Republican Central Army (his Russian identity: Georgi Georgiyevich Morozov); Enrique Líster (Russian identity: Eduard Eduardovich Lisitsyn); Antonio Cordon Garcia, general and chief of staff of the Eastern Army (Russian pseudonym: Anton Antonovich Kuznyetsov).

6. Antonio Cordón García (1895–1969) describes his military career in his memoirs: *Trayectoria: Memorias de un militar republicano*, Barcelona: Crítica, En cubierta trasera, 1977.

7. Manuel Tagüeña Lacorte, *Testimonio de dos guerras*, Capitulo X: "La post-guerra: Dos anos en la Yugoslavia de Tito," pp. 523ff.

33. THREE TITOIST EVANGELISTS, TRIESTE 1945

1. Angleton was head of CIA's counterintelligence operations (ADDOCI) from 1945 to 1975. At the University of Yale, he edited the literary magazine *Furioso*, published the poems of E. E. Cummins and Ezra Pound, and corresponded with T. S. Eliot. During the war, he took over the London-based X-2 Section of the American OSS. After the war, he ran X-2 in Italy, making efforts to help the Christian Democrats beat the communists in 1948. In 1949, he became head of CIA's special ops, in charge of contacts with Mossad and Frank Wisner's offensive actions in Albania and Poland. In Washington, DC, he collaborated with Kim Philby, a representative of SIS. The two were very close. Under directors Dulles, Colby, and Helms, Angleton kept working his way up. However, his suspicions about the omnipresence of Soviet agents turned into paranoia, and he started suspecting everyone, including Henry Kissinger, Olof Palme, and Willy Brandt. He

retired in 1975. Numerous books were written about him. He also served as the inspiration for Robert De Niro's film *The Good Shepherd* (2006).

2. Carlo Troilo, *La guerra di Troilo. Novembre 1947: l'occupazione della prefettura di Milano, ultima trincea della Resistenza*, Soveria Mannelli: Rubbettino, 2005.

34. PLAN MAXIMUM, GRAMOS 1947

1. *Posljednji visit* ... Ruski Istoričeskii arhiv, as quoted in the collection of documents *Tito–Staljin*, Serbian and Montenegro State Archives, Belgrade, 2007.

2. Đilas's subsequent reminiscences, which are just as unreliable as Kardelj's accounts, and the much more reliable notes of Dimitrov and Kolarov.

3. M. Đilas, *Vlast*, London: n.p., 1983.

4. Cabinet of the Marshal of Yugoslavia, KMJ I—3-b/257—Datum: IX—9. XII 1947. Beleška o zasedanju CK KPG i savetovanju vojnopolitickog rukovodstva DAG, saopštenje o radu i rezolucija III plenuma CK KPG od 12. IX 1947. i pismo politbiroa CK KPG s rezolucijom drugog dela politbiroa CK KPG od 2. XII 1947. i zakljuckom o politickom radu u DAG, IX—9. XII 1947. See Nikos Marantzidis: "Η Προσωρινή Δημοκρατική Κυβέρνηση," 7 January 2012, *Kathimerini*.

35. STALIN'S HISTORIC "NYET", DEDINJE 1948

1. The aide in question was William Hilary Young, who was stationed in Berlin between 1945 and 1948. Between 1948 and 1950, he served in Budapest as Wallinger's aide.

2. Ćuruvija, *Ja, Vlado Dapčević*.

3. The Cominform Resolution was publicly issued on 28 June, St. Vitus's Day (the day of the Battle of Kosovo in 1389 and the assassination of Archduke Ferdinand in 1914). This is hardly a coincidence, just like the dates of the Cominform letter (27 March—the eighth anniversary of the Belgrade coup) and its Second Resolution ("Spies and Murderers"—29 November, the sixth anniversary of the Second AVNOJ Session).

36. THE EXCOMMUNICATION, BUCHAREST 1948

1. Robert A. Ventresca, *From Fascism to Democracy: Culture and Politics in the Italian Election of 1948*, Toronto: University of Toronto Press, 2004, p. 152.

2. Yugoslav Archives, Group 507—IX—Commission for International Relations and Contacts of the Central Committee of CPY (KMOV CKSKJ) k.1/8 documents on the Second National Council of the PCI held 7–10 April 1945. Toggliati clearly pointed out that the communists should consider themselves part of the new democratic state. Togliatti rejected the uprising—he supported a democratic revolution by means of a wide alliance with Christian Democrats. He particularly underlined his explicit opposition to the "Greek scenario."

3. Secchia will arrange a transfer of foreign currency with Stalin himself. Stalin asks him if he wants US dollars to be sent via the Soviet embassy or via Yugoslav comrades. Using his experience from his pre-revolutionary past, Stalin explains to him that a million can fit in a relatively small suitcase if "25 dollar bills" are used. Naturally, Secchia prefers the latter solution.

4. Yugoslav Archives, k.1/23, letter of Longo to the Central Committee of the CPY of 7 May 1946. Longo requests repatriation of the Italian Partisans that fought in the Yugoslav Army. The 4th Section (Personnel Department) of the 6th Army is in charge of their affairs.

5. Ibid., information from 1947: "L'apparato militare clandestino del PCI nel rapporto del Console USA di Milano—1947."

6. Ibid., k.1/45 dispatch on the arrival of Longo (codename Gallo) in Trieste on 19 April 1947.

7. Slobodan Nešović, *Bledski sporazum Tito–Dimitrov*, Zagreb: Globus, 1979.

8. Silvio Pons, "Stalin, Togliatti and the Origins of the Cold War in Europe," *Journal of Cold War Studies*, 3, 2 (Spring 2001), pp. 3–27.

37. TARGET: TOGLIATTI, ROME 1948

1. This quote of an unknown union member can be found in a book by renowned historian Paul Ginsborg *A History of Contemporary Italy: Society and Politics, 1943–1988*, Basingstoke: Palgrave Macmillan, 2003.

2. Umberto Terracini (1895–1983), president of the Constitutional Assembly. In the parliament, he allegedly spoke as an "anti-fascist," not just as a member of the PCI.

3. Kardelj was Yugoslavia's foreign minister at the time.

4. Rodion Yakovlevich Malinovsky (1898–1967) took part in the First World War as a volunteer in 1914. In 1916, he was sent to France as part of the Russian Expeditionary Corps. Upon returning to Russia in 1919, he joined the Red Army and worked his way up from platoon commander to corps commander. He completed his studies at the Frunze Military Academy in 1930. From 1937 to 1938, he was a volunteer in the Spanish Civil War. In February 1943, Malinovsky took command of the Southern Front and, in March of the same year, the Southwestern Front. Malinovsky was promoted to marshal of the Soviet Union in 1944. He commanded the Second Ukrainian Front troops that liberated Romania, Hungary, Austria, and Czechoslovakia. As of July 1945, Malinovsky commanded the troops of the Transbaikal Front that dealt the crucial blow to the Japanese in the strategic operation in Manchuria. Years later, in the Khrushchev era, he described his role in the 1949 events to his friend, Yugoslav air force General Dr Zlatko Rendulić, who retold it to the coauthors of this book.

5. Coleman Mehta, "The CIA Confronts the Tito–Stalin Split," *Journal of Cold War Studies*, 13, 1 (Winter 2011), p. 133.

pp. [247–258] NOTES

38. THE MAHARAJA OF THE BALKANS, LONDON 1954

1. Nick Ceh, *US Diplomatic Records on Relations with Yugoslavia during the Early Cold War, 1948–1957*, New York: University of Columbia Press, 2002. "From USMA and USNA Belgrade," incoming telegram from Belgrade–Trieste to secretary of state no. 180 (army message), 29 June 1948.
2. "The policy was not defined in 1948, when George F. Kennan, the then head of the Policy Planning Staff in the State Department, advised that 'Tito's schism' should be capitalized on—although, in fact, it was Stalin who split with Tito—so that Germany could be united and the Soviet domination in Eastern Europe disintegrated." See Stephen Kotkin, *Uncivil Society*, New York: Random House, 2009.
3. The letter of Mikojan to Stalin of 25 August 1946, document no. 183 in the collection of documents *Jugoslavensko-sovjetski odnosi 1945–1956*.
4. Ристо Кирјазовски, "Учеството на македонскиот народ во антифашистичката и граѓанска војна во Грција (1941–1949)," *Egejska Makedonija vo antifašističkata vojna*, Документи, Архив на Македонија, Skopje, 1987.
5. Bojan S. Dimitrijević, *Jugoslavija i NATO (1951–1957)*, Belgrade: Novinsko-izdavački centar "Vojska," 2003, p. 7.
6. Vlado Popović, the ambassador to Washington, DC, was sent to a special mission. He also negotiated the release of Cardinal Stepinac, archbishop of Zagreb, and his internment in his native Krašić in exchange for USD50 million of assistance to Yugoslavia.
7. Dimitrijević, *Jugoslavija i NATO*, p. 15.
8. Michio Kaku and Daniel Axelrod, *To Win a Nuclear War: The Pentagon's Secret War Plans*, Montreal: Black Rose Books, 1993.
9. Darko Bekić, *Jugoslavija u hladnom ratu—Odnosi s velikim silama 1949–1955*, Zagreb: Globus, 1988.
10. *Balkanski pakt 1953/1954—Zbornik radova*, Belgrade: Institut za strategijska istraživanja—Odeljenje za vojnu istoriju, 2008.
11. *Dokumenta o spoljnoj politici Jugoslavije—Jugoslavija–SAD*, messages of presidents of Yugoslavia and the United States SAD, 1944–80, Yugoslav Archives, Belgrade, 2014. Doc. no. 10. President Eisenhower to President Tito, Denver, Colorado, 12 October 1955, p. 27.
12. Ibid. Doc. no. 7. President Tito to President Eisenhower, 5 November 1954, p. 23.

39. L'HOMME NIKITA, BELGRADE 1954

1. Although *Medaljoni*—which included portraits of almost 400 contemporaries—was partly printed in the 1970s, they were not published in their entirety before 2005.
2. *Jugoslavensko-sovjetski odnosi 1945–1956, Zbornik dokumenata*, Ministry of Foreign

380

Affairs of the Republic of Serbia and Ministry of Foreign Affairs of the Russian Federation, Belgrade, 2010. Doc. 291. Letter of secretary of CPSU, N. S. Khrushchev to general secretary of LCY, p. 660.

3. Ibid., p. 672.

4. *Jugoslavija—Sjedinjene Američke Države, Poruke predsjednika Jugoslavije i SAD, 1944–1980*, Yugoslav Archives, Belgrade, 2014, p. 174.

40. A NEW MEDITERRANEAN OFFENSIVE, SUEZ 1955

1. Pablo Molanes Perez, "El Hospital Varsovia de Toulouse, un proyecto del exilio espanol," *Cultura de los Cuidados*, 35 (2013).

2. Comandante Carlos (real name Vittorio Vidali, 1900–83), was born in Muggia, on the outskirts of Trieste. One of the most important Soviet operatives, ranking as high as Walter, as a twenty-year-old Vidali fled from fascist Italy to the Soviet Union and joined the OGPU there. After the founding of the PCI in Livorno, the Red Guard was established in Turin as "armed proletarian detachments of the Third International." Vidali belonged to these structures—Italian "combat cells." From the Soviet Union, he was sent to Mexico, where he became close with communist painter Diego Rivera. Rivera depicted him in his famous mural *Arsenal*, together with some other iconic characters of the Central American communist pantheon. Rivera's wife Frida Kahlo, the heroine and muse with connected eyebrows, sits in the center of the painting, distributing rifles to revolutionaries. Others include Julio Antonio Mella, one of the founders of the Cuban Communist Party; his mistress Tina Modotti; and Vidali, the third member of this revolutionary *ménage à trois*. Vidali's first assignment was to eliminate Mella, because he had become close to Trotsky, who then lived in Mexico City. Mella was shot while walking hand in hand with Tina. She then became Vidali's mistress. The two of them were sent on an assignment to the Spanish Civil War. Vidali and Iosif Romualdovich Grigulevich, a GPU assassin, led a group of operatives of the 5th Regiment, in charge of enforcing the party line and exterminating the members of POUM, an independent grassroots anarchist organization of the revolutionary unions from Barcelona. Vidali then sent Grigulevich and Ramón Mercader from Spain to Mexico. Using the contacts in Rivera's circles, they would become close to Trotsky and kill him in 1940. After the war, in 1947, Vidali was sent to Trieste to prevent the Titoization of the local communist organization. Then he was elected to the Italian Senate. He published ample autobiographical literature. His partner Tina Modotti is even more famous. A member of leftists circles in Mexico City, she was an artist, actress, and photo-model. At least a dozen books were written about her. It seems that in Spain she witnessed some 400 liquidations carried out by Vidali. She died in Mexico in 1942, under suspicious circumstances. Rivera claimed that she had been another victim of Vidali. Her last lover, Pablo Neruda, wrote the epitaph carved on her grave.

3. Svetozar Rajak, *Yugoslavia and the Soviet Union in the Early Cold War 1953–1957*, London: Routledge, 2011, p. 100.

4. Jovan Čavoški, "Arming Nonalignment: Yugoslavia's Relations with Burma and the Cold War in Asia (1950–1955)," Woodrow Wilson International Center for Scholars, working paper no. 61, 2010, p. 25.

41. A PSYCHODRAMA IN TITO'S WHITE PALACE, BELGRADE 1955

1. Mićunović was Ranković's deputy and head of the Belgrade OZNA during the bitter postwar repression. He was later appointed ambassador to Moscow (from 1958 to 1962 and from 1969 to 1971). He went on to publish his sensational diary, *Moscow Years 1956–1958*, which appeared in serial form in *The Sunday Times*.

2. *Jugoslavensko-sovjetski odnosi 1945–1956*, Belgrade, 2010. No. 325, from the minutes of the negotiations of the Yugoslav and Soviet government delegations, 27–8 May 1955, p. 742.

3. Ibid., p. 765.

42. A SECRET WAR IN THE MEDITERRANEAN, ALGIERS 1956

1. Spencer C. Tucker (ed.), *Encyclopaedia of Insurgency and Counterinsurgency*, Santa Barbara, CA: ABC-CLIO, 2013, p. 67.

2. *Jugoslavija—Alžir*, collection of papers from a scientific conference, Yugoslav Archives, Belgrade, 2013, p. 18.

3. Alistair A. Horne, *A Savage War of Peace: Algeria 1954–1962*, New York: New York Review of Books, 1977, p. 102.

4. Archive of J. B. T., KPR, I-2/4–4, shorthand notes of talks of Josip Broz Tito and Gamal Abdel Nasser, pp. 17–18.

5. Minutes from talks between Soviet and Yugoslav government delegations, *Jugoslovensko-sovjetski odnosi 1945–1956*, collection of documents, Ministry of Foreign Affairs of the Republic of Serbia and Ministry of Foreign Affairs of the Russian Federation, Belgrade, 2010, p. 867.

6. Bruce Hales-Dutton, "'Ivan the Terrible' and the Tu-104," *Aeroplane*, Cold War Special Edition (March 2016).

7. A. N. Jakovlev, *Tellegrama posla v Egipte E. D. Kiseleva v MID SSSR, Bližnevostočnij konflikt, I—1*, Moscow: n.p., 1997, pp. 453–5.

8. Guy Laron, "The Czech–Egyptian 1955 Arms Deal: Findings from Soviet and Czech Archives," Fourth Annual Conference on the Cold War, LSE (6–8 April 2006).

43. THE DOUBLE CONSPIRACY, BUDAPEST 1956

1. Béla Miklós de Dalnok was head of the military cabinet of the Hungarian collaborationist dictator Miklós Horthy de Nagybányai, who ended up at the Nuremberg

Trial, but only as a witness at the so-called Ministries Trial of Dr Edmund Veesenmayer, a German Nazi commissar of Hungary, who had organized the deportations of 900,000 Hungarian Jews to Auschwitz. Veesenmayer was sentenced to twenty years but was released as early as 1951. Béla Miklós died in Budapest in 1948 as a free man. Horthy was exiled to Portugal, where he died in 1957.

2. Sentenced to twenty years in prison in 1949, Brankov was allegedly transported to Moscow. He claimed he had spent seven years in solitary confinement there. He was then sent back to Hungary and used the opportunity to escape from the country during the uprising of 1956. He worked as a manual laborer in Paris. He died in 2011, at the age of 100.

3. Roger Gough, *A Good Comrade: Janos Kadar, Communism and Hungary*, New York: I. B. Tauris, 2006, p. 45.

4. Csaba Békés, Malcolm Byrne, and Janos M. Rainer (eds), *The 1956 Revolution: A History in Documents* Budapest: Central European University Press, 2002, pp. 365–6. In an interview given to *Paris Match* on 28 October 1968, after the Warsaw Pact intervention in Czechoslovakia, Tito said: "I have to say something I have never mentioned before in public. Before the well-known Budapest events, Khrushchev, Malenkov, and Mikoyan visited me on the Brijuni Islands. I told them then: the worst outcome should be avoided by all means if possible. But if the developments took such a course that they could turn into a counterrevolution, then it would be a whole different thing. The events in Hungary should not be compared with these in Czechoslovakia. These are two completely different things. Some forces in the West were de facto involved in Hungarian internal affairs. Even in Hungary itself there were forces that had not come to terms with the socialist system. Remnants of the old Horthy regime were also still active." See Zdravko Židovec (ed.), *Josip Broz Tito—Intervjui*, Zagreb: "August Cesarec"—NIRO Mladost, 1980.

5. "From the diary of D. T. Shepilov," 7 November 1956. History and Public Policy Program Digital Archive, published in CWIHP Bulletin 10, pp. 144–5. Translated for CWIHP by Benjamin Aldrich-Moodie; see http://digitalarchive.wilsoncenter.org/document/111100

6. Jenô Györkei and Miklós Horvath (eds), *Soviet Military Intervention in Hungary, 1956*, Budapest: Central European University Press, 1999, pp. 187, 204–205.

44. THE ARSENAL OF THE MEDITERRANEAN REVOLUTION, CASABLANCA 1958

1. As usual, Tito twists the facts. In 1958, after this intervention in the letter to Eisenhower, 121 modern F-86E Sabre aircraft arrived (its superior version Canadair CL-13 mk IV). With these aircraft, Yugoslav pilots broke the sound barrier for the first time. See Bojan B. Dimitrijević, *Jugoslavija i NATO*, Belgrade: Tricontinental/Novinsko-izdavački centar centar "Vojska," 2003, p. 161.

2. *Jugoslavija—Alžir*, Yugoslav Archives, Belgrade, 2013, p. 40.

45. FROM DESERT TO WILDERNESS, GOLD COAST 1961

1. Zbigniew K. Brzezinski, *Africa and the Communist World*, Stanford: Stanford University Press, 1965.
2. Jovan Čavoški, "Jugoslavija, Alžir, nesvrstane zemlje i velike sile u Hladnom ratu 1954–1962," in *Jugoslavija—Alžir*, p. 119.

46. THE THIRD WORLD CAPITAL IN THE BALKANS, BELGRADE 1961

1. The UAR, a short-lived union of Egypt and Syria (1958–61), was formed as an embryo of a future pan-Arab state in the Middle East. Egypt was on the rise, and Nasser both attracted and terrified other leaders. He agreed to a Syrian proposition for the unification, but Lebanon and Jordan (correctly) took it as a threat. As a result, Jordan made an alliance with Iraq in 1958. Meanwhile, Lebanon sank into a civil war when the pro-Nasserite Muslims and Druze clashed with Christian Maronites. As the West believed it would help the expansion of Nasser's hegemony, US marines and British special forces landed in Lebanon. Another coup in Iraq dethroned the Hashemite dynasty there and King Faisal II was killed. They kept only Jordan, and the new regime in Baghdad signed a friendship treaty with Moscow. A coup would also take place in Syria in 1961, when the country will leave the UAR and the union will thus fall apart—another of Nasser's historic failures.
2. DoS, 13 September 1961, Yugoslavia General Folder, National Security Files, Box 209A, JFK Library.

47. CUBA LIBRE, BRIJUNI ISLANDS 1962

1. Open Society Archives (OSA), Box-Folder-Report: 60–4–192, 1962–9–28, by Stankovic.
2. Congress passed a decree abolishing the "most favored nation" status for Poland and Yugoslavia. However, the decree left room for the president of the United States to restore this status by an executive order if deemed to be in the best interest of the United States.

48. A DEFEAT IN THE HIMALAYAS, NEW DELHI 1962

1. Numa Mazat and Franklin Serrano, "An Analysis of the Soviet Economic Growth from the 1950s to the Collapse of USSR," Instituto de Economia de Universidade Federal do Rio de Janeiro, 2012.
2. Yang Jisheng, *Tombstone: The Great Chinese Famine 1958–1962*, New York: Farrar, Straus & Giroux, 2008.
3. Frank Dikötter, *Mao's Great Famine: The History of China's Most Devastating Catastrophe, 1958–1962*, London: Bloomsbury, 2010.
4. Alfred D. Low, *The Sino-Soviet Dispute: An Analysis of the Polemics*, Rutherford, NJ: Associated University Presses, 1976.

5. The underground testing of the Indian nuclear bomb codenamed Smiling Buddha was performed in a Rajasthan desert on 18 May 1974.

49. ENTER THE DRAGON, MOSCOW, 1964

1. Krzysztof Ostaszewski is one of the world's leading statisticians and risk management experts. See Krzysztof M. Ostaszewski, "Laughing at the Regime," Mises Institute, 16 June 2010; https://mises.org/library/laughing-regime

2. Dr Sergo Anastasovich Mikoyan (son of Anastas Mikoyan), a historian and chief researcher at the Institute of World Economy and International Relations at the Russian Academy of Sciences, presented his comprehensive paper at a seminar organized by the CIA at Princeton University in 2001. See S. A. Mikoyan, "Eroding the Soviet 'Culture of Secrecy,'" CIA's Analysis of the Soviet Union 1947–1991, Princeton, March 2001.

3. "The Foreign Policy Views of Mikhail Suslov," CIA National Foreign Assessment Center, July 1987, CIA Historical Review Program Releases, Sanitized 1999.

4. "Soviet Staff Study: Party–Military Relations in the USSR and The Fall of Marshal Zhukov, CAESAR I and II-B-59," Office of Current Intelligence, CIA, 8 June 1959.

5. "July 08, 1963: Meeting of the Delegations of the Communist Party of the Soviet Union and the Chinese Communist Party, Moscow, 5–20 July 1963," Wilson Center Digital Archive, translated from Russian.

6. Ibid.

7. Some of the scenarios developed in the Pentagon were even more far-fetched. What if Suslov is actually planning such an attack using a Golf-type submarine based in Vladivostok, believing that suspicion will fall on China, so that the United States will retaliate against Beijing and topple the regime there—something Moscow is keen to accomplish? This theory became particularly popular after the disappearance of the Soviet K-129 (Golf II) submarine from a Kamchatka base. It disappeared without a trace in the Pacific in 1968. After a long search, the US navy managed to find it at a depth of almost 5,000 meters. The CIA signed a USD350 million contract with Howard Hughes to build a 50,000-ton ship, *Glomar Explorer*, and lift the K-129 from the bottom. The ship did the job, but nothing of any particular interest was found. See *Red Star Rogue*, New York: Simon & Schuster, 2005.

8. According to the claims of Chinese historian Liu Chensan, published in a series of articles in the official press in 2010, in the midst of the 1969 Soviet–Chinese border conflict that began on the Ussuri River and continued with some 400 other incidents (with a total of 4,000 casualties), the Soviet army prepared a preventive nuclear strike against the Chinese nuclear site Lop Nor and notified the Americans of it in advance, asking the United States to stay neutral. President Nixon refused. Chief of Staff Joe Haldeman was the first to write about it in his memoirs. It certainly paved the way for Kissinger's (1971) and Nixon's (1972) visits to China.

50. THE EMPEROR WITHOUT AN EMPIRE, BRIJUNI ISLANDS 1964–80

1. Budimir Lončar, a member of the delegation, said so to the authors. Lončar was the Yugoslav ambassador in Indonesia, assistant minister of foreign affairs, ambassador to West Germany, and the last Yugoslav foreign minister. He later worked as an advisor in the UN and to Croatian Presidents Franjo Tuđman, Stjepan Mesić, and Ivo Josipović.

2. An account from the unpublished second, enlarged edition of the memoirs of Dušan Bilandžić, a member of the Croatian Academy of Arts and Sciences (in possession of the authors). First edition: Dušan Bilandžić, *Povijest izbliza: Memoarski zapisi*, Zagreb: Prometej, 2006.

3. On 16 May 1966, just fifteen days before the Brijuni Plenum in Yugoslavia, the Chinese Politburo published its letter with the instructions for launching the Cultural Revolution. On the very day of the Brijuni Plenum, *Renmin Ribao* published an editorial entitled "Sweep out the Ox-Demons and Snake-Spirits." In China, too, everything started with Mao's wife Jiang Qing's accusations that the chairman had been wiretapped.

4. Jan Pelikán, "Titovi pogovori v Moskvi aprila 1968. in čehoslovaška kriza," *Acta Histriae*, XVIII, 1/2 (2010), pp. 101–26.

5. All the protest leaders suffered some sanctions, except Vuk Drašković, a Montenegrin student. He got a job in Tanjug, the Yugoslav news agency, and was sent to Nairobi as a foreign correspondent. Then he became chief of staff of Mika Špiljak, the then chairman of the Federation of Trade Unions of Yugoslavia. In the Yugoslav wars of the 1990s, Drašković would become the leader of Serbian royalists and Milošević's coalition partner. He would later join the opposition. In the ensuing decades, he would become one of the most influential people in Belgrade. His last book is a hagiography of King Aleksandar I Karađorđević.

6. When Longo succeeded Togliatti in the 1960s, communist cadres were again sent behind the Iron Curtain to attend courses for agents, such as in the special school of the East German Stasi in Berlin, where some of the teachers were Soviet experts. There they would learn how to wage a secret war against the rightist agent network. The leaders of the PCI became concerned after the 1967 "colonels' coup" in Greece.

7. The term was invented by Frane Barbieri, a Yugoslav journalist who worked for the influential Milan daily *Giornale*. His task was to keep contact with Berlinguer and transfer funds to the Italian party. "The name Eurocommunism was first invented in 1975 by a Croatian journalist, Frane Barbieri, working for the Milan daily, *Il Giornale Nuovo*." See Bogdan Szajkowski, "Roots of Eurocommunism," *Contemporary Crises*, 3, 3 (July 1979), pp. 255–67.

8. Growth in Soviet GDP dropped from 5 percent in the 1961–73 period to 3.4 percent in the period 1974–8, but with a huge deficit in agricultural production that reached USD20 billion per year in the mid-1970s. Peasants left Khrushchev's super-kolkhozes and agrotowns. The import of cereals was compensated with the export of raw materials and energy products to the West at low prices. Trade with the

Eastern Bloc countries was based on barter in order to help stabilize their economies and thus maintain Soviet domination. See Mazat and Serrano, "Analysis of the Soviet Economic Growth."

9. In accordance with the Hallstein doctrine, Germany broke off its diplomatic relations with Yugoslavia in 1957, as soon as Tito—at Khrushchev's request—recognized the GDR, the country of his old boss from the Moscow days, East German President Pieck.

10. Following Croatia's independence, Tomac joined the Social Democratic Party (former League of Communists of Croatia) and competed against President Tuđman at the presidential election. Then he converted and became a radical nationalist, Tuđman's follower and believer. He also became a bitter opponent of his former party, all former communists and the left in general.

11. Presidency of SFRY—Service for the Protection of Constitutional Order, state secret—to be kept in a safe, ref. no. 3, Belgrade 1987. Copy in authors' archive.

12. *Peking Review*, no. 36 (2 September 1977).

13. The contact with Gaitskell was maintained by Ante Sorić (1929–2014). He was sent to London as a Tourist Office representative. He also had excellent connections with the highest circles of the Catholic Church, with the Chinese leadership, and South Korean business leaders.

14. This political episode was researched and explained by William Klinger in his article "Continuity Man: La visita di Stane Dolanc a Londra nel 1977," *La Battana, Rivista trimestrale di cultura*, 187 (2013), pp. 77–91.

15. Duško Doder, *Yugoslavs*, New York: Random House, 1978, p. 74.

16. The members of the first generation of the Red Brigades were all arrested by law-enforcement forces under the command of Gendarmerie General Carlo Alberto dalla Chiesa. Only Moretti remained at large. Moretti organized the kidnapping of Moro and ultimately shot him. He was sentenced to six life sentences but was paroled in 1998.

17. Roberto Bartali, "Red Brigades (1969–1974): An Italian Phenomenon and a Product of the Cold War," *Modern Italy*, 12, 3 (2007), pp. 349–369; https://www.tandfonline.com/doi/abs/10.1080/13532940701633817

18. Berlinguer had a serious traffic accident on 3 October 1973 on his way to Sofia airport after a tense meeting with Todor Zhivkov. The episode was hushed up until the fall of the Berlin Wall. Sicilian Communist Emanuele Macaluso was the first one to talk about it in a 1991 interview for the Milan weekly *Panorama*. The program's two reporters later published a book: Giovanni Fasanella and Corrado Incerti, *Sofia 1973: Berlinguer deve morire*, Rome: Fazi, 2006.

19. At the same time as exporting socialism to Asia, the Soviet Union also exported revolution to Africa. After Portugal decolonized Angola in 1975, charismatic Marxist leader Dr Agostinho Neto seized power there. That prompted an immediate reaction from South African mercenaries and armies mobilized by the CIA in neighboring countries. Cuba intervened by sending 25,000 soldiers to Angola.

INDEX

Friuli, 55, 75, 109, 180, 186, 188, 195, 202, 215, 253
Frković, Mate, 207–8
Frol, Frane, 150
Frunze, Mikhail, 66
Frunze Military Academy, Ryazan, 21, 66–7, 215
Fruška Gora, Serbia, 118
FTP-MOI, 213–14, 215

Gagarin, Yuri, 307
Gaitskell, Hugh, 355
Galán Rodriguéz, Francisco, 262
Galbraith, John Kenneth, 319
Galeb, 253, 264, 297, 299, 302
Galicia, 15, 16, 17
Gandhi, Indira, 306, 337
Gandhi, Mohandas "Mahatma", 306
Gang of Four, 353, 354
Garibaldi Brigades, 142, 171, 188, 197, 214, 215, 237, 261
de Gasperi, Alcide, 217, 235, 241, 242, 251
de Gaulle, Charles, 214, 253, 296, 309
Gavrilović, Milan, 106
Gaži, Franjo, 150
Genoa, Italy, 214, 242, 244
George VI, King of the United Kingdom, 251
Georgia, 360
Georgijević, Dimitrije, 20–22, 175
German Democratic Republic (1949–90), 59, 67, 174, 277
  1953 Uprising, 259
  1955 West proclaims Hallstein doctrine, 277
  1957 Yugoslav recognition, 330
  1961 Berlin Crisis, 324
  1967 Stasi training of PCI begins, 357
  1976 Conference of Communist Parties, 352

German Federal Republic (1949–90), 277, 287, 324, 344–5, 346, 357–8
German language, 13, 15
German Occupied Zones (1945–9), 228–9, 247
German Revolution (1918–19), 27, 52, 102
German Reich (1933–45)
  1933 Hitler becomes chancellor, 46, 48, 53, 60, 61
  1938 Anschluss, 95
  1939 invasion of Czechoslovakia, 95; Molotov-Ribbentrop Pact, 94–8, 101, 102, 108, 110, 111, 127, 191, 210; invasion of Poland, 94
  1940 invasion of France, 101; Tripartite Pact, 105–6
  1941 invasion of Yugoslavia, 98; invasion of Crete, 119; arrests of communists, 113; invasion of Soviet Union, 108, 111, 113; occupation of Athens, 113; pacification of Serbia, 119, 124–9; sieges of Leningrad and Sevastopol begin, 125
  1942 Operation Saturn, 128; Hitler orders destruction of Partisans, 136
  1943 Operation Fall Weiss, 137–40, 141, 142; Zagreb negotiations, 140–41; Operation Fall Schwartz, 141–5; Battle of Kursk, 148, 153; Operation Istria, 148, 203
  1944 Battle of Monte Cassino, 153, 195, 273; Operation Rösselsprung, 159–63, 167; Normandy landings, 163, 171, 198; Operation Bagration, 163; Battle of Batinska Skela, 187; Battle of Belgrade, 172, 181, 183–4, 186,

INDEX

INDEX

1941 German offensive, 123–9
1942 Long March begins, 129, 130; prisoner exchange, 134; establishment of AVNOJ, 135–6; arrival in Bihać, 136
1943 Fall Weiss battles, 137–40; Zagreb negotiations, 140–41; Fall Schwartz battles, 141–5; second session of AVNOJ, 149
1944 Operation Bari, 153–8; BAF established, 156–7; German assault, 159–63; transfer to Vis, 163–4, 167–8; Popović appointed commander, 182; Tito–Churchill meeting, 168–70, 172, 173, 176; Overseas Brigades formed, 170, 171, 198; Stalin–Tito meeting, 179–80, 181, 182, 184; Battle of Belgrade, 172, 181, 183–4; liberation of Thessalonica, 172, 188, 193; liberation of Dubrovnik, 188; arrival of Spanish generals, 211; Battle of Knin, 188; Vukovar landing attempt, 187
1945 Alexander–Tito meeting, 199–200; Rijeka Operation, 202–4, 214; ethnic cleansing campaigns, 204–7
Partito d'Azione, 171
Pathet Lao, 307
Patrice Lumumba Student Dormitory, 336
Patton, George, 214
Pauker, Ana, 147
Paul VI, Pope, 342, 356–7
Paul, King of Greece, 253
Paul, Prince of Yugoslavia, 72, 75, 83, 95, 105, 185
Paunović, Davorjanka "Zdenka", 111, 112, 120, 121, 145, 251
Pavelić, Ante, 207, 342

Pavlodar radio, 120, 126–7, 132
Pavlović, Živojin, 73
del Pedro, Carmen, 196
Penezić, Slobodan "Krcun", 112
Perm, Russia, 18, 19
Petacci, Clara, 214
Petain, Philippe, 213
Peter II, King of Yugoslavia, 95, 150, 169, 185
Péter, Gábor, 49
Petőfi, Sándor, 287
Petrograd, Russia, 18–19, 20
Petrović, Drago, 82
Petrović, Nikola, 99, 100, 151, 179
Peza, Albania, 189
Philby, Harold Adrian Russell "Kim", 49, 262
Philip, Duke of Edinburgh, 251, 252
Philippeville, Algeria, 274–5
Pieck, Wilhelm, 58–9, 60, 99, 147
Piedmont, Italy, 215
Pijade, Moša, 41–2, 56, 74, 238
  Constitution (1946), 42
  Đilas resignation (1954), 258
  Hebrang's ouster (1944), 175, 178
  Marić–Miletić conflict (1937), 79, 80, 93
Piłsudski, Józef Klemens, 27
Piraeus, Greece, 222, 253
Pirin Macedonia, 237
Pistoia, Italy, 108
Pius XII, Pope, 342
Piva river, 142, 145
Po river, 171, 195
Podgorica, Montenegro, 98
Podsreda, Slovenia, 12, 93
Polak's mill, Bjelovar, 29, 38
Poland, 65, 228, 270, 278, 356
  Baltic Secretariat and, 48
  Cominform conference (1947), 223
  German invasion (1939), 94

INDEX